Sense, Sensex and Sentiments

The Failure of India's Financial Sentinels

Sense, Sensex and Sentiments

The Failure of India's Financial Sentinels

M R VENKATESH
Chartered Accountant

KNOWLEDGE WORLD
KW Publishers Pvt Ltd
New Delhi

KNOWLEDGE WORLD

KW Publishers Pvt Ltd

4676/21, First Floor, Ansari Road, Daryaganj, New Delhi 110002

E mail@kwpub.in/knowledgeworld@vsnl.net T +91.11.23263498 / 43528107

www.kwpub.in

ISBN 978-93-80502-49-6

Contents

Dedicated to

Baburao Genu – One of India's foremost fighters

Babuji was a four-anna member of the Indian National Congress. His registration number: 81941. On December 12, 1930, Babuji was killed in the most gruesome manner while physically attempting to stop a speeding truck in Bombay (now Mumbai) carrying imported materials from Britain.

Babuji's supreme sacrifice is a message for all Indians – political independence can coexist only with economic independence – a fact that seems to have been forgotten within sixty years of our independence.

Foreword

Welcome to a World Without Rules

John Christensen*

The best estimate I have seen suggests that between USD 22-27 billion of domestic capital flows illicitly out of India every year.[1] India ranks fifth highest overall in the world in terms of scale of its illicit outflows, ranking below Russia (USD 32-38 billion), Mexico (USD 41-46 billion), Saudi Arabia (USD 54-55 billion) and China (USD 233-289 billion). The vast majority of this capital disappears offshore, typically being routed through exotic secrecy jurisdiction islands like Mauritius or my home island of Jersey, to the major financial markets in Europe and North America. Some of this capital returns to India, disguised as foreign investment to benefit from tax holidays and all manner of special treatments. India, like most countries, has fallen victim to a catastrophic failure of financial market deregulation.

Since the late 1970s, capital has been set free to roam the world unhindered, but virtually nothing has been done at the international level to tackle the inevitable side-effects of this liberalisation process, including and especially tax evasion. We are now suffering the consequences of this appalling failure of international cooperation. Tax evasion has become endemic; abetting financial crime has become a major profit centre for banks and other financial intermediaries; tax regimes are becoming increasingly regressive in their impact on the poor, and public services are withering on the vine. Social cohesion across the world is increasingly threatened by levels of inequality not seen since the period immediately before the French Revolution.

At the global level, the scale of illicit financial flows and tax evasion far outweighs aid flows and debt relief programmes. The World Bank's Stolen Asset Recovery initiative reports that the cross-border flows of proceeds from criminal

---

* **John Christensen** is Director of the global Tax Justice Network and a leading authority on secrecy jurisdictions. He has worked in many countries, including India, and has also worked for prolonged periods in London and its offshore satellite, Jersey, where he learned many of the tricks of the trade used by sophisticated tax evaders.

1. Global Financial Integrity (2008), Illicit Financial Flows from Developing Countries, 2002-2006, Washington.

activities, corruption and tax evasion amount to between USD 1 trillion and USD 1.6 trillion a year, approximately half of which originates from the developing and transitional economies. The global stock of wealth hidden away in secrecy jurisdictions by people known in banking circles as high net-worth individuals (or Hen-Wees) has been estimated at USD 11.5 trillion. This wealth is almost entirely untaxed. If it was taxed at even a modest rate, additional revenue exceeding USD 255 billion a year would be available, for example, poverty alleviation purposes. It is time for the international community, and specifically for the Group of 20 countries, which has taken upon itself the role of restoring integrity and stability to the global financial markets, to recognise that secrecy jurisdictions are not minor oddities on the outer fringe of the financial markets, but are in fact a central and highly corrosive part of globalised finance. Being both a victim of the activities of these places and also a member of the G-20, India has the opportunity to both voice its concerns and take direct action to crack down on financial opacity.

At the same time, it also needs to be recognised that the corruption debate, which until recently has largely focussed on the demand side, and in particular on bribe taking and payments of commission kickbacks, needs to widen its focus to include those who provide the supply side of corrupt practices. The supply side includes not only bribe-payers, but also financial intermediaries who create and administer the elaborate legal structures through which illicit cross-border financial flows are routed via Offshore Financial Centres (OFCs) into the mainstream banking system. Crucially, the secretive legal instruments used by multinational companies and Hen-Wees for tax dodging purposes are also used for a wide variety of other criminal activities, including market rigging, insider trading, payment of illicit political donations, embezzlement, fraud, and payment of bribes and commission kickbacks. This underlines the role of secrecy jurisdictions in providing a supply side stimulus that encourages and enables grand scale corruption by providing an operational base for financial intermediaries and their clients to exploit legislative gaps and fragmented regulation. Judging from my own experience of working for many years in the British secrecy jurisdiction of Jersey, legions of lawyers, bankers and accountants are engaged in systematically abusing the laws of other countries, not to mention their own professional codes of conduct, for the simple reason that they can charge gigantic fees for helping their clients evade taxes.

Secrecy, Complexity and Corruption

The majority of illicit financial flows are transacted via complex structures involving legal entities operated by intermediaries working in a variety of secrecy jurisdictions. This is a world of smoke and mirrors, where a typical tax evasion strategy might begin with an offshore trust created in Mauritius, which acts as sole shareholder of an offshore company registered in the Isle of Man using nominee directors and shareholders, with the Isle of Man company serving as the front for a secret bank account in Zurich, Switzerland. The ultimate beneficiaries of this structure will very probably have no apparent connection with the trust, the company or the bank account, and the entire structure, which is expensive to both create and operate, will have been designed to frustrate investigation. Even if investigators were able to penetrate these hidden structures, flee clauses written into trust agreements, and re-domiciliation clauses in corporate memorandum and articles of association, require the financial intermediaries to immediately shift the legal entities to another jurisdiction. All sorts of reasons are offered to justify these devices, including avoidance of political risk and succession management, but tax evasion is almost invariably an outcome of these actions, and banks are actively engaged in providing the enabling mechanisms for dodging taxation.

The use of secrecy jurisdictions is actively marketed by financial intermediaries to potential clients throughout the world. Mainstream newspapers and magazines such as *The Economist* carry advertisements promoting offshore structures and "tax efficient" wealth-managements schemes. These advertisements are an open invitation to illicit financial flows and tax evasion. They reveal a major fault line in the financial liberalisation process. Whilst capital has become almost completely mobile, the ability to police cross-border dirty money flows remains largely nationally based and international judicial cooperation is weak to non-existent.

Capital market liberalisation has stimulated an extraordinary increase in cross-border financial flows, which have increased eight-fold since 1990 to USD 8.2 trillion in 2006. Illicit financial flows constitute around one-fifth of this sum, but, by and large, governments and multilateral agencies have down played concerns about dirty money except when drugs and terrorism are concerned. For the greater part, however, anti-corruption initiatives have focussed on bribery of public officials and politicians, and looting by despots and their cronies, rather than on the workings of a global financial system that encourages and facilitates the laundering of dirty money. Astonishingly, neither the World Bank nor the International Monetary Fund (IMF) has tried to investigate or quantify illicit financial flows and tax evasion. Alarmingly, neither of these agencies has shown any willingness to tackle these problems.

Illicit financial flows persist despite elaborate and expensive "follow-the-money" strategies introduced in the 1980s to tackle narcotics trafficking but subsequently broadened in an attempt to preempt terrorist attacks through tracking related financial flows. The logic of this strategy, which began with the creation of a new offence called money laundering, was to make financial institutions and intermediaries key players in the 'wars' on drugs and terrorism by handing them responsibility for identification of the originators and beneficiaries of financial transactions. These 'know-your-client' rules require bankers and other financial intermediaries to inform the authorities of currency transactions exceeding a certain level (Currency Transaction Reports) and any transaction or transactor that raises reasonable suspicion in the minds of the banking personnel involved (Suspicious Transaction Reports).

However, for all the expense involved in complying with anti-money laundering initiatives, the failure rate for detecting dirty money flows is astonishingly high. According to a Swiss banker, only 0.01 per cent of dirty money flowing through Switzerland is detected. It is unlikely that other jurisdictions perform any better. This is partly due to the narrow focus on money related to illegal drugs and terror, which accounts for only a small proportion of cross-border illicit financial flows, and also because of the extraordinary lax attitude towards commercial trade mispricing and fraudulent invoicing, which account for the majority of such flows. This laxity also extends to tax evasion, which is treated as a predicate crime in some countries, but not others, and is an area where developing countries are particularly vulnerable.

The secrecy provided by secrecy jurisdictions creates an effective barrier to investigation of activities booked through the secrecy jurisdiction, and facilitates the laundering of proceeds from a wide range of criminal and unethical activities, including fraud, embezzlement and theft, bribery, narco trafficking, illegal arms trafficking, counterfeiting, insider trading, false trade invoicing, transfer mispricing, and tax dodging. Elaborate schemes are devised to 'weave' dirty money into commercial transactions and to disguise the proceeds of crime and tax evasion using complex multi-jurisdictional structures. According to one expert investigator:

> *Methods to launder money vary dramatically from low-level, relatively simple to highly-structured and complex business scenarios for transfer of money offshore. What is being increasingly identified is the infiltration of criminal identities into otherwise legitimate business interests. None of these people could get away with a lot of what they were doing if it wasn't for lawyers, accountants, financial advisers, and the like, knowingly assisting them to launder and hide assets.*[2]

2. Detective Superintendent Des Bray, of the Commercial and Electronic Crime Branch, interviewed in the *Adelaide Advertiser*, "Lawyers Helping to Launder Money," June 4, 2007.

Crucially, the techniques used for tax dodging and laundering dirty money involve identical mechanisms and financial subterfuges: multi-jurisdiction structures, offshore companies and trusts, foundations, correspondent banks, nominee directors, dummy wire transfers, and so on. Legal institutions granted special status and privilege by society have been subverted to purposes for which they were never intended. For example, the original purpose of trusts was to protect the well-being of spouses and other family members unable to look after their financial affairs, and to promote charitable causes. Incredible as it must appear to those not familiar with the operations of secrecy jurisdictions, charitable trusts are regularly set up for the purposes of owning 'special purpose vehicles' used for international tax planning and for hiding both assets and liabilities 'off-balance sheet', as happened with Enron and the collapsed British bank Northern Rock.

The scale of the illicit financial economy, and the rapid growth of a globalised infrastructure of lawyers, bankers and accountants willing to cash in on the extraordinary fees earned from facilitating tax evasion, suggest to me that a radical change is needed in the public understanding of what constitutes corruption. The focus needs to shift from individuals to the systems and processes that encourage and enable corrupt activities. Corruption always involves narrow interests, both in the public and private spheres, of those who abuse the common good. It always includes insiders, using guarded information, who can operate with a high level of impunity. And it always corrodes public confidence in institutions, laws, rules and systems that are intended to promote the public interest.

For these reasons, I would argue that it is more useful to think of corruption as *"the abuse of public interest and the undermining of public confidence in the integrity of the rules, systems and institutions that promote the public interest"*. Broadening the definition of corruption in this way creates room for a wider range of actors and their facilitating activities. It widens the focus to include activities such as insider-trading, tax evasion and avoidance, market-rigging, non-disclosure of pecuniary involvement, embezzlement, and trade mispricing, all of which occur in the private sector and are disguised through opaque and complex legal structures. Economic crimes such as these are highly damaging to market economies and social stability. The near collapse of the Greek economy in May 2010 can be directly linked to the astonishing levels of tax evasion in that country, but while Greece is an extreme case in the European context, the scale of the problem in many developing countries, including India, may well be worse.

The Dark Side of Financial Market Liberalisation

Secrecy jurisdictions persist in a world of globalised financial markets solely because they serve the economic interests of powerful and unaccountable people. Most of the problems posed by secrecy jurisdictions could be remedied by strengthening international cooperation. Measures to reduce opacity and strengthen international cooperation in effective information sharing could be implemented in a relatively short time frame. The principal barrier standing in the way of progress towards achieving these goals is the lack of political will on the parts of the governments of leading G-20 nations, most notably the USA and UK, both of which are leading secrecy jurisdictions. The reality of their commitment to 'globalisation' is that they want liberalised capital markets on their own terms but continue to use lax regulation, secrecy and fiscal incentives to distort the markets in favour of domestic interests and to attract capital from other countries.

As this book makes very clear, debates in India, and elsewhere in the world, around development, accountability, corruption and persistent poverty are undergoing a profound shift. The promise that independence held out for India in 1947 cannot be taken for granted: democracy is being challenged by powerful individuals and corporations, who can use secretive offshore structures to subvert political processes while also evading their dues to society. This book is, therefore, a wake-up call to Indian society: in joining the dots between illicit financial flows, tax evasion, corruption, rising inequality and persistent poverty, M. R. Venkatesh tells a much bigger story about how globalisation in its current form has undermined the integrity of markets, the rule of law and democracy itself. It is of paramount importance, for India and the rest of the world, that the issues laid out in this book are debated as widely and openly as possible and that global solutions are implemented to remove the cancer of secrecy jurisdictions.

Preface

I need to make a confession up front: I had named this work long before I had even conceived it my mind. "Sense, Sensex and Sentiments" was just a phrase used by me, almost spontaneously, on the sidelines after one of my lectures while explaining the linkages between markets and sentiments to an enthusiastic participant. The effect of the phrase on my own self was so profound that more I thought about it, the more I got convinced that a deeper exposition of the subject was necessary. With the broad idea having flowed from my subconscious mind, I presumed, it was divine will too.

So, what began as a study of seemingly unrelated aspects that drive global and national economics today – a global regime that allows proliferation of tax havens, national economic policies that are simultaneously the cause and effect of corruption, corruption that eventually results in money laundering, money laundering which, in turn, sustains the economics of tax havens, reverse flow of money from tax havens that cause the boom and doom of markets across continents, exaggeration of boom and exacerbation of doom of the markets being aided and abetted by sections of the media and intelligentsia, the inexplicable but unpardonable apathy of the regulators in India – ultimately culminated in this work.

This work seeks to explore the symbiotic link among all these issues, the state of interplay among the factors that govern the stealthy flow of money to and from tax havens and its impact on markets as well as national economies. *Sense, Sensex and Sentiments*, in short, is the story of how markets run the risk of being dynamited from within and becoming rigged casinos.

This study has simultaneously explored the inability of national governments across continents in their fight against the cabal that runs this global financial chicanery. What is pertinent to note in the Indian context is that it is not only the issue of ability but positive political, bureaucratic, judicial and media patronage that sustains the same. Worse still, all this is rationalised as the inevitable negative consequence of globalisation even by the intelligentsia. That, in turn, stunts any debate. Modern governance, if I may be permitted to state, is defined only by its ability to feed on the gluttonous avarice for limitless wealth of this cabal. Consequently, the growth of Gross Domestic Product (GDP) has become more important than human development, the rise of the Sensex more important than human welfare.

It will perhaps be appropriate at this point in time to refer to the stunning predictions for *Kaliyug*[1] made by Sage Sukhar while he was concluding his 7-day discourse (Chapter II of the 12th Canto of *Srimad Bhagavatham*) to King Pareekshit.

- Wealth accumulation by any means alone will be considered as the purpose of life.
- One who is audacious will be accepted as truthful.
- A man who talks ornamentally will be considered a literate and poet.
- Law and justice will be applied only on the basis of one's power.
- A person will be judged unworthy if he does not have money.
- Hypocrisy will be accepted as virtue.
- As the whole world becomes crowded with a corrupt population, whoever shows himself to be the strongest will gain political power.
- Rulers will be avaricious and merciless and will behave no better than ordinary thieves.
- As the kings will mostly be thieves, the occupations of men will be stealing, lying and needless violence, and all the social classes will be reduced to the lowest levels.

What a precise, extraordinary and insightful clairvoyance and stunning resemblance to all that is happening in India now. What we see are the exact happenings of such divine foretelling, isn't it?

Governance: The Mother of all Issues

Obviously, everything boils down to governance or the lack of it. Corruption is the abject manifestation of poor governance. Corruption results in capital flight from an economy. Capital flight causes poverty, which, in turn, feeds on terror. Terror leads to chaos, crisis and calamity. Importantly, in such a diffused scenario, the corrupt, criminals and terrorists flourish. The net consequence of all these is the lack of governance in India that is increasingly engaging the attention of international players. And that is definitely reaching embarrassing proportions. Commenting on this rather dismal scenario, Mr. Mohan Murti, former European Director of the Confederation of Indian Industry (CII) wrote a rather stunning article in *The Hindu Business Line*, May 31, 2010, titled rather provocatively but aptly, "Is the nation in a coma?" According to him ,"Europeans believe that Indian leaders in politics and business are so blissfully blinded by the new, sometimes ill-gotten, wealth and deceit that they are living in defiance, insolence and denial to

1. *Kaliyug* is the last of four Yugas viz., Krutha, Drethaa, Dwapara and Kali, as per Hindu mythical account of the time lines, totalling 43,20,000 years.

comprehend that the day will come, sooner than later, when the have-nots would hit the streets."

In fact, the article itself was the fallout of the question and answer of a panel discussion in Frankfurt, Germany, organised by Euroforum and *The Handelsblatt*, one of the most prestigious newspapers in German-speaking Europe. That, according to him, was his "moment of truth," which according to Murti, "turned into an hour of shame, embarrassment – when the participants fired questions and made remarks on their experiences with the evil of corruption in India." The questions, according to Murti, ranged from the corruption in the judiciary, the possible impeachment of a judge, the 2G scam to the money parked illegally in tax havens.

If one thought that this was an aberration, one would be sadly mistaken. Referring to a popular prime-time television discussion in Germany, Mr Murti points out that the panelist, a member of the German Parliament, quoting a blog stated: *"If all the scams of the last five years are added up, they are likely to rival and exceed the British colonial loot of India of about a trillion dollars."* Well that is a telling comment of our times. Mr. Murti is not done yet in his article. He goes on to quote from some of the leading newspapers of Europe. Accordingly:

One German business daily, which wrote an editorial on India, said, "India is becoming a Banana Republic instead of being an economic superpower. To get the cut motion designated out, assurances are made to political allies. Special treatment is promised at the expense of the people. So, Ms Mayawati who is Chief Minister of the most densely inhabited state, is calmed when an intelligence agency probe is scrapped. The multi-million dollars fodder scam by another former chief minister wielding enormous power is put in cold storage."

An article in a French newspaper titled "Playing the Game, Indian Style" wrote: "Investigations into the shadowy financial deals of the Indian Cricket League have revealed a web of transactions across tax havens like Switzerland, the Virgin Islands, Mauritius and Cyprus." In the same article, the name of one Hassan Ali of Pune is mentioned as operating with his wife a one-billion-dollar illegal Swiss account with "sanction of the Indian regime".

A third story narrated in the damaging article is that of the former Chief Minister of Jharkhand, Madhu Koda, who was reported to have funds in various tax havens that were partly used to buy mines in Liberia. "Unfortunately, the Indian public do not know the status of that enquiry," the article concluded.

"In the nastiest business scam in Indian records (Satyam) the government adroitly covered up the political aspects of the swindle–predominantly involving real estate," wrote an Austrian newspaper.

That is not all. There have been several unambiguous references by the global media to the levels of corruption in India, sometimes even pointing out to the tacit complicity of the highest of the land. Lest the reader believes that all these are references only to the corrupt practices within the government, he would be sadly mistaken. Increasingly, the world believes that the success of corporates in India is because of their ability to bend and change the rules of the game. And that, to a large extent, dents the image of India, Indians and Indian enterprise.

Money Laundering and Tax Havens

The gargantuan corruption practised in India takes us to the issue of money laundering and parking of it in tax havens. It may be recalled that the General Elections in 2009 generated considerable heat (and very little light, I must confess) on the said subject. Virtually every political party worth its electoral salt vowed to bring back this Indian money parked in tax havens. The then ruling combine promised to bring it back within one hundred days if reelected to power. What is galling is that even after a year, events continue to unfold at a glacial pace on this issue, even as it was reelected.

Estimates of India's wealth parked in these tax havens are varied, depending on the methodology adopted and the assumptions that characterised the methodology in the first place. It is indeed inexplicable that in a country where political parties of all hues have openly admitted to the existence of Indian loot in tax havens, there are no "official" estimates by the Indian government of Indian wealth parked in these tax havens.

Nevertheless, the most reliable estimates of Indian wealth parked in tax havens came from the Task Force of the Bharatiya Janata Party (BJP – the opposition party in India), constituted in the run up to the General Elections in 2009. This Task Force came up with an estimate of the Indian wealth parked abroad that ranged between a conservative USD 500 billion (Rs 25,00,000 crores) to a more aggressive USD 1.4 trillion (Rs 70,00,000 lakh crores). All these were in turn based on several international studies by various organisations and economists of repute. To comprehend even the conservative estimate proffered by the said Task Force, suffice to say that it would be more than the entire tax (customs, excise, direct taxes, service tax all put together) collections of our nation for four full years!

Yet economists and analysts who, were silent all these years when India's wealth was indeed laundered into the tax havens, instantly found fault with the estimates put forth by the Task Force. Of course, one can endlessly nitpick the methodology adopted or relied on by the Task Force. Interestingly, this debate on the precise amount of wealth stashed from a country into tax havens has been an engaging one for most economists across the world. Mr. Raymond

Baker, an acknowledged specialist on the subject, put the entire issue of the extent of amount stashed in tax havens in proper perspective in a speech in June 2007. According to Baker, "We don't ask you to accept these numbers. We ask you to do just the opposite – to produce your own numbers. We ask the World Bank and other international financial institutions and the community of development scholars to do your own analyses. If you do it honestly and thoroughly, you are very likely to come up with numbers that are greater than these." None of the international financial institutions (including Indian economists) have taken up Baker's challenge.

The heat generated in the run up to the 2009 elections died even by the time the last vote was actually cast. Subsequent political debates in India on the convoluted subject of money laundering and tax havens have been reduced to the periphery. Hiding behind the facade of the so-called virtue of tolerance, all of us are going ahead with our lives without realising that it is we—the ubiquitous *Aam Admi*—who have been robbed all these years and it is our money that is parked in these tax havens. Crucially, we do not realise the debilitating impact of all these in our assault against poverty and terrorism.

There is yet another dimension to the issue relating to tax havens. Post the global financial crisis of 2008-09, several countries have been able to prise open the details about the accounts of their rich and famous in these tax havens. For instance, as recently as in July 2010, the revered *Wall Street Journal* carried a story of this data being available to certain individuals. As per this account, Mr. Falciani, a former HSBC bank official, along with a colleague, Ms Mikhael, rocked the financial world by claiming possession of information about thousands of Swiss banking customers from about 180 nations. This information is now in the possession of the French government, which has offered the data to any country that is in pursuit of its tax cheats. The report points out that Spain, Italy and Germany have obtained their share of the data. Intriguingly, there is no mention of India.

But what must agitate the collective conscience of the nation is that such data is increasingly available in private hands. What if such data is traded for a few dollars by such individuals with forces inimical to the country? Surely, the potential for mischief in such cases is immense. Yet, this is one issue about tax havens that seems to have escaped the attention of most analysts, political parties and the media.

While on the topic, I would also like to share the contents of an interesting e-mail sent to me by Mr John Christensen, a resident of Jersey and an expert on these issues, in response to one of my articles on the subject in *Rediff* in 2008:

Last week I stood outside the Jersey branch office of Bank of India with a film crew and asked a simple question: "Why does Bank of India have a branch in Saint Helier, Jersey?" The branch manager told me that their branch provides treasury operations, but the truth is that there is no economic reason for using Jersey for such purposes, and in reality this branch is purely located in Jersey to facilitate capital flight, tax evasion and top end corruption. Very few people of Indian origin reside in Jersey (so there is virtually no need for domestic retail banking purposes), but huge amounts of trade and investment are routed through Jersey and the Isle of Man for tax avoidance or evasion purposes. The UK government is totally complicit with this process because, as Ray Baker comments in his book, We Like the Money!

Mr. John Christensen's response sums up in more than one way our approach to tax havens, money laundering and, of course, fighting corruption.

Sentiments to Make and Mar Markets

Markets, as students of economics tell us, are a function of sentiments. Sentiments, in turn, are fashioned by the collective mood swings of market participants. Naturally, that makes the media an important tool in shaping and de-shaping the sentiments of market participants. But the role of certain sections of the media is not limited merely to this exercise.

Let me elaborate through certain real life developments of the past couple of years. Of late, there is a new class of investors – investment by the financial sector into the commodities futures market. In doing so, the link between the prices of a commodity and the relationship between supply and demand seems to have been completely bypassed. What is worrying analysts is the growing influence of these players, who tend to take positions that exert extraordinary pressure on prices. That, in turn, fuels speculative bubbles. Moreover, their activities are coordinated across currency, stock and commodity markets. Consequently, the rise and fall in commodity prices has nothing to do with demand and supply of that particular commodity. In the process the fundamentals of economics have been short-circuited.

This issue is of particular importance for food commodities in a country like India with constant supply side constraints. Nothing illustrates this paradigm better than a report by Johann Hari: "How Goldman Gambled on Starvation" in the *Independent*, UK, on July 2, 2010, portions of which I am reproducing hereunder:

You want to know how some of the richest people in the world—Goldman, Deutsche Bank, the traders at Merrill Lynch, and more—have caused the starvation of some of the poorest people in the world?

At the end of 2006, food prices across the world started to rise, suddenly and stratospherically. Within a year, the price of wheat had shot up by 80 per cent, maize by 90 per cent, rice by 320 per cent. In a global jolt of hunger, 200 million people–mostly children – couldn't afford to get food any more, and sank into malnutrition or starvation. There were riots in more than 30 countries, and at least one government was violently overthrown. Then, in spring 2008, prices just as mysteriously fell back to their previous level. Jean Ziegler, the UN Special Rapporteur on the Right to Food, calls it "a silent mass murder", entirely due to "man-made actions."

Most of the explanations we were given at the time have turned out to be false. It didn't happen because supply fell: the International Grain Council says global production of wheat actually increased during that period, for example. It isn't because demand grew either: as Professor Jayati Ghosh of the Centre for Economic Studies in New Delhi has shown, demand actually fell by 3 per cent. Other factors – like the rise of biofuels, and the spike in the oil price – made a contribution, but they aren't enough on their own to explain such a violent shift.

For over a century, farmers in wealthy countries have been able to engage in a process where they protect themselves against risk..... When this process was tightly regulated and only companies with a direct interest in the field could get involved, it worked. Then, through the 1990s, Goldman Sachs and others lobbied hard, and the regulations were abolished. Suddenly, these contracts were turned into "derivatives" that could be bought and sold among traders who had nothing to do with agriculture. A market in "food speculation" was born. Until deregulation, the price for food was set by the forces of supply and demand for food itself. (This was already deeply imperfect: it left a billion people hungry.) But after deregulation, it was no longer just a market in food. It became, at the same time, a market in food contracts based on theoretical future crops – and the speculators drove the price through the roof.

In 2006, financial speculators like Goldman pulled out of the collapsing US real estate market. They reckoned food prices would stay steady or rise while the rest of the economy tanked, so they switched their funds there. Suddenly, the world's frightened investors stampeded on to this ground. So while the supply and demand of food stayed pretty much the same, the supply and demand for derivatives based on food massively rose – which meant the all-rolled-into-one price shot up, and the starvation began.

So it has come to this. The world's wealthiest speculators set up a casino where the chips were the stomachs of hundreds of millions of innocent people. They gambled on increasing starvation, and won.

Recall, all this was happening in the full public glare of the intelligentsia, media and analysts. Thanks to the machinations of these financial speculators, grain prices, especially of wheat, rose across continents. The then American President Bush blamed it on the increasing consumption of the Chinese and the Indians. The Indian response was far more bizarre – South Indians were consuming more wheat, which was fuelling global wheat prices! Yet no one, definitely not one trained economist from the establishment, blamed it on the financial speculators and their impact on the grain prices. Either they were all in the payroll of these financial speculators or were simply innocent. And in both scenarios, it does not speak very high of such economists. One of my friends captured the credibility crisis of the economists quite brilliantly at the height of the global financial crisis of 2008 when he said, "It is not merely global economy that is in crisis, globally economists are in crisis." How true.

What is adding fuel to the fire is the role played by the media in the entire affair. Increasingly, it is seen that the lines separating the media and the financial players are getting blurred. The media seeks to be a player in the markets while simultaneously also is a commentator of the markets. That makes it easy for media to make or mar the market sentiments. Naturally with its power and reach, the media has enormous influence over the collective psyche of the people, especially in a country like India. That ensures that the sentiments are always controlled – mostly favourably but, if need be, negatively – by the media. With rumours of anchors (in the case of electronic media) taking enormous positions by the day and the print media investing into companies through an arrangement called private treaties, the media's role as an independent commentator of the markets is suspect.

Consequently, a "report" published in some remote corner on the El-Nino flows or its impact on the Indian monsoon pattern could well trigger a spurt in the food grain prices in India merely in anticipation of a failure of the monsoon. That, when repeated by vested interests in the media at prime time or in the front pages of national dailies, instantly becomes an "impending food disaster waiting to explode."

Naturally, all these add to the overall panic in the economy. This, in turn, leads to hoarding by the "common man." People hoard in anticipation of shortages and not when there is an *actual* shortage. It is this hoarding by the common man that generates demand at the aggregate level, leading to increase in the price of a commodity. Once the necessary threshold level of panic is created, the rest is easy. Rumours, black marketers and hoarders at the retail level then take over and ensure a price rise. In India, it is far easier, with underdeveloped spot markets and poor infrastructure, to create demand-supply gaps easily through this process of creating panic. Speculators and their partners in investment, the media, act in tandem to create this panic. After all, they have taken positions in the futures market quite early, knowing pretty well that it is they who have the ability to hype the failure of the monsoon, leverage it and profit from it.

Commenting on this issue of overhyping the failure of the monsoon in 2009, the Economic Survey for 2009-10 was particularly critical of the government's failure in not being able to check the "hype" over the *Kharif* crop failure, caused by an erratic monsoon, which did not take into account the comfortable food stocks and prospects of *Rabi* production. The Survey further notes that this "may have exacerbated inflationary expectations, encouraging hoarding and resulting in a higher inflation in food items." What is lost in this debate of the absurd is that the government allowed such speculation in the first place and then kept quiet when the players hyped up the monsoon failure.

Some analysts argue that the impact of such "intervention" by such speculators would be purely temporary and prices would return to normal so as to reflect the fundamentals. That is, provided the fundamentals themselves are not subject to such intervention. But the more important question is: what prevents the government from preventing such hyping in the first place?

That makes the study of economics and markets simply fascinating in India. The answer to this question requires a reference once again to the Economic Survey for 2009-10. The Economic Survey further points out to the fact that the minimum buffer stock of rice and wheat required to be maintained in the month of January 2010 was 20 million tonnes. Against the same, the Survey reveals that the actual buffer stock of rice and wheat was approximately 47 million tonnes. In contrast, the buffer stock in January 2009 was 35 million tonnes. In short, in a "drought year" the government actually procured 12 million tonnes from the markets. Conventional economics suggests otherwise – that the government should release buffer stocks to ensure more supply to meet the possible surge in prices.

The reference to the commodity markets mentioned above provides a contextual reference to a larger discussion on the relationship between the triumvirate consisting of the government, media and financial sector.

Participatory Notes (PNs)

As a subset of the policy on foreign direct investment, India allowed investments by foreign institutional investors (FIIs) directly into the stock markets, provided these FIIs register with the Securities and Exchange Board of India (SEBI) and be subjected to its rules and regulations. Readers may be aware that

Participatory Notes (PNs) are derivative instruments issued by FIIs to foreign investors – individuals or corporates – who want exposure to Indian equities but do not want to register with SEBI. However, FIIs are not allowed to issue PNs to Indian nationals, Persons of Indian Origin (PIOs) or Overseas Corporate Bodies (OCBs).

Thus, PNs are a contract between a foreign institution and a foreigner to invest into India. However, the underlying securities of PNs are Indian stocks. In contrast to the stringent Know Your Customer (KYC) norms laid out for resident Indians even for opening a bank account, the norms for PNs are relatively lax. In fact, as we will see subsequently, there are virtually no KYC norms for PNs. That makes transactions relating to PNs incomprehensible. The net result: Indian regulators do not know the names of such investors, or the origin and sources of such funds. Crucially, they can do precious little. No wonder, PNs are referred to as Phantom Notes.

Obviously, suspicions about terrorists operating from some tax haven and routing their investments into the Indian stock market remain. The irony is that if such investments are routed through Mauritius, the Indo-Mauritius Double Taxation Avoidance Agreement (DTAA) ensures that even short-term capital gains are tax free – both in India and Mauritius – again a benefit denied to resident Indians. Consequently, not only is the identity of the investor a secret but also the investment is insulated against any forms of taxation. What more could a terrorist want? The crux of the argument against PNs is that these predominantly comprise round tripping of the corrupt money of Indians, moved out first through the Hawala route and routed back into India, taking advantage of the tax-breaks provided by the Indo-Mauritius DTAA.

Given this background, the Finance Ministry had constituted a high-power committee comprising senior officials and experts from the Ministry as well as from SEBI and the Reserve Bank of India (RBI) in 2005 to look into these issues. In this connection, "The Report of the Expert Group on Encouraging FII Flows and Checking the Vulnerability of Capital Markets to Speculative Flows" was submitted in November 2005, precisely dealing with these issues.

The RBI, which was a part of this committee, was of the view that PNs should not be allowed. In a dissenting note to the expert group, it stated, "The Reserve Bank's stance has been that the issue of Participatory Notes should not be permitted. In this context, we would like to point out that the main concerns regarding issue of PNs are that the nature of the beneficial ownership or the identity of the investor will not be known, unlike in the case of FIIs registered with a financial regulator."

Further, the RBI apprehended that "trading of these PNs will lead to multi-layering, which will make it difficult to identify the ultimate holder of PNs. Both conceptually and in practice, restriction on suspicious flows enhance the reputation of markets and lead to healthy flows. We, therefore, reiterate that issuance of Participatory Notes should not be permitted."

Subsequently, the Tarapore Committee, set up by the RBI in 2006 to recommend steps to usher in Capital Account Convertibility, reiterated its earlier views of banning PNs. In this connection, the report stated, "In the case of Participatory Notes (PNs), the nature of the beneficial ownership or the identity is not known unlike in the case of FIIs. The Committee is, therefore, of the view that FIIs should be prohibited from investing fresh money raised through PNs. Existing PN-holders may be provided an exit route and phased out completely within one year."

Yet PNs continue to dominate the Indian capital markets. But what is disturbing to note here is that despite repeated attempts by SEBI, as exemplified in the UBS and Goldman Sachs cases, it has been unable to get the names of the ultimate beneficiaries of the PNs. The net result is that even to this date, SEBI is unable to get the full details of PNs that are suspected of playing ducks and drakes with the Indian capital markets.

How much of our money was laundered into tax havens? How much of this has reentered India through the PN route using the Indo-Mauritius DTAA to its advantage? How independent is our monetary policy under these circumstances? *Sense, Sensex and Sentiments* seeks to provide answers to these questions.

During the course of a casual conversation, a good chartered accountant friend of mine said: "In India, you have two major classes of citizens: law-abiding and Hawala-abiding." On a pure despondent note, I could have left with saying, "The less said, the better" but I chose exactly the opposite, "The more said, the better," in this work. The work has been written with a constant pang in the heart and a fiery passion in the mind. We cannot, after 60 years of independence, be meek and subservient to the mighty few who have acquired such might in the first place by questionable means. If we continue our indifferent, selfish ways, we will carry the curses of several generations to our graves.

Let me end with what His Holiness Jagadguru Sri Chandrasekarendra Saraswathi Swamigal (Kanchi Paramacharya), the most venerated pontiff of the country in the recent times, once said: *"Our country's welfare demands an organised, sustained movement to reestablish ethical and moral values – signified by the term 'Dharma' – so that the nation could regain its lost direction for a better future for the present generation and for posterity. To remain passive, though distressed at heart, in this hour of all-round crisis is a betrayal of national consciousness and failure in national duty."*

This work precisely is aimed at ensuring that the nation does not remain a passive spectator to the current state of drift. Crucially, we need to debate all our economic policies so as to make the markets functional and efficient.

Acknowledgements

It was a chance breakfast meeting in 2008 with Professor R. Vaidyanathan of the Indian Institute of Management, Bangalore, that eventually became the trigger for this book. Being unscheduled, the conversation was adrift till we accidentally hit upon the issue of tax havens and money laundering. Instantly, Professor Vaidyanathan ended up sowing the seeds for a larger understanding of this vexatious subject within me. But he did not stop there. As this book was written, he engaged me in a continuous debate so as to improve my understanding of this subject, went through the drafts and suggested improvements as only a teacher of his stature and calibre can. Constantly engaging in course correction and giving me the necessary words of encouragement, he acted as a mentor during this entire project. I owe a huge sense of gratitude to Professor Vaidyanathan but for whom this book would have never been possibly conceived even in my mind, leave alone ever been written.

I must also acknowledge the role of Mr. G. Anantharaman, former whole-time member, SEBI, in providing me an overarching understanding on the functioning of capital markets and related regulations. My personal interactions on this subject with Mr. Anantharaman were usually intense and purposeful.

I was fortunate to attend a series of lectures of Mr. S. Gurumurthy in 2000 and 2001 on a range of subjects. Since then, he has had a profound impact on my thinking. Subsequently, my personal interactions with Mr. S. Gurumurthy have revolved around several issues relating to law, economics, politics and spirituality. These interactions have refined my understanding of economics in general, and Indian economics in particular. But for his insightful guidance to several issues from a nationalistic perspective, I would not have been able to appreciate them in all their dimensions, including the present one. I have no words to express my gratitude to Mr. S. Gurumurthy, who has not only provided me the necessary mental endurance to embark on such a mission, but has also constantly monitored me personally as a friend, guide and philosopher.

Over a period of time, I had penned several articles on this subject in various publications. These include the Hindu Business Line, Rediff and the Chartered Accountants' Study Circle, Chennai. My thanks are to the editors of the respective publications for having provided me the necessary opportunity, which allowed me to get my thoughts across on this subject to a wider audience.

But for this interaction with various readers, my understanding of this subject would have been well and truly incomplete.

My thanks are to Mr. P. S. Prabhakar, Chartered Accountant, Chennai, for painstakingly going through the draft and constantly suggesting improvements to the contents. It is impossible, with the limited vocabulary under my command, to describe the monumental efforts undertaken by him. Constantly egging me on, Mr. Prabhakar was indeed an invaluable source of support and encouragement during this physically demanding exercise.

My thanks are also to my partner Mr. G. Srikanth for allowing me the liberty of escaping from the rigours of office to complete this exercise. Srikanth has been God's chosen gift to me. A colleague since school days, Srikanth has been the one to put up (and, perhaps is used to) with my whimsical way of functioning! My thanks are also to Prof Radhakrishnan and to my colleagues, particularly Mr. A.N.S. Vijay, Ms. Kanika and Ms. Srilatha for going through the drafts and suggesting improvements. My thanks are also to my other office colleagues, Mr. K. Vimalnathan and Mr. E. Kumaraguru, for helping me in the completion of this book.

I must also thank the publishers, KW Publishers Pvt. Ltd., New Delhi, especially its Managing Director, Kalpana Shukla and Jose Mathew, for having done a remarkable job. Their professionalism has indeed been admirable. I also take this opportunity of thanking Ms Rehana Mishra for editing this book.

I also thank all my family members for having left me unburdened by the pressures of family life, not only while writing this book but even otherwise. I have no words to express my thanks to my parents, my wife Priya (who has been another God's chosen gift to me) and sons Siddharth and Pranav for their support during this entire project. I am sure they did miss me during my long hours of absence during the completion of this work. I too did miss them.

While ensuring that all references contained in this book are appropriately acknowledged, I must admit that I could have missed some due to oversight. My apologies to all those whose references I might not have acknowledged in the book or recognised their contributions to this work.

Place: Chennai
Date: 01.08.2010

M. R. Venkatesh
mrv@mrv.net.in

CHAPTER 1

The Story of Loot and Scoot from India

Long years ago we made a tryst with destiny, and now the time comes when we shall redeem our pledge, not wholly or in full measure, but very substantially. At the stroke of the midnight hour, when the world sleeps, India will awake to life and freedom.

— Pandit Nehru, on the eve of India's independence.

Immortal words of Pandit Nehru that captured the imagination of the nation then and continues to do so to this day! Never in the history of mankind had a speech inspired a nation of this diversity, population and complexity as much as this address of Panditji did to independent India. Subsequently, two generations of Indians have been motivated by simply watching this grainy footage of Panditji.

Panditji's declaration was as profound as it was pointed on that historical occasion: "A moment comes, which comes but rarely in history, when we step out from the old to the new, when an age ends, and when the soul of a nation, long suppressed, finds utterance. It is fitting that at this solemn moment, we take the pledge of dedication to the service of India and her people and to the still larger cause of humanity." Sixty odd years later, we need to ask ourselves: has the moment arrived? Has the soul of this long suppressed nation found its utterances? Have we delivered on our pledge of dedicating ourselves to the service of India and humanity?

Independence to Panditji, as it was to several others who fought for it, was the "end of a period of ill fortune" and a time for India to discover herself again. Panditji added, "The achievement we celebrate today is but a step, an opening of opportunity, to the greater triumphs and achievements that await us. Are we brave enough and wise enough to grasp this opportunity and accept the challenge of the future?"

Sixty-two years later, we need to answer the question: did we discover ourselves again? Did we attain greater triumphs and achievements in this period? Were we brave and wise enough to grasp the opportunity that was presented to us in these decades following our independence?

To the great sons of India who fought for our independence, freedom was completely intertwined with responsibility. They foresaw the delicate balance between rights and duty, between power and discipline, between authority and responsibility. Panditji puts it brilliantly in his speech then, "The responsibility rests upon this Assembly, a sovereign body representing the sovereign people of India." Six decades later, we need to ask ourselves: did we, as free citizens of a free country, act responsibly and discharge our duties in full? Did we understand the difference between a free country and an independent country? Did we handle independence in a manner that was envisaged by our forefathers who gave their life, liberty and blood for the sake of our independence?

Foreseeing the mammoth task ahead of us, Panditji put us on notice succinctly, "The service of India means the service of the millions who suffer. It means the ending of poverty and ignorance and disease and inequality of opportunity." Several years later, we need to ask ourselves: have we ended poverty, ignorance and disease? Importantly, have we addressed the issue of inequality of opportunity? Better still, have we done enough service for the millions who suffer?

Reflecting the optimism of those heady times, Panditji declared, "The appointed day has come – the day appointed by destiny – and India stands forth again, after long slumber and struggle, awake, vital, free and independent." And Panditji added with great expectation, "It is a fateful moment for us in India, for all Asia and for the world. A new star rises, the star of freedom in the East, a new hope comes into being, a vision long cherished materialises. May the star never set and that hope never be betrayed!" Was Panditji right with his prophecy? Did the new star rise to guide the destiny of the entire world? Did the star deliver the hopes and the vision expected of it?

Panditji told us, illuminatingly, that the future beckoned us. What was the endeavour of free India? What was the end goal of independence? Was it a mere transfer of power from the British to the Indians? Or was it something more? Panditji explained the same with extraordinary clarity, "To bring freedom and opportunity to the common man, to the peasants and workers of India; to fight and end poverty and ignorance and disease; to build up a prosperous, democratic and progressive nation, and to create social, economic and political institutions which will ensure justice and fullness of life to every man and woman." Panditji finally concludes by stating, "We have hard work ahead." Indeed, we had hard work ahead then. The moot question is: did we work hard enough?

This, in sum and substance could be called the charter of our independence, the end game of our freedom movement, the vision of free India. Freedom was not merely political freedom from the British. That would have been tokenism at best. Freedom, therefore, was a much larger idea. Naturally, the idea of freedom finds immediate relevance even today in contemporary India. Have we succeeded as a free country? Have we redeemed our pledge to ourselves in these sixty-odd long years? Did we work hard enough?

Answers to these questions are not easy. While on the one hand, it is easy to be cynical about India, on the other, one should not forget that India is indeed a reasonably successful political story. Not many gave India a chance of survival as a viable political entity at the time of independence. Political experts even went on to predict the disintegration of India within a couple of decades of our independence. India's complexity, given her myriad castes, communities, religions, languages, population and her sheer size were beyond the comprehension of many Western scholars. To them, India did not fit their definition of a country. Since India was incomprehensible, they began doubting India rather than understanding India, as the former was easier. In the process, India's democratic structure was often questioned and its institutions ridiculed by these Western experts.

Yet, six decades later, we have disproved all our critics. Today, we are seen by the world as a vibrant democracy worthy of emulation. This has been possible largely due to civilisational values and cultural ethos that allowed us to embrace democracy in a spectacular fashion. It is, indeed, a compelling story of our times that neighbours who are comprised of our own genetic stock have been extraordinary failures in embracing democracy. Some are rogue states, some are on the verge of becoming one and some are in the process of disintegration. As our neighbours alternate between democracy and dictatorship, India in contrast is seen as a role model of democracy by the entire world.

That is not all. India is seen as an emerging political as well as economic powerhouse. India, that was hyphenated with Pakistan till recently, is now hyphenated with Brazil, Russia, and China. Together, these four countries form what is popularly known as the BRIC countries. In a few years from now, it is quite possible that India would become the third largest economy in the entire world, and by 2050, it is quite possible that we could well overtake the US and become the second largest economy in the world.

Our Incomplete Tryst with Destiny

However, there is a stated failure within our understated success story. It is true we have survived, but barely. It seems, contrary to what Panditji envisaged, we went to sleep at the midnight hour and the world overtook us. Countries with less natural endowments, human capital and those repeatedly ravaged by several natural calamities are placed far higher than India in the Human Development Index (HDI). According to the global Human Development Report 2009, India's HDI rank is 132. That is a sad state of affairs indeed. As we draw up the balance sheet of the country, the liabilities exceed the assets, perhaps by a significant measure. There are tell-tale signs that independent rule has not exactly resulted in independence to several millions of our countrymen. What is depressing is that we have under performed by a significant measure consistently for over six decades. The reason for this under performance is not lack of resources but under utilisation and mis-utilisation of resources.

All these are pointers to the fact that there is something terribly wrong with the way we have governed ourselves since independence. The Goldman Sachs report on these BRIC countries, which is often and widely quoted to prove India's growth potential in the next four decades, has something very interesting to state in the context of India's poor governance.

Seeking to answer a hypothetical question – had a similar study been conducted in 1960, what would have been the projection about India in 2005 – the analysis by the BRIC report is illuminating. The report admits that they would have projected a growth rate of 7 per cent per annum between 1960 and 2005. In short, this is our growth potential. But what we have achieved in this period has been a mere 4 per cent per annum. This difference of 3 percent between the actual and potential growth can be simply attributed to the lack of decisive leadership, faulty administration and lack of capital. It may be noted that as enough has been said on the first two issues by many stalwarts and experts, this book intends to be confined to the third one, in almost all its myriad forms.

Sixty-two years later, it would seem that our tryst with destiny is well and truly incomplete.

Facts often speak louder than comments. To comprehend the size of our failures, let us look into some facts that go on to define what India is today. The following facts are extracted from the Draft Approach Paper to the 11th Five-Year Plan, prepared and published by the Planning Commission. Therefore, these are not mere statistics or unverified facts. Rather, coming from the Planning Commission, they comprise an authentic and grim record of what has gone wrong in the past six decades since our independence. It is not that one can dismiss our progress post-independence. Rather, some of our achievements post-independence are indeed laudable. But our failures seem to overwhelm our successes. Consider these facts from this document of the Planning Commission:

Growth and Poverty

- Preliminary estimates are now available from the latest National Sampling Survey (NSS) thick sample conducted in 2004-05 which provides data that are fully comparable to 1993-94. This shows that the percentage of population below the poverty line in 2004-05 was almost 28 per cent, which is higher than the official figure for 1999-2000 because of the non-comparability of 1999-2000 data. The reduction in poverty between 1993-94 and 2004-05 is 0.74 per cent points per year rather than 1.66 per cent points per year as implied by the earlier 1999-2000 data.
- A more equitable allocation of the state's resources must be an important part of the solution.
- Complete elimination of the abhorrent practice of manual scavenging needs to be accomplished by the middle of the 11th Five-Year Plan. This needs to be done through effective measures of liberation and rehabilitation of scavengers such as sustainable employment and income generating activities. Similarly, total eradication of the practice of bonded labour which especially targets the Scheduled Castes (SCs) and Scheduled Tribes (STs) would be an urgent imperative in the 11th Plan.

Governance

- Some of these services, e.g. education and curative health, are available in the market to those who can afford to pay. However, quality sources of supply are costly and beyond the reach of the common man, and other privately provided services are of highly variable quality. In our situation, access for the mass of our people can only be assured through a substantial effort at public financing of these services.
- A major institutional challenge is that even where service providers exist, the quality of delivery is poor and those responsible for delivering the services can hardly be held accountable. Unless such accountability is established, it will be difficult to ensure significant improvement in delivery even if additional resources are made available. This is a major challenge of governance that must be addressed.
- At present, there is a large number of vacancies of staff in the health and education systems which have not been filled up due to resource constraints.

- The costs of displacement borne by our tribal population have been unduly high, and compensation has been tardy and inadequate, leading to serious unrest in many tribal regions. This discontent is likely to grow exponentially if the benefits from enforced land acquisition are seen as accruing to private interests, or even to the state, at the cost of those displaced.
- Corruption is now seen to be endemic in all spheres and this problem needs to be addressed urgently.
- The legal system in India is respected for its independence and fairness but it suffers from notorious delays in dispensing justice. Delays result in denial of justice.

Agriculture

- Agricultural growth declined from 3.2 per cent observed between 1980 and 1996-97 to a trend average of only 1.5 per cent subsequently. This deceleration is undoubtedly at the root of the problem of rural distress that has surfaced in many parts of the country. What is more, the problem is also not purely a distributional one, arising out of the special problems of small and marginal farmers and landless labour. In fact, the deceleration is general, affecting all farm size classes.
- A second green revolution is urgently needed to raise the growth rate of agricultural Gross Domestic Product (GDP) to around 4 per cent. This is not an easy task since actual growth of agricultural GDP, including forestry and fishing, was only 1 per cent per annum in the first three years of 10th Plan and even the most rosy projections for 2005-06 and 2006-07 would limit this below 2 per cent for the full five-year period.
- The National Farmers Commission has identified the knowledge deficit in agriculture as an important reason why productivity is much lower than what is achievable even with existing technology. To overcome this, farmers will need effective links to universities and best practices. A good extension system is the means for achieving this linkage but, unfortunately, the extension system has virtually collapsed in most states, partly as a result of constraints on non-Plan expenditure.
- No dramatic technological breakthrough comparable to the "green revolution" is presently in sight. We are also not exploiting the potential of existing technology. In fact, most of the growth required in cereals, pulses and oilseeds is possible merely through plausible yield increase in currently low yield regions.

- The result is that farming practices in large parts of the country are sub-optimal. Soil testing to determine optimal nutrient requirements is hardly practised and fertiliser application is often highly unbalanced, with excessive use of nitrogenous fertilisers, often leading to a negative effect on productivity of the soil over time, a consequence that farmers are not fully aware of. These imbalances are themselves to some extent the result of a system of fertiliser subsidy which is irrational and focusses excessively on nitrogenous fertilisers.
- Diversification requires effective marketing linkages, supported by modern marketing practices including introduction of grading, post-harvest management, cold chains, etc.
- The failure of the organised credit system in extending credit has led to excessive dependence on informal sources usually at exorbitant interest rates. This is at the root of the farmers' distress, reflected in excessive indebtedness.
- With an estimated 80 million hectares needing treatment, and average expenditure of Rs. 10,000 per hectare, the total requirement of funds is about Rs. 80,000 crores.

Education

- Literacy is still less than 70 per cent.
- The most difficult task is to ensure good quality of instruction and the position in this respect is disturbing. A recent study found that 38 per cent of children who have completed four years of schooling cannot read a small paragraph with short sentences meant to be read by a student of Class 2. About 55 per cent of such children cannot divide a three-digit number by a one-digit number. These are indicators of how bad things might be in the learning of other school subjects.
- The children must also complete eight years of useful and relevant school education and this remains a problem since the drop-out rate in primary schools for the country as a whole was around 31 per cent in 2003- 04. For some states, it was much higher.
- Data collected in the 60th round of NSS shows that only 3 per cent of the rural youth (15-29 years) and 6 per cent of the urban youth have gone through a formal course of vocational training of any kind. Most of them have acquired the skills they have from taking up, or changing, employment. Therefore, the principal planning issue will be how to expand vocational training from the present capacity of a mere 2 to 3 million to 15 million new entrants to the labour force.

- There is also a serious problem of quality. While some of our institutions of higher education compare well with the best in the world, the average standard is much lower. Disturbingly, the high quality institutions are finding it difficult to get faculty of suitable quality given the enormous increase in opportunities in the private sector for many of the skills most in demand.
- Industry also requires persons skilled in many specific trades and the situation in this area is not comforting. India has historically lagged behind in the area of technical/vocational training and even today, enrolment rates in Indian Institutes of Technology (IITs) and other vocational institutes, including nursing and computer training schools, is only about a third of that in higher education. This is quite the opposite of other Asian countries which have outperformed us in labour intensive manufactures.

Health

	India	Sri Lanka	China	Vietnam
Infant mortality (per 1,000 live births)	60 (2003)	13 (2003)	30 (2003)	19 (2003)
One year olds fully immunised for measles (%)	58.0 (2002-2004)	99 (2003)	84 (2003)	93 (2000)
Population with sustainable access to improved sanitation (%)	30 (2002)	91 (2002)	44 (2002)	41 (2002)
Under-five mortality (per 1,000 live births)	87 (2003)	15 (2003)	37 (2003)	23 (2003)
Births attended by skilled birth attendants (%)	47.6 (2002-2004)	97 (1995-2003)	97 (1995-2003)	85 (1995-2003)
Maternal mortality (per 100,000 deliveries)	407 (adjusted 2000)	92 (adjusted 2000)	56 (adjusted 2000)	130 (adjusted 2000)

Environment

- The impact on water quality of the "Water Quality Assessment Authority (WQAA)" constituted in June 2001, in different states is yet to be ascertained. A workable mechanism will be developed for monitoring and early warning systems for improving water quality.

- However, it is a matter of concern that the quality of green cover has deteriorated. There has been a 6.3 per cent reduction in dense forests, indicating degradation.
- Out of the 14.22 lakh habitations in the country, although more than 95 per cent coverage was achieved prior to Bharat Nirman, about 2.8 lakh habitations have slipped back from the fully covered to the partially covered category. Another 2.17 lakh habitations have problems with the quality of water, with about 60,000 habitations facing the serious problems of salinity or arsenic and fluoride contamination.

Infrastructure and Industry

- The most critical short-term barriers to growth of the manufacturing sector are absence of world-class infrastructure and shortage of skilled manpower.
- The most important constraint in achieving a faster growth of manufacturing is the fact that infrastructure, consisting of roads, railways, ports, airports, communication and electric power, is not up to the standards prevalent in our competitor countries.
- Shortage of electric power and the unreliability of power supply are universally recognised as a drag on the pace of India's development. Our competitors benefit from round the clock supply of power at stable voltage and frequency, but this remains elusive in most parts of India. The management of power systems, especially distribution, is the responsibility of state governments and a decisive improvement in this area is a critical challenge.
- Indian roads are considered very accident prone and claim a large number of casualties, representing an enormous human and economic loss.
- There is a need to ensure that delays in land registration, water and utility connections, environmental and other clearances are minimised through a single window clearance of applications for establishment of industrial units.
- The Mines and Minerals Act and the Mineral Concession Rules as well as the Foreign Direct Investment (FDI) policy have also been revised on several occasions with a view to attracting private investment for exploration of mineral deposits and operation of mines but actual investment in this area has been meagre because of procedural hassles and numerous discretionary provisions in the laws, which discourage prospective investors.
- A key issue in this context is the need for greater flexibility in some of the labour laws. In particular, there is the need to consider appropriate

amendments in Section V-B of the Industrial Disputes Act, 1947, to facilitate exit of labour and the Contract Labour (Abolition and Regulation Act) to give the industry the necessary flexibility to compete in international markets.

- Cross-subsidising passenger traffic through freight traffic, and within passenger traffic, cross-subsidising second class fares by overcharging the higher class of travel cannot be carried beyond a point because overcharged freight migrates to the roads and the overcharged passengers to the air. To put railway fares on a rational basis, it is essential to establish a Rail Tariff Regulatory Authority.
- Manufacturing and maintenance of rolling stock (of the railways) should be corporatised as has been done in China.
- The Accelerated Power Development and Reform Programme (APDRP) initiated in 2001 was expected to bring down AT&C[1] losses to 15 percent by the end of the 10th Plan. In fact, the average loss for all states is closer to 40 per cent (including uncollected bills). State Governments should adopt the goal of bringing down AT&C losses from the current level of around 40 per cent to at least 15 per cent by the end of the 11th Plan. This can be done if managements of State Electricity Boards (SEBs) are professionalised and given autonomy of operation without political interference.
- Coal production is nationalised at present. If petroleum, which is much scarcer than coal, is open to the private sector, there is no reason why coal should not also be opened up, especially if we take a longer term view of energy constraints and also the need to absorb new clean coal technologies.

Even in those idealistic times, immediately following independence, Panditji's soul was tormented. He commented that we have often been unworthy followers of the Mahatma and have strayed from his message. But he hoped that "succeeding generations will remember this message and bear the imprint in their hearts of this great son of India, magnificent in his faith and strength and courage and humility." Given the state of affairs in the country, one shudders to think of what Panditji would have had to say if he were alive today.

Post-independence there is no doubt that we have buried the ideals of the Mahatma and the dreams of our freedom fighters fathoms deep.

---

1. AT&C refers to Aggregate Technical and Commercial losses. This is also referred to as the Transmission and Distribution (T&D) losses.

Corruption and Capital Flight Post-Independence

Of the three ancient civilisations, Greek, Roman and Indian, it is the Indian civilisation that has survived the ravages of time. The reason for the same is not far to seek. It may be interesting to note that while the Greek civilisation depended on beauty and sensual pleasures, and the Roman civilisation was based on military and hard power, the Indian civilisation was based on *Dharma*, which meant that it was based on eternal truth, righteousness and morality. For a civilisation that prided itself throughout its history on being rooted to *Dharma*, it is indeed a sad state of affairs that all the three pillars of our Constitution – the legislature, judiciary and executive – stand significantly corroded within this short period of time and their collective moral authority, considerably eroded. It is this gross degeneration of morality in all walks of life that has brought India where she stands today in the comity of nations.

No wonder, bereft of her civilisational moorings, India is a debilitated democracy, a handicapped civilisation and a challenged society.

Much as we talk of India's poverty, let me hasten to add that we should not forget another dimension of the entire debate about India. It is estimated by various historians that the 90 years of formal British rule between 1857 and 1947 resulted in the transfer of wealth of approximately one trillion dollars at current market prices from India to Britain. We seem to have done far better in sixty-odd years of self-rule, especially in the last thirty years. Various estimates demonstrate that our post-independence rulers have achieved this target far more efficiently compared to what the British did with so much ado in ninety years. Put pithily, if the British took ninety years to transfer one trillion dollars of our wealth, various estimates suggest that our indigenous *Swadeshi* rulers have taken merely thirty years to transfer USD 1.4 trillion (Rs 70,00,000 crores) of our wealth abroad!

It may be noted that all these negative developments were hastened since the Eighties when the Indian economy underwent mild doses of reforms. Contrary to popular belief that liberalisation of the economy would prevent corruption, the deepening of the reforms process since the early 1990s is seen as having increased the opportunities for corruption. The emergence of globalised corporations with huge financial and political powers disproportionate to the power of our local governments, manned by people without *Dharma*, has provided an impetus for a very high level of corruption. Perhaps we began liberalising and globalising the Indian economy without adequate preparation of our men for the same. Consequently, every department of the Government viz., public work, health, sanitation, infrastructure, education, transport, power, law and order, social welfare, public distribution, rural development, state or Centre, are all involved in massive doses of corruption.

Since the late Eighties, the nation has been a silent witness to massive doses of corruption. Bofors, procurement of armaments for our armed forces, imports and exports of various edible items, food for oil and, of course, licensing spectrum for our telecom companies are a few cases in point not to speak of massive evasion of taxes. The corruption involved in all these cases has been huge, so much so that despite the availability of overwhelming evidence, precious little has been done, lest the system becomes dysfunctional. Interestingly, it points to a seamless integration of the state actors and the private sector.

In the Indian context, there is something more – despite such massive levels of corruption, we have not been able to get at the big fishes in the Government in any meaningful manner. Therefore, it is rationalised that scams have become a way of life in India. In the process, scam is India's gift to the English language which suggests the following paradigm – one, that indicates massive levels of corruption; two, the availability of irrefutable evidence; and three, the impotency of the law enforcers. What is traumatising the collective conscience of the nation is the fact that the judicial system has been unable to convict anyone from the ruling elite, despite overwhelming evidence available in such high-profile cases of corruption.

Nevertheless, corruption is not the central theme of this book. Admittedly, corruption in India is massive. Naturally, questions follow: where has this money gone? Is it in India or has it been parked outside India? With increasing liberalisation of the Indian economy, it is easier to park the ill-gotten wealth in some foreign tax havens than parking it in India. Liberalisation of the Indian economy has simultaneously ensured that it is equally painless to get this ill-gotten wealth back into India as either Foreign Direct Investment (FDI) or Foreign Institutional Investment (FII) – an area that has repeatedly escaped the attention of the Government, polity and media. But let us not blame liberalisation either and throw the baby out with the bathwater. *The fact of the matter is that governance is an issue in India.*

Therefore, the focus of this book is actually on the policies that aid and abet this transfer of the loot – yes, loot – out of India, and on those who allow shifting back a portion of such wealth stealthily into India. From an ideological standpoint, it may be noted that capital movement by itself is not illegal but for the fact that the clandestine manner in which this is done deprives the

Central and State Governments of their legitimate share of revenue as much as it encourages corruption. The globalisation of the Indian financial markets and in particular, the poorly regulated movement of funds from secretive offshore financial centres to the Indian financial sector, has facilitated the successful laundering of this dirty money from India and back into India. This underpreparedness of the Indian regulatory mechanism to the process of global integration of its financial sector has ensured a virtual free-for-all where illegal transactions (of crime, corruption and terror) become indistinguishable from legitimate transactions.

Remember, here we are talking of the loot from India by Indians, aided and abetted by policies that ensure such loot. This loot from India is a mere fraction of the total quantum of corruption in India. And that aggregates to a staggering 1.4 trillion dollars or more. Do we need to say anything more? Yet, given this magnitude of loot from India, one is surprised that India is termed as a poor or a developing country repeatedly by economists in India and abroad.

You do not loot a poor country, do you? But that is poor consolation in more ways than one.

Crucially, the impact of this loot on the national development is one of the most understated aspects of modern Indian economics. The net outcome of poor social sector performance and failing infrastructure is both the cause and consequence of this loot. That effectively brings in the question of governance in India. Corruption, it is often said, flourishes in weak states. Therefore, those who are the beneficiary of corruption, seek to ensure that the Indian state remains weak. That means our assault on poverty is superficial and symbolic as the state is unable to deliver either on infrastructure or on social sector indices. Further, poverty fosters crime, and crime has a demonstrable nexus with terrorism. The symbiotic link to all these is corruption – one that unites poverty, crime and terrorism – a linkage that is a central theme of this book. Strangely, the nation seems to be in a state of stupor or remains a silent witness to this continued mess caused by corruption. The plausible reason for the same is pretty obvious – the nation is oblivious of the ill-effects of corruption and its symbiotic link to poverty, crime and terrorism.

Consequently, the "progress" of the nation has remained in its periphery. Given the extent to which corruption, coupled with this gargantuan plunder, has gnawed at the vitals of the nation, to many Indians, independence means very little. Some well meaning Indians have gone to the extent of suspecting that corruption and not anything else will dynamite the unity and integrity of the country in the near future. The spectacular economic growth announced by the Government year after year is meaningless to a majority of our people. It is in this context that it is perhaps necessary to remember the profound observation made by Kanchi Paramacharya H.H. Chandrasekarendra Saraswathi Swami on the very day British left India, viz., August 15, 1947, that while it was true that India had attained freedom, it was a long way from achieving independence. Prophetic words indeed!

All these reflect the mess that is India. Broadly, three factors that have contributed to this mess are:

- The lack of decisive political leadership.
- Systemic flaws in governance which even to this day is modelled on the British way of governance.
- Loot of capital from India (technically termed as capital flight).

Or is it to be sequenced the other way around? Once flight of capital happened on a regular basis, vested interests began to feed on the system and worked their way to ensure a weak leadership and a pliable administration. Definitely, one cannot be original in this debate. It is corruption that makes India poor and our poverty feeds on corruption. It is corruption that is ensuring the continued loot of billions from the poor in India and, thus, holding us back from using our own precious capital required for our development. It is corruption that is preventing better governance in India. It is corruption that feeds on petty crime which in turn leads to terrorism.

This interrelationship between corruption, on the one hand, and poverty, crime and terrorism, on the other, is too well documented by various studies across the globe to warrant a repetition here. But it is a vicious circle that has a debilitating impact on the development of a nation as well as a systemic impact on its economy. And unless we break this cycle, it is impossible to win our war on poverty.

In this connection, it may be noted that Transparency International's "The Global Corruption Report 2009" discusses the means to corruption in business, identifies pressing areas for reform and outlines the challenges that corruption poses to sustainable economic growth and development. Topics covered in this report include bribery and policy capture, corporate fraud, cartels, corruption in supply chains and transnational transactions as well as other emerging challenges. While the rankings provided by this report are admittedly subjective and, hence, at best indicative, the fact remains that India is ranked as a highly corrupt nation by this report.

For a country whose motto is Satyameva Jayate, (truth shall prevail), that is simply unacceptable.

The situation must be remedied forthwith. To get rid of the scourge of poverty, we need to eliminate corruption. Yet most Indians believe that the Government would do the needful, little realising that many State actors in India are the beneficiaries of the system that allows rampant corruption. This is akin to the belief entertained by most Indians that the Government of Pakistan could join the global war on terror. How could the State actors in Pakistan direct the Pakistani Government or its agencies to fight terror when they – the State actors in Pakistan – are beneficiaries of such terror?

Therefore, in this scenario, one must hasten to add that it would be extremely puerile to believe that the Indian establishment (executive, legislature or judiciary) could act decisively on this vital issue. On the contrary, their neck deep involvement in corruption (and as a beneficiary of corruption) makes them a suspect to handle the vexatious issue of corruption.

The time has, therefore, come for the people of India to act in their own supreme self-interest, which in this case approximates to the national interest. That in a way justifies this book.

Debilitating Impact of Capital Flight on a Developing Country

The debilitating impact of capital flight on a developing country can never be understated. To develop, obviously, a country requires capital. This is fundamental economics. A country like India requires a huge quantum of capital, especially as her developmental needs are simply gigantic. Yet, for the past sixty years after our independence, we have turned a blind eye to the idea of capital flight from India. The time has come to recognise the debilitating impact of capital flight from India, prevent any further flight and take the necessary steps to bring back the same back into India.

This flight of capital over the years has prevented India from attaining a developed country status and ensured that we have remained a "developing" one for the past sixty odd years and could continue to be so for a reasonable time in the future. It has left our millions mired in poverty, ignorance and disease. It is the cause of our poor infrastructure, both rural and urban. It has resulted in India being repeatedly hyphenated to sub-Saharan countries or South Asian countries in several human development indices. It is to be noted that capital flight has impacted several developing countries for the past few decades. But that is no solace to a country like India whose real performance, as explained above, has consistently fallen short of her potential. Nevertheless, it is interesting to note the global perspective before we try and appreciate the Indian context.

In a speech delivered by Raymond W. Baker in June 2007, titled "The Ugliest Chapter in Global Economic Affairs Since Slavery," Baker the traces the development of the global structure since the 1960s that facilitated the movement of illicit capital away from the developing countries. Baker captures the prevailing economic paradigm of the 1960s when he states, "Many political leaders and wealthy business people wanted to take money out of these newly independent countries, a desire which was well serviced by Western financial institutions." Baker implicitly alleges that the idea of encouraging capital flows from the developing world is a conspiracy of the developed nations, notably certain Western nations. This capital flight was further encouraged by the proliferation of tax havens since the Sixties that aided and abetted capital flows from the developing countries into the developed ones.

And that applies to India in equal measure. Naturally, capital flight has emerged as the single largest challenge to the sustenance of the Indian economy. There are several seemingly valid economic reasons for the flight of capital from India. Some of these are global and some local. Some of these are typical to India. Some of these are time honoured reasons and some relatively new to the Indian context. All these factors are summarised briefly hereunder:

- Doubts about the very idea of India: Till the 1980s, several political commentators doubted the very idea of India. Western political analysts often predicted the collapse of the country. All these played on the collective psyche of the elites of India, who as a natural de-risking process, simply parked their money abroad.
- Tax Rates: Socialist India in the Sixties and Seventies was subjected to phenomenal rates of both direct and indirect taxes. Some of these rates are too obscene to be quoted now. Naturally, these high rates provided the incentive to park money outside India.
- Draconian Forex (Foreign Exchange) Laws: Till not so long ago, India had one of the most draconian foreign exchange laws in the entire world. That meant Indians who needed Forex even for their legitimate needs, were denied the same. This, in turn, encouraged Indians to park their money outside India.

Post-liberalisation, several of these legislations that implicitly encouraged illegal flow of capital were replaced by far liberal exchange controls as well as tax laws. While liberalisation addressed the issues of capital flows arising due to extraordinarily high rates of taxes, it spawned a new set of reasons for capital flight away from India. With a liberal exchange control regime, it is easier to officially obtain foreign exchange for payments to be made abroad to Indian policy framers for their favours. Simultaneously, the investment regimes too has been liberalised, with several companies reportedly using their foreign affiliates or subsidiaries to make such payments.

Secondly, India is a huge playground for several narco-terror outfits and continues to be a vital link in the international drug smuggling pipeline. Security officials have repeatedly pointed out that several insurgent groups fighting for independence in India's northeastern states have jointly opened up a new front to smuggle drugs abroad and buy weapons from the proceeds. Terrorism, as we understand it, is a costly affair and requires huge amounts of money. Several commercial entities are reported to camouflage their end game of funding terror outfits. All these involve clandestine movement of funds from India to other countries as a first step and then bringing them back into India for illegal operations as the second.

Finally, there is still the old commercial logic that drives capital away from India. Remember, crooks will be crooks. Despite the significant fall in both direct and indirect tax rates over the years, further accentuated by the liberalisation process, some sections of the Indian industry feel that business in India can be carried out profitably only when taxes are evaded. While conceding the fact that our tax laws are still complex and levies higher than the global standards, one is often reminded of the maxim: old habits die hard. All these factors that sustain capital flows away from modern India are summarised hereunder:

- The proceeds of bribery of corrupt Government officials, politicians and perhaps even some judges including members of the higher judiciary.
- The proceeds of criminal activities, often referred to as narco-terror money.
- The proceeds of tax-evasion and laundered commercial transactions.

Nevertheless, over the years, the reasons why Indians parked money abroad changed, the practice did not.

While the reasons for ensuring capital flight changed over the years, the means and destination of this capital flight over the years remained more or less similar. These include under- or over-invoicing in cross-border transactions and transfer pricing with offshore affiliates or subsidiaries. Interestingly, all three forms of capital flight – those arising from corrupt, criminal or commercial activities – often end up using the very same routes for transferring the capital abroad.

As explained above, first, it was mostly by commercial channels. Then, drug peddlers began using these channels. Since the late 1990s, seeing how easy it was for drug dealers to move their profits, terrorists stepped in to move their proceeds from India. Over the years, that was further improvised and improved by newer players. Baker puts it simply, "Drug kingpins, criminal syndicate heads, and terrorist masterminds did not invent any new ways of moving their illicit proceeds. They merely utilised the mechanisms that we had created for the purpose of moving flight capital and tax-evading money."

As briefly mentioned at the outset, India is not the only country facing capital flight. Baker estimates that USD 1 trillion to USD 1.6 trillion of illicit money moves across borders annually. In his celebrated book on the subject *Capitalism's Achilles Heel*, Baker has detailed how he has "conservatively" arrived at this figure. Other experts estimate that the figure could be far higher.

How much of this global capital flight could arise from India? India's GDP is approximately 2 per cent of the global GDP. Prorating (again that could be a conservative basis in the Indian context) this to the global figures mentioned by Baker, one can safely arrive at a capital flight of approximately USD 20-25 billion per year from India. How much of this could have aggregated in the years since independence is anybody's guess. Estimates vary between USD 500 billion (on a conservative basis) to a more aggressive USD 1.4 trillion. In rupee terms and at the present exchange value, it could well mean anywhere between Rs 25,00,000 crores to Rs 70,00,000 crores! We will be dealing with this subject in greater detail in subsequent chapters of this book while dealing with the issue of tax havens.

These amounts need to be put in the proper perspective. Noted columnist Mr. S. Gurumurthy, writing in his column in the *New Indian Express*, an article titled "Secret Wealth Abroad," explained the consequence of bringing even a fraction of this huge amount of money back into India. He wrote, "See the consequence even if part of it is brought back. A portion of it would make India free from all external debts which is now over USD 220 billion; India will transform into an economic superpower; some 10 or 15 Indian rupees could buy a US dollar which today 50 Indian rupees cannot; a litre of petrol on our roadside would cost Rs 15 or even less, against today's 50 plus; the cost of imports in rupee terms would be down to a third or half; India's entire infrastructure needs can be funded; India will become so energy efficient and cost competitive that exporters may need no sops at all; India will lend to – not, as it does now, borrow from – the world; Indian housing can be funded at affordable cost; rural poverty can be wiped out... The list is endless." Indeed. Isn't it?

Several experts have pointed to the overall cost of modernising India's infrastructure. This ranges from a conservative USD 200 billion to an extravagant USD 750 billion, depending on one's definition of infrastructure and modernity. One way of funding our infrastructure requirements including roads, ports, airports, irrigation, power, schools, hospitals, city infrastructure and, of course, cleaning up our environment, apart from repaying our foreign debts, is to retrieve our own money from these tax havens.

Contrast this with the general picture of India portrayed earlier in the chapter by the Draft Approach Paper to the 11th Five-Year Plan issued by the Planning Commission. For eleven successive plans, the Planning Commission has been repeatedly talking of the issue of lack of resources to tackle the socio-economic challenges of the country. But the Planning Commission does not mention our resources in these tax havens even in passing. Neither does it think out of the box and seek to reverse capital flight from India and bring back the stolen wealth of India parked in tax havens. On the contrary, the Planning Commission is known to have a template approach to successive plans, so much so that one of my friends, when asked to comment on the first draft to the 11th Plan, cryptically commented that it was in fact the eleventh draft to the first plan! How true!

The only apparent reason why we as a nation are hesitating and not launching an all out war is that the high and mighty of the land are suspected to have accounts in these tax havens. It is generally believed that several of our politicians, industrialists, celebrities, media personalities, legal luminaries and bureaucrats have accounts in these tax havens. In short, all the three pillars of the Constitution , the legislature, executive and judiciary along with the fourth, the media, seem to be severely compromised and affected by the virus of corruption. That explains the silence of the political class, chambers of commerce, industry, media, intelligentsia, professionals and the administration on this crucial issue of our money parked in tax havens. It makes the battle in India completely unequal – a war between the elites of the country (who have been party to the loot since 1947) and the victims of their loot (who still await the promised tryst with destiny since 1947).

Rajaji, no less famously remarked that it is easier to remove foreign tyranny than the one caused by indigenous, *Swadeshi* self-rule. That was in the early 70s. Approximately four decades later, one cannot but fully appreciate the import of these words. While one can understand the suppressed glee of the looters and appreciate the stoic silence of the looted, the behaviour of the intelligentsia and the civil society on this matter is inexplicable. In the recorded history of mankind, perhaps there is no parallel of the elites and intelligentsia of a nation having betrayed it as much as the Indian elite betrayed the cause of India, especially on this matter of corruption and the looted wealth being parked in tax havens.

Phenomena of Reversal of this Flow Through PNs

There is an interesting twist to this tale of capital flight from the developing countries. To appreciate the issue comprehensively, a reference to the global developments since the last decade or so becomes crucial. China and India are perhaps the only two countries in the world to record robust growth for the past decade or so. What makes India's story particularly spectacular is the fact that India's savings rate has increased from approximately 23 per cent a decade ago to well in excess of 35 per cent of her GDP in 2008-09. This gargantuan amount of domestic savings, by and large, funds the domestic investments. In this connection, the annual report of the Reserve Bank of India (RBI) for 2008-09 states, "Domestic savings financed more than 95 per cent of investment, and the remaining, by capital flows. Domestic investment rate reached 39 per cent of the GDP in 2007-08 from 37 per cent in 2006-07." That makes India's growth story extremely impressive and sustainable. India's savings ensure that India need not significantly depend on the global capital flows for her investment requirement. That insulates India from large scale gyrations witnessed in global capital flows. No wonder, in the aftermath of the recent financial and economic crisis that continues to plague the world, it is India that is one of the very few countries to quickly return to very high growth trajectory.

All these factors make the Indian economy a fascinating investment destination. While liberalisation seems to attract genuine capital flows from abroad both as FDI and FII, there is an interesting phenomenon in so far as it pertains to India. Decades of capital flows seem to be reversing and some of it seems to be coming back into India, masquerading as foreign capital. This reverse flow of capital is attempted not covertly but openly through a large regulatory gap. Naturally, this has set the cat amongst the pigeons. Some economists put forth the moral argument. Why should we be importing such tainted capital back into India? Of course, there are some who put forth the theory of convenience. They argue that it is our own black money that is coming back and is thus an indicator of the confidence that our own people have in the strength of our economy and should, therefore, be welcomed. Accordingly, they rationalise that if capital flight took place in the Sixties and Seventies on account of lack of faith in the country, today, some of it would obviously return, reflecting the inherent strength of India and her economy.

But in real life, situations cannot be evaluated on a binary footing. Rather, life is full of shades of gray, with several arguments and counter-arguments that impact every policy formulation of the Government. The question that needs to be pondered is whether such costs justify the resultant benefits.

One mechanism for such return of tainted capital is known as Participatory Notes (PNs), an issue that seems to have engaged the attention of analysts in the past decade or so. To appreciate the evolution of PNs, a bit of our history of successive doses of liberalisation needs to be traced. It may be recalled that India's development strategy post-independence was largely focussed on self-reliance and import substitution. Further, the meagre current account deficits were financed largely through debt flows and official development assistance. There was a general disinclination towards foreign investment. That was till the Eighties. After the launch of the reforms in the early 1990s, there was a gradual shift towards liberalising capital flows. From September 1992, with certain restrictions, FIIs and Overseas Corporate Bodies (OCBs) were permitted to invest in financial instruments. This policy of liberalisation had further taken the form of:

- Relaxation of investment limits for FIIs.
- Relaxation of eligibility conditions.
- Liberalisation of investment instruments accessible for FIIs.

Originally, the initial limit for an individual FII was 5 per cent of the total issued capital of the invested entity. This was raised to 10 per cent in June 1998 and the ceiling for a single FII was separated from that of a single Non-Resident Indian/Person of Indian Origin/Overseas Corporate Body (NRI/PIO/OCB). Further, the aggregate investment ceiling for all FIIs was raised to 24 per cent of the issued and paid-up capital in a company, subject to passing of a special resolution by the general body of the company. Under eligibility conditions, the definition of broad based funds was relaxed in August 1999, and in February 2000, newer entities, such as foreign firms were allowed to invest as sub-accounts. Subsequently, PNs emerged as an alternative to sub-accounts.

PNs, it may be noted, are instruments used by foreign funds. PNs are like contract notes and are issued by FIIs, registered in our country, to their overseas clients who may not be eligible to invest in the Indian stock markets. PNs are used as an alternative to sub-accounts by ultimate investors generally based on considerations related to transactions costs and record-keeping overheads. What makes the issue of PNs entirely convoluted is that by the process of multi-layering, the identity of the ultimate beneficiary can be kept confidential. The RBI has on several occasions expressed apprehension that some of the money coming into the Indian market through the PN route could be the unaccounted wealth of some rich Indians camouflaged under the guise of FII. What adds fat to the fire is that this money could even be tainted and linked with illegal activities such as terrorism, smuggling and drug-running.

Further, it is apprehended by several financial experts that the PN route is misused by hedge funds (hedge funds are 'unregulated' collective investment vehicles, often organised as private partnerships and residence offshore for tax and regulatory purposes; currently, offshore hedge funds are not permitted to participate in the Indian markets). That raises the risk of significant volatility in Indian markets, undermining the integrity of the markets and making them susceptible to manipulation. But all these arguments were well known to the Securities and Exchange Board of India (SEBI) since 2001 when the issue of PNs had come to rock the Indian stock markets and led to the stock market scam and the subsequent enquiry through the Joint Parliamentary Committee (JPC).

To SEBI, anonymity was not an issue in 2001. Neither does it seem an issue in 2010.

But the anonymity of PNs is an issue by itself, as we will see right through this book. First, anonymity goes against the very idea of modern banking and ethos of the global financial sector. Second, the international financial sector is chary of terrorists infiltrating their operations and, hence, seeks to identify the ultimate beneficiary of every transaction as well as its originator. Finally, with international consensus veering towards identifying and preventing illicit flow of capital arising out of crime, corruption and commercial activities, the global financial system is against allowing anonymous characters to gain access to any financial markets.

Despite these global developments, why anonymity of PNs has never been an issue to SEBI is one of the central themes that runs throughout the length and breadth of this book. We shall be dealing with this issue in greater detail in the following chapters of this book while dealing with the UBS Bank and Goldman Sachs cases.

But first let us examine the link of PNs to the stock markets, and its debilitating impact on the functioning of the Indian stock markets.

Stock Market Scam 2001 was in Effect a PN Scam

In the beginning of January 2001, the Sensex was about 4000. It appreciated by 10 percent in the following weeks to once again slide back to the same levels by February 27. On February 28, 2001, the Budget of 2001-2002 was presented in the Parliament. The gyrations in bourses continued unabated with a definitive downward trend noted in March of that year. This gyration in the index was the result of extreme volatility recorded in select scrips. Consequently, SEBI instituted an investigation on March 2, 2001, which began with six broking entities and was subsequently expanded to cover several other players. Simultaneously, in the first week of March, the members of the Parliament drew the attention of the Government to the ongoing meltdown in the stock market, and their apprehensions that there could be market manipulation. What was bothering the Parliament was that a major stock market operator had taken huge stock positions by misusing bank funds. In a way, the Parliament suspected a stock market scam funded by unscrupulous bankers.

The members of Parliament were agitated about the ineffectiveness of SEBI and the possibility that the stock market had been manipulated. Simultaneously, on March 9, there was a sudden rush of depositors wishing to withdraw their deposits at the Ahmedabad branch of Madhavapura Mercantile Cooperative Bank, the second largest bank in the state of Gujarat. This run on the bank were fuelled by rumours that the bank had extended guarantees to Mr. Ketan Parekh, a leading Mumbai based stockbroker, who had suffered huge losses in his share dealings. On March 13, the bank closed all its operations, unable to meet the run on its deposits.

The matter came up for discussion in the Parliament subsequently. The members drew attention to the volatility in the stock markets and unhealthy practices like insider trading and rampant speculation. They pointed out that SEBI had not kept a close watch on the market. Since SEBI itself was a suspect, the members were of the view that a mere enquiry by SEBI would not serve the purpose. Responding to these charges, the then Finance Minister Mr. Yashwant Sinha stated that "while fluctuations are normal in stock markets and should not be a matter of undue concern, we should be vigilant with regard to any systemic risk or movement driven by any form of manipulation." However, he also gave assurances to the members that he was in turn assured by SEBI that there was no systemic risk to the market and there was no danger of a payment crisis.

Some members were of the view that the damage caused to the share market was of such magnitude that it needed a thorough enquiry and it was, therefore, suggested that a Joint Parliamentary Committee (JPC) should be constituted and a report be submitted to Parliament within a proper time-frame. Consequently, a JPC was constituted in March 2002.

One of the interesting findings of the committee was with respect to PNs. According the JPC report [Para 8.81 of the report], SEBI expressed suspicion that some of the Indian promoters have purchased shares of their own companies through PNs issued by sub-accounts of FIIs. This mechanism enabled the holders to hide their identities and to transact in the Indian capital market. It is obvious that the JPC report concluded that PNs by their very character provide anonymity to their owners.

Anonymity! And that is the Crux of the Issue

The committee further noted that SEBI had since directed FIIs to report details of the PNs as and when issued by them. The committee suggested that failure on the part of FIIs to report on the issue of PNs should be viewed seriously and should entail stringent punitive action. It should also be ensured that this instrument is not misused in any way to manipulate the Indian securities market, the committee had opined.

The response of the Government contained in the Action Taken Report (ATR) to the JPC is interesting: "During the investigation into the last stock market manipulation, SEBI had come across certain cases of Participatory Notes issued by FIIs and OCBs. In order to increase the transparency, SEBI had immediately issued Circular No. FITTC/CUST/14/2001 dated October 31, 2001 to all FIIs and their Custodians advising the FIIs to report as and when any derivative instruments (PNs) with Indian underlying securities are issued/renewed/redeemed by them either on their own account or on behalf of sub-accounts registered under them. Accordingly, FIIs are sending reports from time to time whenever they are issuing PNs. SEBI is considering steps to include disclosure of information about the terms, nature and contracting parties to the PNs issued by FIIs."

Look how the response is worded – clearly ducking the issue of PNs by Indian promoters as well as the issue of anonymity in totality.

In fact, the anonymity issue is what led to the 2001 scam in the first place. The issue raised by the JPC was whether Indian promoters had purchased shares of their own companies through the PN route, obviously using illegitimate funds. The answer of the Government skirts this crucial issue and begins to focus on the proposed reporting structure mandated by SEBI since October 2001, seeking details of PNs issued/renewed/redeemed by FIIs either on their own account or on behalf of sub-accounts registered under them. The obfuscation begins right away.

Subsequently, the first progress report (progress reports on further action taken are reported to the Parliament twice every year – in May/June as well as December; till date, 14 progress reports have been issued by the Government) to the ATR issued by the Ministry of Finance in December 2003 states: "Provision has been made for disclosure of offshore derivative instruments (i.e. PNs) based on underlying Indian securities in the SEBI (FII) Regulations, 1995." SEBI, vide circular IMD/ CUST/8/2003 dated August 8, 2003, has introduced fortnightly reporting of offshore derivative instruments against underlying securities from August 2003.

The first progress report further states, "All FIIs are also required to submit the following undertaking: We undertake that we/associates/clients have not issued/subscribed/purchased any of the offshore derivative instruments directly or indirectly to/from Indian residents/NRIs/PIOs/OCBs during the Statement Period."

The report also points out the fact that "out of a total 508 FIIs registered with SEBI as on August 14, 2003, till October 9, 2003, PN Reports from 467 FIIs have been received in terms of the aforesaid circular. It may be noted that only 12 FIIs have submitted the PN Reports containing information on PNs issued by them, the balance 455 FIIs have submitted 'Nil Reports'. Letter dated September 30, 2003, seeking explanation for the non-submission of PN Reports has been sent to the FIIs who had not submitted the said report."

Look at our fixation at settling the contentious issue by asking for some vaguely worded undertaking from the FIIs. Not only is the undertaking delightfully ambiguous, one is unsure of the inbuilt counter-check mechanism to verify the veracity of the undertaking prescribed by SEBI. That is not all. As we would see subsequently when we deal with the Goldman Sachs case in later chapters, this undertaking suffers from serious legal deficiencies, as dealt with elaborately by the Hon'ble Securities Appellate Tribunal (SAT) order in May 2008. The Progress Report issued subsequently (i.e. in the aftermath of the order of Hon'ble SAT in May 2008) is surprisingly silent on this issue.

Further, the second progress report to the ATR issued in June 2004 pointed out certain regulatory changes brought about in the FII Regulations. It is interesting to note that Regulation 15A provides that after February 02, 2004, PNs can be issued only in favour of regulated entities subject to compliance of the "know your client" (KYC) requirement. It has also been stipulated that an FII or sub-account shall ensure that no further downstream issue or transfer of any PN would be made to any person other than a regulated entity.

What is crucial here is that in May 2004, the Indian stock markets, as a response to the fall of the National Democratic Alliance (NDA) Government witnessed a dramatic fall. Given the gravity of the fall, SEBI sought to investigate into the entire matter and find out as to who all were instrumental in selling such a huge quantum of shares, triggering a dramatic fall in the stock prices in one single trading session. It is in this context that the entire issue of respecting the KYC norms was analysed by SEBI in the context of the UBS case. In the instant case, SEBI suspected UBS of having triggered the fall in the Indian stock markets in May 2004.

However, UBS stated that it did sell shares under the instructions of certain PN holders. When SEBI pursued the matter further to know about the identity of the ultimate beneficiaries of the PN holders, UBS claimed that it could not understand what constituted KYC in the absence of precise guidelines defining the term. Consequently, it did not furnish the same to SEBI. This argument was upheld by the Hon'ble SAT in its order in 2005. Subsequent progress reports issued by the Finance Ministry maintain a stoic silence on this issue. We will also examine the issue of the UBS case in greater detail in later chapters.

Mauritius: The Route to Tax Heaven From Tax Havens

Mauritius is a tiny island tucked deep inside the Indian Ocean. The official website of the country claims that "Mauritius will enchant you, uplift your soul, making you feel that you belong to the chosen few. Every visitor enjoys personal attention. Every encounter is an opportunity to discover a friendly face. Behind each smile lies the promise of a unique holiday. Mauritius, a melting pot where past and present are smoothly blended together, offers an essential beauty that will compel you to return to its shores time and time again. May your stay with us remain engraved in your memory forever." One does not know about the rest of the world being enchanted by this wonderful, idyllic, picturesque island, but surely India has been, and continues to be, for the past two decades, for investment purposes.

The reasons for the same are not just its scenic beaches. Rather it is economics, pure and simple. Interestingly, this tiny island nation is the single largest investor into India. Between 2000 and the middle of 2009, it accounted for approximately 45 percent – yes, 45 – of the total foreign investment received in this period by India. The importance of Mauritius can be gauged by the fact that Singapore is a distant second best, at 9 percent. The USA and UK are the third and fourth best at 7 and 6 percent respectively. That explains our fascination and fixation with Mauritius.

In the early 90s, Mauritius sought to have an image makeover (coinciding with the new economic policy in India). It wanted to transform itself from a sleepy tourist island into a "competitive investment destination." To achieve this objective, Mauritius, launched a global banking scheme, liberalised its tax regime and signed a Double Taxation Avoidance Agreement (DTAA) with select countries. (DTAAs are signed between two countries to avoid double taxation at both ends while simultaneously preventing tax evasion in both countries). Clarity on taxation matters, it is generally believed, goes a long way in ensuring enhanced trade and commerce.

India, prominently figured in this master plan of Mauritius. India, because of her strategic location, size and historical connections, emerged as a preferred investment destination for Mauritius. The Indo-Mauritius DTAA was first signed in a remarkable coincidence on All Fools Day in 1983. The singular attraction of this DTAA is that no "resident" of Mauritius would be taxed in India on capital gains arising out of sale of shares in India. This clause is perhaps deliberately worded loosely enough so that even if any money simply passes through Mauritius, it could be characterised as "investments" arising out of Mauritius. The DTAA virtually gives exemption from capital gains tax arising out of sale or transfer of shares if such investments are routed through Mauritius. According to experts on this subject, no other DTAA signed by India has such peculiar beneficial clauses.

Yet not much sound and fury would have been raised, provided Mauritius levied capital gains tax on such transactions. Mauritius also abolished capital gains tax in the early 90s. Effectively that means as per the DTAA, capital gains arising on investments in shares in India can be taxed only in Mauritius. And the tax rate in Mauritius is zero. That explains why there is clamour for investments into India through Mauritius. No wonder, Mauritius is the largest investment partner of India.

An engaging piece of information: Press reports suggest that a good portion of these investments arise from specific locations in Mauritius, which include the offices of chartered accountants, lawyers and investment consultants. In effect, significant portions of our "global investment" originate from a few offices in a remote island in the Indian Ocean. Obviously, there is nothing foreign about FII.

The *Daily Pioneer* had done some extraordinary investigation on this matter. In a spectacular investigation carried out by Mr. J. Gopikrishna of the *Pioneer*, the inability of big foreign investors to find appropriate office space in Mauritius was brought to public notice in a telling manner. Significant portions of the article are reproduced hereunder to highlight our laxity in dealing with investments from Mauritius.

"The daily updated list of Foreign Venture Capital Investors (FVCI) registered with the Securities and Exchange Board of India (SEBI) shows that out of the total 135 foreign companies, as many as 38 are Mauritius-based, having the same address, phone and fax numbers. It is strange to note that these companies, which pump billions of dollars into Indian market, do not either need or cannot afford separate offices and business infrastructure.

The daily updated list, which exhibits the registered foreign investors from 2001, shows these 38 companies' address as: IFS Court, Twenty-Eight Cybercity, Ebene, Mauritius. Tel: (230) 467 3000 Fax: (230) 467 4000. In fact, 2i Capital PCC is the first firm which was registered with SEBI in 2001 on the abovementioned address. The scrutiny of the addresses leads to one International Financial Services in Mauritius. Apart from these 38 firms, another five FVCIs have also shown their address as 'care of' this Mauritian company, though the street is different.

According to the details provided by the website of International Financial Services, the company was founded in 1993 by one Kapil Dev Joory and Couldip Basanta Lala. The company also claims that they are administering the funds of financial majors like Lehman Bros, AIG, Citi Group, Merrill Lynch, New York Life, AMP, etc.

The Mauritian firm also claims that it is administering the funds of Indian companies like ICICI, HDFC, Tata Group, IL&FS and UTI. The company also claims that it is a member-firm of the Institute of Chartered Accountants in England and Wales.

The Pioneer had sent a set of questions on December 23 to SEBI Chairman C.B. Bhave to know how these companies were registered with SEBI. But there has not been any response from him so far.

As per the claims of SEBI guidelines and circulars, an FVCI has to undergo a series of scrutinies under several committees, including the Reserve Bank of India, to get itself registered. But the question remains as to how SEBI approved 38 companies from Mauritius with the same address, phone, fax numbers.

A scrutiny of SEBI's list gives some more interesting information. Out of the 135 registered FVCIs, pouring billions of dollars into India, barring two each from Singapore and Cyprus, the rest are from Mauritius."

In the Indian context, FII would mean Foreign Indirect Investment.

There are several charges that foreign companies are using "notional residence" in Mauritius to avoid paying capital gains taxes in India, sometimes running into several thousand crores of rupees. Despite such serious charges, successive finance ministers across the political spectrum have supported the said DTAA in its present form. They have repeatedly maintained that changing the structure of the DTAA could lead to flight of capital from the country, slowing down FDI and could lead to the collapse of the stock markets. In this connection, former Finance Minister (FM) Mr. P. Chidambaram is on record as having stated that he didn't want to review it as the subject had been debated threadbare and given the "larger economic, political and diplomatic considerations, we are not proposing any unilateral revision." In real life, the DTAA is not a simple double taxation avoidance agreement, but a larger strategic agreement.

But that is not all. Analysts fear that money arising out of corruption is laundered to various tax havens from India and routed back into India through the Mauritius route as foreign investment. This is termed as round tripping. And the DTAA with Mauritius, for reasons explained above, ensures that there is no tax on incomes arising out of such investment. In modern economics, every country realising the fallibility of its revenue department, is seen entering into some arrangement or the other with another country, preferably a tax haven. This facilitates the return of capital which would otherwise not be available to it for its own developmental needs. For China, it is Hong Kong. Some African countries use Cyprus. The Europeans and Americans have a range of options. In a way, such DTAAs are a triumph of practicality over morality. *Politicians, especially our politicians, are extremely practical.*

The Central Board of Direct Taxes (CBDT) is often referred to the Central Board of Diffused Taxes. But that was not the case with the DTAA with Mauritius. As India opened her stock markets to foreign investments, the CBDT enlightened the world on the zero tax impact of the Indo-Mauritius DTAA. By way of a circular in the mid-90s, the CBDT clarified the abovementioned position of taxing capital gains of any investment made into India by a resident of Mauritius. Further, it clarified that such capital gains would be liable to tax in Mauritius (where the rate, as already mentioned, was zero). This clarification ensured a free flow of foreign capital into the country from Mauritius. FIIs began to invest into India, using this route without the fear of the taxman. All this was acclaimed as brilliant tax planning as FIIs had a zero tax liability on their profits, both in India and Mauritius. Tax consultants were laughing all their way to the banks. Importantly, "ensuring" profits from our stock markets became a lucrative affair for many. And that meant subjecting our markets to repeated cycles of boom, doom and gloom. And should anyone protest against this volatility, he is instantly labelled as ignorant.

India is a very strange country where brilliant minds are constantly at work, sometimes constructively and sometimes destructively, but mostly at cross-purposes. It also depends on where you sit to make that judgement. In 2000, obviously peeved at the amount of taxes avoided by exploiting the DTAA to the maximum, some income tax authorities in India issued show cause notices to FIIs operating in India. The controversial part of this show cause notice was to change the head of taxation – from capital gains to business income. After all, the FIIs were in the business of buying and selling shares. This distinction between "investments" and the "business of buying and selling" shares is as crucial as it is technical. It may be recalled that in the context of the Indo-Mauritius DTAA, one could have a zero tax liability if and only if, one had capital gains arising out of investments. Needless to emphasise, in the case of business income, this is altogether a different subject, falling under a different head of taxation. Sadly, the DTAA, does not offer any such benefits to business income. In fact, in such a scenario, FIIs could be liable to pay taxes at 30 percent plus applicable surcharge along with interest and penalty. Such high levels of taxes could effectively ruin them.

The Income Tax (IT) Department further charged that mostly investments were routed through "shell companies" incorporated in Mauritius, whose main purpose was investment of funds only in India. Consequently, it was alleged that these companies were controlled and managed from other countries and as such they were not "residents" of Mauritius so as to derive the benefits of the DTAA.

As stock markets gyrated on the possible effect of this position of the IT Department, the Government acted with greater alacrity. The then FM issued a Press note on April 4, 2000, virtually disowning the position of the IT Department. Subsequently, the CBDT was pressed into service through a "clarificatory" circular in 2003. After all, the stakes were high and the Indian elites were involved.

The new circular of the CBDT once again clarified the stated positions, which are summarised hereunder:

- The provisions of the Indo-Mauritius DTAA of 1983 apply to "residents" of both India and Mauritius.
- The resident of one state to mean any person who, under the laws of that state is liable to taxation therein by reason of his domicile, residence, place of management or any other criterion of a similar nature.
- FIIs and other investment funds, etc. which are operating from Mauritius are invariably incorporated in that country. These entities are "liable to tax" under the Mauritius tax law and are, therefore, to be considered as residents of Mauritius in accordance with the DTAA.

- Wherever a Certificate of Residence is issued by the Mauritian authorities, such certificate will constitute sufficient evidence for accepting the status of residence as well as beneficial ownership for applying the DTAA accordingly.
- Accordingly, FIIs, etc., which are resident in Mauritius, would not be taxable in India on income from capital gains arising in India on sale of shares as per paragraph 4 of article 13.
- The aforesaid clarification shall apply to all proceedings which are pending at various levels.

The Matters Come to the Courts

Subsequently, this matter was referred to the Hon'ble Delhi High Court through a Public Interest Litigation (PIL) to declare this circular of the CBDT as illegal and void. The Hon'ble Delhi High Court quashed the circular on the following grounds:

- It is beyond the powers of the CBDT to hold that a certificate of residence issued by the authorities in Mauritius is sufficient evidence as regards status of a resident and beneficial ownership
- The income tax officer is entitled to lift the corporate veil in order to see whether a company is actually a resident of Mauritius
- "Treaty Shopping" by which the resident of a third country takes advantage of the provisions of the agreement, is illegal and, thus, necessarily forbidden
- Political expediency cannot be a ground for not fulfilling the constitutional obligations inherent in the Constitution of India and reflected in section 90 of the Act. The circular confers power to lay down a law which is not contemplated under the Act on the ground of political expediency
- Avoidance of double taxation is a term of art and means that a person has to pay tax at least in one country; avoidance of double taxation would not mean that a person does not have to pay tax in any country whatsoever.

The matter reached the Hon'ble Supreme Court and a landmark judgement was given in 2003 on this subject. Rarely has a PIL on a tax matter attracted so much attention as this case did, both in the course of the arguments made out by the Government and the petitioner and subsequently when the judgement was delivered. Disagreeing with the decision of the Hon'ble Delhi High Court, the Hon'ble Supreme Court observed, "An important principle which needs to be kept in mind in the interpretation of the provisions of an international treaty, including one for double taxation relief, is that treaties are negotiated and entered into at a political level and have several considerations as their bases."

It agreed with the contention of the Government that the benefits and detriments of a double tax treaty will probably only be truly reciprocal where the flow of trade and investment between treaty partners is generally in balance. It also agreed on the view that treaty negotiations are largely a bargaining process, with each side seeking concessions from the other; the final agreement will often represent a number of compromises, and it may be uncertain as to whether a full and sufficient *quid pro quo* is obtained by both sides.

Based on these observations, the court did not want to lose sight of the preamble of the Indo-Mauritius DTAA which states that it is for the "encouragement of mutual trade and investment." The court observed that many developed countries tolerate or encourage treaty shopping, even if it is unintended, improper or unjustified, for other non-tax reasons, unless it leads to a significant loss of tax revenues. Moreover, several of them allow the use of their treaty network to attract foreign enterprises and offshore activities. In developing countries, treaty shopping is often regarded as a tax incentive to attract scarce foreign capital or technology. Developing countries need foreign investments, and the treaty shopping opportunities can be an additional factor to attract them.

The court held that in recent years, India has been the beneficiary of significant foreign funds through the "Mauritius conduit." Although the Indian economic reforms since 1991 permitted such capital transfers, the amount would have been much lower without the India-Mauritius tax treaty. Overall, it concluded that countries need to, and do, take a holistic view. The developing countries allow treaty shopping to encourage capital and technology inflows, which the developed countries are keen to provide to them. The loss of tax revenues could be insignificant compared to the other non-tax benefits to their economy.

The court also opined, "There are many principles in fiscal economy which, though at first blush might appear to be evil, are tolerated in a developing economy, in the interest of long-term development. Despite the sound and fury of the respondents over the so-called abuse of treaty shopping, perhaps it may have been intended at the time when the Indo-Mauritius DTAA was entered into. Whether it should continue, and, if so, for how long, is a matter which is best left to the discretion of the executive as it is dependent upon several economic and political considerations."

Given this discretion, more so offered by the apex court, the Government obviously chose inaction over action.

The Hon'ble Supreme Court finally concluded that it cannot judge the legality of treaty shopping merely because one section of thought considers it improper. According to it, a holistic view has to be taken to adjudge what is perhaps regarded in contemporary thinking as a necessary evil in a developing economy.

With due respects to the Hon'ble Supreme Court, one feels that the "Mauritius Conduit" is more of an evil and less of a necessity.

That explains why India is an attractive investment destination for any investments from Mauritius. Given the lack of firewalls that control the flow of capital across borders, India is equally an attractive destination for funds with doubtful integrity. As already pointed out, a significant amount of such monies is routed to India through Mauritius. Routing from Mauritius gives them the tax benefit. Their origins from tax havens make them all the more sinister.

The Government subsequently reacted to these developments in the only manner in which it could – subterfuge, obfuscation and dilation. The Income Tax Act till 2004 empowered the Government to enter into DTAAs with other foreign countries under Section 90 of the Income Tax Act, 1961, for granting relief in respect of income on which income tax was paid both in India and in that other country. Subsequently, the Income Tax Act was amended in 2004 so as to empower the Central Government to enter into various DTAAs to promote "mutual economic relations, trade and investment, besides granting relief on double-taxation." The tectonic change from providing merely taxation relief to promoting economic relations virtually means that the Government can get away with anything through the DTAA. The leeway provided by the Hon'ble Supreme Court had become an expressway by 2004.

Unanswered Questions

It is obvious that the triumvirate of laundering money from India into tax havens, using the anonymous PN route to transfer such money back to India and the Indo-Mauritius DTAA (which provides tax relief for capital gains arising out of such investment) form a formidable challenge to the integrity of the Indian tax system and capital markets, the independence of our monetary policy, and our physical security. Needless to emphasise, there are two dimensions to this: one, it dynamites our commerce as well as economics; and, two, it emboldens narco-terror groups to use these structures to plan, operate and execute terror operations in India.

Given the sensitivities involved, the issue of the Indo-Mauritius DTAA naturally occupied centre-stage in the JPC enquiry. The JPC observed that there were "indications of misuse" of the provisions of the DTAA between India and Mauritius. This aspect, "as in the past," the JPC noted in all seriousness, "should seriously engage the attention of the Government." The Government, as if on cue, did what it did "in the past" – "nothing"! *Well one cannot find fault with the Government for that. After all, it did what was mandated by the JPC.*

Further, the JPC was concerned that this DTAA resulted in substantial financial inflows into India through money laundering by Indian companies making illegitimate use of the same. The committee was particularly disturbed to note that notwithstanding the agreement between both sides to address Indian concerns of receipt origin, little or nothing was done. The committee was of the considered view that although the inflow from Mauritius was "welcome," due care also needed to be exercised about possible misuse of this route. In this connection, the JPC stated, "Instances of such misuse have come to light and misuse of the route appears to have been significantly responsible for market manipulations during the boom of 1999-2000 which led to the bust of 2001." The committee commended the steps taken in July 2002 to amend the DTAA: "Continued vigilance on this front will be necessary to prevent scams of the kind that occurred in 1999-2001 when due attention was not being paid to the dangers inherent in the virtually unregulated Mauritius route."

Prophetic words indeed, as we would continue to see right through this book, how the Mauritius route continues to haunt and plague the Indian financial system!

The Government began its defence – read stonewalling – in right earnest to the JPC report. Pointing to certain cosmetic regulatory changes brought about by the RBI in the context of OCB regulations, the ATR of the Government claimed that "the occasion for the misuse of the DTAA was no longer there." That was pure fiction written in May 2003, while the fact is that in the spring of 2010, Mauritius continues to be the single largest source of foreign investment into India. How much of that is use, misuse and abuse is anybody's guess.

The reply of the Government to the possible misuse of the DTAA was extraordinary. Referring to the fundamentals of the canons of taxation, the ATR pointed to the fact that if the place of effective management of a company is in India, the company would be liable to tax in India. But what about misuse of the treaty – silence. What about shell companies (where locals "operate" the company and thereby shift the effective management to Mauritius) operating in Mauritius – thundering silence. What about Indian money being laundered to

Mauritius and routed back to India? As is its wont, the Government maintained an eloquent silence.

The JPC further observed that the consequent revenue loss arising on account of the misuse of the "residency clause" of the treaty could not be quantified, "but taking into account the huge inflows/outflows, it could be assumed to be substantial." They, therefore, recommended that companies investing in India through Mauritius should be required to file details of ownership with the RBI and declare that all the directors and effective management are in Mauritius. The idea of self-declaration is a bogus one, for crooks never take the trouble of confession through a declaration. There are billions of ways to control a Mauritius company sitting in India. *Benami* in India may come at a cost. *Benami* in Mauritius may come for a professional fee.

Yet, look at the singular purpose with which the Government acts to defeat even this superficial idea of the JPC. The response of the Government was cryptic – the RBI is examining the matter. That was in May 2003. But the query was not closed. Then came the progress report in December 2003. It was obfuscation personified. It stated, "CBDT has informed that RBI has advised against imposition of a condition that companies investing in India through Mauritius should file details of ownership with RBI and declare that all directors and effective management are in Mauritius. They have indicated that such a condition does not apply to Foreign Direct Investment (FDI) from any other country, including European countries and the USA. Further, such a condition about the director's residence does not apply to investment by Indian companies aboard." Sound logic again. But there is a fatal flaw – India does not have a DTAA on similar terms with the European countries and the USA. Why then compare apples with oranges? Well that is another way of diffusing the situation.

Nevertheless, these assertions agitated even the otherwise dormant conscience of the Government. Surely someone's soul was tormented on such partial obfuscation. So, more obfuscation was added to complete the partial attempts at stonewalling in the subsequent progress reports. The reply once again focussed on the concept of "effective management" in India, as explained above. Also, the reply pointed out that "wherever necessary" to check the misuse of the residency clause, the Income Tax Department will carry out the required investigations with the help of the Mauritius authorities. "Wherever necessary" is a fantastic phase – it provides enormous scope for inaction, discretion and consequent corruption. Pray, for the past seven years, how many such actions were initiated?

In the next progress report, more progress was reported. The Government drew attention to the Hon'ble Supreme Court's judgement dated 7.10.2003 in the Azadi Bachao Andolan case and pointed out that the circular on Mauritius (discussed earlier in this chapter) issued by CBDT was valid. Consequently, the reply noted that the "misuse of the residency clause" of the DTAA "was plugged." But, as we saw earlier, the clarificatory circular only clarified the obvious – that the DTAA had huge loopholes. It did not talk of plugging the same. Yet, the answer was acceptable to the Parliament. With this, the Government declared, the *action* was complete.

Fascinatingly, by then, (i.e. 2004) political roles were reversed. The opposition was voted to power and the party in power till then became the opposition. Yet the stonewalling continued in right earnest. And that is Indian democracy for you. You can change the players, game, rules and regulations but not the outcome.

However, crucial questions arise:

- The party in power then is the principal opposition party now. The then opposition party is the party in power now. Yet, there is a convergence on this vital issue. Why?
- The party in power as well as the opposition are ready to accept the repeated obfuscation of the Government as evidenced by the ATR and its subsequent progress reports. Has the bureaucracy been pulling wool over the eyes of our political parties?

All these are not merely limited to the issue of tax avoidance, terror funding and defrauding revenues. The independence of the country's monetary policy comes under extreme strain on account of abrupt surges in the Forex flows into the economy as well as away from it. We shall look into greater detail on the impact of all these on our monetary policy in the subsequent chapters. The issue of Forex management is an extremely dextrous exercise. Sudden inflow could result in abrupt rise in the prices of shares. But in the absence of Chinese walls in the economy between stock markets and other markets, this abrupt inflow of money naturally funds other sectors too. When the stock market rises, the Government claims it is because of its policies. When the real estate price shoots up consequent to this flow of funds, it is called a real estate boom. As next stage, these funds make their destination into the vegetable and food grains market. And when that happens, it is called inflation! In short, booming stock markets fuelled by funds from abroad and a benign domestic inflation are a near impossibility in the Indian context.

Neither is it an issue of markets alone. The surge in capital inflows in 2007-08 caused domestic pressures of its own. Significant capital flows resulted in increased domestic liquidity, asset bubbles, inflation and appreciation of the rupee in excess of 10 per cent. Subsequently, when the position reversed and India witnessed an outflow of a mere USD 15 billion of FII flows in the second half of 2008-09, the rupee depreciated in excess of 25 per cent, and India witnessed a collapse of its stock markets and severe liquidity pressures.

It was, therefore, natural that some right thinking citizens began asking a series of inconvenient questions about all these issues which are interconnected and involve the moral state of play in India:

- Why the Government of India is not taking up the issue of capital flight away from India as a serious economic challenge confronting the economy? Why is the Government in a constant state of denial on the issue?
- Where do we place ourselves in the context of the present global debate on eliminating tax havens? Are we reluctant partners to this global initiative?
- It is estimated that a substantial amount of money laundering takes place from India. Why is it that the Government views the Prevention of Money Laundering Act as an ornamental piece of legislation?
- Why are we hesitant to renegotiate the Indo-Mauritius DTAA despite having overwhelming proof that it has been repeatedly abused?
- Who are the ultimate beneficiaries of these PNs? Why is our regulatory standard on this issue consistently behind the curve?
- What is the hold of PN holders on successive Governments that prevents any meaningful action by the Indian establishment on them?
- Why is the Government of India not banning this obnoxious practice of PNs? In the alternative, why is it not even prescribing meaningful regulations to curb PNs?
- Are all these merely issues of unaccounted money belonging to Indians flowing out through the Hawala route and reentering India through the PN route?
- Does it also include the illegal narco-terror money used to finance terrorism in the country?
- Or is it a case of hedge funds using the PN route to "pump and dump" our stock markets for their spectacular gains?
- Or is it being increasingly used by Indian promoters to purchase their shares, by-passing the takeover code of SEBI and other well-intended regulations of SEBI?

- In the process, are the Indian promoters manipulating the stock prices?
- How does the surge in the flow of Forex into the country and away from it through the PNs impact our monetary policy?
- Consequently, do we have an "independent" monetary policy? Or is it dependent on Forex flows, especially PNs?
- Are our stock markets susceptible to manipulations by entities that cannot even be identified, leave alone regulated, by SEBI?
- Why are our intelligentsia, institutions, industry and media silent on the issue of tax havens and flow of Forex through PNs? Their silence is the most intriguing aspect of this saga.

We attempt to answer most of these questions in this book

Super Senior Citizens Take up the Matter

Nonetheless, a few people chose to seek answers from the Hon'ble Supreme Court. A few concerned "Super senior citizens," including noted criminal lawyer Mr. Ram Jethmalani, the former DGP of Police, Punjab, Mr K. P. S. Gill, the former Secretary General of the Lok Sabha, Mr Subash Kashyap and a few others had filed a Public Interest Litigation (PIL) in the Hon'ble Supreme Court in the run up to the General Elections in 2009. The broad issues covered in the PIL filed by these senior citizens in the Hon'ble Supreme Court are briefly stated hereunder:

- Steps taken by the Government of India on the recovery of Indian money lying in foreign banks.
- Regulatory control exercised by the Government and its regulatory agencies on PNs.
- Action initiated by the Central Government on information received from the German Government with respect to the Indian account holders in the LGT Bank, Liechtenstein.
- Status of the investigations in the case of one Hassan Ali Khan and his alleged co-conspirator Kashinath Tapuria in relation to the alleged illicit deposits made by them in the UBS Bank.

The reply by the Government filed through an affidavit with the Hon'ble Supreme Court was typical of it – embellished with half-truths and half-lies. Stating at the outset a half-truth that the "Central Government led by Dr. Manmohan Singh, Hon'ble Prime Minister, played a major role in the G-20 Summit seeking exchange of information," the affidavit went on to add a half-lie that it persuaded "countries which were not falling in line to review their position." It may be also be noted that never in the history of any multilateral forum has India played a major role (though it does have a role), leave alone the G-20 summit in April 2009. But the half-lie was all the more evident on the persuasion issue. Virtually the whole world had come to believe that the tax havens were one of the primary causes of the global financial crisis. Consequently, the turn of events persuaded countries to go after their national wealth stashed in various tax havens. Given her track record, that ostensibly did not include India! How could a reluctant India have persuaded countries that had already decided to come to the said summit for this purpose? Yet, the affidavit filed by the Government claims the entire credit for the same.

More was to follow. Stating that the Central Government was "constantly alive to the need to be able to retrieve information about the monies which are lying deposited in foreign accounts," the affidavit filed in the Hon'ble Supreme Court further stated that "towards this end, initiatives have been taken on a continuous basis." If the Government was constantly alive to the need to track down the offenders, could not the Government of India track down even one such case in the past several years and showcase it to its citizens? If the initiatives were taken on a continuous basis, what was the outcome of the same? The answers to these questions are obvious.

More infotainment follows. And this entertainment as well as information is not for the weak-hearted. In the process, the Government makes a confession – it claims to be "fully alive." A Government that is alive to an issue of corruption is an inscrutable paradox if not a downright impossibility. Claiming that the Central Government was "fully alive" to the economic well-being of the country, the affidavit throws an unplayable googly. It states point blank that the Government has addressed the economic well-being of the country at "different international fora from time to time." That the Government is addressing the economic challenges of the country is in itself questionable. That it seeks to do so in different international fora from time to time is laughable. That it seeks to trivialise this vital subject is lamentable.

The outcome of the April 2009, G-20 summit is discussed in greater detail in subsequent chapters this book.

On the issue of recovering the money allegedly belonging to Indian citizens, lying in foreign banks, especially in tax havens, the affidavit of the Government seeks to dilute the matter. The affidavit seeks to explain the same as legitimate accounts of either Indians or Indian corporates or Indian mutual funds as permitted by various liberalised schemes of the Government. In the process, it sought to ignore the illegitimate accounts of Indians lying in foreign banks, especially tax havens. The question was about the illegitimate accounts and not the legitimate ones. How could the Government know whether an account is a legitimate one or an illegitimate one, unless it has the details of the accounts, both legitimate and illegitimate? This is the fundamental issue on which the affidavit is silent. Unfortunately, the silence is deafening. Either way, the charade through half-truths, lies and damned lies is repeated all over once again in the context of tax havens and the efforts of the Government of India to recover this money.

On the issue of PNs, the affidavit states that "the issuance of such notes can take place only after complying with know your client (KYC) norms." This is an untenable proposition. As would be seen in the subsequent chapters when we discuss the UBS case in greater detail, the fact of the matter is that even to this date, SEBI has not prescribed the KYC norms to FIIs. Consequently, UBS claimed it was unable to adhere to the KYC norms. Where is the question of adhering to a norm when it is non-existent!

This argument found favour with the Hon'ble SAT. However, SEBI went on to appeal this decision of SAT to the Hon'ble Supreme Court only to backtrack there. On a consent petition filed in the Supreme Court by both SEBI and UBS, the latter agreed to pay the former a fine of Rs 50 lakhs for failing to supply – yes, failing to supply – crucial data pertaining to the holders of PNs. This consent order needs to be looked into in the backdrop of the accusation by SEBI that UBS manipulated Indian stock markets and made profits running into several crores of rupees *Put differently, the cost of manipulating the Indian stock markets can at best be Rs 50 lakhs!* All these matters are obviously not referred to by the Government in its reply filed in the Supreme Court to the PIL.

On the issue of SEBI having all information regarding PNs, the affidavit states, "SEBI regulations provide for disclosure of full information regarding PNs. Further, SEBI is adequately equipped to call for any information regarding PNs." Again, as we would see in subsequent chapters of this book, this response of SEBI is based on an undertaking furnished by FIIs, which was challenged successfully by Goldman Sachs. Once again, the SAT overruled SEBI and questioned SEBI's legal position to call for such undertaking from FIIs.

In short, both KYC norms as well as undertakings about FII dealings with PNs, as explained in the affidavit, are legally untenable arguments. The adherence to the KYC norms and identification of the ultimate beneficiaries of PNs are central to the JPC findings and its recommendations in the aftermath of the 2001 stock scam. Yet, for nearly a decade, the Government of India has been successful in pulling wool over the eyes of the people on precisely these very issues.

This book has been divided into ten chapters. Money laundering, tax havens (discussed in Chapters 2 & 3), the global response to money laundering and tax havens (Chapter 4), the lax regulatory regime prevalent in India (Chapter 5), the issues relating to the PNs in India (discussed in Chapters 6 & 7), their combined impact on the domestic economy, monetary policies, (Chapter 8) and the net impact of all these on the national security (Chapter 9) represent broadly the scheme of the book. The final chapter (Chapter 10) is the concluding chapter that seeks to join the dots and discusses what needs to be done, especially in the context of the national security.

References

1. Speech of Pandit Jawaharlal Nehru on August15 , 1947
2. Draft Approach Paper to the 11th Plan issued by the Planning Commission, June 14, 2006.
3. The Ugliest Chapter in Global Economic Affairs Since Slavery, Speech by Raymond W. Baker, "Illicit Financial Flows: The Missing Link in Development", June 28, 2007.
4. Annual Report of the RBI for 2008-09.
5. S. Gurumurthy, "Secret Wealth Abroad", *New Indian Express*, April 2, 2009.
6. Report of the Expert Group on Encouraging FII Flows and Checking the Vulnerability of Capital Markets to Speculative Flows, Government of India, Ministry of Finance Department of Economic Affairs, November, 2005.
7. Interim recommendations of the Task Force constituted by the Bharatiya Janata Party (BJP) on the steps to be taken by the Indian Government to bring Indian funds illegally stashed away in secret Swiss bank accounts and other tax havens around the world.
8. The Report of the Joint Parliamentary Committee on the stock market scam and matters relating thereto.
9 G-20 Declaration in London, April 2009.
10. Reply (Affidavit) filed by the Government of India in the Hon'ble Supreme Court in connection with the PIL filed in April 2009.
11. Decision of the Hon'ble Supreme Court in the Azadi Bachao Aandolan case - 263 ITR 706.
12. Transparency International's Global Corruption Report for 2009.
13. Indo-Mauritius Double Taxation Avoidance Agreement.
14. Circular No. FITTC/CUST/14/2001 dated October 31, 2001, issued by SEBI.
15. Circular No. IMD/CUST/8/2003 dated August 8, 2003, issued by SEBI.
16. Reply (Affidavit) of the Government of India filed in the Hon'ble Supreme Court to the PIL filed on the issue of tax havens.
17. J. Gopikrishna, "One Address, 38 Investors, all via Mauritius", *Daily Pioneer*, December 28, 2009.
18. Ajay Shah and Ila Patnaik, "Managing Capital Flows: The Case of India", Working Paper 2008-52, May 2008, Research Programme on Capital Flows and their Consequences , National Institute of Public Finance and Policy, New Delhi.
19. Report of the Committee on Liberalisation of Foreign Institutional Investment issued by Government of India, Ministry of Finance, Department of Economic Affairs, June 2004.
20. Human Development Report 2009.

CHAPTER 2

Hawala and Money Laundering

Weapons cannot cut it nor can fire burn it. Water cannot wet it nor can wind dry it.

— Bhagavad Gita, Chapter II (23)

Every Indian movie, even before we attained independence, attempted, albeit crudely, to glorify socialism. This was the dominant ideology, not only in India but in substantial parts of the globe, in those innocent times. Mostly the script revolved around the trials, tribulations and eventual triumph of a poor, educated, honest and hard working young Indian against the shenanigans of a rich Indian. No prizes for guessing – the former was the hero, the latter, the villain. This was how the mass-media of those times prepared the minds of Indians to accept socialism without any demur, on attaining independence.

But that was not all. The villain, if he was rich, had to be dishonest. And by a corollary, only the dishonest could be rich. This bunkum idea continued to gain currency even after we attained independence. And why not? After all, most laws of independent India, including our Constitution, were mere rehashes of the laws laid down by our colonial rulers.

Recall that the core idea of the British Raj centred on commerce till the very end. That meant crushing Indian business through the might of the Government and its oppressive agencies. How then, could they allow the Indian business to flourish right under their very noses? Naturally, in British India, Indian businessmen had to violate every single law to even survive.

People who hoped that things would change significantly after independence were wrong by several miles. After 1947, it would seem that we failed to replace the pre-independence thinking, system or mindset of our Government. Nothing changed expect that the white sahibs had been replaced by the brown ones. That, in essence, captured the "transfer of power" by the British to the Indians. For the outside world, everything had changed. For the Indian business, not much had changed.

Naturally, Indian business continued to be constrained in the first three decades of our independence as it was during the British Raj, perhaps even more. This was done in the name of ideology. In our lofty goal to ensure that the Government occupies the commanding heights of our economy, we condemned our businesses and private initiatives to the gutter.

In the process, exorbitant taxes were levied. Industrial policies successfully duplicated the British model in strangulating the Indian businesses in India. Draconian labour laws were legislated. While they necessarily did not favour the labourers, they were definitely designed to throttle the Indian economy. All these were the outcome of an alien ideology without examining its workability in a country like India.

The net effect was glorification of poverty and simultaneously ridiculing creation of wealth by the society. To be poor and be mired in poverty was glorious in those times. We patented the right to distribute poverty, not wealth. All these were inexplicable in a country which traditionally venerated *Lakshmi,* the goddess of wealth.

Naturally, Indian business could not survive the twin onslaught – the intellectual perversity resulting in the abuse of the very idea of profits as well as the naked aggression of the system, even post-independence, against Indian business itself. The odds were heavily stacked against it. Hence, anyone who was rich and, more importantly, ran a profitable business, was definitely a law breaker. Else, how could he have become rich in the first place? *The unspoken argument was that with a policy which was so blatantly anti-business, there was not even a theoretical chance of anyone running a business legally as well as profitably!*

It was, therefore, well understood by the society that it was impossible to be rich except by breaking the laws of the land. Naturally, all our villains, even in the first three decades of those ideologically heady times, were smugglers, black marketers, racketeers and fraudsters. In these circumstances, it was ideologically unacceptable to be rich and compelling to be poor. The "poor" hero was condemned to fight the rich. It was pure and simple logic, with little scope for any other alternative.

How Much Have Times Changed or Have They?

The years rolled by. By the early Nineties, socialism (whatever it meant), was given a silent burial. People who threatened to set the Ganges on fire to protect socialism, watched silently as the nation jettisoned socialism. That resulted in an extraordinary situation in India. By the next decade or so, ideologues who swore in the name of socialism till then, now swore at socialism. Dominant deformers of the Indian economy acquired a new sobriquet – radical reformers.

Nowhere in history has a nation witnessed such a remarkable makeover in the ideology of its ideologues as India witnessed in the mass conversion of its socialists into champions of free markets, silently but openly, fearlessly yet shamelessly. Socialism, by the next decade, was buried fathoms deep and was left all alone in one obscure corner viz., the Preamble of the Indian Constitution! No explanation was sought and no explanation was ever given.

This mass-conversion of its intellectuals impacted society and, by extension, art forms too. The embracing of reforms and the advent of the new economic policies ensured the arrival of the real India. It unleashed the potential of India – as an economic as well as political powerhouse at the global level. It made us believe that we could perform at the international level and could dominate the best in their home turf. In effect, people realised that it is our systems – a by product of deranged dogma of decades – that are the villains of the piece, the impediments in our progress.

Since then, we began looking at our systems more intensely. Governance and systemic deficiencies came under the intense scrutiny of the society. Today's villain is the dysfunctional or the non-functional Government. Naturally, every Indian movie contrives to ensure that the hero defeats the state. Given the abysmal performance of successive Indian Governments, it is also no wonder as to why the audience began to relish these developments. The modern Indian society laps up every single justification of the hero waging a lonely crusade against his own Government. In the process, it would seem that this was the perfect revenge of the society against the Government for decades of injustices meted out to it by the Government.

But that is not all. The pendulum seems to have now swung to the other extreme. If the Government could do nothing wrong in the pre-liberalisation era, it would, at least, for the movie-makers of the modern era, do nothing right. In these exciting times, the hero had to necessarily be a rebel, even it was to be without a pause, never mind the cause.

Lest one comes to a conclusion that the extant work is on socialism or India's ideological volte-face or the impact of dominant ideology on arts and cinema, let me hasten to assure the reader that this is not so. Yet, despite all the changes evident between socialist India of the past and liberal India of the present, certain ideas never seem to change. Some ideas, it would seem, can never be anachronistic, especially in a timeless civilisation like India.

One such undying idea that seems to catch the imagination of the movie maker eternally is the Hawala transaction. If Hawala was justified in portraying the villain to perfection in yesteryears, now it is justified as the act of the hero who is anxious to ensure that the ends justify the means. In the process, the differentiating lines between the villains of yesteryears and the heroes of modern-day cinema have become blurred like never before. The only exception – if the villain of yesteryears indulged in such acts with trepidation, the modern-day heroes do the same unabashedly. *Nothing, it seems, unites like Hawala!*

Either way, Hawala, is perhaps the only symbiotic link between the socialism of yesteryears and the liberal economic policies since the early Nineties. Perhaps it is one of the few remaining links between independent India and the British Raj.

How much have times changed. Or have they?

Hawala : A Subject Well Appreciated but Least Understood

But what is this Hawala that has retained our attention for over several decades? What is this Hawala that seems to dominate the Indian economy? How is it that Hawala outlives the socialist regime in India and continues to flourish in the new economic order of a globalised India? What made Hawala succeed in those times and what makes it a success in modern times? What makes Hawala timeless, ageless and eternal? We seek to get answers to all these vexed but important questions shortly. But first – what is Hawala?

This is where one needs to get a bit philosophical and, at once, technical. Hawala can be likened to abstract concepts like pain, love and God – one can appreciate their presence but not define them. Hawala is omnipotent and omnipresent. It is virtual as well as physical. It is time-tested as well as time-honoured. It defines time as well as defies it. It disregards history and geography. It is a universal language that is well understood across continents. It is a necessity that has mysteriously made a good bargain at every twist and turn in the history of mankind.

Hawala is a system created by man to defy all other systems put together, individually and collectively. There are well-defined checks and balances within the system that have stood the ravages of time and technology. It has worked well across civilisations, their evolution and even during their collapse. It is perhaps as old as money, wine and crime. As a profession, it could well rival the oldest profession known to mankind. It is a mechanism that has always outlived several empires. One does not recall of any emperor, dictator, king, despot or for that matter any form of democratically elected modern Government being keen on eliminating it. It is the nearest to eternity ever invented by man.

Despite being an artificial construct, the efficiency associated with a Hawala transaction has to be seen to be believed. It has an in-built dispute resolution mechanism that would challenge the efficacy of any formal court. Despite these troubled economic times, left to itself, Hawala is a massive employment generator.

In brief, it is the history of man, his machinations, his Machiavellian approach to life, his contempt for the rules. Hawala is the success of immorality over morality. Put pithily, it is not merely representative of civilisational values, but the aggregate of the negative values of several civilisations all encapsulated in one stroke!

Needless to emphasise, it has constantly engaged the attention of finance professionals, media, policy framers, lawyers, movie producers and, of course, commentators. Hawala has often been a favourite subject of many authors and the subject matter of many bestsellers. Despite such vast attention given to it, the vexed subject is akin to the "other side of the moon" – unexplored, unseen and unheard.

An Informal but Reliable Bank

Hawala is an informal money transfer system without the actual transfer of money in the first place. It is akin to a bank but without any of the trappings of a formal bank. Primarily, it is based on the performance, efficiency and reliability of a network of money brokers. Originally, while these worked within borders or across borders, life was simple.

In a globalised world, the Hawala system could facilitate anyone with ill-gotten wealth to transfer his money from one jurisdiction into another so as to escape the long arm of the law in the country of the origin of such wealth in the first place. A few thousand pounds given in London to a Hawala banker, can turn into Indian currency within a few minutes, thousands of miles away in distant India.

The reverse is also equally possible with the same level of efficiency, reliability and speed. By the same token, the Indian rupee can be converted into USD or Yen or Euro all in a jiffy. The icing on the cake – these services could well be offered at your doorstep, sometimes cheaper, faster and less formal than banks.

Contrast this with the functioning of formal banks. In the case of Hawala transactions, one need not step out into the banks, private public or foreign, and watch the banker's incompetence. Often, his computers don't work. When they do, he doesn't. When both of them are ready, it is usually a holiday in India.

Or it could well be that one of the political parties or the innumerable trade unions have called for a strike or a *bandh*.

And when everything is in order, the banker would invariably come out with the weirdest of explanations to tell you why he is unable to trace your money for the past three weeks or why it has reached China instead of Chennai. But unlike these primordial institutions with Neanderthal technologies, Hawala operators use the latest technologies, codes and crypto to ensure that your money gets transferred across borders with remarkable ease, deadly precision and, of course, absolute reliability.

If only Hawala were a formal system, the formal system called banks could well have been reduced to a relic by now. Often it is suggested, albeit in a lighter vein, that it is a conspiracy of the formal bankers to defame Hawala for rationalising their continued existence!

It is not merely the efficiency in operations that makes Hawala a potent force today across continents. Sometimes, these operators offer better exchange rates than those offered by banks. That often happens depending on the demand-supply position within the Hawala system for a particular currency. That could explain why retail investors are lured to send money through this route.

Lest the reader get me wrong, all this does not only make the small ones depend on Hawala. It is used by the big fish too, big time. It is often found that significant amounts of ill-gotten wealth acquired through bribes or corruption by politicians, bureaucrats, businessmen and even judges are transferred from the jurisdiction of one country to another merely to avoid detection.

Hawala: A Great Leveller

That is why Hawala is often called a great leveller. It is the meeting point of criminals and honourable men, of those who violate the law and those who are the guardians of the law. It is a secular crime that transcends caste and community. No one community, caste or religion can claim exclusivity to it. In a way, it unifies Indians like nothing else would do. Hawala could well symbolise the character of the Socialist, Secular and Democratic Republic of India.

But what has Hawala got to do with those who break the domestic law? Big fishes probably have multiple irritants. It could well be income tax, wealth tax, excise, customs, VAT and service tax or a combination of any or all of these. On top of these revenue laws, we have made life difficult for our rich and famous through other developments viz., corporate governance, vigilance, audits, due-diligence, inspections, enquiries, prevention of corruption laws and, of course, the whistle blower's policy.

But all these do not deter the big fishes. Nevertheless, this ill-gotten money generated in India, is technically prone to searches, surveys, seizures, investigations, assessments, reassessments and vigilance procedures. One must at the risk of repetition add that these laws are for you and me – not for those occupying the higher pedestal in our public life.

For the high and mighty, it is not the law that matters. Rules and regulations are, at best, minor irritants. Nor are they too worried about the loss of their personal reputation. After all, you cannot shame the shameless. A thick skin is definitely a gift from God, not merely to the rhinoceros. When reputation is lost, it is often found that the "source" does not dry up. Rather, it is conclusive evidence of the easy virtue of the man. Taint, if any, to those occupying the high seat of power as a minister, judge or bureaucrat, always ensures continuous flow of ill-gotten wealth. In fact, it perhaps gets accentuated after the first hint.

Therefore, at the rarefied heights of public life, there are no moral scruples or legal issues in breaking such domestic laws for the rich and mighty. However, violating laws is nevertheless a highly cumbersome exercise for them. Only those who break the laws understand the pain and practical difficulty associated with it, especially when the benefits run into several hundred crores of rupees. This, when packed into large suitcases stuffed with even thousand rupee notes could well take quite a few trucks to transport and store.

Therefore, the fact of the matter is that one cannot store currency beyond a point at one's residence or office or elsewhere for obvious reasons – lack of space! Obviously, no one wants to be noted handling truck loads, yes truckloads, of cash. Again, note that this is not on account of shame!

Apparently, Hawala is the only way to get out of the mess of handling such gargantuan quantum of cash generated by violating domestic business laws or money raised through corruption or for that matter any other crime. It is the only mechanism to transfer your ill-gotten wealth – swiftly, reliably and smoothly to some other country or within India for a corresponding payment outside India. It is here that Hawala assures that the transactions are carried out without any evidence.

This is how and why Hawala fits into the scheme of many of our elite, leaders, businessmen and, of course, celebrities. It is safe. It is dependable. It lends itself to absolute confidentiality. There are no audit trail to facilitate snooping investigative journalists. Nor can the media prove a damn. When proved, it can equally be disproved using the same logic, facts and evidence. It is, thus, no wonder that whenever cornered, our rich and mighty never deny their corruption. They are only inquisitive about the evidence and the common refrain is, "Where is the evidence?" With Hawala surely there can be no conclusive evidence.

All this explains substantially if not wholly as to why Hawala has never been tackled seriously by any Government of independent India. Only a fool would kill the goose that lays the golden egg. Our high and mighty may be unabashed, but definitely are not fools.

This necessity to park money reliably outside India or distributed as a part of the Hawala chain within India is not restricted to the high and mighty of the land. It is not the sole prerogative of the ruling elite. One can well imagine as to how much the Hawala system could facilitate terrorists to source funds for their operations from across borders.

Similarly, it is possible for drug peddlers to transfer their sale proceeds from one country to the other without raising any suspicion. Naturally, the illegal arms dealers love it. The underworld relies on it. Terrorists thrive on it. Businessmen fancy it. Celebrities want it. And the polity revels in it.

In a way, Hawala is a wonderful melting pot.

Brief History of Hawala

It is very difficult to trace the history of a subject that is believed to predate history. There are several viewpoints on this subject with a civilisational perspective.

For instance, the Wikipedia states that Hawala has its origins in classical Islamic law, and is mentioned in texts of Islamic jurisprudence as early as the eighth century. Hawala it seems migrated as an idea from the Middle East to Europe in those times. Hawala itself later influenced the financial as well as legal development in Europe and in civil laws such as the *aval* in French law and the *avallo* in Italian law. In fact, the words *aval* and *avallo*, the Wikipedia claims, are derivatives of the word Hawala.

Further, the Wikipedia states that the transfer of debt, which was "not permissible under Roman law but became widely practised in medieval Europe, especially in commercial transactions," and was due to the large extent of the "trade conducted by the Italian cities with the Muslim world in the Middle Ages."

The Hawala mechanism was also "an institution unknown to Roman law" as no "individual could conclude a binding contract on behalf of another as his agent." In Roman law, the "contractor himself was considered the party to the contract and it took a second contract between the person who acted on behalf of a principal and the latter in order to transfer the rights and the obligations deriving from the contract to him." On the other hand, Islamic law and the later common law "had no difficulty in accepting an agency as one of its institutions in the field of contracts and of obligations in general."

Finally, the Wikipedia concludes that Hawala is believed to have arisen in the financing of long-distance trade around the emerging capital trade centres in the early medieval period. In South Asia, it appears to have developed into a full-fledged money market instrument, which was only gradually replaced by the instruments of the formal banking system in the first half of the twentieth century.

Just as you are perhaps led to believe that Hawala was a medieval idea coinciding with the emergence of Islam, I have to request you to pause a little. In a paper prepared in early 2009 titled "Controlling Money Laundering in India – Problems and Perspectives", Mr. Vijay Kumar Singh captures the entire subject in a nutshell rather brilliantly. According to him, "Hawala is an alternative or parallel remittance system. It exists and operates outside of, or parallel to, traditional banking or financial channels."

Interestingly, he states that the idea of Hawala originated in India. In this connection, he states, "It was developed in India, before the introduction of Western banking practices, and is currently a major remittance system used around the world." Obviously, Singh was referring to the age-old Indian practice of issuing Hundis. That means that Hawala could well be traced to the period even before Christ!

Further, explaining the precise *modus operandi* of a typical Hawala transaction, Mr. Singh explains succinctly: "In Hawala networks, the money is not moved physically. A typical Hawala transaction would be like a resident in the USA of Indian origin, doing some business, wants to send some money to his relatives in India. The person has the option either to send the money through the formal channel of the banking system or through the Hawala system. The commission in Hawala is less than the bank charges and is without any complications for opening an account or visiting the bank, etc. The money reaches the doorstep of the person's relative and the process is speedier and cheaper."

Whatever be the origins of the system, what is of relevance to us here is that the Hawala system provides a person service like that of a regular bank, but with virtually no documentation. Naturally, as the system works purely on trust, Hawala provides virtually complete anonymity, secrecy and security. On top of all this, the system is efficient, effective and cost competitive. This success is not because of one factor, efficiency or secrecy, but both. That makes it attractive to all types of users – the innocent ones as well the notorious ones.

This idea of Mr. Singh that Hawala must be predominantly a South Asian idea gets further credence by a document by Mohammed El-Qorchi, senior economist, Monetary and Exchange Affairs Department, International Monetary Fund (IMF), who, in an article in *Finance and Development in 2002,* comes to a similar conclusion. According to El-Qorchi, international fund transfer mechanisms, were, in earlier times, used for trade financing. Obviously, they were created because of the dangers of travelling with gold and other forms of payment on routes beset with bandits.

El-Qorchi goes on to demonstrate that Hawala was indeed a global idea, perhaps predating the first wave of globalisation itself. Tracing its worldwide presence, he states, "Local systems were widely used in China and other parts of East Asia and continue to be in use there. They go under various names – Fei-Ch'ien (China), Padala (Philippines), Hundi (India), Hui Kuan (Hong Kong), and Phei Kwan (Thailand)."

The conclusion from his paper is revealing: "The Hawala (or Hundi) system now enjoys widespread use but is historically associated with South Asia and the Middle East. At present, its primary users are members of expatriate communities who migrated to Europe, the Persian Gulf region, and North America and send remittances to their relatives on the Indian subcontinent, East Asia, Africa, Eastern Europe, and elsewhere."

But there is yet another dimension to Hawala. Remember, I had told you that it was perfectly secular idea. If that were so, could I leave out Christianity, especially having covered its origins through the Islamic laws and the Hindu precepts? Dan Brown in his bestselling novel *The Da Vinci Code* suggests that secrecy, banking and Hawala transactions were intricately linked to Christianity.

Whether Hawala is a Hindu, Islamic or Christian idea, the choice is entirely yours. But whatever it might be, it surely is a system that has evolved by a cross-fertilisation of ideas over generations, religions and civilisations. Nevertheless, the point that I need to make repeatedly is that it is an extraordinary secular idea! Exactly as E. M. Forster said in a *Passage to India*: "Nothing in India is identifiable." How true. Not even Hawala.

The US Department of State in its International Narcotics Control Strategy Report for 2009 explains the linkage of Hawala with the Indian society rather bluntly. It encapsulates the entire paradigm by stating, "Hawala is an alternative remittance system whose deep roots in South Asia make it popular among all strata of Indian society, not only immigrant workers." It also points to the relative ease of documentation in a Hawala system, better rates, and efficiency while simultaneously providing anonymity and security for its customers as reasons for its popularity.

Whatever be it, Hawala as a system is deeply ingrained in the collective psyche of Indians.

Hawala: How it Works and Why

The US State Government Report on the subject points to a different need for Hawala transactions which cannot be ignored in the Indian context. Hawala, the report points out, can also be used to circumvent foreign exchange restrictions imposed by the Government of India and to avoid scrutiny of financial transactions. Many Indians, the report states, especially among the poor and illiterate, do not trust banks and prefer to avoid the lengthy paperwork required to complete a money transfer through a financial institution. That in a way explains why Hawala flourishes in this country.

But what is the precise manner in which the actual transactions take place? First and foremost, what needs to be understood is that a large number of Hawala transactions into India are believed to be "routine ones." That implies involving the transfer of remittances from migrant workers, especially from the Gulf regions, to their relatives in India. It has been often seen that many NRIs prefer to use the Hawala system for reasons already explained.

Thus, in a simple Hawala deal, a migrant in a foreign country, say the Gulf, seeking to send some remittances to his relatives in India approaches a Hawala dealer. The dealer, in turn, directs his agent in India to deliver an equivalent amount to the relative in India. One such group actively involved in squaring Hawala transactions in recent years has been suspected to be software companies. Experts believe that some money receivable out of India is brought safely back into India as proceeds of software exports. Under some conditions, these export proceeds are exempt from tax. Using fictitious agencies, sham-employees and dubious sub-contractors, the export proceeds are suspected to be distributed across the country.

But that is part one of the entire transaction, which, as can be seen, is fairly simple. It does not need any seer to understand that Hawala funds that come into India need to be matched by a corresponding movement of funds in the opposite direction so as to "square" off the accounts between the Hawala dealer abroad and his agent in India.

The mechanism by which the Hawala dealer compensates his agent forms part of the second leg of the Hawala mechanism. This is done over a period of time through a variety of methods – systematically, scientifically and methodically. These include cash transfers from other sources within

India to their relatives outside India, that is, those who may be in need of delivering foreign exchange outside India. In such a scenario, the agent becomes the Hawala dealer and the dealer becomes his agent. But again, these are two simple transactions working in opposite directions, cancelling out each other.

Gold: The Big Daddy of Hawala [1]

But life is not so simple. Nor are these innocent transactions the subject matter of this book. Sometimes, cash is required in bulk for distribution in India for the equivalent foreign exchange received abroad by the Hawala dealer. Who on earth has such a huge amount of cash, that is, crisp currency notes aggregating to several lakhs or perhaps several crores, that too, on call? Remember, we are talking about hard cash and not about balances in current accounts in a bank.

The answer to this question is obvious. This is where the rich and the mighty in India having "excess cash", or if you permit me to say, "truck loads of cash" fit into the scheme of Hawala transactions. But if they are in a position to provide such a huge quantity of cash in India, it is obvious, that the Hawala dealer must be in a position to provide an equivalent amount of foreign exchange outside India. Simply put, only when you have cash either in India or abroad, you are eligible to be part of the Hawala mechanism.

Sometimes, it has been observed that it is not merely cash that is preferred as a mode of settlement. Others include gold, diamonds, consumer or manufactured goods, machinery, or invoice manipulation in a fake export-import business.

In such cases, settlement in a Hawala transaction happens without movement of currencies. But recent developments dovetail smuggling other illegal activities into the "sublime" idea that is Hawala.

Invoice manipulation of cross-border trade, for example, offers the Hawala agents in India the perfect cover for their "unofficial remittance business." Many Hawala agents are also often involved in businesses where the transfer of money on a regular basis arouses little suspicion. Experts believe that one possible leg of the Hawala transaction could come to India initially in the form of gold bars brought in through "regulars." It may be noted that we have liberalised the gold import laws to allow every air passenger who has stayed in a foreign country for a minimum of six months to bring in a maximum of 10 kg of gold.

1. Fake currency is another method of settling Hawala transactions. However, that is beyond the scope of the present discussions.

In typical Hawala style, the funds reach the final destination, possibly from the proceeds of the sale of gold in India. It may be noted that the sale of gold is predominantly carried out in India by cash. That would help any Hawala transaction run its full course. But all this comprises Hawala at a relatively retail level. Neither is one finding fault with these nor is it humanly possible to eliminate virtually all possible sources of Hawala transactions in a globalised economy.

Whatever be the manner of settling the accounts, Hawala dealers, it may be noted, leave no trail for investigators and rarely has it been possible for investigators to get to the second stage of these Hawala transactions, leave alone the entire Hawala transactions in totality.

Naturally, law enforcing agencies are worried about the increasing likelihood of such Hawala routes – used by traditional customers for their cost-effectiveness, efficiency, reliability, lack of paper trail and for tax evasion – becoming instruments of money launderers, smugglers, drug dealers and, of course, the big daddy of all of them, terrorists.

Whenever the Hawala chain runs out of cash, it is usually a messy affair. It may be recalled that in at least two instances, the national media had reported that members of a Hawala network had withdrawn huge amounts running into a few crores from banks. One way of looking at it was to dub these as crude operations – money was stuffed in gunny bags and transported by trucks.

The other way of looking at the entire issue is that the operators were undeniably brazen. When confronted, they confidently explained that they were merely "withdrawing money from their personal accounts for honouring business commitments!" One is reminded of the cardinal rule of explanation – never explain, your friends do not need it and your enemies will not believe you anyway.

According to press reports, in one instance, the investigating officers found a list on the basis of which money withdrawn from a bank was distributed among "unidentified beneficiaries." The biggest share delivered was marked as Rs. 25,000, and officials were told that the entire cash was distributed in a day among several hundred beneficiaries.

One Can See the Levers of this Pulley – Can You?

In this connection, one is reminded of the speech of the then Finance Minister Mr. P. Chidambaram in his Budget speech of 2005-06, made in the Parliament on February 28, 2005. According to the Hon'ble Minister, "The NCMP requires the Government to introduce special schemes to unearth black money and assets. I am obliged to carry out the mandate, but without giving undeserved relief or an amnesty. I am concerned about large cash transactions, especially withdrawals of cash, when there is no ostensible purpose to withdraw such large amounts of cash." That was perfect. Then came the knock-out punch: "These cash withdrawals leave no trail, and presumably become part of the black economy."

The diagnosis was spot on. Now for the prescription that had the nation in absolute disbelief – if not for its novelty, at least for its weirdness. The Hon'ble Finance Minister concluded, "Therefore, I propose to introduce two anti-tax evasion measures: Firstly, I propose to levy a tax on withdrawal of cash on a single day of over Rs. 10,000 or more from banks at the rate of 0.1 percent. Thus, a person withdrawing Rs. 10,000 in cash would have to pay a small sum of Rs. 10."

One distinctly recalls that there was manifest unease in several quarters after this measure was announced. One felt that Pandora's Box had indeed been opened. Most believed that one could have collected the necessary details without levying such tax. Of course, these cash withdrawal limits were subsequently raised following a huge public uproar. But the new tax remained. Obviously, one believed that the Government had indeed become serious in tackling such huge withdrawals of cash which ostensibly formed part of the Hawala chain. Whether it was effective is another matter which we will examine shortly.

In his budget speech for the year 2007-08, Mr Chidambaram stated what apparently seems to be a pat on his own back: "The Banking Cash Transactions Tax (BCTT) continues to be an extremely useful tool to track unaccounted monies and trace their source and destination. It has led the Income Tax Department to many money laundering and Hawala transactions."

While one is not sure as how many such Hawala transactions were discovered and acted upon by the Government, surely, it was indeed a laudable attempt by the Government. Ostensibly, it was intended to tackle significant cash withdrawals and subsequent distribution in India.

This "useful tool" facilitated authorities, perhaps for the first time in independent India, to keep track of people who withdrew huge sums of money for whatever purpose. Nevertheless, in the information technology era, it is indeed strange that the Government had to rely on age-old data collection techniques. It becomes all the more bizarre that the BCTT has become virtually irrelevant when most banks have computerised their operations and all such information may be collected by the mere click of a mouse. Strange are the ways of the Government! In short, minus the levy, the BCTT was a brilliant idea.

Subsequently, in February 2008, presenting the Budget for 2008-09, Mr Chidambaram went on to state, "The Banking Cash Transaction Tax (BCTT) has served a very useful purpose in enlarging the information system of the Income Tax Department." It seemed for a moment it was the customary pat on his back. Yet, what was to follow was inexplicable.

The Hon'ble Finance Minister ended the nation's brief tryst with this "useful tool" by proposing to do away with the same. Perhaps the useful tool was inconveniencing someone high up within the Government itself! The reasoning provided by the Hon'ble Finance Minister is worth recalling here: "Since the information is also being gathered through other instruments introduced in the last few years, I propose to withdraw this tax with effect from April 1, 2009." The Government was indeed prompt in notifying the scrapping of the tax on April 1, 2009.

I am not sure what the "other instruments" are that are presumably in action and hurting Hawala operators. Let us bear in mind a simple proposition of governance – if it is not hurting someone, it is not working at all in the first place. To my mind, not many have been hurt by the BCTT or the invisible "other instruments" till date. Or it might have hurt someone high up within the Government that warranted the withdrawal of this measure. Either way, the BCTT is now history.

Before I conclude on the BCTT, just a piece of irrelevant statistics for the reader – it is a remarkable coincidence that the elections to the fifteenth Lok Sabha commenced a few days after the date on which the BCTT was eventually scrapped, i.e. from the middle of April 2009. *I am reminded of my high school teacher who often used to tell us that coincidence is the word we use when we can't see the levers and pulleys. In this case, I do. Do you?*

Similarly, with the abolition of the recipient based Gift Tax a few years ago, the field was open to every recipient of such cash distribution to explain the same as "gift." Subsequently, the Income Tax Act was amended several times over to ensure that income included gifts made by those who were not relatives. Of course, the Income Tax Act included a list of persons to be relatives. That meant one could get cash as a gift only from relatives. Subsequently, the Income Tax Act was amended to include even non-cash gifts as income in the hands of the recipient of such gifts. Again all these mundane references to laws, rules and regulations are for you and me – the rich and the mighty need not worry. They can carry on without any let or fear.

It would seem that the more complex we get with our laws, the more we are in effect, deluding ourselves. In this connection, one is reminded of the immortal words of Sir Walcott: "Oh what a tangled web we weave, when first we practise to deceive."

If Hawala is Sin, Money Laundering is Recompense

Money laundering is far more an exotic subject than Hawala. Hawala is crude, dirty and elementary. Money laundering is an extremely complex, sophisticated and intelligent exercise. If Hawala is usually associated with dirty money; money laundering is the act of cleansing the dirt associated with such money. It is the saint who removes the taint.

Jeffrey Robinson, a recognised expert on organised crime, fraud and money laundering, explains the concept succinctly, "Money laundering is called what it is because that perfectly describes what takes place – illegal, or dirty, money is put through a cycle of transactions, or washed, so that it comes out the other end as legal, or clean money. In other words, the source of illegally obtained funds is obscured through a succession of transfers and deals in order that those same funds can eventually be made to appear as legitimate income."

In effect, the money after the cleansing process must be available to a person as if it originates from a legal source. This cleansing is done usually on a foreign soil, though at times it can be done within the country's borders too. Naturally, all laundering activities are not associated with cross-border transactions.

Some laundering activities are purely domestic transactions arising out of domestic tax compulsions carried out in full public glare. One of the well-thought out plans popular in India even till a few years back was the pyramid money spinner scheme. This receipt of money from unknown persons who successively become part of the pyramid chain is perhaps a well-known case of money laundering using internal resources, transactions and persons. This was often explained as gifts, especially in the aftermath of scrapping of the Gift Tax Act. Of course, with the amendment of the Income Tax Act to include cash gifts from non-relatives as income, these schemes have lost their potency.

It is pertinent to note that such schemes were introduced predominantly by persons to create a "source" for income tax assessees by brilliant tax practitioners. The problem usually encountered by most assessees is that they have purchased assets or have incurred some expenditure with tell-tale evidence from incomes that have not been disclosed to the taxman. Naturally, they become paranoid when questioned as to the "source" for the purchase of such assets.

Further, under the income tax law, no one (even one who is not even an assessee) can take loans in excess of Rs 20,000 from another person in cash. That restricts their "source" apart from what they legally declare to the taxman. Therefore, assessees who have unaccounted income, end up having corresponding unaccounted expenditure or assets purchased or investments made from such undeclared income. That makes them potential targets for the Income Tax Department to carry out searches. That is, of course, provided that the Income Tax Department is serious.

To amplify further, a trip to Singapore along with his family members may cost a person say Rs 2,50,000 in a particular year. Further, he might have invested in shares of a company aggregating to say Rs 2,00,000 and purchase of gold aggregating to Rs 50,000.

Assume further that the annual salary of that person is Rs 4,00,000 only. Apparently, it is clear that his expenditure and investments – of Rs 5,00,000 in the instant example – exceed his known source of income. Therefore, the person in question has what is technically called a "source" problem – an issue that is often confronted by tax practitioners. That would explain petty money laundering in the Indian context. In the instant case, the assessee in question has to ensure that he has sufficient "source" not only to explain his trip to Singapore with his family, but also his investment in shares and gold.

The reverse is equally true. It might be appreciated that just because one has undeclared income, it cannot be put to sleep. For instance, one cannot keep it as currency in one's lockers or under one's pillows. Such income, whether legal or otherwise, needs to be put to immediate productive use. Therefore, it is imperative, that at the earliest opportunity any unaccounted income is legalised, especially if it needs to be put to productive use. And when a person converts his illegal income into legal income through a series of transactions (or for that matter by "explaining" his source as briefly stated above) – it is money laundering. Sometimes, the person even pays a commission to buy such "source." In fact, many tax practitioners derive their major source of income not by providing advice on tax laws, but by providing a legitimate "source" to an assessee who does not have a legal source.

Another popular way of conferring legitimacy on unaccounted income is by accounting for it as agricultural income. This is simply because farm incomes are not taxable under the Indian Income Tax Act. The age-old trick is to buy farm lands in remote areas and claim to cultivate them. The sale proceeds of the farm products from the (non-existent?) farm are then accounted as agricultural income in their books. Have you ever wondered why some famous personality suddenly begins to sell spinach in the city streets with the same verve as Popeye, the cartoon character? Never mind if the spinach has been purchased from the local wholesale markets.

Interestingly, such events are also covered by the media with great fanfare. All these are part of a grand design to create evidence. After all, when the assessment is done after a couple of years, all these could be submitted as part of evidence to the assessment officers. In the alternative, you cannot take the spinach produced in your farm a few years back as proof to the assessment officer. Can you? And as a customary practice, such evidence usually stands in good stead with the Income Tax Department. That is foresight for you. Or is it skulduggery, plain and simple? Whatever be it, this is surely in the eye of the beholder.

Yet all these money laundering techniques have been practised for ages within India. All that has been stated above comprises merely simple ideas. Today's complicated world has moved beyond all such plain vanilla money laundering ideas. Complex problems naturally cannot afford simple solutions. And in a globalised era, solutions too have to be from abroad. After all, we live in a globalised world, don't we?

The Origins of Money Laundering

As pointed out earlier, if Hawala is associated with any taint, money laundering removes that taint. Put differently, it provides legitimacy to an unlawful or illegal source of income. Under this process, money that is illegal or dirty, is put through a series of transactions so that it comes out lily white at the other end. While Hawala ensures confidentiality of the transactions, money laundering ensures that such illegally (or unlawfully) obtained funds are eventually made to appear as legitimate ones.

Money laundering is not a simple crime. It is a cover up for many crimes committed. In the process, it seeks to remove the taint of illegality associated with money obtained from criminal acts. Money laundering is a necessary follow-up required to hide several crimes. It is the restitution process with the inevitable recompense.

Money laundering is invariably linked to criminals, especially big criminals. Conversely, big crimes usually have a money laundering dimension. It is akin to spraying chilly powder in a scene of crime. That would not only distort evidence but also derail any further investigation. Money laundering is precisely aimed at all that – it not only cleanses the illegal money but also derails investigation into serious crimes.

In contrast to most other types of crimes, money laundering is noted for the ingenuity of its operators and diversity of its forms. What is indeed consternating bankers worldwide is that they end up, unwittingly though, providing some sort of services to their clients, without realising that they themselves have become a part of the laundering process.

According to Billy Steel, the term "money laundering" is said to originate from the US Mafia ownership of laundromats in the early part of the twentieth century. Gangsters earning huge sums in cash from several illegal businesses needed to show a legitimate source for these earnings. The gangsters chose laundromats because they were obvious cash businesses. Nevertheless, linking the term "money laundering" to those times is probably far-fetched, though the linkage to laundromats is indeed revealing.

One of the high profile gangsters who was prosecuted and convicted in October 1931 for tax evasion was Al Capone – the notorious Mafia head of those times. It is interesting to note that he was not sent to prison for the predicate crimes that generated his illicit income in the first place but ostensibly for tax evasion.

Another famous American criminal, Meyer Lansky, was particularly affected by the conviction of Capone for tax evasion. Determined that the same fate would not befall him, he set about searching for ways to hide his money. Before the year was out, he had discovered the benefits of numbered Swiss bank accounts. This appears to be the advent of money laundering.

The term "money laundering" is nevertheless of fairly recent origin. The first documented mention in a newspaper about money laundering is attributed to a report about the Watergate scandal in the United States in 1973. Since then, the term has been widely accepted and is in popular usage throughout the world.

The Three Steps to Laundering

How does money laundering operate? What exactly are the steps in the same? A 2002 report of the Governors of the US Federal Reserve System quoted by the Peterson Institute, describes money laundering as having three sequential elements: placement, layering and integration. In a succinct explanation of the series of transactions that go on within a laundering process, this report explains the three processes rather explicitly, leaving nothing to imagination.

According to the report, "The first stage of the process is placement. The placement stage involves the physical movement of currency or other funds derived from illegal activities to a place or into a form that is less suspicious to law enforcement authorities and more convenient to the criminal. The proceeds are introduced into traditional or non-traditional financial institutions or into the retail economy."

The trickiest as well as the most difficult stage of any money laundering process is the first one, akin to a rocket launching process. One of the several ways of doing this is by intelligently parking criminal money into the legal financial system by opening up several bank accounts in the name of individuals (sometimes non-existent) or organisations (often shell companies) and depositing the money in those accounts.

Experts opine that laundered money is most vulnerable to detection at the placement stage. Consequently, globally, regulators and law enforcement agencies have developed sufficient safeguards to make it difficult to place substantial amount of cash into accounts without detection. These include mandating maintenance of records and reporting of large or unusual currency transactions, including large cash deposits and withdrawals from banks as well as reporting on suspicious transactions.

It is in this connection that one may note that the KYC – "know your customer" – norm assumes significance. Every single banker or those in the financial sector are mandated by various regulators and law enforcing agencies to know their customers. Put pithily, if placement is the first stage in money laundering, strict adherence to the KYC norm is the first but surest step in an anti-money laundering measure. It is this subject that will haunt us during the entire length and breadth of this book, especially in the later chapters while we discuss the matters relating to the UBS and Goldman Sachs decisions.

In 1997, the Basel Committee issued its Core Principles for Effective Banking Supervision which provides a comprehensive blueprint for an effective bank supervisory system and covers a wide range of topics. Of the total 25 Core Principles, Core Principle 15, deals with money laundering; it provides: "Banking supervisors must determine that banks have adequate policies, practices and procedures in place, including strict 'know your customer' rules, that promote high ethical and professional standards in the financial sector and prevent the bank from being used, intentionally or unintentionally, by criminal elements." In addition to these, the Basel Committee issued a "Core Principles Methodology" in 1999, which contains 11 specific criteria and five additional criteria to help assess the adequacy or otherwise of KYC policies and procedures.

It is obvious that it is these "know your customer" or "KYC" policies and procedures that have become, over a period of years, a crucial part of an effective Anti-Money Laundering/Counter-Terrorism Financing (AML/CFT) institutional framework in every country. Naturally, the identification of the client (in the case of an individual) or the beneficiary holders (in the case of a legal entity) has become a crucial part of an anti-money laundering exercise.

Now let us get to the second stage of money laundering. The US Federal Reserve Report referred to earlier goes on to add, "The second stage is layering. The layering stage involves the separation of proceeds from their illegal source by using multiple complex financial transactions to obscure the audit trail and hide the proceeds."

To specifically comprehend what is stated here, a reference to elementary Physics is inevitable. The concept of centrifugal force represents the effects of inertia that arise in connection with rotation at high speeds. This is experienced by objects subject to such rotation as an outward force away from the centre of rotation. This idea is often used in separating several ingredients, say, in a mixture. Ingredients with varied specific gravity behave differently when put through high speed revolutions. Using appropriate separators, these ingredients of the mixture are collected.

To illustrate, centrifugal force is used by allowing blood to be put through a high speed rotating device that separates each of the ingredients of blood viz., platelets, white blood cells, red blood cells, etc according to the speed of the rotating device. These are then collected at various chambers. By this mechanical process, the ingredients of blood are separated without any hassle.

This is again similar to the process that our grandmothers used by churning buttermilk to separate butter from the curd just as uranium is separated from plutonium in a nuclear plant using a centrifuge. You need not be a scientist from CERN, the European Organisation for Nuclear Research, to understand what was stated above. After all, what is stated above is only an adaptation of the great churning of the ocean seen in Hindu mythology.

Separation in a money laundering act involves the same principles of high speed revolution and centrifugal force. Once illegal money is put through this, the money gets separated from illegality. Remember the operational words here are speed, complexity and multiplicity. One has to be extremely dextrous. This is ostensibly done to conceal an audit trail and simultaneously remove the taint of illegality from the money that is being laundered. Once it is done, the money becomes legal, regains respectability and is ready for all uses by all respectable men and, to be fair to the other gender, women too!

One favourite route to ensure multi-layering in a money laundering transaction is by moving money to offshore bank accounts or what are popularly called tax havens. These bank accounts offer complete anonymity and secrecy to the operators of the accounts.

Further, different exotic commercial techniques such as mergers, acquisitions, special purpose vehicles and valuations are reportedly used by various experts in this step. The method to be used in each transaction is extremely case sensitive and requires significant intervention of finance professionals. The idea is often to jump across jurisdictions, mostly through tax havens, so as to add not only complexity to these transactions but in the process ensure multi-layering while innocently claiming to avoid taxes or optimising the tax impact.

The US Federal Reserve Report details the third stage in a money laundering process as one where the money, once having retained its legality, is put through normal financial transactions, perhaps in the very jurisdiction it originated or gained its illegality. In this connection, the report states, "The third stage in the money laundering process is integration. During the integration stage, illegal proceeds are converted into apparently legitimate business earning through normal financial or commercial operations."

The idea here is plain and simple – money that is cleared of its taint is eminently eligible for being used in all transactions. A well known mechanism is to open shell companies abroad, again in tax havens with lax supervisory mechanisms. Money from these tax havens enters a country without any let or fear. Quite the contrary, it even gains some respectability while reentering a country as it is now christened as Foreign Direct Investment (FDI) or Foreign Institutional Investment (FII).

That is why most of the enlightened debate on the subject in the higher echelons of banking, finance and commerce in some countries is to refrain even from transacting with these jurisdictions in the first place. This stems from the fact that tax havens, by their very arrangement, are anachronistic to the modern-day management philosophies of transparency and openness. Further, tax havens offer extraordinary secrecy along with enormous scope for multi-layering.

No wonder, banks globally are increasingly demonstrating their reluctance in dealing with tax havens *per se*. Why choose to sup with the devil and then complain about the devil? Slowly but surely, the once unthinkable idea of imputing untouchable status to tax havens is gaining currency in the Western world. Unfortunately, this idea of refraining from dealing with the tax havens is still in its embryonic stage in India. Needless to emphasise, such a policy requires greater pressure from the civil society.

We will revert to this exotic subject of tax havens in the context of money laundering and some of the recent developments pertaining to them globally in the next few chapters of this book.

Explaining the Symbiotic Link Between Money Laundering and Terrorism

The World Bank, in a document titled "Reference Guide to Anti-Money Laundering and Combating Financing of Terrorism," puts all these discussions in the proper perspective by explaining money laundering as the conversion, concealment, acquisition, possession or disguise of the true nature, source, location, disposition, movement, rights or transfer of a property, knowing that such property is derived from any offence or offences, for the purpose of concealing or disguising the illicit origin of the property or of assisting any person who is involved in the commission of such an offence or offences to evade the legal consequences of his actions.

Naturally, in all these transactions, knowing the ultimate beneficiaries in every financial transaction becomes as crucial as knowing those originating the transactions. It is possible that every innocent transaction put through by your neighbourhood bank could well be carried out by a terrorist or by someone with an illegal source, merely with an intention to remove the taint associated with it. The following chart prepared by the World Bank in the above mentioned document puts the issue of money laundering in the context of these discussions.

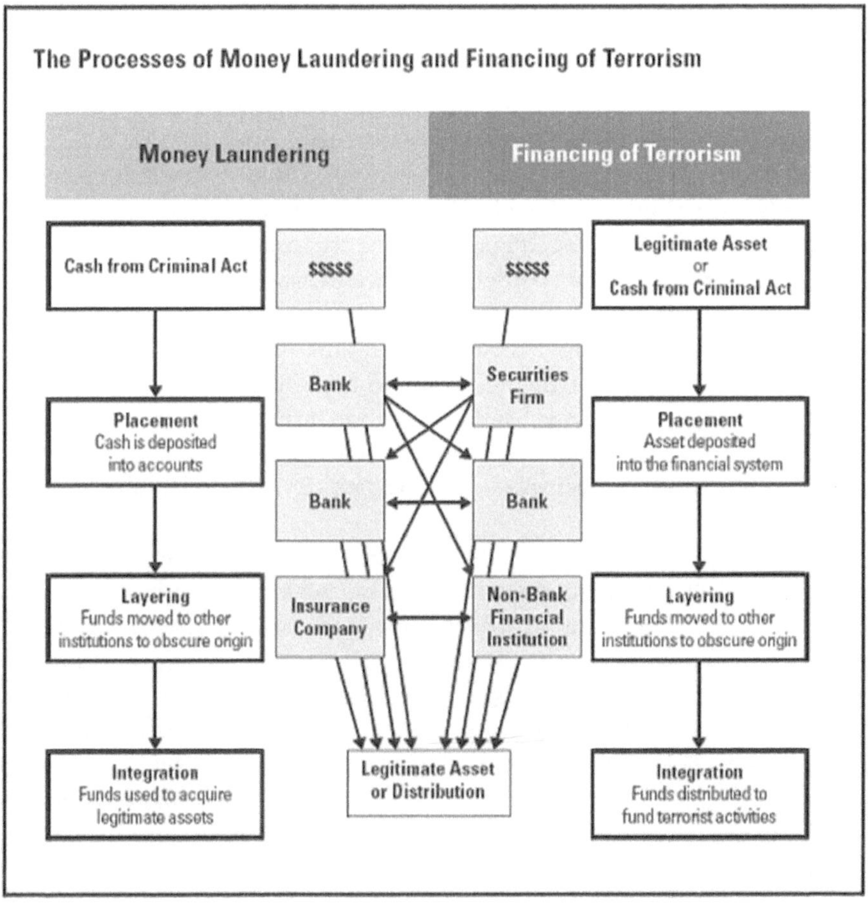

There is yet another side to money laundering. By its very nature, money laundering lends itself to a host of criminal activities. The criminal offences associated with money laundering can be classified into the following broad categories:

- Drug distribution.
- Bribery.
- Corruption.
- Tax violations.
- Foreign exchange violations.
- Terrorism.

As already discussed in the early part of this chapter, apart from terrorism, the world has been witnessing all the other crimes for ages. However, it was only after the terrorist attacks in the US on September 11, 2001, that the link between terrorism and money laundering came to be explored. Consequently, anti-money laundering steps were taken in right earnest worldwide in order to curb terrorism. It is in this context that one has to appreciate the approach of Governments across continents towards money laundering post 9/11.

What is worrying analysts across the world is that the techniques used to launder money are virtually identical to those used for terrorist financing. However, there is a significant difference in the origin of the source. Funds used to support terrorism may even originate from legitimate sources. Or they could possibly be from criminal activities.

Therefore, for effective terrorist activities and to ensure that the authorities do not get a whiff, concealing the source becomes important, irrespective of whether it is legal or otherwise. If the source can be concealed, it remains free from any investigation even after the act of terrorism and, more importantly, from the terrorists' perspective, remains available for financing future terrorist activities.

Terrorism Adds a New Dimension in Combating Money Laundering

Given these developments in recent times, the banking system has come increasingly under the scrutiny of Governments across continents. More so, given the unfortunate developments in the United States on September 11, 2001, money laundering, because of its links with funding of terrorism, has attracted the serious attention of Governments. In this connection, it is well understood by Governments that banks, because of their ability to move funds rapidly, are extremely vulnerable to money laundering. And, hence, the spotlight is constantly on the financial sector, more so on the banks.

Explaining the risk to the banking sector, the Basel Committee on Banking Supervision (BCBS), in a document listing out the initiatives needed by the banking sector to tackle the twin menace of money laundering and financing terrorist activities, states, "The account holder can be a customer who does not present himself or herself for interview at the bank or one introduced to the bank by a third-party. It may also be a legal entity interposed between the ultimate beneficial owners and the bank, or a professional intermediary depositing fund that it manages for its clients."

The Basel Committee further points out the types of customers who carry a higher probability of money laundering and specific activities where the fear of possible money laundering is higher. These include:

- Customers who use fronts to open an account so as to hide their true identities.
- Private banking operations, which by nature involve a large measure of confidentiality.
- Customers who are politically exposed persons may significantly raise the potential for reputation risk.
- Introduced business, where a bank may place undue reliance on the due diligence conducted by an introducer
- Correspondent banking business, especially where banks do not fully understand the nature of the respondent banks' business, or if the respondents are shell banks or located in a jurisdiction which has poor know-your-customer standards.

Therefore, the issue of money laundering and putting across appropriate checks and balances within the financial sector have gathered steam since the terrorist attacks in the US. The BCBS, in October 2001, as a consequence of these terrorist attacks, issued prudential guidance for Customer Due Diligence (CDD) with a view to tackle money laundering on a war-footing.

The said document sets out standards and provides guidance for the development of appropriate practices by banks in this area. Emphasising the need for adequate due diligence on new and existing customers, the BCBS expected banks to develop policies and procedures in key areas such as customer acceptance, customer identification, ongoing monitoring of high-risk accounts and risk management.

The essential elements for these were presented in the paper, together with recommendations for more rigorous standards of due diligence for higher-risk areas. Specific areas for banks to act are:

- Banks should take decisions to enter into business relationships with higher risk customers at the senior management level.
- Banks should identify the *beneficial owners* (emphasis added) of all accounts. Guidance is provided on the persons to be identified where the customer is a non-natural person, such as a trust, corporate, or professional intermediary. If a bank is unable to identify the beneficial owner to its satisfaction, it should refuse the business.
- Banks should apply enhanced due diligence for private banking operations. There should be policies and procedures for handling banking relationships with politically exposed persons.
- Banks should use the conditions below when determining whether it can rely on introducers. These conditions also apply to a number of other areas, e.g. to assess whether reliance can be placed on the due diligence performed by professional intermediaries and respondent banks in a correspondent banking relationship.
- The introducer complies with the minimum CDD standards required of banks.
- The CDD procedures of the introducer are as rigorous as those which the bank would have conducted itself for the customer.
- The bank must satisfy itself as to the reliability of the systems put in place by the introducer to verify the identity of the customer.
- The bank must reach agreement with the introducer that it will be permitted the right to verify the due diligence undertaken by the introducer.
- All relevant identification data and other documentation pertaining to the customer's identity are immediately submitted by the introducer to the bank.
- For correspondent banking, banks should fully understand the nature of the respondent bank's management and business; should refuse to enter into, or continue, a correspondent banking relationships with foreign shell banks; and should pay particular attention when continuing correspondent banking relationships with respondent banks located in the jurisdiction with poor know-your-customer standards.
- In addition to customer identification, the CDD paper provides recommendations for the ongoing monitoring of accounts; appropriate compliance and internal audit functions within the bank; application of an accepted minimum standard of KYC policies and procedures on a global basis.
- Supervisory obligations and powers in the implementation of KYC in a cross-border context.

Among the more fundamental issues addressed by the paper is the identification of beneficial owners, especially where the customer is a non-natural person through the KYC norm.

It may be understood that KYC is the first step to ensure transparency and regulatory regime. It is effectuated through a technical process of due diligence to know the full particulars and details about a client. Banking regulations globally demand that financial institutions must perform this due diligence at the outset to identify their clients. The ostensible purpose of the same is to ascertain relevant information pertinent to doing financial business with them.

In the USA, KYC is a policy implemented to conform to a customer identification programme mandated under the Bank Secrecy Act and the US PATRIOT Act. Know your customer policies have become increasingly important globally to prevent identity theft fraud, money laundering and, of late, terrorist financing. Globally, these rules relating to personal particulars and business details are usually templates. Nevertheless, they are designed to know some definite particulars about the clients, should the need arise in the course of any investigation. Also, such a due diligence facilitates financial institutions to carry out their risk assessments of that particular client.

While these are fundamental details, over a period of time, KYC norms have evolved significantly and cannot be limited to a predetermined template. As it evolves, KYC is all about ensuring that the customer is not on any list of known fraudsters, terrorists or money launderers, and tracking persons or individuals with high-risk owing to negative reports in the media about them or in public records.

Consequently, given the complexity of issues involved, banks have developed special software to monitor Anti-Money Laundering (AML) and Counter-Terrorism Financing (CTF), using particularly names analysis and trend monitoring software. This software generates instant alerts i.e. on real-time basis to identify unusual activity or flag certain off-beat transactions. These transactions are then subjected to further due diligence processes. This helps to determine whether a transaction or activity is suspicious and requires reporting to the appropriate authority in-charge of anti-money laundering or combating financing of terrorism. These transactions have increasingly come to be known as Suspicious Activity Reporting (SAR).

Obviously, as can be seen from the above, information or the names of the account holders is the beginning of any monitoring or reporting in an anti-money laundering exercise. That explains why getting the names of the account holder becomes critical in any financial transaction. Sans the names, no investigation can even commence, let alone be taken to a logical conclusion.

An anti-money laundering monitoring mechanism that cannot have the names would be akin to Hamlet without being the Prince of Denmark. Or, if you may permit me, *Ramayana* without Lord Rama!

Yet India Continues to Remain in Complete Denial

It is indeed strange that we hear about all these regulatory changes only in the context of developments post September 11, 2001. Nevertheless, the chain of such terrorist events in the US was a rude wake-up call to the entire global financial sector. It may be noted that all that has been stated above in this chapter vis-à-vis developments relating to SAR refers to a document in 2001 which was issued by the Basel Committee, no less.

But that was merely the beginning. In the subsequent chapters we would see how Governments worldwide have been keen on the issue of tackling the menace of money laundering. This is not merely because money laundering is merely an economic crime but invariably interlinked, intertwined and interrelated to funding terrorism.

Till 2001, money laundering was explained by some Western economists as an inevitable outcome of capital, like water finding its own level and capital flowing to countries that offer higher security and returns. After all, when taxes are high, draconian exchange control laws exist; it is human nature to bypass all of these. Economists in India and other developing countries could never counter this argument effectively. In the absence of any effective counter-idea, Indian economists too rationalised these arguments of the Western economists.

But all this has changed in the past decade. Today, fighting terrorism has become the key challenge to countries. The economic rationale that justified money laundering from the developing countries into the developed ones has given way to patriotism and pragmatism. In the process, economic tenets of the past have been given the go-by and it is a no entry for flow of dirty money between countries.

Further, in the developing world too, tax rates have been moderated. Exchange control laws have been liberalised. So has a host of rules and regulations under the reforms process.

But what is forgotten in the entire debate is that the modern-day Hawala and money laundering in India are rooted in corruption, especially at high places. It is nurtured by a selective approach to reforms by the Government, thrives on ingenious interpretation by the legal fraternity and, of course, survives, and is sustained and supported directly and indirectly by a pliable media. It is blessed by the intellectuals and consecrated by the trade and industry. Everyone, especially in the higher echelons of the Government, loves it as virtually everyone is a beneficiary of the system. Therefore, it is no wonder that Hawala and money laundering survive, endure and thrive in India.

Hawala and money laundering unfortunately are not merely the symbiotic link between socialist India and modern, liberal India. Hawala and money laundering are symptomatic of a larger malaise afflicting the Indian economy – corruption. For the corrupt to thrive and corruption to proliferate, Hawala is essential and money laundering vital.

In the process of turning a blind eye to money laundering, little do we realise that the terrorists too thrive. Such a rampant system is the obvious choice for the terrorists as well as the enemies of the nation to operate in India. It is not that corruption, Hawala and money laundering do not exist in other countries. They certainly do. But in the aftermath of the events on September 11, 2001, nation-states have begun to realise the crucial importance of curbing Hawala and money laundering so as to curb terrorism. And that is the crux of the issue. Naturally, post 9/11, the grammar of anti-money laundering operations is being rewritten at the global level. But the moot question remains: is it being rewritten in India?

In essence, on issues relating to money laundering, it is often seen that corruption coexists and is co-terminous with terrorism. And a lax anti-money laundering regime is a boon to both the corrupt as well as the terrorists. One begets the other, so much so that lines differentiating the two get blurred over a period of time. The World Bank has observed, "The absence of, or a lax or corrupt, anti-money laundering regime in a particular country permits criminals and those who finance terrorism to operate, using their financial gains to expand their criminal pursuits and fostering illegal activities such as corruption, drug trafficking, illicit trafficking and exploitation of human beings, arms trafficking, smuggling, and terrorism."

Strangely, despite these global developments to fight money laundering, the fight against terrorism in India has been relegated to the background. So what if a few thousand innocent Indian lives are lost every year due to terrorism? What if India is one of the biggest victims of terrorism? We will examine in greater detail the contrast in the global and the Indian policy responses to these issues in the following chapters.

It would seem that in their choice between filthy lucre and the compelling need to combat financing of terrorism post September 2001, most nation-states made their preferences obvious. The point is that from now on, it becomes extremely difficult for someone to fight corruption without fighting terrorism and vice versa. In the process, if there is action on one, there would be collateral damage on the other. It is a trade-off with dual benefits – if we eliminate one, the other gets automatically eliminated.

The moot point is: where are we positioning ourselves as a nation on this crucial issue? Somehow, we as a nation seem to dither, hesitate at every step and lack conviction to carry on our fight against terrorists. For a country which has been one of the worst victims of terrorism over the centuries, it is indeed strange that we are not yet tired of death, blood and gore. On the contrary, it would seem that we have taken to extreme pacifism to tackle violence, terrorism and death. It is indeed inexplicable that as a nation we do not have the necessary willingness to fight terrorism, with the sole exception of sloganeering.

Terrorism, unfortunately, cannot be fought merely through slogans. The will to counter terrorism is a painful process. It is to be tackled at the ground level as much as at the political as well as economic levels. Fighting terrorism at the economic level involves investigating the sources of funding as well as establishing their channels of laundering. That could possibly lead to some inconvenient truths coming out of the closet.

What else could explain why successive Governments have been soft on terrorists, especially investigating their source of funding, their ability to park money, as well as their established routes to launder money into, as well as away from, India? In our anxiety to protect the reputation of the high and the mighty of the land, are we suppressing our collective national will to fight terrorism?

How long will we continue to remain in complete denial of all these issues?

References

1. Paul Allan Schott, *Reference Guide to Anti-Money Laundering and Combating the Financing of Terrorism*, The World Bank, 2006.
2. Vijay Kumar Singh, Assistant Professor of Law, Hidayatullah National Law University, Raipur, Chhattisgarh, *Controlling Money Laundering in India – Problems and Perspectives.*
3. Billy Steel, Money Laundering – A Brief History from Billy's Money Laundering Information Website.
4. Dr. Peter Mihalyi, Head of Banking Program Partners for Financial Stability (PFS) Program, USAID – East-West Management Institute, Inc, The Prevention of Money Laundering: A Key Component of the Partners for Financial Stability (PFS) Program's Banking Activities.
5. The US State Department International Narcotics Control Strategy Report of 2009 – Country Reports – India – As submitted to the US Congress.
6. Dan Brown, *The Da Vinci Code.*
7. The Report of the Board of Governors of the Federal Reserve System (2002).
8. The Hawala Alternative Remittance System and its Role in Money Laundering Prepared, by Interpol General Secretariat, January 2000.
9. The Wikipedia.
10. Budget Speeches of the Hon'ble Finance Minister of 2005, 2007 and 2008.

11. Mohammed El-Qorchi, Senior Economist, Monetary and Exchange Affairs Department, IMF, *The Hawala System*
12. Krishna Kumar, "A Hawala Tunnel," *Frontline.*
13. Initiatives by The Joint Forum of the Basel Committee on Banking Supervision, International Organisation of Securities Commissions and the International Association of Insurance Supervisors to Combat Money Laundering and the Financing of Terrorism
14. Baggage Rules 1998, [M.F. (D.R.) Notification No. 30/98-Customs(N.T.), dated 2-6-1998, as amended].

CHAPTER 3

Tax Havens: The Contrasting Debate Elsewhere and in India

I have to challenge some of my own inherited perceptions that London is safe, Lagos is not. Britain is free of corruption, but Nigeria is not. Much of the corruption stems from London and Washington. Many of the mechanisms that keep Nigerians poor – the networks of offshore bank accounts that companies use to bleed Nigeria dry of its profits – are based in tax havens that were set up by the British and other colonial powers.

— Andy Rowell

Money laundering is the culmination of several predicate crimes that necessitate money laundering in the first place. Bringing back laundered wealth into mainstream economies as good clean money is crucial to ensure that such money is put to profitable use. The end game of a money laundering exercise is to ensure that money is cleansed of all its criminality. This has been discussed in some detail in the previous chapter. But all that has been stated till now pertains to money laundering at the retail level i.e. through individual transactions, piecemeal attempts and in driblets. Obviously, all these take time, money and efforts. Therefore, it is risky, uneconomical and time consuming. Moreover banks, financial institutions and other financial intermediaries are constantly on the lookout to detect such transactions and move to penalise all those who are behind it. All these make money laundering on a retail basis, inconvenient, uneconomical and cumbersome.

Hence, in these days of instant nirvana, there is a natural need for a wholesale money laundering mechanism. For modern economies, there is a necessity for large scale money laundering without the concomitant risks of the traditional routes. Modern global financial architecture allows money laundering at the wholesale level through a simple process – So, Welcome Tax Havens! People park and route their wealth in tax havens not merely because these levy no or abysmally low taxes. Rather, they do so as these jurisdictions operate on intense secrecy. At an operational level, this translates into offering complete anonymity to those who operate from these tax havens. In the process, the money that emerges from the tax havens is completely sanctified, pure and ready for legitimate use. If the ultimate source of the money is not identifiable, where is the question of alleging any taint? It is this anonymity offered to the money emerging from tax havens that is both its strength and, as we would see increasingly in this chapter, its Achilles' Heel.

Tax Havens – Exotic, Esoteric and Erotic

Before we proceed any further, a word about the world of tax havens. These are the most glamorous of places in the entire world – places where one would expect Bond movies to be shot. They are located in the most distant places on the planet. Yet they are accessible from virtually every country. They number approximately seventy, of which forty are very active and well known. Yet, not many can point out the names of even a few. They entice, encircle and enchant you. They may be well known as tourist centres. Yet, it is their banking mechanism that is notoriously famous and famously notorious.

Therefore, their USP is their secrecy. This includes:

- Bank secrecy – information cannot be obtained from banks and other financial institutions for official purposes such as tax collection.
- Secrecy about the beneficial ownership of the entities incorporated in such jurisdictions.

Most of the banks in these tax havens operate through numbered accounts. A numbered account can consist of a name, a number or a combination of both. The beneficiary is anonymous and only a very limited number of people have access to the details. To meet strict confidentiality rules, certain precautions are obligatory. These include:

- Bank statements must be sent to a post-box, or to a legal representative of the account holder.
- There is no cheque book, credit cards or other means of transferring funds: they leave too many traces.
- Any payment into the account by a third party must be formally authorised.
- Bankers advise clients to avoid accessing their account over the internet, because of security concerns.
- The same applies to the telephone; clients are advised to use public call boxes.

The icing on the cake is that such returns attract little or no taxes.

Naturally, not even saints can resist their seductions. Those who have not yet used the services of tax havens are not virtuous. No wonder it is often remarked that only the ignorant, incompetent and foolish stay away from tax havens.

Tax havens seek to attract investments from outside their borders offering stringent financial secrecy laws. But their idea is not merely to retain investments. They offer a host of financial services, of course, ensuring complete anonymity to those who operate from there. Secrecy is the chief driver that sustains a tax haven. These investment models are sustained through elaborate networks. All these are not simple issues relating to tax havens alone. Rather the very idea of tax haven is a by-product of the modern global financial architecture. Tax havens are a modern day invention. And, as the adage goes, necessity is the mother of all inventions.

Tax experts have opined that they have never come across any reason for people to set up an entity in a tax haven other than to avoid tax. However, tax havens are not merely limited to avoiding taxes. They have a much larger role in the modern globalised world of finance, trade and services. In fact, some financial experts believe tax havens to be a conspiracy of the Western world against the rest. By allowing the proliferation of tax havens in the twentieth century, it is argued by some economists that the Western world explicitly encourages the movement of scarce capital from the developing countries to the rich. It is the missing link in the explanations of economists who fail to explain why capital flows "upwards" from the poor and developing countries to the rich and developed ones. Consequently, some conclude that globalisation itself is a deep-rooted game that facilitates this upward flow of capital from the developing to the developed world. Tax havens seek to avoid taxes, avoid anti-money laundering mechanisms and, of course, recycling this illicit wealth into the financial markets of the world, all in one go.

This cloak of secrecy practised in these places is like the proverbial iron curtain of Kremlin of the Stalinist Russia – it covers up everything. Wealth passing through these tax havens is cleared of illegality and criminality. Since the secret accounts remain anonymous, they are also out of the bounds for the authorities of other countries. Since criminal laws of several countries operate not on preponderance of probabilities but on exacting standards of evidence, (where one is held innocent till proved guilty) the anonymity offered by these tax havens provides a perfect hideout for illegal wealth.

An ordinary Indian may not be exactly aware of how such secret accounts operate and what are the rules and regulations that go on to govern such tax havens. However, one may well be aware of "Swiss bank accounts," the shorthand for murky dealings, obfuscation and secrecy. Further, it is common knowledge that over one-half of global cross-border trade is routed on paper through tax havens, and about one-third of the assets of the global rich are held in offshore structures. That makes tax havens the centrifugal force in the world of economics and finance.

Geographically, the majority of these offshore tax havens are located on small island economies dispersed across the spectrum of time zones. From a political economic perspective, these offshore jurisdictions are inextricably linked to developed countries, mostly Organisation of Economic Cooperation and Development (OECD) members. It may be noted that the term offshore is merely a political statement. Professor Vaidyanathan of the Indian Institute of Management, Bangalore, an acknowledged expert on this convoluted subject, adds, "The largest concentrations of assets are attracted to the stable secure environments of the established tax havens – those that have existed for a number of years and enjoy the diplomatic protection of former colonial powers." In short, this overt blessing by an economic superpower sustains the existence of a tax haven.

According to literature available in the public domain on the subject, nearly forty countries aggressively market themselves as tax havens. The popular ones are Switzerland, Luxemburg, Liechtenstein, Isle of Man, Channel Islands and Bahamas. Of these, some have gone so far as to offer asylum or immunity to criminals who invest sufficient funds. They permit the formation of companies without any proof of identity, perhaps even by remote instructions through the internet with minimal hassles and bare minimal capital. It is impossible to extract details of beneficial ownership of these companies in such countries, unless someone has a distinct taste for imprisonment. All these make the tax haven a perfect rendezvous for the notorious and the terrorists.

Tax Haven and its Intimate Link to the World of Finance

The defining feature of a tax haven is the element of secrecy it provides predominantly through banking secrecy laws. Secrecy, it may be noted creates an effective barrier to investigation by any authorities, and paralyses any anti-money laundering efforts. John Christensen of the Tax Justice Network (TJN) calls this as "a major fault line in the financial liberalisation process." In this connection, he further points out that while capital has become well and truly global, the fact of the matter is that the ability of Governments to police cross-border money movements, especially dirty money, is extremely limited. It is further hindered by the lack of cooperative arrangements between national authorities on certain predicate crimes. And even when such money is traced, the laws in these tax havens are so loaded in favour of their clients that it is virtually impossible to get the money back from these places.

Service providers in tax havens as well as their clients know that their actions are veiled from the tax authorities of other countries by banking and commercial secrecy. The *modus operandi* of these service providers is similar: they create paper entities (through remote instructions) and shell companies to disguise the real parties to the transactions. Further, in some cases, many such service providers are willing to create false documents to disguise the real nature of transactions. This is done professionally and with the help of professional accountants and lawyers in such locations. Some global accounting firms specifically deal with this convoluted subject in a dextrous manner. In the process, dealing with the tax havens has been converted from an art into a science. We will examine the role of these professionals shortly.

The increased movement of capital recorded in the past several years on account of liberalisation of the financial markets worldwide is believed to have provided sufficient opportunities for the proliferation of tax havens. It may not be out of place to mention that capital account liberalisation is alleged by some to be one of the fundamental conditionalities imposed on various countries by the International Monetary Fund (IMF) right throughout the 1990s as a part of their structural adjustment programme. In fact, some analysts suggest that capital account liberalisation (one that allows free entry and exit of capital into an economy without any restrictions whatsoever) became a benchmark for evaluating the "extent of globalisation" achieved by countries, under the "Washington consensus" – a term coined by economist John Williamson – to denote the package of ten conditionalities repeatedly imposed by the IMF on all its "client nations."

The efficacy of this particular liberalisation process has been increasingly questioned by economists as diverse as Paul Krugman and Joseph Stiglitz. However, the question that remains unanswered is whether capital account liberalisation is a mere ideological fixation of the IMF or a ruse to allow free transfer of wealth from the developing countries to the others, notably the tax havens.

Writing in his celebrated book *Globalisation and its Discontents*, Nobel Laureate Joseph Stiglitz states, "There are no smoking guns here. You won't find hard evidence of a terrible conspiracy by Wall Street and the IMF to take over the world. I don't believe such a conspiracy exists." Yet he goes on to add intriguingly, "The truth is subtler. Often it's a tone of a voice, or a meeting behind closed doors, or a memo that determines the outcome of discussions."

Whether capital account liberalisation is a by-product of such conspiracy of the IMF or a genuine economic idea oversold by the IMF is left to the perception of the reader. Nevertheless, this idea of capital account liberalisation, the flight of capital from the developing countries which require capital the most for development, and its linkage to tax havens remains one of the most uncritiqued aspects of globalisation.

Christensen argues that the globalisation of financial markets and capital account liberalisation and in particular the creation of a poorly regulated globalised structure of secretive offshore financial centres has facilitated the cross-border transfer of good money and simultaneous laundering of dirty money. A combination of all these factors, as already pointed out earlier, has resulted in a virtual free-for-all.

And that is the beauty of a tax haven – it mixes the good and evil and leaves no trace of either.

It is in this context that one has to view the repeated yet allegedly dogmatic prescriptions of the IMF to ensure full capital account convertibility across those client countries that approach it for assistance. One does not recall of any other idea being sold with such missionary zeal by any multilateral organisation as much as the IMF "sold" capital account liberalisation to their hapless victims – read client countries. Was it plain ideological fixation? Was it, in turn, being arm-twisted by superior forces to prescribe the outlandish as good economics? Whatever it may be Christensen and Stiglitz suggest that the idea of capital account liberalisation was definitely not merely ideological as it appears on a superficial reading.

Liberalisation of capital movement globally, the breakthrough in internet technologies and proliferation of predicate crimes have led to the explosion of tax havens in the past several years. But all these are not random, unrelated and distant events. It is true that some of these developments, especially on the technological front could be completely unrelated to the scheme of tax havens, as envisaged originally. However, every single development in the technological world has been brilliantly put to use more for these transactions rather than for any legitimate use. The dovetailing of these developments in modern international banking and thereby allowing the flow of funds into and from tax havens has been near perfect.

Digital Dollar, Virtual Finance, Electronic Economics[1]

To explore the relationship between tax havens and global financial architecture, it is imperative that we have a closer look at the latter. The importance of finance in a globalised world can never be underestimated. The globalised world is nothing but globalisation of its capital; one that allows free movement of capital from one country to the other. Movement of global capital (and not any other factor of production) from one country to the other has often been held by analysts to be the last mile connectivity of a country in its process of globalisation.

In fact, for the past few decades, no other factor of production – labour or, for that matter, technology – has invited as much attention and discussion at the global level as the movement of finance has. It may not be out of place to mention that having realised the potency of this arrangement, the developed countries, notably the US, have lost interest in the Doha Round of trade negotiations under the aegis of the World Trade Organisation (WTO). Why produce, trade, take risks and complicate issues when one can profit merely through movement of finance? Put pithily, the one who controls global finance, controls the world of trade, commerce, business and the course of geo-politics.

The manner in which the world of finance dominates the global economy, its disproportionate influence in shaping and de-shaping the global economy while managing to remain virtually uncritiqued is one of the most perplexing aspects of modern life. To understand this architecture, a reference to the developments since World War II which led to the formation of the World Bank and the IMF is inevitable. Under this arrangement (also called the Bretton Woods arrangement), each participating Government guaranteed to exchange its own currency on demand for US dollars at a fixed rate. The underlying argument that led to this arrangement was that stability of exchange rates was crucial for the development of the global economy. In turn, the US Government guaranteed to exchange dollars for gold on demand at a rate of USD 35 per ounce of gold. This effectively placed all the currencies on an indirect gold standard, backed by the US gold reserves. Governments, thus, came to accept US dollars as gold deposit certificates and held the USD as a global currency.

This arrangement was based on a fundamental premise that the US economy would always remain strong enough to support its dollar. But the cost of the Vietnam War considerably weakened the faith of the rest of the world in the dollar as the *de facto* global currency. This situation had the potential to lead to a run on the US dollar, with countries and investors surrendering

1. A term coined by Mr. S. Gurumurthy.

the excess dollars and asking for gold in return. To preempt such danger, the then US President, Richard Nixon, removed the convertibility of the dollar to gold in August 1971. This completely dynamited the very structure of global finance conceived by the Bretton Woods meet. But in the process, the world had inevitably got habituated to the US dollar as the global currency by virtue of the rules adopted earlier. The fixed exchange rate of the Bretton Woods system of the post-World War II was replaced by a floating exchange rate mechanism. With the result that the global financial architecture post 1971 was a virtual antithesis when compared to that of pre-1971. Crucially, what was sought to be avoided (volatility of the exchange rates) by creating the IMF was legitimised through the IMF itself partially due to changed global economic scenarios.

It is such chain of developments that led some economists to pronounce the death of the US dollar. As events of the subsequent decades bear out, it would seem that the prediction of the demise of the US dollar was vastly exaggerated. The US dollar has not only survived all these days without the explicit backing of gold, but has spawned the global financial architecture that was unthinkable even in the early Eighties. This, in turn, ensured the growth of the financial sector which was not foreseen at the same time. Naturally, the question arises: was the collapse of the Bretton Woods Agreement in 1971, the rise of the dollar and also the global financial sector a mere coincidence? Or is it something far more sinister? Certainly uncertain!

But the remarkable string of coincidences does not end here. The proliferation of tax havens is one such event intimately linked to the tectonic changes witnessed in the global financial architecture in the Seventies and Eighties. Naturally, since their very evolution, tax havens have been symbiotically linked to the world of finance. The only question that remains unanswered is: was it a part of a greater design or did all this happen by sheer coincidence?

Thus, on the one hand, begins a fascinating dollar game. And, on the other, begins the proliferation of tax havens. Apparently, it is difficult to link one with the other. To do so would require some further understanding. After the currencies were floated against one another with no single reference point, the US began to manipulate the new financial floating exchange architecture so as to ensure that surplus dollars, which had accumulated in the hands of other countries, were brought under its control. Surplus dollars circulating globally were not in its interest as anything in surplus could see its value getting eroded.

It is believed that it was precisely to suck out the excess dollar circulation that the very idea of the petrodollar was conceived. Or was it sheer coincidence

– one would not know. But the fact remains that immediately after the collapse of the Bretton Woods Agreement, the US persuaded the Organisation of Petroleum Exporting Countries (OPEC) (the global oil cartel) to carry out a steep increase in the price of crude. It may be noted that even today, as against the estimated cost of production of a barrel of crude at less than USD 15, the international selling price is several times over the figure.

This sucked the excess US dollars circulating globally into the hands of a handful of oil producing and exporting countries. Obviously, the dollars thus sucked by the OPEC countries could not be invested anywhere except predominantly into the US, as no other country could absorb such gargantuan investment.[2] So these petrodollars were invested back into the US economy by OPEC members as long-term investments, at times at less than even one per cent per annum. It is these investments at subsidised rates of interest that continue to fuel the growth of the US. In effect, the explicit gold standard of pre-1971 had given rise to an implicit crude standard of the Seventies. And this was further expanded to include the entire global trade and multi-commodity regime since the Eighties. The WTO regime only implicitly legitimised this arrangement.

But the dollar game did not stop here. The floating exchange rate mechanism of post-1971, particularly with an unprecedented expansion of various financial instruments, mechanisms and structured products, had the net effect of giving rise to what is colourfully termed by experts as "virtual finance." And then with the proliferation of technology, this arrangement itself morphed into digital economics overwhelming the real or actual economics. What is crucial to note here is that the sheer size of the virtual financial market viz., the world of virtual finance and digital dollars outnumbers the real economic transactions by approximately over a hundred times. This would give the extent of the mind-boggling influence of the virtual finance over the actual in sheer size. Naturally, this translates into a dominance of the world of finance over the real economy.

This dominance subsequently expanded into an elaborate network of derivatives market – estimated to be several times over when compared to the global GDP of approximately USD 60 trillion and global trade of goods and services not exceeding USD 15 trillion. The world of derivatives, at present, is beyond the power of any regulator or monitoring mechanism. Naturally, this led to a complete disconnect between the global financial system and the global production mechanism. In the process, the production sector has been completely marginalised by this global financial order. It may be noted that

2. India could have been an investment destination for such surpluses. However, with a closed economy, India did not encourage foreign investments till the early 90s. For such myopic policies, we cannot blame anyone.

global trade heavily depends on this financial system, which, in turn, by its very unstable nature, causes currency instability and derails the global economy, trade and commerce. In short, when currencies become commodities and begin to be traded on a virtual basis, with complete disconnect to the real economy, the consequences are indeed disastrous.

Crucially, all these arrangements are suspected to have the tacit blessings of the IMF. In fact, as already pointed out, the IMF is accused of having encouraged countries to liberalise capital controls and facilitate their financial sector to enter into this game of speculation, virtual finance and, of course, digital economy. All these have made the world of finance extremely volatile. This, in turn, has the calculated effect of destabilising the real economy. Increasingly, as Governments battle this volatility within the financial sector (notably the value of their currency) in order to protect their real economy, volatility drives and feeds the financial market players. This, over the years, has resulted in the full blown war between Governments and participants in the financial sector. Increasingly, as finance gets global, national Governments realise that they are completely incompetent to deal with the situation. Nevertheless, as Governments seek to lay their hands on such financial players wherever it is possible, it is seen that most financial market participants now operate within the safe sanctuary of the tax havens. It is interesting to note that the IMF has never castigated the tax havens nor protested against the operations of major financial sector players emanating from there.

Readers may note that the monitoring of the global economy is carried out by the IMF through a defined surveillance programme. It has a mandate to oversee the international monetary system, assess the economic and financial developments across continents and advise on risks to global financial stability as well as to suggest appropriate policy adjustments.

Yet, despite this seemingly overwhelming concern for finance, it is indeed bewildering to note that the world of finance is increasingly coming under extraordinary stress. In fact, some experts opine that it has already reached the breaking point as recent events in the US economy and financial markets demonstrate. Further, the recent gyrations witnessed in the commodities, currency and stock markets in 2008 and 2009 at the global level are all products of systemic failures, unregulated markets and bad surveillance.

The element of surprise is not merely on the size of the crisis, which in my opinion is secondary. What is galling to note here is that such serious systemic flaws have crept in undetected for over a couple of years despite multilateral supervision and surveillance. It is in this connection that it is indeed perplexing to note that the IMF – the high priest of supervision of global finance – has expressed surprise, yes, surprise, on the latest crisis that has engulfed the world of finance, its extent and the consequent implications. One wonders what the IMF has been doing all these years.

Naturally, questions arise. Has the IMF merely winked at these negative developments in the world of finance because of some external pressure or does it not have the appropriate competence to carry out the surveillance of the global financial architecture? Is it a classical case of misplaced trust?

It may not be out of place to mention that the IMF has repeatedly pointed to the virtues of financial sector liberalisation and its calculated effect of rewarding the productive and the prudent while ruthlessly punishing the unproductive and the profligate. Countries, which approached the IMF for financial assistance under the structural adjustment programme, were "persuaded" to liberalise their financial sector. Recall what Christensen states on the issue of capital account liberalisation. Given such enormous stakes, it was, therefore, of extreme importance to monitor the global financial architecture, capturing the risks to the movement of global capital as well as the risks arising of the sudden reversals in the flow of global capital. The entire global financial architecture has been constantly monitored and certified by the IMF, giving rise to the collective belief that all is well in the world of finance. But as events turn out, we all now know that it has been a case of misplaced trust.

IMF: Programmed to be Incompetent?

The IMF presents a biannual report titled the Global Financial Stability Report (GFSR) as a part of its surveillance programme. Yet, in its GFSR report released by the IMF in April 2008, it points out that the events of the past six months have demonstrated the "fragility of the global financial system" and raised "fundamental questions about the effectiveness of the response by institutions."

What is indeed appalling to note here is that the IMF suggests that the global financial system seems to have come under increasing strain since "October 2007." The key and recurrent themes that are repeated in this report of April 2008 include:

- There was a "collective failure" to appreciate the extent of leverage taken on by a wide range of institutions.
- There was a "supervisory failure" to comprehend the evolving risks through appropriate risk management systems, update disclosure norms and improve financial sector supervision so as to meet the rapid innovations and shifts in business models.

- There was a failure to detect the transfer of risks off the balance sheets by banks. Consequently, as the risks have materialised, it has placed enormous pressures back on the balance sheets of banks.

Naturally, this lack of appropriate supervision and risk management, according to the IMF, encouraged extreme leveraging. And as deterioration of the credit quality "exacerbated the de-leveraging process," the global financial system increasingly came under extraordinary strain.

Strange as it may seem, especially with the benefit of hindsight, one can safely state that the IMF has been perhaps oblivious to the negative developments in the global financial architecture since the past couple of years. In this connection, it may be noted that in the absence of any specific warnings on the risks embedded in the global economy, the IMF has been certifying all the developments between 2002 and 2007 as positive.

Recall that the April 2006 GFSR states, "The positive assessment contained in the September 2005 GFSR that the global financial system has yet again gathered strength and resilience has been validated by recent developments."

It does not stop there. It further states, "In particular, the emergence of numerous, and often very large, institutional investors and the rapid growth of credit risk transfer instruments have enabled banks to manage their credit risks more actively and to outsource the warehousing of credit risk to a diverse range of investors. A wider dispersion of credit risk has 'de-risked' the banking sector."

And wherever it has mentioned the potential risks arising from the lending to sub-prime borrowers or for that matter any other risks, it remained muted and suppressed – akin to the statutory health warning on cigarette packets. As events in 2008 turned out and given the positive language of assurance contained in the GFSR 2006 report, one is certain that the global economic surveillance of the IMF has indeed misled the world of finance.

But this failure of the IMF to detect the extant global crisis is not an exception. In the past decade, the world has been witness to several major financial crises: the East Asian crisis, the collapse of Long-Term Capital Management, the Russian crisis, the Argentinean crisis, the Dotcom bubble and, of course, the latest sub-prime crisis of the US as well as the unfolding Euro crisis. And on every occasion, the IMF simply failed to identify the crisis ahead of time. Of course, the IMF has repeatedly, after each of these crises, come out with appropriate reasoning, identified policy failures and provided prescriptions to prevent such crises in the future.

In retrospect, it is clear that there was a failure on the part of the IMF in identifying these risks even as they were manifesting. And now when the IMF is innocently terming the extant crisis as a "collective failure," one is constrained to believe that there is something more than meets the eye. The crucial question that arises from all these is a simple one: is the IMF merely incompetent to monitor or is it a case of incompetence compounded by a conspiracy? The one continuing thread that runs through these crises is that first a bubble was allowed to be built right under the nose of the IMF, and then it went bust.

This cycle of boom and bust was later rationalised through elaborate reports, studies and findings. One may state that the recurrent boom and bust cycle witnessed across the globe leads to extreme volatility. While the real economy abhors volatility, financial markets love it. In fact, volatility is the elixir that drives the financial markets. Therefore, it is not merely a question of the competency of the IMF that is central to the discussion on hand. Rather, it is all about the clout of the global financial sector and its need for volatility. The potency of these firms and the disproportionate clout that they wield on the global financial markets is central to the issue. And it is these players from the US financial markets that dominate the global financial architecture. Naturally, the allegation, however, outlandish it may seem, that the IMF merely reflects its master's voice has been gaining currency in the past few years.

For instance, an article in *The Economist,* quotes a study of BCA Research, a Canadian economic-research firm, that traces the rise of the American financial sector. The total corporate profits, the report points out, grew from 10 per cent in the early 1980s to 40 per cent by 2008, and its share of stock market value grew from 6 per cent to 19 per cent. It may be further noted that financial services account for only 15 per cent of corporate America's GDP and a mere 5 per cent of private sector jobs.

This clearly illustrates the disproportionate influence of the financial sector on the US economy, US Government and its continued interest in ensuring the proliferation of the global financial architecture. This allows gyrations, volatility and, of course, in the process, provides significant opportunities to these players to make profits, even at the cost of taking the entire global economy to the very brink. Given this paradigm, it is also natural to suspect the profound impact of the global financial sector on the IMF and the manner in which it works.

Globalisation requires global systems and global governance. In the absence of a global Government, multilateral arrangements have been worked out as a substitute by all nations. But the experiences of the past decade now tell us that this unaccountable and unsure system is untrustworthy, unworkable and, hence, unacceptable. That explains the continued diffusion of the IMF while the global economy swings from one crisis to another. Till date, the debate on the IMF has primarily been on its incompetence. The time has come to evaluate whether the IMF was designed to be incompetent.

Tax Havens: Part of the Grand Design

Tax havens, a sub-set of the global financial architecture, are definitely a part of this "grand design." John Christensen captures the entire paradigm brilliantly: "The IMF promoted capital account liberalisation despite the evidence that offshore secrecy would hinder investigation efforts and make tax evasion virtually undetectable, especially in the case of developing countries with limited resources available for tax fraud detection. Predatory financial intermediaries recognised that profitable fees could be earned from selling tax dodging services on an industrial scale, and a culture of 'crime pays' became rampant."

Deploring the lackadaisical attitude of the IMF and the World Bank towards tax havens, Christensen states, "By and large, Western governments and multilateral agencies have downplayed concerns about dirty money except when drugs and terrorism are involved. For the most part, however, the political and media focus has been on looting by despots and their cronies rather than on the workings of a global financial system that encourages and facilitates the movement of dirty money." Christensen poses an intriguing question: "... whether The IMF anticipated this outcome but considered tax evasion a minor evil or whether this was an unintended consequence of its commitment to the Washington Consensus."

In effect, he had put his finger right at the centre of the problem. If despots in every country are one half of the problem, the global financial architecture is the other half. The extant global financial architecture (which tacitly encourages the proliferation of tax havens) is as much a cause as crooks in various parts of the globe for this state of affairs. *No wonder, it is often remarked in this context that when normal men go berserk, they are called crooks and when crooks go berserk, it is called the global financial system.* Astonishingly, Christensen concludes, "Neither the World Bank nor the IMF has tried to investigate or quantify capital flight and tax evasion."

Estimates of Wealth in Tax Havens

With nations ineffective and multilateral agencies perhaps programmed to be incompetent, the net impact of these tax havens on the world of finance and trade is mind boggling. Till date, there have been only intelligent guesstimates of the wealth stored in these places. Needless to emphasise, there are no credible studies by multilateral agencies, much less audited, figures of the wealth stashed into these tax havens from various countries. Naturally, private estimates are based on a variety of research reports, economic intelligence and the propensity of various other countries to allow their capital to flow into these tax havens. For instance, throughout the socialistic period in India, underinvoicing of exports and overinvoicing of imports was rampant. These funds were subsequently siphoned off to tax havens. This was primarily on account of the following two reasons:

(1) The rupee was artificially overvalued by the Indian Government till the early Nineties when India gave up socialism and embraced the new economic policies. Storing wealth in dollars outside the country meant that in the case of the rupee finding its actual level through devaluation, one could gain significantly. And when that eventually happened in the early 1990s, one's guess is that a good section of such people benefited.

(2) Secondly, India had a stringent exchange control regime till a few years back. That meant that Indians needing foreign exchange always had to grovel before some officer of the RBI to get even their meagre quota of foreign exchange. Having a few dollars outside India, albeit illegally, helped such account holders tremendously in those troubled times.

But high tax rates and stringent exchange laws are not the only reason for stashing wealth away from developing countries. And all that is stated above is of socialist vintage. Modern days are all about nanotechnology, biometrics and genomics. The larger and modern reason for transfer of wealth away from developing countries like India is often found to be gargantuan corruption. Obviously, the compelling reasons that necessitate laundering through the tax havens are that it removes all taints (and the resultant stains) from ill-gotten wealth. The other set of people using tax havens are the terrorists, drug peddlers and their ilk, for obvious reasons.

Crooks in different countries have a varied rationale for exporting their wealth to these tax havens. However, one can safely surmise that irrational tax laws and perversely strict exchange controls were the primary reasons for such transfer of wealth away from India in the yesteryears, while it is corruption, drug trafficking and terrorism now. Whatever it may be, tax havens have a justification at every turn of modern life.

All these factors make the wealth deposited in the tax havens completely difficult to predict. That these caches of wealth are secret may not be a secret, but the estimates of their size vary significantly. In March 2005, the Tax Justice

Network (TJN) published a research finding demonstrating that USD 11.5 trillion of personal wealth was held offshore by rich individuals across the globe. The annual worldwide income on these undeclared assets is estimated at about USD one trillion. Simultaneously, the annual worldwide tax revenue lost on such undeclared income is about USD 250 billion. This figure significantly exceeds the sums needed to finance the UN's Millennium Development Goals.

The findings of the TJN estimate was that a large proportion of this wealth was managed from some 70 tax havens. Further, augmenting these studies of TJN, Raymond Baker in his widely celebrated book titled *Capitalism's Achilles Heel: Dirty Money and How to Renew the Free Market System* estimates that at least USD 5 trillion has been shifted out of the poorer countries to the West since the mid-1970s.

All these figures, it may be noted, are pure estimates. And these have been done by experts like, for instance, Baker, as mentioned above, using several techniques. Nevertheless, they are intelligent guesses. The choice of whether they are to be accepted or dismissed merely as guesses is entirely yours. Raymond Baker put the entire issue of the extent of amounts stashed into tax havens in the proper perspective in a speech in June 2007. According to Baker, "We don't ask you to accept these numbers. We ask you to do just the opposite – to produce your own numbers. We ask the World Bank and other international financial institutions and the community of development scholars to do your own analyses. If you do it honestly and thoroughly, you are very likely to come up with numbers that are greater than these." No wonder no one has taken up this challenge.

Baker further adds, "Be prepared to produce a range of numbers, highs and lows, best estimates and deviations from such estimates. We will not reach certainty about these illicit and hidden flows, just as we do not have certainty about how many poor people there are in the world. But we can reach clarity as to the order of magnitude of the problem and consensus on the importance of the issue."

Further, according to Raymond Baker, reported in the *Financial Times* in 2004, up to USD 500 billion of capital flight funds flow out of developing countries each year. He has suggested that this figure has three components:

- USD 50 billion of funds flowing from corrupt practices.
- Up to USD 200 billion arising from commercial exploitation of taxation weaknesses within the developing world.
- USD 250 billion of "capital flight" money arising from criminal activity.

To put this figure into perspective, the UN Millennium Project report estimated an improbable tripling of the global aid budget to USD 195 billion a year by 2015. That would be enough to halve world poverty within a decade and prevent millions of unnecessary deaths in the poor countries.

But this flight of illegitimate capital has yet another unintended consequence: the flight of legitimate capital. It is in this connection that Léonce Ndikumana and James K. Boyce present a stunning analysis of capital flows to and from Africa. According to them, "The analysis of capital flows to and from Africa presents a stunning paradox. On the one hand, African countries are heavily indebted. On the other hand, African countries have experienced massive outflows of private capital towards Western financial centres. Indeed, these private assets surpass the continent's foreign liabilities, ironically making sub-Saharan Africa a 'net creditor' to the rest of the world."

The flight of illegitimate capital from Africa deprives Africa of the much needed capital to sustain itself in economic terms and meet its vast infrastructure and social needs. Naturally, when that happens, sensing a bleak future for Africa, legitimate capital too follows suit. In effect, while Africa becomes a net creditor to the rest of the world, at the ground level, it continues to suffer for want of capital to develop itself. Yet Africa the lender is labelled as a Third World country and the Western financial centres – the borrowers – are called First World. Modern economics is well and truly beyond the understanding of the common man and his brand of common sense!

What is true for Africa applies in some measure to India too. The cause may vary but the effects may not. Such capital flight from India robs the Government of the much needed revenues to launch an assault on poverty. Crucially, such capital flight moves capital from the public to private hands and from the poor to the rich. The net result is that we as a nation are capital starved and resource handicapped. Consequently, we are caught in a vicious cycle of poverty, poor development and lack of investments.

In the Indian context, there is yet another dimension. We first allow capital flight to take place on a sustained basis away from India into tax havens and then allow capital to flow from abroad by adopting liberal economic policies. Surely, the Indian policy framers have forgotten the age-old adage – a bird in hand is worth two in the bush.

The reason for the same is not far to seek. Foreign capital flows often come about through policy interventions that favour such investment – often at the cost of domestic industries and the locals. Secondly, such investments are often found to have a debilitating impact on the domestic industry. Third, it is often found that the profits earned by such investment fleece the domestic economy several times over the benefits that it apparently seeks to bring about in the first place.

In this connection, John Christensen opines, "The ability of multinational businesses to structure their trade and investment flows through tax haven subsidiaries provides them with a massive financial advantage over nationally based competitors. Local firms, regardless of whether they are technically more efficient or more innovative, find themselves competing on an uneven basis. In practice, this market distortion favours the large business over the small, the international business over the national, and the long-established business over the start-up."

Trade fundamentalists have persistently turned a blind eye to this practical problem. For Christensen, the blatant unwillingness of key players like the IMF, the World Bank and the UK Government to tackle these global market failures "says a lot about their real intentions." Surely it does.

India's Share in This Global Loot

Experts estimate that one per cent of the world's population holds more than 57 per cent of total global wealth, routing it invariably through these tax havens. How much of this is from India is anybody's guess.

What is to be noted here is that most of the wealth parked in these tax havens is illegitimate money acquired through corrupt and illegitimate means. Naturally, the secrecy associated with the bank accounts in such places is central to the issue, not their low tax rates as the term "tax havens" suggests. Remember Bofors and how India could not trace the ultimate beneficiary of those transactions because of the secrecy associated with these bank accounts even two decades after the pay-offs were made? All that is known after approximately two decades of painstaking investigations by some of the best minds in the country is that the money was deposited in numbered accounts in Switzerland: 5A5151516L and 5A5151516M. Beyond this, not much is known officially.

Professor R. Vaidyanathan, writing his columns on this subject in a Chennai-based daily, has pointed out that "Zurich is the only European town where Hindi slogans are written on the sides of the tram-cars." Isn't this straight from Ripley's Believe it or Not? But the professor is not done. He adds, of course, with his tongue firmly in his cheek, "Of course, it is supposedly linked to Bollywood, but the Indian traffic to Zurich has to be seen to be believed. It is suggested that at least 60,000 Indians visit Switzerland – not all going there for skiing." Given their shape and size, it is a miracle that most can even walk. Why then talk about skiing. Obviously, they are out there on some more serious business than merely skiing.

The reasons, according to the professor, for such heavy Indian traffic to Zurich are obvious. The secrecy laws of these banks mandate personal presence in these tax havens, along with passports to operate accounts: passport numbers are perhaps crucial to determine the secret code for opening and operating these bank accounts. No wonder, many people keep their old expired passports as prized possessions. Apparently, this is not to show their grandchildren where they travelled in their younger days.

All these are pointers to the stashing of wealth from India. But they do not point out to the extent of the loot. And that is a study in itself. Recall that the extent of global loot into these tax havens is at best a guess. Naturally, the Indian portion of the loot – the subset of the larger figure – too would be a guesstimate.

In this connection, it is pertinent to keep in mind the following facts:

- In 2006, the Global Financial Integrity study estimated that the developing countries lost annually an estimated USD 859 billion to USD 1 trillion in illicit financial outflows.
- Even at the lower end of the range of estimates, the volume of illicit financial flows leaking out of developing countries increased at a compound rate of 18 per cent over the five-year period analysed by this study
- Further, on an average, for the five-year period of this study, Asia accounts for approximately 50 per cent of overall illicit financial flows from all developing countries.
- This study shows that the average money taken away from India annually during 2002-06 works out to USD 27 billion. This means that during the five-year period, the amount stashed away equals USD 135 billion.
- Another important point is that the study pertains to only five years. So the loot for the first sixty years of our independence would be several times the abovementioned amount. Experts estimate that the Indian money stashed abroad may be of the order of USD 1.4 trillion.

At Rs 45 to a US dollar, that works out to approximately Rs 70,00,000 crores – roughly equivalent to the GDP of India. One can endlessly question these figures. Similarly, one can question ceaselessly the quantum of the Indian portion of the global loot parked in Switzerland or in Liechtenstein or for that matter in the Bahamas. The issue is not one of loot – the fact of it is now proved beyond any doubt. It is only the quantum which is in debate. Yes, secret money is no longer a secret but the extent of this secrecy continues to be a secret.

Therefore, the next question is whether the loot is a lot or not. In this connection, addressing a press conference to commemorate 60 years of Indo-Swiss Friendship Treaty, the Swiss Ambassador to India said, "Switzerland was accused of giving shelter to black money and there has been a lot of inflow of such wealth from India and other countries of the world. I would not say it would be stopped 100 per cent (under a new law). But through this measure, it would be controlled up to a certain limit."

What is the precise quantum of this "a lot" is anybody's guess. But definitely it is not an insignificant sum even for the usually indifferent Indian Government, lethargic bureaucracy and unresponsive Indian media to ignore. At every turn of this debate, we must bear in mind that in the murky world of tax havens, precise numbers do not matter, unless, of course, you are an account holder! Yet the collective silence of every single institution in this country is deafening as well as defining the very character of the modern secular, socialist republic of India.

What is interesting to note here is that over the years, some of these tax havens have emerged as the prime destination for outbound FDI from India. It is indeed weird that industrialists from a poor, capital-starved, developing country yet populous like India with a robust economy could choose some of the most secretive tax havens, with tiny markets and scant populations running into mere thousands, for gargantuan investment. It is indeed strange that some of the best minds of the country have chosen to invest in such remote places known at best for some secret banks and, of course, casinos. It is presumed that a good portion of this money comes back into the Indian stock market through the Mauritius route – read the PN route.

But that is not all. The Indian tourism to these tax havens seem to have picked up significantly of late. It is not that Indian celebrities, industrialists, media personalities and bureaucrats take a holiday trip to these tax havens. It may be recalled that it is believed that one has to be personally present with one's own passport in certain tax havens to operate the accounts.

It is in this connection that *India Today*, a weekly of repute, in its February 2008 issue, had revealed the international travel particulars of some of the ministers of the Indian Government till November 2007. Some of these international travels were official and some were obviously personal. While the story focussed on the travel expenditure of our ministers (pointed out wryly as the cost of running a coalition Government), it did reveal some amazing truth on the travel profile of our ministers, their places of travel interest and, of course, the perks arising from such hard labour in the form of accumulation of frequent flyer miles.

Nevertheless, in the melee, the story threw up some interesting details. Amongst those which were personal visits, included travel to some of the well known tax havens, including Switzerland. Some went there repeatedly. God only knows for what but ordinary mortals can at best hazard a guess!

The following are some of the interesting excerpts from this issue of *India Today*:

- In the 1,287 days of the UPA Government till November 30 2007, its ministers travelled an incredible 1 crores km (10 million km)-plus on trips abroad, official and personal, but mostly official. It means that the ministers made more than 256 trips around the globe, considering the earth's circumference of 40,008 km. Among the 71 ministers (excluding the prime minister) who went on foreign trips during their tenure, 47 ministers spent over Rs 27 crores.
- In fact, some spent more time abroad on personal trips than on official visits.
- Praful Patel, [the then Minister of State (MoS) for Civil Aviation], MoS for Human Resource Development M.A.A Fatmi and D. Purandeswari, Minister for Information and Broadcasting Priya Ranjan Dasmunshi, Minister for Mines Sis Ram Ola, MoS for Petroleum and Natural Gas Dinsha J. Patel, Minister for Corporate Affairs Prem Chand Gupta and MoS for Steel Akhilesh Das were the ministers who recorded more days outside the country on personal visits in comparison to official visits.
- In any event, it took over four months and 59 Right to Information (RTI) applications to various ministries apart from the Prime Minister's Office (PMO) and the Cabinet Secretariat, before the information could be compiled and made available
- In many instances, the connection between the destination and the portfolio is difficult to decipher. Why would an MoS for commerce and textiles visit Uzbekistan thrice? Or what is the attraction of Serbia for ministers?
- Here's another interesting detail. Italy, Congress President and UPA chairperson Mrs. Sonia Gandhi's country of birth, attracted the largest number of ministerial visits, private and official. No less than 20 ministers visited Italy, and they include Prasad, Sushil Kumar Shinde, Nath, Kantilal Bhuria, R. Velu, Santosh Mohan Dev, Ambika Soni, Subodh Kant Sahay, Shankersinh Vaghela, Vilas Muttemwar, S. Jaipal Reddy, Oscar Fernandes, P.R. Kyndiah, Akhilesh Prasad Singh, Ashwini Kumar, Sriprakash Jaiswal and Renuka Chowdhury.
- Ms Ambika Soni (the then minister for culture) spent 23 days abroad on personal trips – which included Italy, as a destination – of which itineraries for 11 days were not disclosed by the PMO.

Any student of geography would instantly tell you that Italy and Switzerland are neighbours. There are enough means of transport even for common folk (for ministers that could come as official transport even when they travel on personal visits) between these two countries. It is quite possible that some of them could have visited Switzerland – either to ski or to carry out some personal banking business. Obviously, all these are not to suggest that every minister who goes abroad, especially on a personal visit to a tax haven, is a suspect. Quite the contrary, it is exactly the opposite. But if the minister concerned has not clarified as to the personal nature of the visit to tax havens, the needle of suspicion will definitely go berserk.

MAF: The Lynchpin in Money Laundering

Let us once again revert to the issue of tax havens. India's tryst with tax havens is pretty old – perhaps since independence. Yet, there was a partial disconnect between the Indian economy and the tax havens. Loot and scoot into tax havens had not become a national obsession till, say, the mid-Eighties. There was a sense of remorse. Remember, only the villains dealt with the tax havens, heroes were yet to open their accounts. All this changed virtually since the past two decades or so when the national morality plummeted beyond the tipping point.

It may be recalled that in the early 90s India faced a severe foreign exchange crisis. Recall that India was desperate for foreign exchange. We approached the IMF for a bailout package while having a quick rethink on the entire Nehruvian economic policies that had guided the nation since independence. Overnight, we gave up socialism and approved of the new economic policies.

Simultaneously, as we were negotiating with the IMF, perhaps one of the very few conditionalities put forth by the IMF was to allow the entry of the Multinational Accounting Firms (MAFs). The MAFs began to set foot on Indian soil primarily as consultants in terms of the "unstated" stipulations laid out by the IMF. In fact, allowing the MAFs to enter India preceded the New Economic Policies of the 90s. The entry of MAFs was rationalised to facilitate free flow of capital into India and from India to the other countries under the new economic regime. It was suggested that global investing bankers would "only be comfortable" with their own consultants as advisors to help them invest in India. Naturally, these decisions were taken at the highest level in the Government, perhaps without any great thought. Eighteen years later, i.e. today, we need to revisit the entry of these MAFs into India in the context of the current discussions involving the global financial architecture, the role of the financial sector in a globalised world, the competency of the IMF and, of course, the role of tax havens.

It is in this context that one has to examine the role of these MAFs. As briefly explained above, the entry by the MAFs into India was stealthy. Neither did the accounting profession know about it nor was its regulatory body, the Institute of Chartered Accountants of India, consulted before this unilateral opening up of the profession. It is a fact that the initial "mistake" could probably be attributed to the RBI and the Government. Obviously, the Indian establishment, already reeling under an unprecedented economic crisis, did not have the time, money or mental strength to conduct an appropriate due-diligence on these MAFs. Therefore, an introduction to these MAFs, a brief overview of their operational strategies and their symbiotic links with the tax havens would be appropriate. First, some questions: what are these MAFs? Where are they located? Where is their headquarters? Who owns them?

The answers to these questions are both interesting and intriguing. The very secrecy of the operations within a tax haven ensures that it is a perfect interface between the illicit and licit economies. In this exercise, everyone is involved – global investment bankers, global consultants, multilateral funding agencies, global law firms, global analysts and, of course, all other financial players. Yet everyone who is involved in this exercise has a façade of innocence and even that of a co-victim. If secrecy is the first line of offence, the façade of innocence is the first line of defence. The fundamental rule of the game is to pretend to be of complete virtue, never mind that one might be neck deep into money laundering or even operating from a tax haven. The art of money laundering has been well and truly converted into a science, especially when it is routed through tax havens. But for that we require some professionals. Don't we?

It is precisely for this reason we have Multinational Accounting Firms (MAFs) – the high priests of global finance – to bless, dress and stress the deal. They are the lynchpin between all the players listed above. Without them, it is impossible to deal with tax havens – why, it may be impossible to deal with the convoluted world of global finance. They are the gateway to the heavens and tax havens.

First, we invent the tax havens and then the MAFs to legitimise and optimise operations from tax havens. Or is it the other way around? I am not sure of the sequence – but surely one of the two remains the cause, the other, naturally, the effect. In the instant case, tax havens and MAFs are made for each other. Located inside tax havens, MAFs have elevated laundering illicit money from an art form into a perfect science. The MAFs, in fact, have commoditised these laundering mechanisms; so much so, some of their services are even branded and advertised, of course, without any let or fear.

Let us at this point examine as a case in point the role of MAFs in greater detail. In its 2007 survey on "Global Anti-Money Laundering", KPMG, a leading audit and consulting major, states, "Estimated money laundering flows are reported to be in excess of USD 1 trillion being laundered every year by drug dealers, arms traffickers and other criminals. Recent years have seen rapid change in the financial services industry and growing regulatory expectations and pressures. Combating money laundering and terrorist financing continues to be a major challenge for the banking sector, as gatekeepers to the legitimate financial system."

Look at the concern of KPMG on the vexed issue of money laundering. The disquiet is palpable. Their apprehension is completely genuine. The trepidation perfectly justified. Their angst is absolutely in place. Yet, there is something that is missed in the melee.

One may be stunned to know that KPMG is itself headquartered in tax havens, has been allegedly involved in money laundering and its global ownership is unknown. Yet, it pontificates on the issue of money laundering. Usually, it has been my experience that it is only the devil who quotes the scriptures, verb and prose, without any remorse. No wonder, KPMG is reported to have famously stated on another occasion that "tax avoidance does not damage corporate reputations and may even enhance them."

Yet no one submits even a token protest or questions them regarding their conduct. And men (and women) who do not matter, may point to all these, only to be brushed aside or summarily dismissed. In the alternative, men (and women) who matter i.e. those who remain at the helm of the affairs of the country and could protest, do not. The reason for the same is obvious – they could be clients of these very MAFs that continue to play havoc on the global finances. They are the high and the mighty in every country. Naturally, a corrupt bureaucracy, lax judiciary, tainted businessmen, a pliable media and, of course, the dirty politician – in short, the elite of India – are all beneficiaries of this mechanism to cleanse their ill-gotten wealth. They are the natural clients of these MAFs. They need MAFs to cleanse their money as much as the tax havens. That explains why MAFs were welcome into India without much ado in the early Nineties. Their entry through stealth is primarily aimed to manage the wealth of some of our rich and mighty.

The very operations of these MAFs were brought out in a US Senate enquiry revealing the internal communications of KPMG. That contained a warning from one senior tax adviser that if KPMG were to comply with the legal requirements of the Inland Revenue Service of the US relating to the registration of tax shelters, the company would place itself at a competitive disadvantage and would "not be able to compete in the tax advantaged products market." The Senate enquiry surmised that KPMG went ahead with these schemes "knowingly, purposefully and wilfully violating the federal tax shelter law." Yet nothing happened. In fact, who cares? KPMG flourishes in the US as it does in the rest of the world. After all, even the US has its share of corrupt bureaucracy, lax judiciary....

Further, during its enquiries, the Senate Committee discovered that KPMG had devised over 500 "active tax products", some of which may have been illegal. Just four of those 500 products cost the US Treasury USD 85 billion annually in lost tax revenues, whilst KPMG booked USD 180 million in fees! Speaking after the conclusion of the Senate Committee's enquiries, senior ranking Democrat Senator Carl Levin said: "Our investigations revealed a culture of deception inside KPMG's tax practice." Notice that what is allegedly practised by KPMG is a "culture of deception." But what else does one expect from a firm headquartered in a tax haven?

If you thought this was an exception, consider this: KPMG has been repeatedly alleged to have been involved in money laundering across continents. A White Paper released by the Chennai based Chartered Accountants' Action Committee (CAAC) in 2003 on the Multinational Accounting Firm (MAF) dealt extensively with the issue of the role of these firms in money laundering. According to this White Paper, KPMG was perceived to be involved in laundering the corrupt and ill-gotten wealth of Ferdinand Marcos of Philippines to the tune of over USD 400 million.

This fraud has been brilliantly exposed by Lucy Komisar, in an article under the title "Marcos' Missing Millions." This article dated August 2, 2002, has been carried in the website "The Catbird Seat." The relevant portion of this article is reproduced below for a full understanding of the culture and drive of the MAFs, and particularly KPMG which is believed to be involved in this fraud.

> *Corporate corruption scandals roil the United States, dragging down with them the reputations of the major accounting firms that signed off on – or even designed – fraudulent financial practices. These global auditors were supposed to keep corporations honest. But a closer look at Switzerland, the birthplace of financial legerdemain, shows that accounting deceit is nothing new. Western financial managers cut their teeth designing systems for third world dictators to loot their countries.*

Perhaps the most notorious example is Ferdinand Marcos, who is suspected of stealing at least USD 10 billion from the Philippines before being overthrown in February 1986. The Philippine Government has spent more than 15 years trying to track and recover the money, some of which was secreted away by Swiss bankers and stashed in offshore havens.

Now, a former attorney with accounting firm KPMG in Zurich has come forward claiming she has evidence that on March 23, 1986 – just a day before a freeze would be placed on Marcos' accounts – KPMG secretly transferred USD 400 million from Credit Suisse Zurich to a Liechtenstein trust on the ex-dictator's behalf. The attorney, Marie-Gabrielle Koller – named in this article for the first time – first testified about the events behind closed doors before a French parliamentary commission in May 2000. Its report referred to her only as "Madame Z."

According to this testimony in the dead of night on March 23, 1986, lawyers for KPMG (then known as Fides, a subsidiary of Credit Suisse) moved USD 400 million of Marcos' funds to a Liechtenstein trust, Limag Management und Verwaltungs AG, which dispersed the money via new secret "foundations."

This is merely one unknown facet of KPMG – the global audit giant that claims presence in over 140 countries with revenues running into billions of dollars. Its website claims to have employed several thousands of accounting and auditing professionals. It does provide you every detail about itself except that it does not produce the names of its ultimate owners. Crucially, it is a network of firms based out of Switzerland – the grandmother of all tax havens.

And, if you thought that KPMG had patented all these in one go, hold your breath. In fact, all that has been stated above could equally be true of the other three – PricewaterhouseCoopers, Deloitte Touche Tohmatsu and Ernst & Young. These three, along with KPMG, constitute what are called Multinational Accounting Firms – each one competing with the other in the race to infamy and notoriety. Remove KPMG from the above paragraphs and substitute it with the others, one could be spot on.

So, even as they claim to be global firms, they are actually accused of being global dodgers of several national laws. That is contrary to the very purpose of their being – these firms which exist to ensure transparency in business, accounts and finance are themselves secretive. They use this secrecy to claim to be global when it comes to seeking business opportunities, and disclaim being global when it comes to answering investigators from other countries.

They are the firms that make tax evasion exotic through specific schemes, encourage corruption as well as flight of capital and, if need be, help you stash your ill-gotten wealth. Crucially, it is from the developing countries to the developed countries.

From a professional view-point, MAFs legitimise, bless and sanctify tax havens.

Yet, the world believes that they are the ones who would fight corruption, establish and maintain accounting standards and bring about benchmarks for audits and ethical functioning! It would seem that the entire world has suspended its complete sense of disbelief on MAFs.

Surely, at this point, Stiglitz and Christensen look increasingly credible.

Recall what we discussed about the IMF, its inability to supervise the global financial architecture and its repeated failure to foresee the extant global financial crisis. In that context, we did discuss the disproportionate power of the US financial sector. The linkages between MAFs and the world of finance (read US financial sector) are too intimate to warrant a repetition here. It is this triumvirate comprising the US financial sector, IMF and, of course, these MAFs that continues to dominate the collective thinking within our financial sector too.

And one of the emerging issues in managing our financial sector is the linkages of our elite with our financial sector, its liberalisation and tax havens. No wonder, even before the battle against tax havens has begun, we seem to have lost the war.

Further, all this partially, if not substantially, explains why most of the elites of India are silent on the issue of tax havens.

The G-20 Initiative in April 2009

Nevertheless, the associated problems of capital flight and tax avoidance – both being simultaneously the cause and consequence of corruption – are fast emerging as the next major global issue requiring urgent multilateral attention. Consequently, the global community has come under increasing pressure to deal with the issue of increasing share of global wealth that is now held in tax havens. As this ill-gotten wealth is beyond the reach of national tax authorities, national as well as global authorities are now coming to a consensus that unless this issue is tackled forthwith, the millennium development goals of the UN cannot be achieved, even partially, by 2020.

But that is one part of the story. The prevailing economic crisis in the West has caused the collapse of several financial institutions which have withstood even the great depression. This, in turn, has forced many Western countries to do a quiet but quick rethink on the wealth secreted in these tax havens. Consequently, secret banking and by extension, tax havens became the target of most Western countries. Politicians are politicians – be it in India or elsewhere. And all politicians like to open a newer, bigger and better can of worms. At least, it helps to deflect their failures partially, if not totally. And frankly what difference does it make if tax havens are the cause of the global meltdown in 2008-09 or not? To me, what matters is that now there is a window of opportunity unavailable till date to any previous Indian Governments.

Be that as it may, one must concede at the outset that the linkages between the global economic recession and the tax havens are quite contrived at a superficial level. By allowing volatility in every market – currency, commodity, stocks and real estate – Governments realise that they have been taken for a ride by their own act of recklessly liberalising the financial sector. The reliance on deregulated markets went to the extent of allowing the financial sector to operate without even an effective regulator. And wherever such regulators were appointed, they were more ornamental than effective supervisors. Naturally, the seeds of the extant crisis came about when the regulators turned a Nelson's eye to the rapid build-up of bubbles in every market since 2001.

The beneficiary of all this happened to be the financial sector that was more often than not found to be operating from tax havens or with their beneficial ownership situated in such tax havens. At best, the linkages of the tax havens to the latest financial crisis can be traced thus far and no further.

If all that is stated above is an explanation for targeting tax havens by various countries, there is yet another mundane reason for the same. On account of this economic crisis, nation-states are forced to have massive spending programmes, prop up failing industries, nationalise companies and guarantee bank deposits. For all these acts of "benevolence," they are finding it extremely difficult to raise revenues. How can one raise tax revenues when the economy is facing recession? However, for most countries across the world, developing as well as developed, additional tax revenues are desperately needed. As most countries scrape the bottom of the barrel, tax havens are obviously a good target!

By blaming tax havens for everything from the present global economic crisis to taxation shortfalls, the developed nations are now seeking to eliminate tax havens. This act of the developed nation reminds one of the age-old ruse of the "foreign hand" repeatedly used by the Indian political leaders to deflect their domestic failures. The foreign hand theory is sometimes right, mostly exaggerated and certainly cannot be true at all times. Yet our leaders do not hesitate to blame the ubiquitous foreign hand for even the failure of monsoon, or for that matter, any other act of nature. Politicians are politicians – whether they are in India, the US or in the Philippines.

What is engaging the attention of observers is that as pointed out earlier, the political class has been the beneficiary of the largesse of this financial sector over the years. Naturally, one is surprised at the alacrity with which Governments have proceeded against the financial sector and tax havens. One is concerned whether all of this is temporary or whether there would be a sustained action against these tax havens. Whatever it may be, the net result of all these developments is that the Western nations have virtually begun a crusade against tax havens.

Tax havens and MAFs are, therefore, part of the problem facing the global economy. What is adding fuel to the fire is that technological changes in the financial sector and increasing capital account liberalisation worldwide facilitate movement of money easily. This has created problems because in a world of globalised financial markets, tax regimes and financial regulations remain largely national. In addition, because of the stringent laws on secrecy, the operations of a company in such offshore jurisdiction need not be recorded with the Government of such tax haven. Sometimes, even if the law there requires the names and addresses of the shareholders and directors to be reported, it is almost never mandated that these be on public record. Further, local nominees are allowed to camouflage the names of the ultimate beneficiaries. (A nominee is a person who is paid a small fee to say he is a director of a tax haven company when, in fact, he has no real involvement in its operation.)

To add to all this, many tax haven companies are owned by trusts. These trusts are themselves set up in another offshore entity with their ownership spread across several offshore entities. The trustees of that trust will be invariably located in a third tax haven territory. Given this expertise in managing the affairs of an organisation operating out of a tax haven (of course, perfected by the MAFs), it is generally found that such complicated yet seamless structuring of entities across tax havens often makes it very difficult for any authority in any country to meaningfully investigate the origin and flow of funds.

The net outcome of routing money through such a maze of networks and entities is that the tax haven activity appears to take place nowhere, no one is accountable and no one needs to report to anybody. No one's presence can be confirmed or denied. There are no regulators, no reporting standards and no one to monitor. It is indeed an absolutely free world.

Given this paradigm, it is impossible to conceive of the possibility of combating corruption at the global level without simultaneously tackling the broader issues of tax havens. Also, it is futile to address the issue of tax havens around the world without addressing the continued flow of funds to the global economy from these tax havens. No wonder, the entire world is perturbed by the tax havens and the manner of dealing with the same.

It is in this connection that the decisions made by the leaders of leading economies (G-20 Summit) in the London Summit on the global plan for recovery and reform in April 2009 need to be analysed. Leading Western countries invariably hold these tax havens as one of the reasons for the extant global economic crisis. The said communiqué issued by these global leaders agreed "to take action against non-cooperative jurisdictions, including tax havens."

To effectuate this plan, the G-20 had made out a separate declaration on strengthening the financial system. This declaration states *inter alia*, "It is essential to protect public finances and international standards against the risks posed by non-cooperative jurisdictions. We call on all jurisdictions to adhere to the international standards in the prudential, tax, and AML/CFT areas." Obviously, non-cooperation and adherence to the international standards is the core of the issue.

To address this issue, the G-20 calls on the "appropriate bodies to conduct and strengthen objective peer reviews, based on existing processes, including through the FSAP process." It also mandates countries to adopt the international standard for information exchange endorsed by the G-20 in 2004 and reflected in the UN Model Tax Convention. It also notes that the "OECD has today published a list of countries assessed by the Global Forum against the international standard for exchange of information." Using the carrot and stick policy, the declaration "welcomes" the new commitments made by a number of jurisdictions and encourages them to proceed swiftly with implementation.

It also states, "We stand ready to take agreed action against those jurisdictions which do not meet international standards in relation to tax transparency." To this end, the declaration mandates countries to develop effective counter-measures, such as:

- Increased disclosure requirements and extra weight to be given the principles of tax transparency.
- To report transactions involving non-cooperative jurisdictions.
- Withholding taxes in respect of a wide variety of payments.
- Reviewing tax treaty policy with such jurisdictions.
- Asking international institutions and regional development banks to review their investment policies.

The G-20 declaration also adds, "We agreed that the FATF should revise and reinvigorate the review process for assessing compliance by jurisdictions with AML/CFT standards, using agreed evaluation reports where available. We call upon the FSB and the FATF to report to the next G-20 Finance Ministers and Central Bank Governors' meeting on adoption and implementation by countries."

It is indeed surprising that the West has prescribed all these when all along it is suspected that the West itself that has been the beneficiary of these tax havens. It is also surprising that the Western world of late has risen up against these tax havens. If at all, one idea that unites in these troubled times the leaders of the US, France, Germany and Japan, it is that they are united against the very idea of tax havens. Similarly, they are united on the prescriptions to tackle tax havens. Whatever be the inherent fallacy behind this drive against the tax havens by the Western nations, the fact remains that they are now preparing for action against the tax havens. How long this will last is anybody's guess for if the global economic scenario undergoes a change, the approach of these countries towards tax havens could well undergo a shift.

Surprised?

But more is to follow. The approach of the Indians – who have been the traditional victims of capital outflows through tax havens over the past several years – has been one of being extremely squeamish. First, it would seem that we are in a state of complete denial about the problem pertaining to tax havens. Secondly, it would seem that the Government of India would not act till it is very clear about the exact amount stashed in these tax havens. Third, the behaviour of the Indian establishment seems to suggest that it is convinced that the tax havens are having a positive impact on the Indian economy.

We will revert to the Indian position shortly. First, the global attempt at dealing with tax havens.

Liechtenstein: The Beginning of the End

This is the dirtiest of all tax havens. Strangely, it is this offshore jurisdiction that has spelt trouble for the tax havens. It encapsulates all that is wrong in the dark dirty world of tax havens. It is the envy of even Switzerland – it is the place where the Swiss send criminals whom even they themselves cannot handle! It is often remarked, albeit in jest, that it is the place where the Swiss go to hide their money. The tiny country, just 72 miles east of Zurich, is the place where the Swiss send their dirtiest customers. It is Liechtenstein – the ugly wart on the face of Europe.

Liechtenstein has gotten rich by laundering the money of "drug traffickers, Mafiosi, tax cheats and other criminals." A 1999 report from the German secret service described Liechtenstein as a criminal state in the middle of Europe. The then German finance minister denounced the country as "a worm in the European fruit." Strong words but perhaps deserved ones.

Putting it brilliantly in his inimitable style, Prof. Vaidyanathan states, "You need to be careful if you are jogging in Liechtenstein as you may enter the next country. You need to carry your passport in your jogging shorts." The reason for the same is obvious – jog a little extra and you could cross over to a neighbouring country. Yet, it is this place to which the rich and famous of the world rush – not to jog – but to carry out banking operations.

Recently, Liechtenstein was in the news and for pretty interesting reasons. It had become the Achilles heel for the world of tax havens. The dirtiest of all tax havens had fallen from its lofty perch, the high pedestal and fallen to ignominy. For long, Liechtenstein prided itself on its secure and secret banking systems. Situated in the heart of Europe, it had been the home of laundered money from across the world, mostly the European countries. Naturally, most European countries were worked up with it for providing a sanctuary to criminals, money launderers and, of course, tax evaders. It was the cynosure of all criminals and the envy of all nation-states. All that was till early 2008 when the world of secrecy normally associated with tax havens, more specifically Liechtenstein, was bought crashing down. And the manner in which the rogue amongst tax havens was waylaid, attacked and destroyed is a story in itself.

For long, German intelligence and LGT, a bank in Liechtenstein owned by its first family, were often at loggerheads on the issue of Germans parking their ill-gotten wealth in the LGT Bank. LGT would be ready to provide details if and only if Germany could prove the illegality of the money held in its bank. And the Germans could never prove the illegality in the first place since they never had the names of the account holders! It was a classical 'egg and chicken' case.

Given the stonewalling of the LGT Bank over the years, Germany did what it deemed it best for its interests. Fascinatingly, the Germans used "national" interests in a globalised world to justify their actions! In a globalised world, borders became suddenly relevant. Capital, inexplicably seem to have acquired some colour. Crucially, there was a clamour for "our" capital, "your" capital as much as "good" capital and "dirty" capital. But globalisation was all about world without walls (www), wasn't it? The story of tax havens seems to demolish several popular economic ideas, doesn't it?

Germany, sought to cut diamonds with diamonds. Germany's intelligence agency paid an unnamed employee of the LGT Bank more than USD 6 million for confidential and secret data about clients of the LGT group in a computer disc. Perhaps never in the history of mankind had the data of less than 2,000 individuals cost so much. Neither has one caused so much anxiety and consternation across continents.

The unnamed employee is also reported to have been granted asylum by Germany. The relationship between the two countries was marginally better than that between India and Pakistan at the best of times before this coup was carried out by the German intelligence unit. After this daring and successful attempt, Germany's relationship with its neighbour plummeted drastically, so much so that today it must rank far below that of the US and North Korea. This successful operation of obtaining details from a bank located in a tax haven, had several fallouts. Some of them were felt in distant India too.

The revelations of the LGT Bank immediately led to the resignation of the head of Deutsche Post – the former German mail service that is currently one of the world's largest logistics companies.

Naturally, the Liechtenstein leaders were furious and focussed their ire at the data theft. What was lost was not merely data but their credibility, assiduously built over decades. But that was not all. According to the *Deutsche Welle–DW-World.DE* (a respected German newspaper), in its issue dated 18.07.2008, judges in Bochum handed a two-year suspended prison sentence to a 66-year-old real estate tycoon, Elmar Schulte, in one of the first cases brought to justice in Germany in a major Liechtenstein tax evasion scandal. He would probably receive a suspended term of two years' jail for evading Euros 7.5 million (USD 11.8 million) in tax between 2001 and 2006. Elmar Schulte, from the western city of Bad Homburg, was found guilty of six counts of tax evasion after depositing several million euros in the Alpine principality of Liechtenstein and failing to declare the interest made. He had reportedly paid Euros 7.5 million in taxes and fines to German tax authorities.

Ever since the German foreign intelligence service bought the data on the trusts managed by the Liechtenstein bank LGT on behalf of wealthy tax-shy Europeans, the world of tax havens has indeed turned upside down. Prosecutors in Bochum said they have opened enquiries against about 700 tax dodgers all over Germany. Under the German tax law, they were supposed to report all dividends and interest earned abroad by trusts that they fully controlled. According to various press reports, the German Government has raised about Euro 200 million till April 2010 in taxes from secret accounts in Liechtenstein in the two years since it bought the stolen bank data to track down tax evaders.

Now the Heat is on Switzerland

But while Liechtenstein may have been the trigger for all the action against the tax havens, experts are quite convinced that Switzerland is the real culprit. Switzerland, after all, is a major tax haven with more than a third of global private funds deposited in its banks. While the fact remains that tax havens have grown phenomenally in the last couple of decades, the West now sees these tax havens, notably Switzerland, as the villain of the piece. And why not? According to Richard Murphy, Switzerland has become a paradise for foreign capital on which tax is not paid. The uproar from foreign Governments is understandable. Murphy estimates that around 30 per cent, or CHF 1,000 billion, of the CHF 2,800 billion or so of foreign assets in Swiss banks is untaxed black money. These assets are beneficially owned by non-Swiss individuals who could easily be illegally avoiding tax on them in their home jurisdictions

A reference in this context to certain interesting historical facts about Switzerland would be in order. During World Wars I and II, one may recall, countries around it in Europe fought against each other. Yet Switzerland was never a victim of any aggression in both these World Wars. It is stated in lighter vein that the leaders of several countries in Europe, even in those times, had stashed their ill-gotten wealth in Switzerland. Hence, attacking it would effectively mean shooting oneself. Naturally, this beautiful nation became the common friend of both the Allied and Axis powers, at war with each other. But neutral Switzerland, a friend of all even as recently as during World War II, is relatively friendless today. Again the reason for this is fairly obvious. What was once its strength – its powerful banks – has now become its nemesis, its Achilles' heel.

The nature of the loot deposited in Switzerland by the neighbouring countries can be understood by a recent event pertaining to Italy. The Italian Government announced amnesty to those Italians who brought back their ill-gotten wealth from Switzerland. Some Euro 97 billion came back in the next few months. And that is estimated to be a mere fraction of what the Italians have stored in these banks! Obviously, dealing with Switzerland is priority number one for any country that seriously seeks to deal with the extant issue.

In this connection, let us just examine as a case in point as to how the US has begun dealing with UBS Bank, the financial giant from Switzerland. It may be recalled that the US Government initiated stringent action against UBS on the issue of secrecy of its banking operations. Further, the US Inland Revenue threatened the largest Swiss bank, UBS, with a lawsuit – that would have bankrupted it – unless the bank disclosed the names and accounts of American tax dodgers. UBS wilted under the onslaught and forthwith surrendered all the data to the US. According to press reports, this was done on a weekend so as to prevent the move of account holders through any intervention of the courts in the following week. Strangely, even before the US could precipitate the matter, escalate it and ensure that it reached a logical conclusion, UBS capitulated and agreed to part with the details of the tax evaders.

It was a remarkable capitulation of a bank that is known to maintain secrets at any cost. Crucially, it has done so for several decades. Contrast this with what UBS did to the Indian authorities, notably SEBI, in the infamous UBS case which we will discuss in great detail in subsequent chapters. Did UBS get away in the Indian context? Or was it allowed to get away quietly? A fifty-lakhs rupee question indeed!

As the global crackdown on tax havens gathered momentum following the G-20 meeting in London, several Swiss banks, including UBS, which is the world's largest manager of private wealth assets, have issued travel directives to their "client-facing" staff not to visit foreign countries for carrying out what are called offshore wealth-management banking services. UBS, has also asked its wealth management staff not to travel abroad to meet clients.

Meanwhile, based on this revelation by UBS, a wealthy client of UBS became the first US citizen to be arrested for tax evasion stemming from an investigation into secret offshore accounts at Zurich. Michael Steven Rubinstein, a 55-year-old yacht company accountant was charged with one criminal count of filing a false and fraudulent tax return in the US District Court in Fort Lauderdale, Fla. Mr. Rubinstein deposited more than USD 2 million in Kruggerand gold coins into his UBS accounts and bought securities worth more than 4.5 million Swiss francs through the accounts from 2001 to 2008.

UBS is under criminal investigation for helping US citizens hide nearly USD 20 billion and evade taxes through secret offshore accounts that went unreported to the Internal Revenue Service (IRS). In February 2009, UBS admitted to conspiracy to defraud the IRS and paid USD 780 million to settle the charges. Federal prosecutors say Mr. Rubinstein is the first US citizen to be criminally charged in the UBS case.

Anyone looking for signs of how the US Government will carry out its crackdown on the use of Swiss accounts to evade taxes now has a case to examine: Michael Steven Rubinstein of Boca Raton, Fla., is the first person to be prosecuted since the Government's recent agreement with UBS AG (UBS). In naming Rubinstein, the Department of Justice and Internal Revenue Service alleged that from 2001 through 2008, Rubinstein communicated with UBS bankers regarding an account held in the British Virgin Islands, directing the purchase and sale of securities valued at 4.5 million Swiss francs, or about USD 4 million at current exchange rates.

According to the Government's filing, Rubinstein didn't disclose the existence of the UBS account, as required by law, in his 2007 income tax return, nor did he report income from the account on the return. UBS also agreed to pay USD 780 million in fines and penalties.

Further, the OECD has published a list of these tax havens and categorised them according to the level of non-cooperation. The Obama Administration is now reportedly working on a legislation to deal a severe blow to these tax havens. As already stated, one is not sure how long all this will last. But for a country like India which must have a vested interest in getting at the loot parked in these tax havens, the going could never have been so good. This, in a way, explains why the issue of tax havens is discussed so passionately "now" in the Indian context.

Further, according to press reports and under pressure from US federal authorities, UBS is closing down hidden offshore accounts of its American clients. This has the potential to allow secrets of such clients to spill out into the open. According to Prof. Vaidyanathan, "In a step that would have been unthinkable at one point in the rarefied world of Swiss banking, UBS will shut about 19,000 accounts that prosecutors suspect have gone undeclared to the Internal Revenue Service." It is expected that UBS will transfer the assets to other banks or other divisions within UBS, or mail cheques directly to account holders, creating audit trails for prosecutors who are examining whether UBS clients used such accounts to evade taxes in the US.

The clients now face stark choices: they can encash their cheques and, thereby, alert the authorities to any potential wrongdoing, or not encash them and lose their money. Surely, an unenviable position to be actually in! UBS – the largest banking institution in Switzerland – has also committed to provide the names of top 250 persons who have kept money in offshore accounts out of 19,000 accounts to the US authorities. The US State Department having tasted blood, is insisting on the further disclosure of American accounts kept with UBS.

Switzerland is now under tremendous international pressure. *Der Spiegel* a German magazine of repute, wrote that for generations, the Swiss had held bank secrecy as "not negotiable," and added that it was "no longer" so. The magazine quoted Swiss Finance Minister Merz as saying that they would have "to compromise". The Swiss justice and foreign ministers, the magazine reported, had hinted that the country might have to stop protecting tax dodgers. Subsequently, a nervous Merz met the then Prime Minister of UK, Gordon Brown on March 14, 2009, with a deal to prevent any move in the G-20 to blacklist his country. The deal was that Swiss banks would adopt the bank transparency rules of the OECD countries. Brown claimed that it was "the beginning of the end of banking secrecy."

Another interesting development taking place is the outcome of the crackdown in Germany. A report by Reuters says, "A crackdown on tax havens that prompted Switzerland to loosen its banking secrecy is encouraging more and more Germans to come clean about foreign accounts they use to evade taxes. Berlin has waged a very public campaign to stamp out tax evasion since Klaus Zumwinkel, then chief executive of Deutsche Post and one of Germany's top businessmen, was arrested in a major tax probe last February."

"Zumwinkel kicked off a bit of an avalanche," said Andreas Boehm, a lawyer based in central Berlin. "Afterwards, the number of people coming clean with us... rose by about 400-500%. And that level has been maintained." This is a positive outcome of the LGT affair

Given these developments across the globe, there has been tremendous demand by the civil society in several countries to tear off the veil of secrecy over these tax havens, particularly Switzerland. Apart from the G-20 action, as explained above, the OECD has been the main forum that has consistently been used by countries to deal with this vexed issue. Let us examine in some detail the efforts of the OECD on this sensitive yet vexed issue.

In the third quarter of 2008, the OECD fired the first salvo by threatening to blacklist Switzerland for protecting tax evaders. The OECD has also published a list of these tax havens and categorised them according to the level of non-cooperation.

It is, therefore, perfectly logical that Switzerland is specifically mentioned among all the tax havens as it is the largest and the oldest and also the most uncooperative. Equally, it is dogged and unrepentant. For instance, a report dated April 10, 2009, mentions that the head of the OECD, Angel Gurria, referred, in a letter to Swiss President Hans-Rudolf Merz, to the "inaccuracy" of charges of unfair treatment made by Swiss officials. Switzerland had originally expressed its disapproval of being targeted as a tax haven by refusing to authorise a budget contribution to the OECD.

"There are no 'blacklists' and the OECD did not include or 'threaten to include' Switzerland on any black list," Gurria wrote, according to a statement made available by the OECD. "We only shared the criteria that have been approved by our committees and the jurisdictions that were adopting or not the OECD standard," and added, "As you know very well, Switzerland does not yet have a single agreement on the exchange of tax information that conforms to the OECD standard." That was diplomacy at its very best. No wonder, Switzerland is feeling the global heat.

But the US Does One Better

Interestingly, as all these events unfolded in various parts of the globe, the US did one better. It virtually cracked open the Swiss secrecy laws and brought the UBS – the largest Swiss bank – on its knees. The story – available on the internet – by Lisa Jucca gives us an insight to the extent to which the US tax and other authorities have travelled even at the height of the 2008 crisis to get at the tax defaulters and recover the tax money from the Switzerland. The unedited story by Lisa Jucca is produced hereunder.

> *"Investors the world over breathed a sigh of relief on October 16 when the Swiss government rescued UBS. But unbeknownst to them at the time, the bank faced a potentially devastating crisis on a very different front.*
>
> *One day after the bailout, top executives from UBS and Swiss regulators were summoned to a closed-door meeting in New York by US officials who were conducting a wide-ranging tax fraud investigation that centered on the bank.*
>
> *The UBS delegation, led by newly-appointed Group General Counsel Markus Diethelm, arrived armed with the results of an internal report highlighting instances of tax fraud within the bank, insiders told Reuters. The plan was simple: admit guilt, settle the case quickly and move on.*
>
> *But Kevin Downing, the US Department of Justice Tax Division Attorney who had been investigating UBS since the middle of 2008, chose that meeting to drop a bombshell: he wanted the bank to disclose names of US tax evaders as a condition for a settlement.*
>
> *That put UBS in the nightmarish position of either breaching nearly a century of Swiss bank secrecy or risking indictment in the United States.*
>
> *"UBS was already in a position of weakness from the credit crisis," said one person who attended the meeting and spoke to Reuters on condition of anonymity. "It became crystal clear at that meeting that without addressing the issue of client names, no settlement could be found."*
>
> *Interviews with insiders and a review of documents reveal previously undisclosed details about how the sprawling tax case was resolved – at several points in the process, for example, Secretary of State Hillary Clinton was involved.*
>
> *The confrontation also pushed UBS closer to the brink than is commonly realized. And while the bank ultimately defused the situation by coughing up $780 million and agreeing to hand over some client names, the damage to its huge and increasingly important wealth management operation still weighs heavily on the Swiss banking flagship.*

In the months ahead, UBS' new management team will try to stabilise its battered wealth management division, whose advisers have been bolting and taking clients with them.

All of this, in turn, has forced the bank to confront a broader, more existential question: what exactly is UBS today? An asset-gathering megabank or a leaner player, more attentive to its wealthy clients' needs.

For UBS and other Swiss banks, the implications of the New York meeting on October 17, 2008, were hardly trivial.

Sharing bank client data would have been against UBS' core principles: confidence, security and discretion, symbolised by the three keys of its 70-year-old logo. Doing so might also shatter wealthy clients' trust in the bank – and in the whole Swiss financial center.

Under scrutiny by the Department of Justice (DOJ) was the so-called US cross-border business of UBS. This consisted of wealth management services offered to American residents outside the United States. It operated out of Switzerland and was separate from UBS' New York-based Americas wealth management business.

In documents relating to the UBS case, the DOJ said the bank helped some 52,000 Americans hide billions of dollars of untaxed assets in secret Swiss accounts between 2000 and 2007. According to settlement documents, UBS sometimes used shell financial entities to hide the money, depriving the Internal Revenue Service of hundreds of millions of dollars of tax revenues.

The business was referred to by some UBS executives as "toxic waste" due to the risks it carried under US law. But UBS bankers, seemingly unaware of the legal consequences, made 3,800 trips to the United States to visit these clients in 2004 alone.

The cross-border accounts were hardly a big part of the bank's business. They added up to almost $20 billion, or less than 1 percent of UBS' total invested assets of about $2 trillion (2.174 trillion Swiss francs) at the end of 2008.

The business was so small it was initially below the radar screen of Swiss financial regulator FINMA, at the time known as the Federal Banking Commission. The agency's main concern back then was the systemic risks posed by UBS's increasingly wobbly fixed-income division.

Passing on some UBS client data to the United States was possible under certain strict conditions under an existing US-Swiss tax agreement. US authorities put in a request for the client data to Berne, but the process was cumbersome and slow and the Department of Justice grew increasingly impatient.

The investigation was launched by the US Securities Exchange Commission, which suspected that UBS had breached US securities law. But when the Department of Justice became involved, raising the prospect of criminal prosecutions, Swiss regulators became alarmed.

Their concerns grew in April, 2008, when US authorities briefly detained Martin Liechti, the Zurich-based head of UBS's US cross-border business, while he was visiting Miami. Then in May, Bradley Birkenfeld, a former UBS financial adviser who famously admitted smuggling a diamond in a toothpaste tube on behalf of a client, was arrested. He began a 40-month sentence in January.

Those cases got the Swiss Federal Banking Commission's attention. As the summer wore on, the agency started pressuring UBS to speed things up. But the bank, still in the throes of the financial crisis, was preoccupied with its own survival.

UBS had recently removed its all-powerful chairman, Marcel Ospel, who had blessed UBS big expansion into the United States a decade earlier and fostered the risky US investments that eventually brought UBS to its knees. Peter Kurer, a well-known Swiss lawyer who had joined the bank in 2001 as its general counsel, replaced Ospel as chairman in April 2008.

Kurer took months to appoint Diethelm as UBS top lawyer. That lengthy process did not help the bank's dealings with US authorities.

Diethelm, an ambitious former chief legal officer at Swiss Re, had made his name in the legal community by negotiating a multi-billion-dollar settlement between a group of insurers and a developer of the World Trade Center.

But within weeks of taking on the job, he found himself working for a nearly crippled lender that was facing indictment in the United States.

Hoping to come to the rescue in what was clearly becoming an untenable situation for UBS, the Swiss Finance Ministry sent a letter to its US counterparts to make clear that Berne was willing to find a solution to the UBS case despite the obvious legal constraints.

That did not sit well with US officials, who saw the letter as political interference, insiders say. The Swiss never got an official response. Instead, the next time US officials contacted the bank, on November 12, it was to inform UBS that Raoul Weil, its global head of wealth management, was being indicted.

"That was a clear message," said a high-level Swiss source. "One can imagine that without the letter they would have at least delayed the indictment of Weil."

Executives inside the bank feared that Chief Executive Marcel Rohner and Chairman Peter Kurer would be next, although neither had been named in court documents, these insiders say.

The indictment of Weil, who immediately stepped down from the executive board and has denied all wrongdoing despite remaining a fugitive in Switzerland, jump-started the negotiations.

In November, the Department of Justice asked UBS to submit a collateral consequences study, normally one of the last steps before an indictment of a company. "They said: we have now the authority from the highest level of government to proceed with an indictment," the UBS source said.

Inside the Federal Reserve Bank of New York, officials were also alarmed. They feared the indictment of UBS could panic already jittery financial markets. But the N.Y. Fed could not interfere in the DOJ's affairs.

"UBS has to find a way to disclose the taxpayer names to DOJ in order to avoid the potentially catastrophic consequences of an indictment," Thomas Baxter, the New York Fed's general counsel, told a Swiss interlocutor, according to another person familiar with the discussions.

In December, UBS held an intense board meeting at which top executives examined alternatives and assessed risks. Kurer, who had recused himself because of pending UBS litigation, could not take part.

At the meeting, directors discussed the possibility of "Notrecht" – German for emergency law, which the government could use to bypass bank secrecy rules and rescue UBS.

But the board decided that the bank should act within the parameters of existing Swiss law. "UBS had to go back to the drawing board," said one insider.

Was the Department of Justice really going to pull the trigger? Would it risk pushing over the cliff a bank with three times more employees than Lehman Brothers, about 27,000 of whom were based in the United States?

No one knew for sure, but the Swiss decided not to take the risk. On a cold night on February 18, the Swiss government convened an emergency late evening Cabinet meeting in Berne and gave its blessing to a hefty $780 million criminal settlement.

More painful than the money, though, was an agreement by UBS to deliver about 280 names of serious US tax avoiders. The government had essentially traded nearly a century of Swiss bank secrecy for UBS' survival.

This was done with the blessing of Swiss regulators, who had to draft an emergency regulation to bypass the court system to save UBS from the risk of failure.

A day after the settlement, the US Internal Revenue Service shocked the Swiss government by demanding that UBS disclose the names of 52,000 possible US tax evaders. The Swiss had clearly failed to take both the criminal and civil investigation into UBS off the table, and pressure on their treasured bank secrecy laws continued.

Finding someone to take on the job of steadying the UBS ship amid financial turmoil and a US criminal investigation was not easy. "No one wanted to talk to us because of this thing," said a senior UBS source.

In the weeks running up to the February 18 criminal settlement, Kurer interviewed three candidates. One of them was German-born Oswald Gruebel, a former Chief Executive of Credit Suisse, credited with turning around the second largest Swiss bank at a difficult time. Gruebel had retired with a bitter taste in this mouth after losing a battle to become chairman of the bank he had spent 22 years with.

On February 26, 2009, barely a week after the settlement of the criminal side of the UBS case, Gruebel agreed to take on the challenge. He immediately signaled a change of tune by announcing sharp cost cuts in an interview with local media. He said it would take him two to three years to rebuild the bank.

Kurer reluctantly left the bank and was replaced by former Swiss finance minister Kaspar Villiger. UBS was counting on Villiger's political ties to help it settle the remaining leg of the US tax case, known as the John Doe summons.

A former trader of humble origins and no formal university education, Gruebel is an outsider in what remains a close-knit hierarchical world of Swiss banking. Born in East Germany in 1943, he fled through the Iron Curtain as a 10-year-old orphan and learned the ropes of the business on Deutsche Bank's bond trading floor in the 1960s.

A straight-talking banker with a dry sense of humor, he is described as "cold" and "tough" by close aides and tends to avoid the limelight. Yet Gruebel is admired by peers as a fighter who possesses deep knowledge of investment banking, wealth management and commercial banking at a time when most banking executives tend to be specialised.

When Gruebel took the job of chief executive in February, the bank had just been stabilised, thanks in part to a loan from the Swiss state. It was also safe from US criminal charges after its February settlement.

But UBS was by no means out of the woods. It still faced a civil tax litigation that threatened the confidentiality of thousands of US clients and led to an exodus of clients and financial advisers. And the bank remained far from profitable, losing over 21 billion Swiss francs in 2008, the biggest annual loss in Swiss corporate history.

The John Doe summons represented a real legal headache for UBS. While it had been possible to stretch Swiss law to settle charges of tax fraud, the summons breached new ground by targeting tax evasion, an area in which the Swiss do not offer international cooperation.

Insiders say that by early March, it was clear that without Swiss government intervention, UBS would face another damaging legal clash that threatened Switzerland's relationship with the United States.

While UBS continued talks with the Internal Revenue Service and the Department of Justice, the Swiss Foreign Ministry got in on the act, sending officials to visit the US State Department in late March. The following month, Swiss Finance Minister Hans-Rudolf Merz, who at the time also held the rotating post of Swiss President, met with US Treasury Secretary Tim Geithner in Washington.

By their own reckoning, the Swiss were in a weak negotiating position: on April 2, the Group of 20 nations had put them on a list of tax havens and the US Administration was pressing ahead with legislation against illicit tax gains in offshore centers.

But they had a few things going for them. The US State Department was grateful for the nation's diplomatic support – such as representing US interests in places like Cuba and Iran and helping to broker a deal that normalized relations between Turkey and Armenia. The pact was signed in Switzerland last October.

This, insiders said, helped create what they called a "certain atmosphere" that made it possible for Swiss Foreign Minister Micheline Calmy Rey to have numerous phone calls with US Secretary of State Hillary Clinton and to meet her face to face three times in the run-up to the August deal.

In the end, at a crucial July 31, 2009 meeting, Clinton and Calmy Rey were able to agree on a deal in principle to avert a damaging court case against UBS.

The Swiss, constrained by their red tape, could not guarantee the timing of the delivery of any client names. But the IRS was satisfied with reassurances that Swiss authorities would eventually do so.

A US State Department official said the United States welcomed the deal "and the continued efforts by the Swiss government to ensure that its obligations under the UBS Agreement are met." The State Department declined further comment for this story.

UBS and the United States settled the civil leg of the case on August 19. There was no fine involved this time around, but a promise to hand over another 4,450 names within a year."

Well, the US did get UBS by its neck – didn't they?

The Indian Response – A Study in Contrast

In contrast to the global response to the convoluted issue of tax havens, the Indian response to the entire subject is a study in contrast. It is filled with deception, loaded with stratagem and coloured with conspiracy – all aimed to defraud its own citizens. As the tax havens near extermination, the global mood is one of jubilation – at least that is what the global leaders want us to believe. In comparison, the Indian Government, media, intelligentsia, professionals, trade and industry bodies and, of course, the all pervasive Indian bureaucracy seem to be melancholic over the probable death of tax havens. This is all the more intriguing given the fact that we have been the victims of tax havens since our independence. Naturally, when the whole world is planning action against those who have for centuries perpetuated this fraud on humanity, we in India are suddenly and strangely hesitant. We do not seem to realise that we have nothing to lose.

It is often found that only in India will a victim sympathise with his own hunter. We rationalise his action, defend his deed. It would seem that there is nothing called enlightened national self-interest when it concerns India. Indeed, we are beyond understanding even for our own selfish interest. No wonder, others are often flabbergasted while interacting with us, especially on matters concerning our own supreme self-interests.

It may be recalled that the JPC Report on the securities scam in 2001 noted that various acts of omission and commission having been clearly established, the committee urged that the Government should take all necessary steps to finalise proceedings against Ketan Parekh entities and ensure that suitable action is taken against them without delay. The committee also urged that expeditious action should be taken to ascertain the facts regarding the Swiss bank account of Ketan Parekh and to follow up the matter. Yet, several years later, till 2010, nothing seems to have even moved on this account.

The reply of the Government in May 2003 to the JPC Report cryptically noted that regarding the Swiss bank accounts of Ketan Parekh, the Swiss authorities had intimated in December 2002 that the Letter Rogatory sent in this matter cannot be executed because of the directions of the High Court at Zurich. Obviously, the Swiss do not seem to care even for the report of the JPC with all its authority, evidence and directions. Or is it that our Government is merely incompetent, unable to proceed any further on such sensitive cases?

Ever since the debate of tax havens exploded in the run-up to the General Elections of 2009, the infamous Indian habit of stonewalling seems to have begun to protect and prolong tax havens. No wonder, the entire world, especially the developing world, which has often looked to the Indian leadership on such crucial issues, is dismayed with the Indian approach to this issue. Several poor and developing nations are quite aghast at the national apathy displayed by India on this crucial issue. Many of these countries feel that it is India and India alone that can provide leadership for the world. Instead, India seems to endlessly procrastinate.

While one may not able to exactly fathom as to why and what is occupying the mind of the Indian Government, one can make some intelligent guesses. Recall that the German Government had obtained data from the LGT Bank. The said DVD obtained from Liechtenstein contained names of several Germans. Interestingly, it contained the names of persons of several other nationalities too. The Germans unusually were willing to play ball to all those countries that were willing to officially write to it.

Three bits of evidence expose the Indian Government's lackadaisical approach to this issue. First, when Germany offered the LGT Bank's secret data to any country that needed it, the Indian Government did not go for the jugular and ask for it despite various press reports suggesting that it contained several Indian names. Second, Transparency International noted India's "stoic silence over the issue" and that it "has not approached the German Government for the data." Third, the revenue secretary in Delhi "reportedly advised the Indian ambassador in Berlin not to push Germany" for the details as Germany might not like it – clear proof that the Government was scuttling, not getting, the details. All this obfuscation is remarkable considering the fact that the rest of the world has been displaying amazing alacrity in obtaining details from Germany.

Remember, all this is only pertaining to the data relating to Liechtenstein. On matters relating to the tax havens, the Indian response has been uniform over decades – shoot the messenger, question his integrity, express concern on his intention, abuse his character and provide the standard defence in such situations: "foreign hand." In fact, one can standardise the response of the Indian Government over the decades as hereunder:

- Question the political colour of the person who raises the issue. As every political party in India has an embarrassing history, this question would be sufficient to put any political party on the defensive.
- Question the timing – why now? This can never be answered. One can always ask why the first Government under Panditji did not do anything on this score? In the process, little do we realise that there is no perfect time to

catch a criminal. Today, there is a strategic opportunity available globally in dealing with the extant issue. Why not make hay till the sunshine lasts? It would seem that the Government is there only to ask questions and sow doubts in the mind of our people. It would never act to answer the questions relating to tax havens.

- Charge the person raising the issue of being politically motivated. Politics is a dirty word in India – being politically motivated is, in fact, an extreme form of abuse in our political theatre. In the process, little do we realise that even the Mahatma, Nehru, Rajaji, Subhash Chandra Bose and all those fought for our freedom were politically motivated.
- Assure action only when the precise sums are known. It would seem that the Government will act only if it has the precise figures (i.e. to the last dollar) and will not act if it is a penny more or a penny less in the ultimate analysis. Crucially, the onus of providing such details of the tax havens lies with the accuser. The Government will not move its little finger on this count too.
- The previous Governments did not do anything. So that justifies our inaction. In the process, everyone in power since August 1947 can be absolved and every future Government too can be absolved.
- Diffuse the situation. "We have written to the Japanese under the Indo-German Double Taxation Avoidance Agreement so that we can get details about Indians who have illegal accounts in Switzerland." For an outsider, that would look like all action. Yet, ordinary people, if they apply their mind, would know that this is an ultimate exercise in obfuscation. And this effectively prevents the Japanese, Germans and, of course, the Swiss from taking any action.

That, in effect summarises the (in)action of successive Indian Governments!

The response of the Government on the issue of the LGT Bank has been highlighted in the response of the Government in the Hon'ble Supreme Court in the matter of the PIL filed by a few enlightened citizens on the issue of tax havens. The affidavit states, "...that immediately after becoming aware through media reports published on 27.02.2008 that the German Government was willing to share information available with it in respect of account holders in LGT Bank, Liechtenstein, a letter was addressed by the Central Government seeking such information on 27.02.2008. The German Government responded vide letter dated March 17, 2008 that they were not in a position to provide that information sought but would inform as soon as they had detailed findings about whether and to what extent Indian taxpayers were involved."

Further the affidavit adds that "on account of persistent follow-up by the Central Government, the German Government, on 16th March 2009, informed that they were in a position to provide the information and the said information was made available to the Central Government on 18.03.2009. However, I state and submit that the said information was made available on the condition of strict confidentiality of contents under the Double Taxation Avoidance Agreement."

The moot point is: did the information contain the names of some Indians? If so, what has the Government done subsequently with the said list? It is speculated in the media and political circles that a list of fifty names has since been received by our Government. Strangely, the Indian Government has maintained silence ostensibly on the plea that the Germans have imposed certain legal preconditions on such disclosure. What is entirely unusual in this request is that Germany has released its own list while our Government wants to us to believe that Germany had issued this precondition to the Indians. (Subsequent press reports suggest that the Income Tax Department has issued notices to all those named in the said list. The outcome of all these may take several years.)

Or is it our own reluctance to disclose the names? It does not take much to analyse this response of the Indian Government. Unless the most powerful of this country are involved, the Indian Government would not have stonewalled to this extent. Unless someone very highly placed within the bureaucracy are involved, the extent of obfuscation would not be so brilliantly effectuated. Unless some portions of the judiciary are involved, no one within the Government would be doing all this so brazenly. Finally, unless powerful sections of the media are involved in this, all the other three pillars of the Indian Constitution – the legislature, the executive and the judiciary – would not have been able to successfully manage the fallout.

In short, every pillar of our sublime Constitution is involved in the mess called tax havens.

Naturally, it is in nobody's interest – except, of course, minions like you and me – to unearth the truth in India. We had already looked into the stonewalling of the Government of India on this issue in Chapter I. We will continue to look into this issue in subsequent chapters, especially in Chapter 9 which deals with Indian policy responses in greater detail.

References

1. John Christensen, Tax Justice Network, "Mirror Mirror on the Wall, Who's the Most Corrupt of all?", World Social Forum, Nairobi, January 2007.
2. *India Today*, Issue dated February 18,2008.
3. KPMG Global Anti-Money Laundering Survey (2007), "How Banks are Facing up to the Challenge".
4. Léonce Ndikumana and James K. Boyce Department of Economics and Political Economy Research Institute University of Massachusetts, Amherst *New Estimates of Capital Flight from Sub-Saharan African Countries: Linkages with External Borrowing and Policy Options.*
5. John Christensen in the *London Review of Books* (Vol. 27, No. 19, dated October 06, 2005), while reviewing *Capitalism's Achilles Heel: Dirty Money and How to Renew the Free-Market System* by Raymond Baker
6. "Tax us if You Can – The True Story of Global Failure" by Tax Justice Network.
7. White Paper on Multinational Accounting Firms Operating in India, prepared and published in public interest by the Chartered Accountants' Action Committee for a level playing field.
8. Professor R. Vaidyanathan, "Time to get Back India's Sovereign Wealth Fund," *The Hindu Business Line*, dated March 28, 2008.
9. August 2009 edition of the *Swiss Review*.
10. Press statement by Mr. L.K. Advani, dated March 29, 2009.
11. *Economic Times*, May 25, 2008.
12. Mr. S. Gurumurthy ,"A Deafening Silence on Funny Money" April 3, 2009.
13. Special Report: How the U.S. Cracked Open Secret Vaults at UBS - http://www.reuters.com/article/idUSTRE6380UA20100409, by Lisa Jucca
14. "Italy Amnesty Yields Euros 97 Billion, Bulk from Switzerland," *Reuters*, June 21, 2010.
15. Globalisation and its Discontents by Joseph E. Stiglitz.
16. "The Financial System: What Went Wrong," *The Economist*, Issue dated March 19, 2008.

CHAPTER **4**

Global Response to Money Laundering and Tax Havens

Only the paranoid survive.

— Andrew Grove of Intel

In the aftermath of the unfortunate events in the US on September 11, 2001 (9/11), the world seemed to have become paranoid. The economics of terror and terrorism on a country's economics have become the emerging frontiers of transnational challenges since then. Naturally, fighting terror and the economics that encourages and sustains terror became the big time objective of Governments. Zero-tolerance to terror is the buzz word. Naturally, that means zero tolerance to all the mechanisms that drive, sustain and nourish terrorism. But the problem with this approach is that funding terrorism is interlinked, intertwined and integrated to money laundering and tax havens. Therefore, Governments across continents are veering to the view that actions to thwart the efforts of criminals and terrorists have to be directed towards curbing money laundering and tax havens. But that is easier said than done.

As explained in the previous chapters, money laundering is often seen to be the end game of an illicit source of income. Pre-9/11, international efforts were predominantly directed towards targeting money laundering in the context of drug trafficking activities only. The international effort to curb money laundering began with the recognition that drug trafficking was an international problem and could only be addressed effectively on a multilateral basis. Consequently, anti-money laundering efforts were linked to crimes relating to drug trafficking only. But those were relatively innocent times where the biggest crime known to mankind was drug trafficking.

The first multilateral effort involving several countries to tackle money laundering through drug trafficking was launched in the early 90s. Due to growing concern about increased international drug trafficking and the tremendous amounts of related money entering the banking system, the United Nations initiated an international agreement – also called the Vienna

Convention – to combat drug trafficking and the consequent money laundering arising out of such drug trafficking. This agreement of 169 countries primarily deals with provisions to fight the illicit drug trade and free movement of the sale proceeds arising out of such illicit businesses.

In view of the fact that the entire issue of tackling money laundering was in an embryonic form, the Vienna Convention neither used the term money laundering, nor defined it or addressed the preventive aspects of money laundering. The reasons for such a limited view on the subject even as late as in 1990 need to be appreciated. First, it is to be understood that terrorism was a local phenomenon till the US got a taste of global terrorism in September 2001. Remember, once the US gets involved with something, it is always global! Till terrorism exploded in the face of America, it was considered by Americans as a local phenomenon in Asia, Africa or Europe. When that happened in the US, apart from domestic efforts to contain terror, the US ensured that it used several multilateral forums to tackle terror. That, in turn, meant that fighting terrorism became global! Second, the internet revolution had not yet taken over the world. Consequently, the world of finance was still using Neanderthal technologies to transfer funds even across continents. Only when the ideas of electronic transfers emerged, especially through tax havens, did the world of finance and with it ideas relating to money laundering, underwent a tectonic change.

The Response to Money Laundering pre-9/11

As more crimes, especially terrorism, lend themselves to money laundering, several countries now include a wide range of offences as predicate crimes to money laundering. Apart from such national efforts, it has been seen of late that anti-money laundering efforts have increasingly become multilateral. Post-9/11, anti-money laundering efforts have been dictated more by the need to fight terrorism than other predicate crimes. But that does not mean that the other predicate crimes do not warrant such anti-money laundering efforts.

Given the developments of the decade between 1990 and 2000, the first concerted multilateral steps in using anti-money laundering mechanisms were taken under the aegis of the UN in 2000. The International Convention Against Transnational Organised Crime (2000) – also called the Palermo Convention – contains a broad range of provisions to fight several types of organised crime. Further, in order to bind countries to the declaration contained in the said convention, it commits countries that ratify this convention and to implement the same by legislating appropriate domestic laws.

The Palermo Convention specifically obligates each ratifying country to:

- Criminalise money laundering.
- Include all serious crimes as predicate offences of money laundering.
- Establish regulatory regimes to deter and detect money laundering, including "customer identification" and "reporting of suspicious transactions."
- Cooperate in the exchange of information amongst countries that are signatories to the convention.
- Establish a financial intelligence unit to collect, analyse and disseminate information relating to money laundering.

While the Palermo Declaration was being adopted globally only in 2003, the UN adopted the International Convention for the Suppression of Financing of Terrorism. This convention came into force in 2002. It is obvious that both these multilateral efforts were by-products of the attacks on the US in September 2001. This UN Convention mandated ratifying states to criminalise terrorism, terrorist organisations and their acts. Under the convention, it is unlawful to collect funds with the intent or the knowledge that the funds will be used to carry out any of the acts of terrorism. Yet more was to follow in the aftermath of the 9/11 incidents.

Global Response to Money Laundering post-9/11

Post-9/11, the global response to terrorism and money laundering underwent a significant change. As the world watched in great horror the events that unfolded before it on 9/11, Governments across continents felt increasingly threatened. The US, with all its anti-terror mechanisms, could not prevent the worst attack since World War II on its soil. On September 28, 2001, the UN Security Council adopted Resolution 1373 which obligates countries to criminalise actions to finance terrorism. It further obligates countries to:

- Deny support for terrorists, including freeing funds or assets of persons, organisations or entities involved in terrorist acts;
- Prohibit active or passive assistance to terrorists; and
- Cooperate with other countries in criminal investigations and sharing information about planned terrorist acts.

It may be noted that unlike other international conventions, which required ratification by the UN member country by the passing of appropriate domestic laws, a Security Council Resolution passed in response to a threat to international peace and security under Chapter VII of the UN Charter, is binding upon all UN member countries.

As noted above, Resolution 1373 was adopted by the UN on September 28, 2001. This, again, was in direct response to the events of September 11, 2001. That resolution made it mandatory for all member countries to take specific actions to combat terrorism. The resolution, further established a Counter-Terrorism Committee (CTC) to monitor the performance of individual member countries in building a "global capacity against terrorism." Through the CTC, the UN seeks to establish a dialogue between the Security Council and member countries to ensure that the objectives of Resolution 1373 are achieved.

As a sequel to these, the UN further requires countries to submit a report to the CTC on the steps initiated to implement the measures contained therein on a periodic basis. Further, the CTC has requested each country to perform a self-assessment of its existing legislation and mechanism to combat terrorism. Over and above all these, the CTC performs the role of an adviser by identifying areas where a country needs to strengthen its counter-terrorist mechanisms.

The FATF and its Recommendations

The next major step in fighting the issue of money laundering post-9/11 was the setting up of a specific body to combat money laundering. In this connection, the Financial Action Task Force (FATF) on Money Laundering was activated. This is an inter-Governmental body whose purpose is to develop an international response to combat money laundering. The FATF also sets standards, develops and promotes policies to combat money laundering and terrorist financing. Though constituted in 1989-90, the Task Force expanded its mission in October 2001 (again within weeks of the attacks in the US on 9/11) to include Combating the Financing of Terrorism (CFT). FATF is an apex level policy-making global body, which brings together legal, financial and law enforcement experts to achieve national legislation and regulatory AML and CFT reforms.

Currently, its membership consists of 34 countries (including India which became a member in June 2010) and two regional organisations. In addition, FATF works in collaboration with a number of international bodies and organisations. FATF's primary functions with regard to money laundering are:

- Monitoring progress in implementing anti-money laundering measures across countries.
- Reviewing and reporting on laundering trends, techniques and counter-measures.
- Promoting the adoption and implementation of FATF anti-money laundering standards globally.

FATF has adopted a set of forty recommendations (thoroughly reviewed in 2003 to take into account changes in money laundering and anticipate future potential trends) titled "The Forty Recommendations on Money Laundering." These constitute a comprehensive anti-money laundering framework. While the forty recommendations set out principles for action, they also permit member countries flexibility in implementing the principles according to each country's own particular circumstances and constitutional requirements. Although not binding as law upon a country, these recommendations have been widely endorsed by the international community as the applicable international standards for combatting money laundering. It may be noted that these recommendations have been recognised *even* by the International Monetary Fund and the World Bank as the international standards for combating money laundering and the financing of terrorism.

Money laundering, thanks to the explosion of the internet technology and innovativeness of the criminals, crooks as well as terrorists, is getting increasingly sophisticated. Further, the proliferation of tax havens, "continuous flow of judicious professional advice" and flows of funds from one jurisdiction to the other, make detection of money laundering virtually impossible. In this connection, the introduction to the FATF note issued by the FATF Secretariat in France notes, "Combinations of techniques, such as the increased use of legal persons to disguise the true ownership and control of illegal proceeds, and an increased use of professionals to provide advice and assistance in laundering criminal funds." All these have made money laundering extremely difficult to detect. Given this background, the FATF's forty recommendations were made extremely comprehensive.

Apart from providing information to all the members of the FATF, in situations where the ability to obtain information sought by a foreign competent authority is not within the mandate of its counterpart, countries are also encouraged by FATF to permit a prompt and constructive exchange of information with non-counterparts. Cooperation with foreign authorities other than counterparts could occur directly or indirectly. When uncertain about the appropriate avenue to follow, FATF suggests that the competent authorities should first contact their foreign counterparts for assistance.

Countries are also necessitated by FATF to establish controls and safeguards to ensure that information exchanged by competent authorities is used only in an authorised manner, consistent with their obligations concerning privacy and data protection.

Over and above these forty recommendations, at an extraordinary Plenary on the Financing of Terrorism held in Washington, D.C. on October 29 and 30,

2001 (again in the aftermath of 9/11) the FATF expanded its mission beyond money laundering to focus its energy and expertise on the worldwide effort to combat terrorist financing.

During the extraordinary Plenary, the FATF issued new international standards to combat terrorist financing, in which it calls on all countries to adopt and implement nine special recommendations (over and above the said forty recommendations) ostensibly aimed at denying terrorists access to the international financial system. The agreement on the Special Recommendations commits members to:

- Take immediate steps to ratify and implement the relevant United Nations instruments.
- Criminalise the financing of terrorism, terrorist acts and terrorist organisations.
- Freeze and confiscate terrorist assets.
- Report suspicious transactions linked to terrorism.
- Provide the widest possible range of assistance to other countries' law enforcement and regulatory authorities for terrorist financing investigations.
- Impose anti-money laundering requirements on alternative remittance systems.
- Strengthen customer identification measures in international and domestic wire transfers.
- Ensure that entities, in particular non-profit organisations, cannot be misused to finance terrorism.

In taking forward its plan of action against terrorist financing, the FATF sought to intensify its cooperation with the FATF-style regional bodies and international organisations and bodies, such as the United Nations, the Egmont Group of Financial Intelligence Units, the G-20, and International Financial Institutions, that support and contribute to the international effort against money laundering and terrorist financing

International Organisation of Securities Commissioners (IOSCO)

Till now, we had been dwelling on the overall aspects of the financial institutions and the approach of the authorities worldwide, multilaterally or otherwise, to tackle money laundering and combating terrorist activities. Now let us turn to the securities market, regulators and the manner in which the world has been preparing and positioning regulators of various securities markets to tackle these emerging issues.

IOSCO is the global apex standard setter for the securities market. The organisation's wide membership regulates more than 90 per cent of the world securities market. Consequently, IOSCO is the world's most important international cooperative forum for securities regulatory agencies.

In 1998, IOSCO adopted a comprehensive set of objectives and principles which have become the regulatory benchmark for all securities markets. Further, the organisation endorsed in 2003 a comprehensive methodology (again after 9/11) that enabled an "objective assessment" of the level of implementation of the IOSCO principles in the jurisdiction of its members.

In 2005, the organisation endorsed the IOSCO Memorandum of Understanding (MoU) as the benchmark for international cooperation amongst securities regulators. It sought the effective implementation of the IOSCO Principles which are considered primary instruments to facilitate:

- Cross-border cooperation.
- Reduce global systemic risk.
- Protect investors.
- Ensure fair and efficient securities markets.

The Preamble to IOSCO's by-laws states:

- Securities authorities resolve to cooperate together to ensure a better regulation of the markets, on the domestic as well as on the international level, in order to maintain just, efficient and sound markets:
- To exchange information on their respective experiences in order to promote the development of domestic markets.
- To unite their efforts to establish standards and an effective surveillance of international securities transactions.
- To provide mutual assistance to ensure the integrity of the markets by a vigorous application of the standards and by effective enforcement against offences.

To achieve this, the IOSCO document on Objective and Principles of Securities Regulation sets out "30 principles of securities regulation." The 30 principles need to be practically implemented under the relevant legal framework to achieve the objectives of regulation described above. The principles are grouped into eight categories.

Joint Forum of BCBS, IAIS and IOSCO: Further Developments to FATF

Simultaneously, the Basel Committee on Banking Supervision (BCBS), International Association of Insurance Supervisors (IAIS) and International

Organisation of Securities Commissions (IOSCO) published a joint note on the subject of anti-money laundering and steps taken by each one of them. It was aimed at providing a consolidated record of the initiatives taken by each sector viz., banks, insurance and securities to combat money laundering and the financing of terrorism. This note was aimed at providing an overview of the common as well as overlapping standards that apply to all three sectors. Simultaneously, it sought to carry out an assessment as to whether there are inconsistencies in the approaches in the respective sectors. The abovementioned joint note was prepared in November 2004 to capture the AML/CFT developments in the three abovementioned sectors. It focusses on recent guidance for addressing the vulnerabilities identified in the earlier report and ongoing and future work. These are stated hereunder in brief:

Guidance Provided to Address Vulnerabilities: Banking

The BCBS noted that it had issued a paper for *Customer Due Diligence* (CDD) in October 2001 (again after 9/11). Further, it issued prudential guidance for CDD in the context of AML/CFT, setting out appropriate standards and guidance for the development of appropriate practices by banks. It was clearly emphasised in these papers that adequate due diligence by banks on new and existing customers was the key element in an AML/CFT mechanism. It was further emphasised that banks must develop appropriate policies in key areas such as customer acceptance, customer identification and consequential risk management.

The BCBS also issued a consultative paper titled, "Consolidated KYC Risk Management," in August 2003. This paper, which has since been revised to incorporate comments received from relevant stakeholders, examines the critical elements for effective management of KYC risks. The Consolidated KYC paper highlights that policies and procedures should be designed not merely to comply strictly with all relevant laws and regulations, but more broadly to identify, monitor and mitigate reputation, operational, legal and concentration risks. To this end, banks are expected to implement a fully effective consolidated KYC risk management programme.

Further, the BCBS consultative paper emphasises the banks' compliance to be carried out through an appropriate audit mechanism and to evaluate adherence to all aspects of the global standards for KYC.

What is crucial is that these discussions needs to be juxtaposed in the context of the UBS case as well the Goldman Sachs case, discussed in the subsequent chapters. The BCBS notes that an important topic that needs to be addressed is the issue of legal impediments to sharing of customer account information. The comments by the industry on the consultation draft noted that some countries have rigorous bank secrecy or data protection laws that prevent, or can be interpreted as preventing, the transfer of information for risk management purposes.

Brushing aside these concerns, it is interesting to note that the revised paper (arising out of the consultative draft and subsequent comments from the industry) recognises that although such impediments may exist there are possible "gateways for passing information in most countries." It stresses that it is essential that all jurisdictions that host foreign banks provide an appropriate legal framework which allows information for KYC risk management purposes to be passed to the head office/parent bank.

Furthermore, the revised version of the paper notes that there should be no impediments to onsite visits by head office auditors, risk managers, compliance officers, or home country supervisors, nor any restrictions on their ability to access all the local office's records, including customers' names and balances. Head office staff granted such access should not be restricted from reporting such information back to the head office. All information gathered during information-sharing processes should be subject to the applicable privacy and privilege laws.

Guidance Provided to Address Vulnerabilities: Insurance

In October 2003, the IAIS revised and expanded its insurance core principles and methodology by issuing a guidance paper. Consequently, the new revised principles dealt specifically with the anti-money laundering and combating the financing of terrorism issues through insurance companies. This new guidance paper takes into account the revised FATF 40 Recommendations of June 2003 and the methodology for assessing compliance with the FATF 40 Recommendations.

In the light of the FATF 40 Recommendations, the IAIS considered that there was need for specific guidance for the insurance sector. One of the new elements of the recommendations provided in the said guidance note is the concept of Customer Due Diligence (CDD). This had been tailored to the specific features of the insurance industry and its supervision.

In accordance with the FATF 40 Recommendations, the guidance paper applies entirely to insurers dealing with life insurance. However, the IAIS, as it is also concerned about the potential risks to types of insurance other than life insurance – non-life insurance and reinsurance – seeks to apply the same principles to other types of insurers too. The guidance paper also offers a range of possible measures, procedures and best practices from which the supervisor should select those most appropriate to effectively and efficiently deal with the risks.

Guidance Provided to Address Vulnerabilities: Securities

A Task Force of the IOSCO prepared a document titled Principles on Client Identification and Beneficial Ownership for the Securities Industry. These principles were approved by the IOSCO at the IOSCO Annual Conference on May 17-20, 2004. Again, notice the coincidence – May 17, 2004! That very day, certain PN holders were selling shares in the Indian securities markets through UBS in substantial quantities. We will be looking into this issue in greater detail in the following chapters.

The IOSCO Statement of Principles provides a comprehensive framework relating to client and beneficial ownership identification and verification CDD requirements. It seeks to take into account the priorities and perspectives of securities regulators. It also ensures complementing the standards of other bodies, such as the FATF's 40 Recommendations relating to anti-money laundering.

In addition to client and beneficial ownership identification and verification, the principles provide guidance to industry on:

- Identification and verification requirements with respect to omnibus accounts;
- Ongoing due diligence obligations;
- Record keeping requirements for client identification information; and
- Third party reliance.

These principles also address the securities regulator's role in monitoring for industry compliance with AML obligations and cooperating with domestic and foreign authorities. Further, they also provide for the regulator to obtain and share client identification and beneficial ownership information with foreign counterparts.

It may be recalled that the primary focus of IOSCO relating to CDD is sought to be achieved by fulfilling its specific mandates of protecting investors, assuring that markets are safe, and preventing systemic risks. The paper concludes that observance of these principles by IOSCO members should contribute to the fulfilment of the FATF's missions of preventing money laundering and terrorist financing.

Financial Intelligence Units (FIUs)

In 1995, a number of Governmental units known today as FIUs began working together and formed the Egmont Group of Financial Intelligence Units

(Egmont Group). As part of the effort to fight money laundering, Governments have created agencies to analyse information submitted by covered entities and persons pursuant to the money laundering reporting requirements. Such agencies are commonly referred to as Financial Intelligent Units (FIUs). These units serve as the focal point within a country to implement anti-money laundering programmes. They also provide for the exchange of information between financial institutions and law enforcement agencies across countries.

The purpose of the group is to provide a forum for FIUs to improve support for each of their national AML programmes and to coordinate AML initiatives. Because money laundering is practised on a worldwide scale, there has also been the need to share information on a cross-border basis. This support includes the exchange of financial intelligence information, improving expertise and capabilities of personnel, and fostering better communication among FIUs.

The mission of the Egmont Group was expanded in 2004 to include specifically financial intelligence on terrorist financing. Only a central, national agency that is responsible for receiving, analysing and disseminating to the competent authorities can be a member of the Egmont Group. Disclosure of financial information expected of the members of the Egmont Group includes:

- Concerning suspected proceeds of crime and potential financing of terrorism; or
- Required by national regulation, in order to counter money laundering and terrorist-financing.

A member, the Egmont Group mandates, must also commit to act in accordance with its Principles for Information Exchange between FIUs for Money Laundering cases. These principles include conditions for the exchange of information, limitation on permitted uses of information, and confidentiality.

Further, there have been several other international endeavours on the issue of tackling money laundering and combating financing of terror. Some of these have been dealt with briefly in this chapter. There are a few others which have not been dealt with in the same manner for three reasons – one, for the sake of brevity; two, some of these efforts are repetitive in nature and duplicate earlier efforts; and, three, some of these are beyond the scope of the issues that are sought to be addressed by this book. Nevertheless, some of these efforts include certain model legislations issued by the UN. These are listed out hereunder:

- Merida Convention: UN Convention Against Corruption, December 14, 2005.
- International Convention for the Suppression of the Financing of Terrorism 1999
- IMF/UNODC Model Legislation on Money Laundering and Financing of Terrorism, 2005.
- UN ODCCP Model Legislation on Laundering, Confiscation and International Cooperation with Regard to Illicit Traffic in Narcotic Drugs, Psychotropic Substances and Precursors, 2003.
- Commonwealth Secretariat, IMF, and UNODC Model Provisions on Money Laundering, Terrorist Financing, Preventive Measures and Proceeds of Crime, 2009.
- UNDCP Model Mutual Assistance in Criminal Matters Bill, 2000.
- UNDCP Model Foreign Evidence Bill, 2000.
- UNDCP Model Extradition (Amendement) Bill 2000.
- UN Model Treaty on Mutual Assistance in Criminal Matters, 1990.
- Commonwealth Model Law for the Prohibition of Money Laundering and Supporting Documentation, 1996.
- OAS – CICAD Model Regulations Concerning Laundering Offences Connected to Illicit Drug Trafficking and other Serious Offences
- UN Model Terrorist Financing Bill, 2003.

Now Where Does India Figure in all These?

We will be specifically looking to India's policy responses to the entire issue of fighting Hawala, putting in place anti-money laundering measures and, of course, combating financing of terrorism, in subsequent chapters of this book. However, in this chapter, we will specifically look into how the world measures our approach to these developments, our responses to the threats and the manner in which we as a nation are reacting to these international standards on combating funding of terror activities and complying with the anti-money laundering programmes.

But before we proceed any further, a brief reference to the series of terror activities in India in 2008 would be in order. It may be recalled that in 2008, India ranked among the world's worst terrorism-afflicted countries. Some of these terror acts are listed out hereunder:

- On November 26, 2008, terrorists struck at several locations in Mumbai, killing at least 183 people, including several foreigners. Over 300 more were injured.
- On May 13, 2008, Jaipur experienced serial bomb blasts at crowded market

areas and at Hindu temples. At least 60 people were killed, and more than 150 injured.

- On July 25, 2008, serial bombs were set off in Bangalore in both business and industrial areas. At least one individual died, while eight were injured.
- On July 26, 2008, 21 devices exploded in Ahmedabad, killing 54 and injuring at least 156.
- On September 13, 2008, terrorists detonated serial bombs in India's capital, New Delhi.
- On October 30, 2008, terror outfits detonated a series of bombs throughout Assam, killing over 100 people.

The list could go on. The names of cities of India and the numbers of those killed change. But the story of terror does not. The Government of India often does not provide the complete picture on this matter of the state of terror in India. In fact, at every turn, we as a nation suppress the number of those killed during such activities.

Surely, it must be conceded that we fared far better in 2009 than in 2008. But that could be more out of the benevolence of the terror groups than affirmative action by the Government of India. According to the Government of India, several South Asian Islamic extremist groups including the Lashkar-e-Tayyeba, Jaish-e-Mohammad, and Harakat-ul-Jihad-i-Islami (Bangladesh) as well as indigenous groups were behind these events. And it is well known that all these groups are intimately linked to several international terror groups including Al Qaeda and the dreaded Taliban. Interestingly, none of the perpetrators of these attacks have been prosecuted.

Naturally, the world looks upon us as a weak state.

Contrast this to the elaborate exercise undertaken by the world in the aftermath of the attacks in the US on September 11, 2001. The US was able to marshal its entire diplomatic energies to ensure counter-terror activities across the globe. No wonder, post-9/11, there have been no further attacks in the US. What is interesting to note here is that the US monitors the operations of terror groups worldwide and the manner in which other countries are combating terror.

In this connection, we shall refer to the International Narcotics Control Strategy Report, 2009, issued by the US Department of State. The 2009 International Narcotics Control Strategy Report (INCSR) is an annual report by the Department of State to Congress prepared in accordance with the Foreign

Assistance Act (FAA). The FAA requires a report on the extent to which each country or entity that received assistance under Chapter 8 of Part I of the Foreign Assistance Act in the past two fiscal years has "met the goals and objectives" of the 1988 UN Drug Convention.

While the UN Convention is generally worded, requiring the parties to take legal measures to outlaw and punish all forms of illicit drug production, trafficking, and drug money laundering, the US statute lists certain actions initiated by foreign countries to evaluate their performance under the 1988 UN Drug Convention. It is in this context that this report is made out to the US Congress. The relevance of examining this report for the purposes of this work includes the view of the US State Department on India's handling of illicit cultivation, production, distribution, sale, transport and financing of drug trafficking, money laundering, asset seizure, extradition, mutual legal assistance, law enforcement and transit cooperation in the context of money laundering and combating terrorism.

Obviously, the US feels that it is in its supreme national interest to monitor AML and CFT measures undertaken by the rest of the world so as to secure itself against possible terrorist attacks emanating even from foreign soil in the future. One way of looking at the exercise undertaken by the US is to dismiss it as the supreme arrogance of the sole surviving superpower. The other way of looking at it is to appreciate the manner in which the US is approaching the issue of terror funding and money laundering. This book seeks to take the second approach.

In this modern world of terrorism caused by religious fundamentalism, it is obvious that only the paranoid survive and the US is paranoid about terrorism, especially caused by religious fundamentalism.

In this report of the US State Government, apart from India, the US tracks the following countries/jurisdictions as it feels that these countries are major centres for money laundering: Afghanistan, Antigua and Barbuda, Australia, Austria, Bahamas, Belize, Bolivia, Brazil, Burma, Cambodia, Canada, Cayman Islands, China, Colombia, Costa Rica, Cyprus, Dominican Republic, France, Germany, Greece, Guatemala, Guernsey, Guinea-Bissau, Haiti, Hong Kong, Indonesia, Iran, Isle of Man, Israel, Italy, Japan, Jersey, Kenya, Latvia, Lebanon, Liechtenstein, Luxembourg, Macau, Mexico, Netherlands, Nigeria, Pakistan, Panama, Paraguay, Philippines, Russia, Singapore, Spain, Switzerland, Taiwan, Thailand, Turkey, Ukraine, United Arab Emirates, United Kingdom, Uruguay, Venezuela, and Zimbabwe.

The report is made out in two volumes. Volume I covers drug and chemical control activities. Volume II covers money laundering and financial crimes.

This report dwells at length on various countries' responses to AML/CFT, including India, in Volume II. Further, this report highlights the issues relating to global money laundering, terrorist finance and other financial crimes. Tainted funds, the report notes, have the potential to destabilise economies, weaken the integrity of the international financial system, subvert rules-based international commerce and corrupt Governments. For the US, this is an important study at an international level on money laundering.

The 2009 and 2010 Reports on India

The report also bring about the new emerging frontiers in money laundering. They point out that trade is used to launder money. Experts estimate that billions of dollars are laundered through trade – trade-based money laundering (TBML) as well as through services (SBML). This is purportedly done through overinvoicing and underinvoicing of trade. The observations contained in the reports make interesting reading. Some of the excerpts of the reports are laid out hereunder for ready reference as to whether India has met the international standards in the "eyes" of the US Department of State.

The 2009 report notes that India's "emerging role in regional financial transactions, its large system of informal cross-border money flows, large underground economy, widespread use of Hawala, and historically disadvantageous tax administration all contribute to the country's vulnerability to money laundering activities." The report concedes that criminal activity contributes substantially to money laundering from India which is rooted to the traditional causes specific to India.

Further, the report blames India's "Hawala" or informal money transfer systems for laundering money. According to Indian observers, estimated funds transferred through the Hawala market are between 30 to 40 percent of the formal market. The 2009 report quotes certain RBI sources which estimate that remittances to India sent through legal, formal channels in 2007-08 amounted to USD 42.6 billion. The 2010 report states, "According to Indian observers, funds transferred through the Hawala market are equal to between 30 to 40 percent of the formal market, totalling between USD 13 and USD 17 billion. The RBI estimates that remittances to India sent through legal, formal channels during fiscal year 2009 (ending March 31, 2009) amounted to USD 46.4 billion."

The 2009 report notes with "satisfaction" that the RBI issued guidelines requiring financial institutions, to follow "know your customer" details. The report also notes that the RBI has been taking additional steps to crack down on unlicensed money transmitters and increase monitoring of non-bank money transfer operations like currency exchange kiosks and wire transfer services. Further, the report notes that due to the liberalisation of tariff barriers, the rise in foreign companies working and investing in India, and increased Government monitoring, India has been able to significantly bring down the Hawala payments arising due to smuggling. The 2010 report notes that the RBI has tightened the KYC norms for authorised money transfer service agents, requiring enhanced due diligence for new customers based on a customer's risk profile and increased monitoring of receipts considered especially risky, based on indicators such as country of origin, sources of funds, and type of transaction. We will revert to the convoluted issue of KYC norms in the context of the UBS case which we will refer to in the subsequent chapters.

In the aftermath of the September 11, 2001, terrorist attacks in the United States, in January 2003, the report points to the fact that India joined the global community in addressing concerns about money laundering and terrorist finance by implementing the Prevention of Money Laundering Act (PMLA). The PMLA in India criminalised money laundering, imposed reporting and record keeping requirements on financial institutions and established a Financial Intelligence Unit (FIU). The report also notes that the legislation outlines the predicate offences for money laundering which are listed in a schedule to the Act.

Even so, the 2009 report pointed out to the fact that Indian law enforcement agencies do not have the necessary capacity to identify individuals who could be subjected to asset seizure and in tracing assets to be seized. The report further points out that the operative recommendations of the FATF on combating illicit finance, recommending a much larger group of predicate offences, including organised crime, fraud, smuggling and insider trading are not within the framework of these developments within India.

Interestingly, the 2009 report points out that in April 2002, India passed the Prevention of Terrorism Act (POTA), which criminalised terrorist financing, among other provisions. In March 2003, the Government of India (GOI) announced that it had charged 32 terrorist groups under POTA. In July 2003, the GOI arrested 702 persons under POTA. In November 2004, the report notes that due to "concerns that the overall law permitted overreaching police powers not related to the terrorist financing provisions, the Parliament repealed POTA." Simultaneously, the report notes that India amended the Unlawful Activities (Prevention) Act 1967 to include POTA's salient elements such as criminalisation of terrorist financing. The 2010 report, however, is silent on the issue of POTA.

The 2009 report notes that as part of the PMLA mandate, India's FIU was established in January 2006 to combat money laundering and terrorist financing. Over the last three years, the FIU has become fully operational and disseminates reports to law enforcement and intelligence agencies to investigate and prevent money laundering and curb financial crimes. Quoting the FIU's annual reports for 2007-08, the 2009 report points out that the FIU received more than 2,733 Suspicious Transaction Reports (STRs), of which about 1,396 were shared with the relevant law enforcement and intelligence agencies. Accordingly, income tax evasion has been readily detected in the STRs and has also led to the arrest of suspected terror operatives. According to the 2010 report, in 2008-09, the FIU received 4,409 STRs, of which, 2,450 were shared with the relevant law enforcement agencies.

The 2009 report seems to be satisfied with the efforts initiated by the Indian Government since October 2006, to reconcile its list of predicate crimes under the PMLA with that of FATF recommendations. Having made some progress towards that commitment, India gained FATF observer status in February 2007 with aspirations that in a two-year probationary period, it will adopt FATF core recommendations towards gaining full membership. India gained full-fledged membership in June 2010.

The key recommendations of the FATF evaluation of India as it was admitted to the membership of FATF are summarised as hereunder:

- Address the technical shortcomings in the criminalisation of both money laundering and terrorist financing and in the domestic framework of confiscation and provisional measures;
- Broaden the CDD obligations with clear and specific measures to enhance the current requirements regarding beneficial ownership;
- Improve the reliability of identification documents, the use of pooled accounts, PEPs, and non-face-to-face business; ensure that India Post, which recently became subject to the PMLA, effectively implements the AML/CFT requirements;
- Enhance the effectiveness of the STR reporting regime; enhance the effectiveness of the financial sector supervisory regime and ensure that India Post is adequately supervised;
- Ensure that the competent supervisory authorities make changes to their sanctioning regimes to allow for effective, proportionate and dissuasive sanctions for failures to comply with AML/CFT requirements.

On the functioning of the financial sector, the 2009 as well as the 2010 report note that the regulators involved viz., RBI, SEBI and IRDA have adopted anti-money laundering policies. SEBI has also issued a circular to all registered intermediaries on their obligations as financial institutions to prevent money laundering. This includes guidelines on maintaining records, preserving sensitive information with respect to certain transactions, and reporting suspicious cash flows and financial transactions to the FIU.

It may be noted that the report points out the inherent weakness in the functioning of SEBI. It points to the fact that there is no requirement that SEBI-regulated entities screen the collected KYC data, under the presumption that in any non-cash transaction, Indian banks have already screened the parties or, if coming from abroad, they have registered with SEBI as a foreign institutional investor. It is this Achilles' heel of the Indian financial system that continues to haunt the Indian authorities, especially SEBI, over the past few years. It is, thus, no surprise that the US Government makes a passing reference to the same.

On the issue of foreign contributions, the 2009 report points out to the fact that the Foreign Contributions Regulation Act of 1976 mandates any non-Governmental entity to register or request permission from the MHA (Ministry of Home Affairs) before receiving foreign donations. The Government requires registered entities to submit annual reports documenting foreign contributions and their use. Clearly not satisfied with the quality of monitoring on these remittances, the report goes on to elucidate that the regulations governing charities remain "antiquated." There are no guidelines or provisions governing the oversight of charities for AML/CTF purposes, and there is insufficient integration and coordination between charities' regulators and law enforcement authorities regarding the threat of terrorist finance.

In conclusion, the 2009 report as well as the 2010 report urge India to become:

- A party to the UN Convention Against Transnational Organised Crime.
- Ratify the UN Convention Against Corruption.
- Attain full-fledged membership of FATF. (Subsequently, as already pointed out, India gained full-fledged membership by June 2010.)

In short, what has been done by India till date to combat terrorism and take effective anti-money laundering steps is, by and large, ornamental. Much concrete work needs to be done. The world, while encouraging India to attain global standards on these issues, is actually worried. India, it may be noted, is a hotbed of terror activities, a centre of drug trafficking and a country with a high level of corruption. Naturally, a significant quantum of money gets laundered from India and such money invariably reaches the ultimate destinations. And all these channels invariably benefit terror outfits as they do other criminals. Obviously, the rest of the world is not amused by our responses in combating terror as well as taking effective anti-money laundering measures. We will seek to address these issues in greater detail in the final two chapters of this book. But first we will look into how our regulators – read watchdogs – have reacted to the developments in the capital markets during the past decade.

References

1. The Vienna Convention.
2. The Palermo Convention.
3. International Convention for the Suppression of the Financing of Terrorism.
4. Security Council Resolution 1373.
5. Security Council Resolution 1267 and Successors.
6. The Counter-Terrorism Committee.
7. The Forty Recommendations on Money Laundering, issued by the Financial Action Task Force on Money Laundering.
8. The Basel Committee on Banking Supervision of Statement of Principles on Money Laundering, Core Principles for Banking and Customer Due Diligence.
9. Declaration of the International Organisation of Securities Commissioners.
10. The Egmont Group of Financial Intelligence Units.
11. International Narcotics Control Strategy Report, 2009, issued by the US Department of State.
12. International Narcotics Control Strategy Report, 2010, issued by the US Department of State.
13. Financial Intelligence Unit – India Annual Report 2008-09.
14. FATF Mutual Evaluation Report (Anti-money Laundering and Combating the Financing of Terror) of India – June 25, 2010.

CHAPTER 5

When Watchdogs Sleep

When stock markets were rising, there was general lack of concern to see that such a rise should be in consonance with the integrity of the market and not the consequence of manipulation or other malpractice. On the other hand, when the markets went into a steep fall, there was concern all over. Such dissonance in the approach to issues of regulation and good governance needs to be replaced with effective regulation which concentrates on market integrity and investor protection, whether at any given point of time the market is buoyant or not.

— The report of the JPC on the stock market scam in 2001

Every morning in South India, hundreds of astrologers sit below a shade, usually a tree and predict the future of their "clients." Their tool is a caged parrot. The mechanism: the parrot, when allowed to come out of the cage, is trained to pick up one booklet from the many that the astrologer spreads out. And based on the clues printed in that particular booklet, the astrologer predicts the future of his clients. Mostly, the questions are predictable – problems relating to cash flows, business, finance, health, children and, of course, marriage. Years of experience have taught the astrologer to give non-standard yet satisfactory replies to these standard questions even to the most intelligent clients. Interesting, isn't it? Or is it mastery of the human psyche?

Cut to the metros. Every morning, across the country, commentators on stock markets begin their work as meticulously as the parrot-astrologers mentioned above, but with a crucial difference. Instead of the parrots, they use high-end computers, and instead of the unsophisticated printed booklets, they rely on sophisticated software. Crucially, they are programmed to talk only when the lights are on and the cameras begin to roll.

Expert Advisers, Anchor Investors and Market Analysts

"They" provide us a running commentary from morning till evening – nonstop for seven or eight hours. "The first hour is crucial." And if you thought that was a cricket commentator talking about the first hour of play, you are sadly mistaken. We are talking of stock market commentators. "Then the middle session is crucial" and, finally, "the final hour of trade is crucial." Little do these commentators realise that the trading beyond the first hour is as crucial as the last hour. Repeated use of the word crucial is aimed to titillate the viewer into believing that something crucial is happening. Crucial yes, but for whom?

They top this with further expert analysis which continues after the end of the day, right through the evening till late night. If you thought they were merely commentators, you are wrong. *They have a deeper and a far sinister agenda – of influencing the minds of the viewers and simultaneously manipulating the markets.* The idea is to obviously bamboozle viewers and ensure that they lose their ability to judge the markets. Reactions invariably arise instantly on every corporate announcement. Round the clock telecast allows every channel the luxury of "Breaking News" on events that are far too innocuous to warrant even a relook. But one does not blame them – twenty-four hours is too long a period in time.

Celebration or mourning of any news is determined by these experts. They can be bullish on one company and bearish on the other for the same reason. Notwithstanding such apparent contradictions, they are experts in conditioning the minds of their viewers. That facilitates them to make or break the market. That in effect is the power of the media at the end of the first decade of the twenty-first century in India.

This power of the media in conditioning the minds of the people was best captured by *Tono-Bungay,* a novel written exactly a century ago in 1909 by H. G. Wells. It is a realist semi-autobiographical novel, narrated by George Ponderevo, a science student who is drafted in to help with the promotion of Tono-Bungay, a harmful stimulant disguised as a miraculous cure-all, the creation of his ambitious uncle. As the tonic prospers, thanks to the power of the "media, advertisement and the resultant brand building" (do we not hear all these repeatedly even after a hundred years?), Ponderevo experiences a swift rise in social status, elevating him to riches and opportunities that he had never imagined, nor, indeed, desired. H. G. Wells, even a hundred years ago, had demonstrated in a spectacular fashion the power of the media in conditioning the minds of the people.

The character of the media has not yet changed even a wee bit for the past hundred years.

If you thought that these are hard-working experts who can be forgiven for their overzealousness, think again. These experts are anchors in front of the camera and possibly investors behind it. It is one link that cannot be forgotten. Virtually everyone has an agenda. Former SEBI Chairman Mr. M. Damodaran is reported to have famously remarked on the new phenomenon of an anchor-investor. In an interview (with senior Editor Mr. Shekhar Gupta in the Walk The Talk programme), he stated, "When we heard the term anchor-investors first, I thought an anchor-investor was the guy that brings in a lot of money initially into a project, around whose reputation others invest. I am beginning to believe at the end of my three-year tenure that an anchor-investor is one who is an anchor and an investor put together."

In that interview, Mr. Damodaran refers to a letter written by an aggrieved investor to the anchor of a widely viewed business channel (with a copy marked to several persons in the media as well as Mr. Damodaran himself). Mr. Damodaran said that he found merit in the investor's charge that the channel did not criticise the Reliance Power issue while it was open for subscription and found everything wrong with it once it was listed. Let us look at what the investor, Rakesh Mundra, wrote to the channel.

> *"I have been listening to your coverage of the Reliance Power IPO since it was launched on CNBC TV18. It is a sorry state of affairs that pre-IPO, there were hardly any negative remarks by you or any of the analysts, while suddenly post-issue/listing all of them turned negative, including you and your colleagues. On the contrary, when the issue got a huge response on the first hour/day you were all praising ADAG (Anil Dhirubhai Ambani) Group.*
>
> *Why don't you organise a debate among analysts and merchant bankers who have justified the premium for a meaningful analysis of the issue pricing? Prima facie almost all the investors are well aware that NTPC is a much better bet; if so, why did the merchant bankers and regulator (though legally, regulators may not have a say but they can always prevail) approve a price of Rs450.*
>
> *The merchant bankers are answerable to the whole country. As you are aware, almost five million people have applied to the issue, which is a sizeable population; if you add their dependants, it is in excess of 20 million, i.e., 2% of the urban population.*
>
> *What you are doing as of now is only asking analysts to give their point of view on the issue price. All are negative for obvious reasons. This is resulting in more selling pressure; consequently, the price is going down and harming the general public.*

> *The QIB portion to RPL was subscribed over 82 times and 446 QIBs had put in bids. They have allotment of over 15 crores shares (60% of the issue), you should find out who are these QIBs; and why have they subscribed at this price?*
>
> *As I understand, before investing, all QIBs have to complete in-house due-diligence and it goes through many channels before getting a final nod. How did they suddenly turn sellers on the first day of listing, that too below the issue price? In fact, in my opinion, it is a case for thorough investigation by the regulator and other agencies and if it comes out that the issue was overpriced or hype was created, the company should be asked to refund the money to all investors or at least they must refund the excess premium charged. This is nothing but daylight robbery. Is Mr Anil Ambani not accessible? I do expect a reply from you."*

Subsequently, Mr. Anil Ambani issued a statement demanding a SEBI investigation into the "vicious and orchestrated campaign of market manipulation and market abuse". Although he named no one, the target was clearly a rival corporate group. Crucially, what did SEBI do about the allegation contained in the letter of Mr. Mundra? Precious little. Or what did SEBI do about such anchor-investors? Virtually nothing. Or what did SEBI do about the role of the media in such cases? Absolutely nothing.

Little does SEBI realise that what happened during the run-up to and after the said IPO is market manipulation. If it was not, then what else was it? If this was not a fraud perpetuated by the media on the innocent investors, what was it? Was it not manipulation by some misusing their position as anchors, analysts and the power of the media to defraud millions of small investors? Inexplicably, despite the demand by the promoter of the company to carry out an investigation on these developments, SEBI has not carried out one. Why? Your guess is as good as mine.

When that can happen to one of India's largest business groups, one can realise the impact of the same for smaller corporates and small investors. In the process, "talking up" the prices of the shares of a corporate or "talking down" is as common as is taking sides in corporate wars. In fact, all these through the tacit silence of SEBI has now come to be accepted as market practices.

At the height of the stock market collapse in October 2008, even the Government of India was finding itself clueless to act against the loaded presentation of the global economic crisis. With the stock markets tumbling by the hour, media players had a field day. In a way, it was a self-fulfilling prophecy. The more they created panic in the minds of their viewers, the faster the markets collapsed. And that, in turn, triggered a further fall. The then finance minister had to intervene on several occasions before the media to address the concerns of the investors.

On October 13, 2008, Mr Chidambaram, given the virulence with which the media had begun to talk down the Indian economy, stated, "We must remain confident and respond to the situation in a cool and mature manner. We must banish fear. Especially, depositors have nothing to fear because their deposits in banks are safe. Investors must take informed decisions. Before you sell, you must remember that for every seller there is a buyer. You must ask yourself why the buyer is buying in these times of perceived uncertainty and, therefore, ask yourself the further question, whether there is a need to act in haste or in panic. In my view, there is no reason at all to act in haste or to give room for panic." It was obvious that the media was creating panic and even the Government of India was powerless to deal with such errant players.

It is rumoured that such market experts have positions in the market running into several hundred crores of rupees at any given point in time. Obviously, the only factor that determines the approach of these media, experts and anchor-investor for the day would be their positions, not the performance of the economy, policy initiative or for that matter, even the global economic crisis. Some are known to be in regular touch with the promoters. Some are known to fashion corporate announcements. Some go the "whole hog" to maximise their profits and are even alleged to force promoters into certain announcements to suit their positions.

The present disclosure norm followed by such experts is a huge sham. Mr. Damodaran puts the entire matter in clear perspective: "There are people who make statements that are very clear indications of talking up or talking down stocks. And what do we have by way of investor protection? A disclosure that says, is this person having a position in that stock? Earlier, we had statements like 'not really', 'may be', 'it's likely that my clients have'. Today, you get a broad spectrum such as, 'It is entirely possible that I have this.' Not even God can figure out what such a disclosure means.

All these may not exactly point out to a grand covert alliance between regulators and market manipulators. Nevertheless, the only way SEBI (or for that matter any other regulator) can disprove such rumours, which are getting shriller by the day, is by taking affirmative action against errant players. It needs to investigate the ugly nexus between the media and the markets. The sooner it does and clears the air, the better. But the billion dollar question is, will it? Again, my guess is as good as yours.

Bamboozling Viewers 24/7

In this sinister world of twenty-four by seven news channels, the business of the media is distinct from the media's business interests. Talk shows, analysis, chat shows, interviews, comments and all other sundry programmes in these channels invariably have a latent commercial aspect to the same. News is secondary, collateral and incidental. Manipulation of stock markets for personal as well as business gains is rumoured to be the main objective.

These experts understand the fundamental human psyche far better than other professionals with the sole exception of the parrot astrologer. They know the proclivity of businessmen (as of their viewers) to make quick money. They understand the power of greed. They also love the publicity weakness of businessmen. They love viewers who suspend their sense of disbelief. Such people are perfect lambs to be led to the slaughter. In fact, they encourage them to dream big, bigger and better. After all, when you dream, it is money for them. Only the extremely lucky escape from the heady brew that they concoct.

Their fundamental *mantra* is to constantly refer to the corporate earnings before depreciation, interest, tax and appropriation – popularly jargonised as EBDITA margins. They can choose to term a 4 per cent variation as serious or dismiss a 40 per cent deviation as immaterial. For them, short-term is "a few minutes" and long-term is "a few hours". And they have the innate ability to link everyone from Obama, Iraq, oil, Pakistan, Taliban, global cues, fiscal deficits, appreciation and depreciation of the rupee, interest rates – for that matter anything and everything. Cause and effect can be turned upside down to suit their arguments. In the process, the differences between the two get blurred.

But if you still understand what they do, they will continue to confuse you by talking endlessly in terms of IRR, cash flows, MAT, dividend tax, tax-shield, leverage buyouts, takeover codes, open positions, fiscal deficits, etc so as to flummox anyone. For a break, there could be some exotic ideas like corporate governance, accounting standards, IFRS, XBRL, derivative positions, mergers and acquisitions little realising the disconnect between the picture they paint and the reality.

If you still manage to survive the same, they have some of the most exotic technical analysis which perhaps not even almighty can comprehend. Technical charts are all encompassing. The managements of most corporates waste millions of precious man-hours to check and recheck all they say as if it is the Bible, Koran and Veda all rolled into one. In the alternative, they can convert a subjective debate into an objective one, or an advertisement into "breaking news," or negative news into positive news. Little do viewers realise that they chuckle in front of you and have a hearty laugh behind you!

The earnings per share of 30 companies that determine the BSE index aggregates to approximately Rs 1,000. They multiply the same with a Price Earning (PE, which is their Holy Grail) multiple of say 12 or 15 or even 21 to arrive at the BSE index. Much of all this is voodoo economics. When it is a bull market, they point to markets that have a higher multiple and justify such higher prices. When it is a bear market, they point out to markets with lower PE multiples to justify the market prices of shares. Remember, comment in every programme is intended for their possible commerce and gain.

But what is surprising is that despite what they blatantly do, it remains beyond the radar of any regulator, notably SEBI. Consequently, as a class, they remain uncritiqued, unexamined and uninvestigated. And should that happen at all, the stench emanating from such investigation would be unbearable. No wonder, as the cliché goes, what is obvious is usually the most oblivious. This allows these experts, like the astrologer in the streets of South India, to endlessly play on the psyche of men and their greed.

Let us not forget that the media is often referred to as the fourth pillar in a democracy. It has a much larger role to play in the context of the nation's development. The degradation of moral values in any country is often linked to the fall in the moral values of the media. India is no different. The fall in the moral values of the media actually precedes the fall in the morality of a nation. One fears that media is no longer a watchdog in our democracy. Quite the contrary, it is feared that it is increasingly getting programmed by vested interests for command performances. With the fear of the media no longer remaining, stock markets will be increasingly prone to manipulation.

This is what happens when the watchdogs fail to perform their duty.

Private Treaties and Public Menace

But if you thought that this phenomenon of influencing markets and carrying out market manipulation is limited to the electronic media, think again. The print media does it equally brazenly but with a different model. The print media houses of late have entered into contracts with corporate houses. Interestingly, this is marketed as a "business strategy" under a novel concept of "Private Treaties" (PTs). PTs are commercial agreements between media houses and corporates, linking the business interests of both through advertisements and equity. What is interesting in this contract is that the corporates allot shares to the media houses. In consideration, the media houses allow advertisement space for the corporates. As someone famously remarked, the business of the media is different from the media's business interest. In the process, the Chinese walls observed by the media between advertisement and editorial in the past have virtually collapsed. On their ruins, we have a new concept of 'advertorial'.

The *Times* Group, one of India's well-known media houses of repute, rationalises PTs as an open brand building exercise. Fascinatingly, several of its competitors who found fault with the *Times* Group for this business strategy, later on began adopting the same model with missionary zeal. Only the contractual terms varied. So did the parties. But not the idea. Is not imitation the best form of flattery?

Competitors even accused the others of using editorials as part of the deal. This is neither confirmed nor denied. Needless to emphasise, on account of shares acquired through PTs, "positive coverage" of corporates is assured. Negative news is tactically shunned. The seeming success of PTs has led competing media houses to embrace and deploy the model. The *Times* Group claims to have entered into over 200 deals worth USD 700 million (Rs 3,500 crores) in the past few years.

In an article on the ethics of PTs, Ms. Sucheta Dalal, one of India's well known and widely respected journalists, has quoted from a 2007 letter from Rahul Joshi, editor of the *Economic Times* to his colleagues: "At ET, we are carving out a separate team to look into the needs of Private Treaty clients. Every large centre will have a senior editorial person to interface with Treaty clients. In turn, the senior edit person will be responsible, along with the existing team, for edit delivery. In this way, we will be able to incorporate PT into the editorial mainstream, rather than it looking like a series of press releases appearing in vanilla form in the paper."

Explaining the idea of brand building through PTs, a presentation available on the *Times* Group Web site explains the idea through a rhetorical set of questions. How do you invest in building a brand and manage cash flows at the same time? How do you convince the cold-blooded accounting department that brand equity can perhaps be your single biggest asset? And yes, where's the money going to come from? Seeking to answer these questions, the power point presentation states, "We invest in the long-term potential of your brand. We believe that strong products and services, when branded right, have the power to transcend their natural growth paths and turbo-charge their balance sheets." It would seem that branding can come about only through advertisement in the media and that too with the *Times*. Such positioning by the media would not have been possible even a decade back. But today it is the in thing.

How much have the *Times* changed?

Proudly claiming that over "200 companies are on our roster," the presentation adds, "We believe in partnering ideas because every brand was once an idea and every idea has the potential to be a brand. We believe in brand building and that is why we are more than willing to ride their downside as well." Well, PT is now a brand by itself. Others in the media have simply latched on to it.

Dwelling further on the idea of brand building – an idea that requires enormous and sustained financial investments – the presentation points out that advertising is a key pillar and an intrinsic component of the brand building process. This, it explains, is the eternal conflict between advertising and other critical resources in terms of fund allocation. The power point presentation seeks to resolve this dilemma: "Private Treaties, a unique model from the *Times* Group empowers fast-growing organisations to create, build and nurture their brand through increased advertising by leveraging their company equity in lieu of cash payments." The operative words are leveraging advertisement through equity. Or is it leveraging equity investments through advertisement?

Ms Sucheta Dalal sums up the issue brilliantly when she states, "Media insiders know that the power of the advertising buck effectively blocks objective coverage, especially by those who have the most to gain."

The salient features of PTs are mentioned below:

- For every advertisement released in the media, the media company will bill only a portion of the advertising cost (which will be settled through cash) while the balance (which is usually the substantial portion) will be allocated towards the PT deal.
- The media company would subscribe to share warrants in the company equal to the value of amount allocated to the PT deal. The share warrants would be converted into shares at a predetermined date and at a preset price or in a predetermined manner.

Obviously, investment in PTs turns positive if and only if the advertiser's stock performance is positive, which thus means that the success of PTs is intrinsically linked to the success of their clients. While there is nothing illegal about the contract, what needs to be factored in the context of the present discussions is that PTs are a potential source of misrepresentation in the markets.

Yet media houses claim that they have created perfect Chinese walls to maintain the integrity of their editorials. "As a concept, it (Private Treaties) is an innovative and aggressive prescription" says Shekhar Gupta, the editor-in-chief of The *Indian Express*. "But, given the commitment made to the (investee) companies in such deals that you will promote them and build consumer and investor confidence around them, it is challenging to keep the editorial integrity." Challenging to keep the editorial integrity? Well, that could be putting things mildly.

What is to be noted here is that other large media publications viz., *Hindustan Times*, NDTV, *Dainik Bhaskar* and Network18 are some of the leading media houses that are reported to have entered or are in the process of entering into PTs with corporates. Which means that for every news item published, especially positives ones, one has to perhaps factor for a possible PT link between the corporate and the media house. In the case of the negative ones, it is quite possible that it is a competitor at war – competitor of one corporate using another media house. Or it could be media houses at war, with corporates only used as a referral point. Or it could be promoters at war with each other, using the markets and media as a battlefield. Either way, the potential for mischief is enormous. And with each passing day, with several rumours doing the rounds in the gossip mill, the credibility of the media is increasingly at stake.

This mischief came to the forefront when in December 2008, a fake order, purported to be written by SEBI, was circulated by some unscrupulous persons using a (forged?) letterhead of SEBI. The fake order directed one of the promoters of the company to give an open offer to purchase 20 per cent of the company's shares from the public at Rs 250 per share. The company in question allegedly had a PT with the *Times* Group. Subsequent investigation into the matter by SEBI, no less, exposed the dark underbelly of the PT. One of the persons accused of fabrication and dissemination of the said forged letter by SEBI happened to be an assistant editor of the *Economic Times*.

Following investigations, SEBI found that the forgery was done primarily to manipulate the stock price of the said company and one of the directors of the company was alleged to be one of the major beneficiaries of the said fake order. The assistant editor of the *Economic Times* was alleged to have played a key role in the dissemination of the fake order which led to the increase in the prices of the company's share till SEBI declared the order to be a fake one. That was in December 2008. And till June 2010, SEBI has been unable to figure out who committed the forgery.

It is interesting to note that despite all this, only one TV anchor till date has been directed by SEBI to "cease and desist" from recommending any investment in the public media. More often than not, persons attached to the media, electronic and print, get away by violating the PFUTP regulations of SEBI (Prohibition of Fraudulent and Unfair Trade Practices related to the securities market), 2003. Either these regulations do not apply to the media (which is not the case as per my understanding) or SEBI simply does not seek to punish such errant persons within the media.

To restore the credibility of the media as well its own as a regulator, it is time that SEBI suggests an appropriate regulation for the media in general, and anchor-investors in particular, and the manner in which they have to make disclosures. Else both will end up being "laughing stocks."

ICAI: A Watchdog That Refuses to Bark or Bite

The fetish to consider a rise in the stock markets as conclusive evidence of the performance of the economy is peculiar to very few countries. India is one of them. Likewise, a fall in the stock markets spells doom across the country. This is all the more peculiar considering the fact that a miniscule portion (less than 3 percent) of our population is directly linked to the stock markets. Further, it is estimated that the companies listed in the Indian bourses contribute less than 10 percent to our GDP. All this does not mean that the stock exchange in India can be dispensed with. Rather, these statistics are pointers to the importance of the stock markets in the overall Indian context.

Yet, consider this pearl from the official journal of a leading professional institute from India: "The Indian stock market today has the potential to lift all boats across the entire social spectrum of the country and this potential needs to be exploited to the fullest if the Government wants to realise the dream of reducing the poverty rate to single digits."

Nowhere in the world is the stock market capable of addressing the issue of poverty nor is it considered to be capable of lifting all the boats across the social spectrum. Surely, somebody has mixed developmental economics with the stock market and passed it off as an original thought. All that is stated here is not from the research paper of an amateur economist. Neither is it Captain Haddock, speaking in his usual inebriated stage. Nor is this another typical gaffe of an uninformed politician. One may be stunned to know that this is the editorial comment – yes, editorial comment – of the official journal of the Institute of Chartered Accountants of India (ICAI) in its December 2007 issue.

If you thought that this was an unintended slip, please have a rethink. The editorial continues with its usual dose of rambling "With the Sensex having crossed the so far unheard of 20,000 mark recently, the burgeoning Indian capital market is making waves across the globe, indicating the boom time and bright future prospects of the country's economy." Burgeoning capital markets? Boom time? Bright future prospects for the country? Well nothing could have been more hilarious than this editorial in the Journal of the ICAI.

The ICAI's crude attempt to provide comic relief to its readers through its editorial does not stop there. The same editorial states in the first paragraph, "The Indian stock market is no real guide to the economy and that is why serious economists do not take it seriously." Pray, why such senseless references to stock markets in the following paragraph? If stock markets are not to be taken seriously, how could they then lift all the boats across the social spectrum? How is this to be linked to the statement that stock markets are to be fully exploited to reduce poverty to single digits? Why not milk the stock markets a bit more and reduce poverty rates to zero?

While the editorial provides further comic relief, let me stop here. There seems to be a fatal flaw in our approach to stock markets. When it comes to the bourses, invariably intellectuals in this country become incoherent. Interestingly, since that editorial by the ICAI in December 2007, the Sensex, along with its global peers, tumbled down dramatically beginning January 2008. So much for the ability of the ICAI, the premier accounting body of the country to understand, foresee and articulate economics. But to the eternal credit of the ICAI, it is not seen in isolation on this matter. In fact, it has illustrious company on this particular issue.

This editorial comment of the ICAI on its understanding of stock markets is the smaller order of the smalls. It has a larger role in the orderly functioning of the capital markets. The spate of scandals that rocked the Indian stock markets recently has brought the role of the ICAI into sharp focus. To understand the same, a reference to the powers conferred by the Chartered Accountants Act on the ICAI is inevitable. The ICAI is a statutory body established under the Chartered Accountants Act, 1949, for the regulation of the profession of accounting and auditing in India. The institute is the premier accounting body in the country. The ICAI has been involved in the fields of education, professional development, prescribing as well as maintaining accounting, auditing and ethical standards.

The total membership of the institute is about 150,000 and over 650,000 students are pursuing the chartered accountancy course. Out of the total members, it is estimated that approximately 50 per cent are in active practice. What makes a practising member of the ICAI so special is that any financial statement attested by him becomes "audited" in the eyes of the law. Naturally, the functions of the ICAI become crucial in ensuring that its members in practice carry out the attesting functions by maintaining the strict professional standards prescribed by it.

What if a member fails to carry out his duties diligently? What if he attests his signature to financial statements wrongly, knowingly or unknowingly? This is where the ICAI as a regulator of the accounting profession steps in. The ICAI has put in place a disciplinary mechanism to ensure compliance of professional ethics and a code of conduct as prescribed by it. The provisions contained in the code of conduct of the institute are theoretically the most stringent ones as compared to any other in the world. The actions taken by the ICAI against the defaulting members are also very stringent. There are hardly a few cases, (some seniors in the profession 'vouch' for this) where the Indian courts have taken more stringent action against the members than what is proposed by the institute. On the other hand, there are a number of cases where the courts have reduced the punishment prescribed by the ICAI. The institute not only entertains complaints from an affected party but also takes *suo moto* action in cases which come to its knowledge through external information.

But all this comes to play provided the ICAI takes action in the first place. That happens more often than not when it involves youngsters and minor infractions of the law. Then it goes about trumpeting about its role as a stringent regulator. When the courts knock down the punishment, it maintains a stoic silence. But what is unknown to many is that the ICAI is known to stonewall when the issue concerns the biggies of the profession. The time taken for the adjudication of any disciplinary case is extraordinary, especially if it involves the high and mighty of the Indian audit fraternity. However, recently, the ICAI has brought about a number of changes to its disciplinary mechanism so as to expedite the same. One needs to wait for a few more years to find out whether it would be a classical case of old wine in a new bottle or not.

While laws, rules and regulations can be changed, what cannot be changed is the attitude of an institution. Nothing illustrates better the attitude of the ICAI in protecting the big daddies of the accounting profession than its reply to the JPC contained in the ATR submitted to the Parliament in May 2003. Mercifully, the ICAI accepts the fact that it was "aware" of the 17 cases listed by the previous JPC investigating the 1991 scam. Apart from these 17, the ICAI had also identified 48 other entities based on other reports such as the Janakiraman Report. The status with regard to these 65 entities is as follows:

1. Filed on *prima facie* stage – 35 (a decade later, i.e. in 2003 the Council of the ICAI was still to decide beyond this stage).
2. Referred to Disciplinary Committee – 30.

   Of which:

   - Number of entities where the respondents are exonerated (at the Council level) – 13.
   - Number of entities in which there is punishment (at the Council level) – 06 (this has to go to the courts for confirmation where a few more could possibly get exonerated).
   - Pending with Disciplinary Committee – 02.

- Pending with Council for consideration of Disciplinary Committee Report – 09.

This was the status approximately ten years after the previous scam. If this is the state of affairs in the ICAI on matters relating to the disciplinary issues concerning only a very small section of our society, why then do we blame the judiciary for extraordinary delays?

Let us now return to the 2001 scam. In the context of this scam, the JPC had drawn the attention of the RBI to the functioning of the Global Trust Bank (GTB) in its report. The report, as one may recall, was made public in December 2002. The charges against GTB in the said JPC report were:

- It funded the stock market operations of Mr. Ketan Parekh which subsequently turned bad.
- It allowed Mr. Ketan Parekh to open several accounts and carry out huge transactions with some of the OCBs having a meagre paid up capital of USD 550 to 5,000, for pumping a substantial amount of money into the stock market.

The JPC directed the RBI to enquire into the role of the auditors on these matters. The first ATR of May 2003 cryptically commented, "As regards any dereliction of duty on the part of the Bank Auditors, the matter has already been brought to the notice of ICAI by RBI." Then for the next couple of years, there was complete silence on this matter. One suspects, especially given how the facts unfold subsequently, that the ICAI was doing its bit to protect the auditor in question.

As fate would have it, on July 24, 2004, the RBI placed a three-month moratorium on the deposits and loans of GTB. This was the first time a new generation private sector bank had gone bust. That brought the role of the auditors of GTB into sharper focus for the first time. And as it happens in all such cases, it brought back the charges made out by the JPC. The past, it seemed had caught up finally with GTB and its auditors.

Unending Progress

Subsequently, the bi-annual "progress" reports to the ATR of the JPC were silent till July 2005. The July 2005 progress report presented to the Parliament by the Finance Ministry stated that ICAI informed the ministry that they had called for the comments of the auditors concerned on February 25, 2005. The auditors for the years 2001-02 and 2002-03, in turn, had sent in their respective responses dated May 20, 2005 which were received by the ICAI on May 24, 2005.

In the said response, the auditors "categorically" stated that since the RBI has not provided the relevant Annual Financial Inspection(s) and the basis/ parameters adopted by the special auditors and has also restrained the ICAI from parting with the Special Audit Report for perusal, they are not in a position to offer any view/explanation thereon. So the matter was referred back to the RBI. The volleyball match was in full steam.

Taking forward the matter, the December 2005 Progress Report noted that the documents sought by the auditors for submission of their respective explanation were received by the ICAI from the RBI on August 4, 2005, and the same were forwarded on August 5, 2005, to the auditors with stipulations that their explanations/comments should reach the ICAI by August 31, 2005. The respective respondent-firms furnished their explanation/comments vide their letter dated September 15 and September 10, 2005, respectively and the same was being examined and processed by the ICAI. Note the extent of "progress" being made.

The May 2006 Progress Reports states, "ICAI have informed that they are hopeful to complete the exercise shortly."

Then comes the Progress Report in December 2006 which informs us that the ICAI have informed that based on the examination of "latest inputs" received from the Oriental Bank of Commerce, along with the earlier papers received from the RBI, special auditors, clarifications of the statutory auditors and other documents, a finality has been reached and show cause notice(s) have been issued to the concerned auditors. Extraordinary progress, one must admit!

The May 2007 Progress Report states that the ICAI have informed that replies had been received and the matter would be placed before the Council in its next meeting, scheduled to be held in the month of June 2007. Look at the progress being made at a glacial pace several years after a scam takes place. And note that this is on a matter that the JPC had mandated subsequent investigation.

The December 2007 Progress Report tells us that the matters relating to all the three years i.e. 2000-01, 2001-02 and 2002-03 have been considered by the Council at its meeting held between August 16 and 18, 2007 for its *prima facie* opinion and the Council has referred all these matters to the Disciplinary Committee for enquiry. The matters have been fixed for hearing by the Disciplinary Committee scheduled to be held between December 13 and 15, 2007. Wonderful progress!

The May 2008 Progress Report states that at the meeting held on December 13, 2007, the RBI, which was cited as one of the witnesses in these matters, had sought adjournment on the grounds that they needed time to send the documents, and the Disciplinary Committee adjourned these matters to April 22 and 23, 2008.

During the hearing on April 22, 2008, the auditors requested the committee that they require 30 to 45 days time for submitting their working papers which are quite voluminous in number. After considering the request of the auditors, the Disciplinary Committee, on grounds of "natural justice", gave the "last opportunity" to the auditors to present their defence and, consequently, adjourned the hearing.

Further "progress" is reported in December 2008. The hearing for the matter relating to the year 2000-01 took place on August 1, 2008, at Mumbai and the same was concluded on that day itself. The auditors were requested to send certain documents as directed by the Disciplinary Committee at the time of the hearing and the same have been received from them. The report of the Disciplinary Committee is under preparation.

Well, this is called treadmill progress – where there is seemingly tremendous activity but nothing concrete emerges. The answer to that is not far to seek. The auditors in question were M/s Lovelock & Lewes, Chartered Accountants, Kolkata (for the year 2000-01) and M/s Price Waterhouse & Co., Chartered Accountants, Kolkata (for 2002-03). According to press reports, RBI blocked the reappointment of Lovelock & Lewes (ostensibly, it was not satisfied with the quality of work) as auditors of GTB and went on to confirm the appointment of M/s Price Waterhouse & Co as auditors of GTB in 2002-03. The remarkable coincidence in the entire appointment is that both Lovelock & Lewes as well as Price Waterhouse & Co are the Indian audit arms of the global audit major Price WaterhouseCoopers (PWC), with possible common partners between them and open sharing of common infrastructure and other facilities.

It may not be out of place to mention that two members of the Council of the ICAI, the apex decision-making body, were partners of firms affiliated to PWC during the entire process. So much for corporate governance within the ICAI!

Is that why these investigations got delayed? Your guess is as good as mine. Regarding matters relating to the years 2001-02 and 2002-03, the matter was adjourned to October 6 and 7, 2008 at Mumbai. On October 6, 2008, the matter was part heard and adjourned to November 8, 2008.

For the first time, the June 2009 Progress Report reported some *real progress* on this matter. It confirmed that the hearing in the matter(s) relating to the years 2000-01 and 2001-02 has been concluded by the Disciplinary Committee and the said reports included in the agenda of the Council Meeting for its final consideration. If these reports are accepted by the Council, the Progress Report points out, it would be recommending the punishment to the High Court for its final approval. Well, after eight long years, the first hurdle was cleared in this matter. Now if you thought things would be smooth from now on, have a rethink. For what is to follow is far more bizarre.

On matters relating to 2002-03, the Progress Report points out that the hearing was concluded on 23.03.09 by the Disciplinary Committee of the ICAI. Thereafter, the auditors had filed a Writ Petition before the Hon'ble High Court of Bombay. The Hon'ble High Court has passed its orders and the same are under consideration by the Disciplinary Committee for further course of action.

But that is not all. In another extraordinary level of coincidence, the managing partner of Price Waterhouse was arrested in an altogether different issue – the Satyam computers imbroglio in January 2009. Obviously, no further hearing could be held in the said case! Thanks to these developments, the Government of India was saved further embarrassment of reporting further progress in its June 2009 Progress Report. We will revert to the Satyam imbroglio shortly where a different technique was adopted to diffuse the matter. Now let us once again continue our grand affair with the auditors of GTB and their disciplinary proceedings within the ICAI.

The clock ticks on and the Government is forced to table the next Progress Report in December 2009, irrespective of the progress or action taken. But there was more than the usual share of progress in this Progress Report.

This Progress Report points out that in the matter relating to the year 2000-01, the hearing by the Council post submission of the report of the Disciplinary Committee was originally fixed in the months of March and April 2009. However, as an adjournment request from the auditors were received and acceded, this matter was included in the agenda of the August 2009 Council Meeting. In the said meeting, the auditors, namely, Mr. P. Ramakrishna and Mr. Manish Agarwal requested for further adjournment on the ground that their partner, Mr. S. Gopalakrishnan (who was incarcerated in the Satyam imbroglio since January 2009) was not available. Consequently, the Council adjourned the matter for the last time and further directed the office to have a copy of the Disciplinary Committee Report served on Mr. S. Gopalakrishnan in the jail which was duly served on him in the jail.

Accordingly, the said report of the Disciplinary Committee would be placed before the Council at its next meeting to be held on December 16 and 17, 2009.

With reference to the hearing relating to the year 2002-03, things get far more complicated. The Progress Report points out that the auditors had filed a Writ Petition in the Hon'ble High Court of Bombay and the Hon'ble High Court vide its order dated April 16, 2009, had given certain directions to the Disciplinary Committee. In compliance with the directions of the Hon'ble High Court of Bombay, the Disciplinary Committee passed its Speaking Order dated July 8, 2009, and the same was informed to the auditors vide the institute's letter dated July 18, 2009, in which fresh date (s) of the hearing were also intimated to them i.e. on August 20 and 21, 2009, at Mumbai.

On receipt of the notice fixing the hearing in the month of August 2009, the auditors again raised certain issues relating to the enquiry, which were clarified. In furtherance to that, the Progress Report states that the auditors moved the Hon'ble High Court in the month of August 2009 and the same came up for hearing on August 15, 2009 (one is not sure how a hearing could have come up on August 15), wherein the Hon'ble High Court directed the Disciplinary Committee to give all the documents which were relied upon by the Disciplinary Committee against the auditors within two weeks' time.

In compliance with the order of the Hon'ble High Court of Mumbai, all the documents were provided to the auditors. Yet, all the documents as received from the witnesses i.e. Reserve Bank of India and the Special Auditors, were sent once again to the auditors and notices were issued for the next date of the hearing, to be held on of September 16 and 17, 2009. The said notice was issued on August 25, 2009, to the auditors, including the witnesses. The auditors moved a contempt petition in the Hon'ble High Court of Bombay against the Disciplinary Committee of the institute on September 9, 2009. The said matter came for hearing on September 11, 2009, for which a short adjournment was sought and the same came up for hearing on September 15, 2009.

It was brought to the notice of the Hon'ble High Court that all the documents as received from the witnesses had already been given to the auditors and the letter to the said effect had also been sought from the Reserve Bank of India which was placed before the Hon'ble High Court. Once again, all the documents which were earlier provided to the auditors, were again given to them before the Hon'ble High Court. The said hearing in the matter was again postponed which was scheduled to be held on of September 16 and 17, 2009, on the directions of Hon'ble High Court. The Progress Report points out that the next date of hearing in the said matter was fixed on January 15 and 16, 2010. We will revert to this disciplinary matter shortly.

The Satyam Link to the Stock Market Scam of 2001

There is yet another interesting dimension to this entire issue. The JPC as early as in its report in December 2002, urged SEBI, the Department of Company Affairs and other investigative agencies to expedite and complete their investigations into the involvement of promoters/corporate houses in the manipulation of prices of certain scrips which were found to have undergone unusual volatility. One of the companies listed for such investigation was M/s Satyam Computers Limited, yes, the infamous Satyam Computers.

Now look into the progress made on this account. Till December 2008, nothing is heard about this company or the progress made on investigating this company. For ten Progress Reports till 2008, the government forgot Satyam and its promoters. Suddenly, the December 2008 Progress Report stirs the entire issue. The December 2008 Progress Report had this to state, "Investigations completed. Complaint filed by I.O. for contravention of provisions of FEMA is under consideration for issuance of SCN." Suddenly, after six long years after the JPC report, the investigations for FEMA violations are complete. Yet, the Government is contemplating issue of the Show Cause Notice (SCN). Remember, when the Government contemplates some minor action on an issue, it is usually stated that the matter is under "active" consideration. And when a government seeks to brush things under the carpet, it simply states that the matter is under consideration. In the case of Satyam, it was merely a case of consideration and not active consideration.

What follows is even more inexplicable. The July 2009 Progress Report states that the proposed SCN was not issued in this case due to the "recent developments" in the detection of fraudulent export documentation adopted by the company over the years. This had cast serious doubts on the extent of actual export proceeds outstanding. Hence, the matter was reported as being looked into afresh. Six years of labour had yielded zilch. It is indeed a pathetic state of affairs that Satyam could hoodwink the RBI for six years despite a FEMA investigation being carried on against it for as much time. Or was the entire investigation a sham in the first place? But surprises never cease. Do they?

The December 2009 Progress Report adds, "As reported earlier, the extent of actual export proceeds pending realisation is now being reconfirmed in the light of the allegation of fraudulent exports documentation in the charge-sheet filed by CBI. Fresh enquiries are under way." Obviously, the Government does not want to comment anything afresh on the convoluted subject of Satyam.

In another interesting coincidence, Mr. Krishna G. Palepu, an acknowledged specialist in corporate governance, was on the Board of both GTB and Satyam Computers. Both had accounting scams. Interestingly, and in another remarkable coincidence, both companies were audited by the same audit firm. Both GTB and Satyam were indicted by the JPC. The GTB was accused by the JPC of funding stock market operations in gross violations of RBI norms. Similarly, the promoters of Satyam Computers were suspected by the JPC of manipulating prices in the stock markets by violating FEMA. An investigation went on for six long years and yielded practically nothing. All of them operated well before and after the JPC report of 2002, without any let or fear. Every regulator seemed to play ball with them subsequently. Even when they went belly up, efforts were made to bail them out by the Government (both the GTB and Satyam were bailed out by the Government). The ICAI, as can been seen, is playing its part by going soft on their auditors.

But GTB and Satyam are not the only ones named by the JPC. In fact, there are several companies, promoters, banks, auditors who have been named by the JPC and continue to operate without any regulatory restraint, fear or investigation. Of course, Progress Reports of the Finance Ministry have repeatedly pointed to some "progress" or the other against these companies and their promoters. But the progress, as we repeatedly saw above, was specious.

But the "efforts" of the regulator do not end here. Interestingly, the press note leading to the appointment of the inspection officer under the SEBI Act issued by SEBI on January 7, 2009, states *inter alia*, that SEBI had "ordered an investigation into the affairs relating to buying, selling or dealing in the shares of Satyam Computer Services." Further the order of the proceedings of the whole time member appointing the investigating officer states, "The Securities and Exchange Board of India (the Board) is satisfied that it is in the interest of investors and public interest to investigate into the affairs relating to buying, selling or dealing in the shares of Satyam Computer Services Ltd and more particularly to ascertain whether the provisions of the SEBI Act, 1992, and following Rules and Regulations made thereunder have been violated."

What is crucial to note here is that the Board is "satisfied" to investigate into the affairs of the M/s Satyam. But under Section 11 C of the SEBI Act, an investigating officer can be appointed only when the Board has "reasonable grounds to believe" that the emergent situation warrants the appointment of an investigating officer to investigate the state of affairs. To a lay reader, the difference between "satisfied" and "reasons to believe" may perhaps sound like an empty exercise in semantics.

But in the eyes of the law, it is not. The Hon'ble Supreme Court in S Ganga Saran and Sons (P) Limited Calcutta Vs Income Tax Officer (1981 AIR 1363) in a similar circumstance (but under the Income Tax Act) went on to explore the difference between the two. The court observed, "The important words under

Section 147(a) are 'has reason to believe' and these words are stronger than the words 'is satisfied'. The belief entertained by the Income Tax Officer must not be arbitrary or irrational. It must be reasonable or in other words, it must be based on reasons which are relevant and material. The court, of course, cannot investigate into the adequacy or sufficiency of the reasons which have weighed with the Income Tax Officer in coming to the belief, but the court can certainly examine whether the reasons are relevant and have a bearing on the matters in regard to which he is required to entertain the belief before he can issue notice under Section 147(a). If there is no rational and intelligible nexus between the reasons and the belief, so that, on such reasons no one properly instructed on facts and law could reasonably entertain the belief."

In short, satisfaction is subjective and abhorred by law and reason to believe is objective and is the cornerstone of modern administrative law. Consequently, forget the investigation on this matter by SEBI, even the SCN of SEBI surviving a cursory glance of the higher courts looks doubtful. Obviously, SEBI seems to be engineered to come second best in such circumstances.

The question remains: Why was the Finance Ministry silent all along? Why is SEBI silent? Why did the RBI's investigation mechanism fail all along when the promoters of Satyam were fooling investors? Why did the ICAI keep quiet for over five years before it began acting against the auditors of GTB?

The Progress Report of May 2010

The Progress Report of May 2010 forgets the previous SCN under FEMA completely and now points out that the CBI's investigations in the accounts forgery case revealed as many as 7,561 fictitious invoices. Since, a substantial portion of the company's income was against exports, the veracity of the exports is being examined to arrive at the correct amount of export proceeds which are actually outstanding. On completion of these investigations, we are informed, the necessary Show Cause Notice under FEMA would be issued. Well that may take several years from now.

As regards the disciplinary case of the auditors of GTB pending with the ICAI, the Progress Report points out that the Council of ICAI accepted the Report of the Disciplinary Committee (2000-01) with respect to Chartered Accountant (CA) P. Rama Krishna and held the respondent guilty of professional misconduct falling within the meaning of Clauses (6), (7), (8) & (9) of Part I of the Second Schedule to the Chartered Accountants Act, 1949 and recommended to the concerned High Court that his name be removed for five years from the list of members. Thereafter, he has filed a Writ Petition in the Hon'ble Delhi High Court. A counter affidavit has been filed by the institute and the respondent has sought time from the court to file a rejoinder and, accordingly, the case was listed for hearing on April 12, 2010 and no further progress has been received.

What is missed out by the Progress Report is that on April 16, 2010, the Hon'ble Delhi High Court quashed the decision of the council on technical grounds (W.P. (C) No. 1721 of 2010 and C.M. No. 3432 of 2010) that the ICAI had all along followed a wrong procedure. The court ordered that the proceedings against the auditors will now recommence under the amended Section 21 of the CA Act before the Director (Discipline) who will proceed in the matter in terms of what is stated in the said order and in accordance with the amended CA Act and CA Rules. To compound the misery of the ICAI, the court ordered the costs of Rs. 10,000 to be paid by the ICAI within a period of four weeks.

The efforts of the past several years have come to naught! Once again, the matter has to be heard afresh under the new procedure. Several years will pass and perhaps by that time, the horses may well fly. For other two years (2001-02) and (2002-03) the volleyball match continues...

Well, watchdogs in the Indian context refuse to bark. But pray why?

When Watchdogs are Ideologically Silenced

To answer these questions, a reference to the JPC report of 2001 is inevitable once again. "There was some vague idea about this, but they were not under our control." "They" referred to the Participatory Notes (PNs). But who is the person who has only some vague idea about this? "There was no means of knowing it," he adds. "They are not issued in India. They are extra-territorial documents. We do not have any control over that." "They" once again referred to PNs. But who is the person speaking? Who is "we?" The answers to these questions are illuminating in the context of the manner in which India is administered. It may be recalled that the JPC went into the stock market scam of 2001 and investigated matters relating thereto. During the course of its investigation, it chose to enquire from SEBI about the practice of FIIs issuing PNs. "We" refers to SEBI, and the person answering the question was no less than the then SEBI chairman.

It did not, therefore, come as a surprise that on the JPC's investigations into the stock scam in 2001, SEBI reported that more than 80 per cent of OCBs were registered in Mauritius. If that was astounding, the JPC was further startled to note that some of them seemed to act as a front for promoters of certain Indian companies. All this when the JPC noted that SEBI's attempt to gather information about the actual beneficiaries of suspected OCBs, their source of funds, their net worth, etc. had not met with success. Despite such happenings right under the nose of SEBI, the then chairman of SEBI claims a "vague idea" about investment through the PN route.

If one assumes that the Government had heeded the well-intended recommendations of the JPC and fulfilled its promise to the JPC, one would be sadly mistaken. Even to this day, SEBI may possibly be clueless about the ultimate beneficial ownership of the PNs. If the questions are repeated to the present SEBI chairman, one is unsure about his response about the ultimate beneficiaries of the holders of PNs. We would be examining these issues in greater detail in Chapters 6 and 7. Suffice to state that between 2001 and 2009, we seem to have been standing still on the subject.

Globalisation and integration of financial markets pose significant challenges to the domestic markets. The Indian experiences of the past decade demonstrate that cross-border flows into India could be significantly impacted by global events. Therefore, in a global and integrated environment, regulators must be in a position to assess the nature of cross-border conduct if they are to ensure the existence of fair, efficient and transparent markets. Flows from tax havens dynamite this very fundamental prerequisite of every market regulator, especially SEBI, in the Indian context.

Further, capital markets are still in the nascent stage in India. With burgeoning savings (India's savings stand at 38 per cent), it is possible that a significant portion of India's savings will begin to be routed to the capital markets. Further, Indian businessmen will be increasingly dependent on capital markets for their capital requirements. Therefore, the integrity of capital markets becomes extremely crucial. Further, since retail investors are placing an increasing proportion of their money in mutual funds and other collective investments, the securities markets have become central to individual wealth and retirement planning.

It would seem that like what the JPC pointed out – as quoted at the outset to this chapter – the entire country seems to suspend its sense of disbelief whenever there is a bull run. In the process, little do we realise that every rise of the stock market in India contain the seeds of a scam. This is what happens when the watchdogs fall asleep, or play ball or even refuse to bark. The watchdogs in question are SEBI, ICAI and RBI. In effect, upward manipulation of the markets is acceptable to, why even welcomed by, our regulators, media and industry. Sometimes, they encourage it openly, sometimes, tacitly, and at times, by their eloquent silence. The only challenge for the regulators is that the markets must be constantly on an upward movement. *The previous scams came to light only when people involved in the scam stopped, paused or fatigued by their misdeeds, sought to reverse their frauds.* Or else, it could have carried on merrily, never to be detected by any of the regulators with the extant system. This is simply because political parties in India have come to accept that the rise of the stock markets is conclusive evidence of the performance and maturity of the Indian economy.

The International Standard Against Market Manipulation

All these bring the role of the regulator – in this case SEBI – into sharper focus. The International Organisation of Securities Commission (IOSCO) has issued a detailed document on the Objectives and Principles of Securities Regulation. The document sets out thirty principles of securities regulation, which, in turn, are based upon three objectives of securities regulation. These are:

- The protection of investors.
- Ensuring that markets are fair, efficient and transparent.
- The reduction of systemic risk.

SEBI has developed a reasonably good risk management system. Over the years, consequently, there have been no defaults in meeting payment obligations. The robustness of the system was put to extreme test on several occasions when stock markets had collapsed dramatically as well as recorded abrupt surges. On all these occasions, though there were constant fears about some payment defaults, in practice, there has been none. That, in effect, takes care of the third objective: reduction in systemic risk.

We shall now concentrate on the other two broad objectives of securities regulation viz., protection of investors and ensuring that the markets are fair, efficient and transparent. In a way, there is a convergence in both these objectives as only a fair, efficient and transparent market can protect the interests of the investors, not otherwise. Again, fairness is interlinked to efficiency which, in turn, is interconnected to transparency. The delay of the ICAI in adjudicating on the disciplinary issues in the GTB case as well as the previous stock market scams (discussed in some detail above) is a clear pointer to the fact that the ICAI is not geared to meet the challenges posed by the Indian economy. The extraordinary delay is ample proof of its efficiency. SEBI, by its tacit silence, is party to the obfuscation of the ICAI and its inefficiency.

Similarly, SEBI is also a silent witness to the constant manipulation of the stock markets by the media. Disclaimers provided by the anchors are as reliable as those of the Pakistani establishment to India on containing export of terror from its soil. SEBI has learnt to ignore such open defiance of its regulations. Private treaties proliferate right under the nose of SEBI. The media does not do it on the sly, but quite brazenly. In the process, the regulatory might of SEBI is constantly challenged. And SEBI capitulates even before the fight begins.

Further, the IOSCO document seeks to protect investors from misleading, manipulative or fraudulent practices, including insider trading. It is pertinent to note that globally, it is agreed that an informed investor is an enlightened investor. Therefore, full disclosure of material information is the most important means of ensuring investor protection and de-risking his investment. By full disclosure, the IOSCO document explains, "Investors are, thereby, better able to assess the potential risks and rewards of their investments and, thus, to protect their own interests."

SEBI, precisely to tackle these issues has put in place the Prevention of Fraudulent and Unfair Trade Practices (PFUTP) regulations. These regulations are vital as, in them, "fraud" is sought be defined. Accordingly, "fraud" includes any act, expression, omission or concealment committed whether in a deceitful manner or not by a person or by any other person with his connivance or by his agent while dealing in securities in order to induce another person or his agent to deal in securities, whether or not there is any wrongful gain or avoidance of any loss. One can well appreciate that the definition of fraud is sweeping enough to encompass most of the programmes, PTs, editorials, chat shows and interviews pertaining to the media and the manner in which stock markets are sought to be manipulated. All it requires is to scratch the surface and conduct some honest surveillance and detailed investigation. Yet SEBI refuses to act.

Highlighting the importance of inspection and surveillance, the IOSCO document points out, "There should be a comprehensive system of inspection, surveillance and compliance programs. Investors in the securities markets are particularly vulnerable to misconduct by intermediaries and others, but the capacity of individual investors to take action may be limited."

Obviously, what seems to be holding back SEBI is the power of the media and its powerful connections. Certain sections of the media have, as demonstrated earlier in this chapter, put in place an elaborate mechanism as well as defined structures to carry out its market operations without any let or fear. To many it would seem to be market manipulation. Yet no one acts. Not a little finger is raised. The watchdog in the Indian context refuses to bark, leave alone bite. And should they attempt to bark, vested interests within the system would ensure that they are silenced.

In contrast, commenting on the need for swift decisive action on matters relating to market manipulations, the IOSCO documents states, "Further, the complex character of securities transactions and of fraudulent schemes requires strong enforcement of securities laws. Where a breach of law does occur, investors should be protected through the strong enforcement of the law." The law in India, the IOSCO should realise, is usually comprehensive. It has been our experience that we as a nation lack the political will to enforce the law. That explains why the media is able to get away with such daylight manipulation of the markets. But that in a way is the story of independent India – extraordinary laws coupled with very poor implementation.

Regulatory Shortfalls Waiting to Explode

Market manipulation robs fairness out of the markets. Hence, it is imperative that the regulations should detect market manipulation at the earliest, and penalise manipulators through extraordinary deterrents, possibly hefty fines and, if need be, even a term in prison. In this connection, the IOSCO document states, "Regulation should also promote market practices that ensure fair treatment of orders and a price formation process that is reliable. In an efficient market, the dissemination of relevant information is timely and widespread and is reflected in the price formation process."

To ensure that the regulator is competent to tackle the menace of market manipulations, the IOSCO documents prescribes certain principles relating to the regulator itself. These include:

- The responsibilities of the regulator should be unambiguous.
- The regulator should be accountable in the exercise of its functions.
- The regulator should have adequate powers, proper resources and the capacity to perform its functions and exercise its powers independently.
- The regulator should adopt consistent regulatory processes.
- The staff of the regulator should observe the highest professional standards.
- The regulator should have comprehensive inspection, investigation and surveillance as well as enforcement powers.
- There should be ongoing regulatory supervision of exchanges and trading systems which should aim to ensure that the integrity of trading is maintained through fair and equitable rules.
- Regulation should promote transparency of trading.
- Regulation should be designed to detect and deter manipulation and other unfair trading practices.

Needless to emphasise, the role of SEBI in preventing market manipulation requires greater scrutiny. If Indian promoters could manipulate the bourses through OCBs in the run up to the 2001 scam, it is quite possible that Indian stock markets could be under the influence of a tacit alliance between the media and the Indian promoters now. In the interregnum, too much water has flowed down the Ganges. We have significantly liberalised our outward capital flows. It is a remarkable coincidence that this has led to significant FDI flows to business affiliates and subsidiaries of Indian corporates outside India. Incidentally, the media too have developed symbiotic business connections outside India. If corporates and media houses are brazenly entering into agreements within India, it is equally possible, given the lax regulatory mechanism available on PNs, that the media and corporates, all combined could be putting such regulatory laxity to devastating use.

It may be recalled that the 2001 JPC was triggered by a mere few hundred points rise and subsequent fall in the Sensex. Since 2004, a few hundred points rise or fall of the Sensex in a trading session does not excite many. Over the years, a 9 per cent or a 10 per cent fall has caused a minor storm in the teacup. Despite all these hiccups, the response of SEBI has been uniform – that the Indian stock markets are sound and well regulated. Perhaps the nation is increasingly getting used to this volatility and accepting it as a way of life, little realising that this volatility is orchestrated by the media which acts in concert with speculators and promoters.

Unethical media houses, unscrupulous promoters and, of course, PNs form a sinister triumvirate who continue to have a stranglehold on the Indian stock markets. SEBI seems to be turning a Nelson's eye towards the first, is oblivious about the second and completely incapable of bringing any regulatory change towards the third.

Despite the repeated assurances of SEBI, in the present scenario, the risk of a scam always remains. For a change, this time it would be bigger and better. As a scam explodes, the nation will go through the entire rigmarole of a JPC enquiry, then the report of the JPC, ATR and the subsequent progress report by the Government. As a nation, we are used to this. For a change, can we have something different?

SEBI needs to explain the efficacy of its surveillance system, especially in the context of the anonymous route offered by PNs. For starters, it needs to explain that in the context of the 2001 stock markets scam and the recommendations of the JPC. How can it effectively have a surveillance programme when it allows anonymity within its system? How can it effectively carry out the surveillance routines when ultimate beneficiaries are operating from the safety of some exotic tax haven? How can it be confident of the robustness of the system when it is quite possible that even to this date the Mauritius route could possibly be misused by unscrupulous Indian promoters? There are several unanswered questions in the context of the Indian capital markets.

Plainly put, SEBI has lot to explain about how Indian capital markets are regulated according to global standards. Merely asserting that Indian capital markets are well regulated would not suffice any longer.

Unfortunately, for the nation, all these issues could have come into sharper focus if and only if the stock markets had not recovered by mid-2009. But, as luck would have it, the stock markets recovered significantly. Recall what the JPC had to say on the performance of the stock markets quoted at the outset to this chapter. And in real life, nothing succeeds like success. But little do we realise that the apparent success of the Indian capital markets has been built on several regulatory shortfalls.

Naturally, all these mean that the efficacy of SEBI in monitoring the Indian stock markets is suspect. The recommendations of the JPC in the context of the stock market scam of 2001 continue to haunt SEBI even to this date. The discussions contained in this chapter demonstrate that market manipulators or violators will be treated with kid-gloves by the regulators, be it SEBI, RBI or ICAI.

All that has been stated in this chapter merely provides a contextual reference to the discussions on hand. We will now move to specifics and far serious issues. We will now have a closer look at the regulatory developments on the PN issue between 2003 and 2009 in the context of the recommendation of the JPC report. We will examine these developments in the next two chapters in the context of two cases that came up before SEBI on the contentious PN issue.

Reference

1. Report of the JPC on the stock market scam of 2001.
2. The Action Taken report and all the fourteen Progress Reports on the action taken pursuant to the recommendations of the Joint Parliamentary Committee on the stock market scam and matters relating thereto.
3. *The Journal of the Institute of Chartered Accountants of India*, vol. 56, No 6, December 2007, p. 903.
4. 60th Annual Report of the ICAI for the year 2008-09.
5. Sucheta Dalal, "Anchor Investors and Related Issues", February 22, 2008.
6. Siddhartha Kumar, "Should Private Treaties be Made Public to Newspaper Readers?" Zest Media January 28, 2008.
7. Private Treaties brochure issued by the *Times* Group.
8. Objectives and Principles of Securities Regulation, issued by the International Organization of Securities Commissions, May 2003.
9. Walk the Talk – Interview of former SEBI Chairman Mr. Damodaran by Mr Shekhar Gupta, Editor of *Indian Express* on February 18, 2008, transcripts available on www.indianexpress.com
10. Sugata Ghosh, "RBI Against Another Term for GTB Auditors", *Economic Times* September 14, 2002.

11. Sugata Ghosh, "Lovelock & Lewes Under RBI Fire for GTB Audit", *Economic Times*, April 25, 2003.
12. Sucheta Dalal, "Ring of Thieves", May 6, 2009.
13. Anchor Investors and Related Issues by Ms Sucheta Dalal, February 22, 2008.

CHAPTER 6

Where the Hunter Becomes the Hunted

Those who stand for nothing will fall for anything

— Alex Hamilton

Just as the Joint Parliamentary Committee (JPC) had submitted its report to the Parliament in late 2002, its recommendations had come up for intense scrutiny. Readers may recall the background of the entire stock market scam of 2001. The 2001 scam, as we discussed in greater detail in Chapter I, was an outcome of a lax regulatory regime that allowed PNs to be issued by FIIs.

One of the important findings of the JPC was that PNs enabled their holders to hide their identities and to transact in the Indian capital market without any let or fear of the market regulator. Further, the committee suggested that any failure on the part of FIIs to report on the issue of PNs should be viewed seriously and should entail stringent punitive action. It also opined that SEBI should also ensure that this instrument is not misused in any way to manipulate the Indian securities market. In effect, regulation of PNs through SEBI was the core of the 2001 JPC report. Let us now see how effectively this recommendation of the JPC was put into practice by SEBI.

It is in this context that an order was passed by SEBI in September 2006, that is, a full three years after SEBI had pulled up a market player – Goldman Sachs – for an alleged violation of failing to furnish certain details pertaining to PNs in 2003. It may be recalled that the JPC had directed SEBI to collect the details of PNs issued by every FII. Subsequently, in August 2003, SEBI had in turn mandated that every FII shall provide the necessary undertaking in line with the suggestions of the JPC. We will revert to the alleged violation of the regulations by Goldman Sachs in greater detail shortly.

But first let us dwell on the delay in the first place of three years by SEBI for an alleged violation of its own regulations. It may be noted that the key operating word in any regulation, especially those relating to financial markets, is speed. One is not sure what was the end game contemplated by SEBI through such delayed action. In three years too much water would have flowed under the bridge. As Benjamin Franklin remarked famously, "Time is money." But SEBI is never known to act with any great speed.

The implicit idea in providing sweeping legal powers to any regulator is to ensure that regulators act with great alacrity. They are often manned by specialists. They have special powers, including preventive ones. Financial markets involve transactions that could run into hundreds of crores of rupees every minute. And in the process, the fortunes of innocent millions could be made or marred. In fact, the very purpose for setting up such regulators, apart from the ideological reasoning, stems from the fact that ordinary courts are structurally incapable of acting dexterously in similar circumstances.

Incidentally, the preamble of the SEBI Act states that it is "an Act to provide for the establishment of a Board to protect the interests of investors in securities and to promote the development of, and to regulate, the securities market and for matters connected therewith or incidental thereto." The operative word is "protect." Yes, protect.

"Protect" by taking an action after three years? One is reminded of Galbraith who said, "A wrong decision isn't forever; it can always be reversed. The losses from a delayed decision are forever; they can never be retrieved." Protection after three years is nothing but justice delayed. And justice delayed is justice denied. But who can regulate the regulator – SEBI, in the instance case?

Regulators in this country are a law unto themselves.

PNs and Indian Stock Markets – Made For Each Other

But this delay is the smaller order of the smalls. It is merely highlighted to point out to the reader as to how, within a decade or two of being set up, SEBI, has meandered into a labyrinth of bureaucracy, where routines matter much more than results. It is more like an army column that moves its hands and feet, only to find itself at the same place even after a considerable period of time. It is indeed paradoxical to see that on the one hand, SEBI has been vested with enormous regulatory powers under Chapter IV of the SEBI Act, yet when it comes to direct action, especially with respect to the big players, SEBI invariably acts like a frightened fawn caught in front of dazzling headlights on a highway. Whatever be the reason for such action or, for that matter, inaction, SEBI's delay or its inaction, though unjustified, is definitely not the subject matter of this work.

Rather, our discussion in this chapter pertains to the regulatory powers of SEBI, the manner in which the Indian stock markets continue to be manipulated by PNs through inflows from abroad and the effectiveness or otherwise of

SEBI in regulating the extant situation. It may be recalled in the context of the observations made by the JPC that FIIs were prohibited from issuing of PNs to a certain class of persons and entities. These included resident Indians, Non-Resident Indians (NRIs), Persons of Indian Origin (PIOs) as well as Overseas Corporate Bodies (OCB).

In order to analyse the issues raised in this chapter, a detailed reference at the outset to the JPC report on the securities market scam is inevitable. In the said report, the JPC had made various recommendations effectively prohibiting investment into the Indian stock markets by OCBs through FIIs using the PN route.

The Recommendations of the JPC

In the context of the violations by OCBs, the JPC contended, "SEBI's investigations have brought out several instances of violations by OCBs such as non-delivery of shares, purchase of shares on adjustment basis, booking purchase orders without sufficient balances in their accounts, exceeding the prescribed ceiling of 5 per cent for individual OCBs and violations of 10 per cent aggregate ceiling, etc." [Para 8.76.]

Explaining that the OCBs have been used, misused or abused to circumvent the takeover code, indulge in circular trading and build-up positions, the JPC stated, "Certain OCBs and sub-accounts of FIIs also violated the SEBI (Substantial Acquisition of Shares and Takeover) Regulations. SEBI has mentioned five OCBs and two sub-accounts of FIIs which have aided, assisted and abetted in creation of artificial market and volumes, circular trading and building up concentrated positions in a few scrips." [Para 8.76.]

Further, in the context of OCBs and their functioning the JPC added, "In the Committee's view, there is a need to have a fresh look at OCBs' operations after an in-depth study of inflows and outflows on a holistic basis covering their PIS and non-PIS transactions. The exercise should also include identification and plugging of loopholes and possible establishment of a proper regulatory set-up with stringent penal provisions for violations. The regulatory provisions should *inter*-alia enable detection of cases where the same set of individuals have formed more than one OCB and have their investments spread across the OCBs to escape provisions of the SEBI Takeover Code." [Para 8.80.]

Interestingly, in this context of regulating OCBs, the JPC suggested, "The Committee feel that the suggestions made by RBI for stipulation of a minimum paid up capital for OCBs and adoption of the same registration procedure as applicable to FIIs deserve careful consideration by the Government. The

Committee would like the Government to review the ban imposed on OCBs in the light of the above and clearly lay down the responsibility to a particular agency to oversee the OCB operations." [Para 8.80.]

It may be stated at the risk of repetition that the subject of PNs being issued to OCBs by FIIs was central to the stock market scam of 2001 and the JPC investigation, its report and recommendations. It is in this connection that the JPC recommendations are extremely crucial.

The JPC concluded, "SEBI has expressed suspicion that some of the Indian promoters have purchased shares of their own companies through Participatory Notes issued by sub-accounts of FIIs. This mechanism enables the holders to hide their identities and enables them to transact in the Indian Capital Market. The Committee note that SEBI has since directed FIIs to report about details of the Participatory Notes as and when issued by them. The Committee suggest that failure on the part of FIIs to report about the issue of PNs should be viewed seriously and should entail stringent punitive action. It should also be ensured that this instrument is not misused in any way to manipulate the Indian Securities Market." [Para 8.81]

The aforesaid JPC observations exposed the soft underbelly of the Indian stock markets in 2001. PNs, OCBs and the Indian promoters formed an impregnable yet obnoxious troika that could make and mar the markets. It was natural that the JPC suggested steps that would break this ugly nexus between the OCBs and Indian promoters so as to ensure that the markets were not manipulated.

What was causing consternation to the JPC was the unholy practice of issuing PNs which guaranteed absolute anonymity to the entire transactions. In the process, there were no audit trails, evidence or confirmation for SEBI to act further on the matter. That meant that more often than not, SEBI was left groping in the dark. Surely, this was not the role envisaged for SEBI in the first place.

As a response to this scenario, SEBI introduced a significant piece of regulation in October 2001. The contents of the said circular are reproduced hereunder: "It has come to the notice of SEBI that some FIIs are issuing derivative/financial instruments against underlying Indian securities. These instruments are known by various names such as Participatory Notes, Equity-Linked Notes, Capped Return Notes, Participating Return Notes, etc."

But that was not all. SEBI went on to bring in the regulatory oversight on the said vexatious subject by seeking to bring FII investments through PNs under its supervision. In this connection, the circular of October 2001 stated, "With a view to monitoring the investment by FIIs through these derivative

/ financial instruments, it has been decided that FIIs may report issuance / renewal / cancellation / redemption of the aforesaid instruments to SEBI with immediate effect as per the format enclosed as Annexure."

The circular also added, "It is further advised that this report shall be submitted by only those FIIs which issue such instruments. Further, these reports are to be submitted only on issuance / renewal / cancellation / redemption of the aforesaid instruments and only for the month during which the FII has issued / renewed / cancelled / redeemed the aforesaid instruments." As per the circular, the FIIs were requested by SEBI to submit these reports on a monthly basis.

Subsequently, SEBI had issued another circular dated August 8, 2003, with a view to revise the format of reporting by FIIs. According to SEBI, "This was done with a view to monitor the investment by FIIs through these derivative / financial instruments and to revise the format for reporting the issuance / renewal / cancellation / redemption of the aforesaid instruments."

This reporting was to be submitted in two forms which were enclosed with this circular as Annexures A and B. For the first time, the reporting format included an undertaking. Annexure A is a one-time report to be submitted once only in which the FII is required to indicate the outstanding PNs as on August 15, 2003. After furnishing the requisite information in the one-time report, the FII or the sub-account, as the case may be, is required to furnish the following undertaking: "We undertake that we/associates/clients have not issued/ subscribed/purchased any of the offshore derivative instruments directly or indirectly to/from Indian residents/NRIs/PIOs/OCBs."

Information as required by Annexure B was to be submitted for every fortnight from the first day of the month to the 15th day of the same month and from 16th day of the month till the last day of the month. The reporting in Annexure B commenced with effect from the fortnight ending August 31, 2003, The information for each fortnight is required to be submitted within three working days from the closure of the fortnight. The fortnightly report is also required to contain an undertaking by the FII as the case may be, in the following words: "We undertake that we/associates/clients have not issued/ subscribed/purchased any of the offshore derivative instruments directly or indirectly to/from Indian residents/NRIs/PIOs/OCBs during the Statement Period."

Goldman Sachs

Goldman Sachs Investments (Mauritius) Limited is a registered sub-account with SEBI and Goldman Sachs and Co. is registered as an FII with SEBI. On

November 25, 2002, Goldman Sachs as a sub-account issued PNs to its affiliate namely, Goldman Sachs International Ltd. England, with the shares of Himachal Futuristic Communications Ltd. as the underlying security. The affiliate, in turn, issued PNs on the same underlying security on a back to back basis to Magnus Capital Corporation Limited (MCCL) which is an OCB.

It may be noted that at the time when these PNs had been issued, the revised format for reporting had not been prescribed.

That is where things get interesting. In response to the aforesaid circular, Goldman Sachs filed a statement vide letter dated August 20, 2003, which did not contain the clause of the undertaking as prescribed in Annexure A of the said circular. The following was the undertaking in Annexure A of the statement:

"Goldman Sachs Investment (Mauritius) International Ltd., (MCCL) undertake on behalf of itself and its affiliates (Goldman Sachs) that as far as it is aware, Goldman Sachs has not entered into any offshore derivatives on Indian Underlyers directly with Indian Residents, NRIs or OCBs (each as defined under relevant Indian laws and regulations) during the statement period. As agreed with SEBI, this undertaking does not extend to Persons of Indian Origin, whether comprising part of the above categories of persons or otherwise."

However, later, in continuation of this, another statement was made out by Goldman Sachs. SEBI, based on investigation, alleged that despite issuance of PNs to an OCB, namely MCCL, Goldman Sachs gave an undertaking which, in the opinion of SEBI, was not to its satisfaction. Consequently, this mis-wording of its undertaking was viewed very seriously by SEBI. In this context, SEBI recalled that the JPC report on the securities market scam had made various observations with respect to the role of FIIs vis-à-vis the investment made by OCBs.

In this connection, it may be recalled that the JPC pointed out that certain OCBs had aided, assisted and abetted in the creation of an artificial market and volumes, circular trading and building up concentrated positions in a few shares.

The law which prohibits OCBs to invest in Indian securities came into force with effect from February 29, 2000. That was the ostensible intention of SEBI in amending the FII Regulations by introducing a proviso to Regulation 13(1)(b) in the first place, which states that "a non-resident Indian or an overseas corporate body registered with RBI shall not be eligible to invest as sub-account or as FII." It is to be noted that the alleged transactions of MCCL and Goldman Sachs relate to a subsequent period i.e. November 2002.

Naturally, SEBI was not at all amused as the undertaking was not in the format prescribed by it in its circular dated August 8, 2003. At many places in the reply, SEBI found Goldman Sachs seeking repeated clarification from SEBI on the extant issue. In the process, Goldman Sachs sought to repeatedly demonstrate its ignorance of law about prohibition on dealing with OCBs.

SEBI, nevertheless, held that Goldman Sachs was consciously aware of the importance of the declaration and that is why it avoided filing the declaration in the first place. So, according to SEBI, there were twin violations: one, when Goldman Sachs violated the SEBI circular by not providing the declaration; and two, when after all of its discussions with the SEBI, Goldman Sachs claimed to have complied with the SEBI circular by filing a declaration entirely different from the prescribed format.

Such Compliance is no Compliance

SEBI strongly objected to the move of Goldman Sachs to amend or change the prescribed format of the undertaking as per the SEBI circular, to suit its fancy. SEBI opined that "if this is the way a registered entity complies with the SEBI circular, I would say it is no compliance." Secondly, on the issue of MCCL being an OCB, SEBI concluded that "it is clearly observed from the communication from the Reserve Bank of India (RBI) dated December 26, 2003, addressed to SEBI, that Magnus Capital Corporation, Mauritius is an Oversees Corporate Body (OCB)." SEBI was in no mood to buy the argument of Goldman Sachs that the latter was ignorant of this fact.

SEBI noted that Goldman Sachs was having a global presence. Naturally, it was expected by SEBI to have compliances of the highest level. Yet, in the instant case, SEBI was of the opinion that Goldman Sachs had failed to give significant information to the regulator on the PNs issued to OCBs. According to SEBI, "It is common knowledge and a fact that OCBs had mis-utilised the PN route to park their illegal money and to manipulate the Indian securities market without the fear of their identity getting detected." So SEBI concluded that Goldman Sachs had violated the declaration furnished in the statement on issue of PNs to SEBI.

Goldman Sachs contended that the FII regulations do not explicitly prohibit the issue of PNs to OCBs. In this regard, SEBI pointed out that FII Regulations provide that "a non-resident Indian or an overseas corporate body registered with RBI shall not be eligible to invest as sub-account or as FII." This condition can only be met, according to SEBI, if OCBs are also "denied making investments as clients of sub-account or FII, otherwise the legislative intent and the object of the provision would get defeated." It is in this context that Goldman Sachs was alleged by SEBI to have violated the FII Regulations.

SEBI naturally felt that the violation of the same by Goldman Sachs that had a global presence in the financial markets, should be dealt with firmly. SEBI concluded that it "is required to ensure that law of the land, especially when the efficacy of Indian securities market is at stake, is enforced to the maximum and a message is given to the other market players that they need to be cautious in their dealings in the securities market."

Further, SEBI relied on the JPC report which stated that "failure on the part of FIIs to report about the issue of PNs should be viewed seriously and should entail stringent punitive action." After all, the JPC report was formulated by members of both Houses of Parliament and expressed the supreme will of the people of this country.

In view of the seriousness of the violation, SEBI imposed a penalty of Rs one crores on Goldman Sachs.

SEBI Proposes, SAT Disposes

Goldman Sachs immediately went on an appeal to the Securities Appellate Tribunal (SAT), the appellate authority for all matters decided by SEBI. Under the SEBI Act, any party aggrieved by an order of SEBI could proceed to appeal to SAT. It may be noted that SAT is an appellate forum that enjoys legal power on par with that of the High Court. Under the provisions of the SEBI Act, an order of the SAT can be appealed in the Supreme Court.

The fundamental question on which Goldman Sachs proceeded to appeal against the order of SEBI was whether SEBI could ask for an undertaking that they had not dealt in respect of PNs with Indian residents, NRIs, PIOs or OCBs in the absence of a legal bar on such deals.

In this connection, let us at the outset, refer to power of the Board of SEBI under Chapter IV of the SEBI Act. It may be further noted that SEBI acts through a duly constituted Board comprising its members. In this connection, the SEBI Act provides:

- It shall be the duty of the Board to protect the interests of investors in securities and to promote the development of, and to regulate, the securities market, by such measures as it thinks fit.

- The Board has the power to regulate the business in stock exchanges and any other securities markets.
- The Board shall prohibit fraudulent and unfair trade practices relating to securities markets and insider trading in securities.
- The Board shall regulate substantial acquisition of shares and takeover of companies.

To achieve these objectives, the Board shall:

- Call for information, undertake inspection, conduct enquiries and audits.
- Call for information and record from any bank or any other authority.
- Call for, from any agency, such information as may be considered necessary by the Board.
- Undertake inspection of any book, or register, or other document or record of any listed public company.

For these purposes, the Board is empowered to:

- Direct the discovery and production of books of account and other documents, at such place and such time as may be specified by the Board.
- Summon and enforce the attendance of persons and examine them on oath.
- Inspect any books, registers and other documents of any person or a company.
- In the interests of investors or the securities market, take any interim measures, either pending investigation or enquiry or on completion of such investigation or enquiry.

Over and above these, the Act empowers the Board to conduct investigation in certain circumstances, subject to certain conditions, internal checks and balances.

Readers may wonder why such elaborate reference to the powers of the Board is made here. It is relevant to note here that the question raised at the outset with Hon'ble SAT by Goldman Sachs on the appeal preferred by it relates to the very power of the Board of SEBI to seek an undertaking from a market participant. It is a matter, (as would be seen shortly), that would continue to haunt SEBI.

But as we would see right through this book, the issue is not merely a legal interpretation of the law relating to SEBI and the powers of the Board. Rather, it remains at the root of all that goes on to create a market regulator in the first place, provide it with sweeping power for the orderly conduct of the market, and take punitive steps against errant players.

For over two decades since the enactment of the SEBI Act, legal experts on stock market regulations have been seemingly at ease with a world-class legislation. We went on patting ourselves to glory. But that was on the drafting of the Act, which as any student of law would tell you, is the easiest part. The real challenge is often found in the administration of the Act. For the travails of SEBI, well, read on.

Check and Mate

In its appeal with Hon'ble SAT, Goldman Sachs raised a fundamental question – i.e. the power of the Board to seek information from FIIs. The question raised was whether the Board was at all justified in the first place in asking the FIIs to file undertakings in a prescribed format contained in the circular of August 8, 2003. In effect, Goldman Sachs was raising questions about the powers of the Board to issue a circular in order to obtain the said undertaking from FIIs.

It is indeed interesting to note that the arguments of Goldman Sachs were premised on the fact that till such time the circular was issued, there was *no bar on the FIIs to deal in PNs* with Indian residents/NRIs/PIOs/OCBs. The bar on FIIs to deal in PNs with the prohibited categories as discussed above was issued way back in February 2000 and then subsequently in October 2001 when the original reporting format was suggested.

Consequently, Goldman Sachs, while conceding that it had been dealing with such categories in the past, argued that in the absence of such bar, the Board could not, by the circular in question alone, require FIIs to furnish such an undertaking, that too on a retrospective basis!

Fascinatingly, SAT found "considerable force in this contention."

Goldman Sachs argued that it was in pursuance to the powers conferred by Regulation 20 of the FII Regulations that the circular dated October 31, 2001, was issued requiring FIIs to merely "report" the issuance/ renewal/ cancellation/ redemption of the PNs against underlying Indian securities issued by them.

But Goldman Sachs pointed out that there was no bar on the FIIs to issue/subscribe/purchase any PN to/from Indian residents/NRIs/PIOs/ OCBs. Consequently, it conceded that it would be reasonable to presume that many FIIs must have dealt with such persons in the course of their business activities. When this was the position, Goldman Sachs contended, SEBI had "suddenly amended" the reporting requirements by the FIIs on August 8, 2003, by prescribing the revised reporting format. In short, their argument was that the legal bar had to precede the SEBI reporting requirement, not otherwise.

Hon'ble SAT found these arguments absolutely tenable. It reasoned, "We wonder how they could be asked to furnish such an undertaking in the absence of any bar to deal with such persons. This requirement of an undertaking appears to us to be opposed to all norms of reason and is totally devoid of logic."

Taking strong exception to the very issue of the circular itself in the first place, Hon'ble SAT went on to chide SEBI for the same in strong language. It added, "In fact, it borders on absurdity and is arbitrary. When the FIIs have not been debarred from dealing in ODIs with Indian residents/ NRIs/ PIOs/OCBs and many of them would have dealt with the latter, they could not be asked to furnish the undertaking."

Hon'ble SAT agreed on the proposition of Goldman Sachs that "even as on today, there is no provision either in the Act or in the Regulations which debars FIIs or their sub-accounts from dealing in PNs with Indian residents/NRIs/PIOs/OCBs." In short, the very contention of Goldman Sachs was that there is no legal prohibition on FIIs to issue PNs to any of the four categories viz., Indian residents, NRIs, PIOs and OCBs. This contention effectively dynamites the JPC recommendations and subsequent amendments made to the FII regulations by SEBI. In the process, it renders the very purpose of the formation of the JPC otiose.

On the issue of Goldman Sachs dealing with Magnus and thereby violating the proviso to Regulation 13(1) of the Regulations, Hon'ble SAT dealt with the same, both on facts as well as law. According to SAT, the proviso to Regulation 13(1)(b) states, "Provided that a non-resident Indian or an overseas corporate body registered with the Reserve Bank of India shall not be eligible to invest as sub-account or as foreign institutional investor."

According to SAT, the said proviso debars a non-resident Indian or an OCB from investing in India only "as sub-account or as foreign institutional investor." Hon'ble SAT observed that it is nobody's case that Magnus has invested in India either as a sub-account or as an FII. Quite the contrary, Goldman Sachs had repeatedly maintained that Magnus had invested as a client of an affiliate and, therefore, the bar envisaged in the proviso to Regulation 13(1) is not attracted.

Therefore, SAT was critical of the observations made by the adjudicating officer and it chastised SEBI. According to SAT, the interpretation of SEBI so as to include Magnus as a client within the ambit of the proviso to Regulation 13(1)(b) was "absurd." According to SAT, such an interpretation would tantamount to an attempt to "rewrite the Regulation."

Secondly, it was the case of Goldman Sachs that when it issued the PNs in November 2002, it did not know that Magnus was an OCB. OCBs wanting to carry on activities in India are registered with the Reserve Bank of India, which maintains their list. SAT agreed with the contention of Goldman Sachs that the list of OCBs is not in the public domain nor is it on the website of the Reserve Bank of India and, therefore, not easily accessible to anyone.

According to SAT, "It is clear from the record that even SEBI came to know that Magnus was an OCB only when it received the letter dated December 26, 2003, from the Reserve Bank of India. This letter is a part of the show cause notice issued to the appellant and we have perused the same. It appears to us that even the Reserve Bank of India before confirming that Magnus was an OCB, took up the matter with the designated Bank of OCB i.e. Hong Kong & Shanghai Banking Corporation Ltd."

Obviously, SEBI itself could not have been aware and neither was the Reserve Bank of India clear about the status of Magnus till December 2003. Therefore, SAT did not think that it was fair and reasonable to charge Goldman Sachs for having dealt with Magnus as an OCB.

In addition, Goldman Sachs also contended that Regulation 15A of the FII Regulations which was inserted on of February 3, 2004, points out to this stated position i.e. there is no bar under the FII regulations or for that matter any other regulations issued by SEBI that effectively bars an FII from issuing PNs to OCBs.

A reference to Regulation 15A becomes crucial at this point, which states:

(1) A Foreign Institutional Investor or sub-account may issue, deal in or hold, offshore derivative instruments such as Participatory Notes, Equity Linked Notes or any other similar instruments against underlying securities, listed or proposed to be listed on any stock exchange in India, only in favour of those entities which are regulated by any relevant regulatory authority in the countries of their incorporation or establishment, subject to compliance of "know your client" requirement:

Provided that if any such instrument has already been issued, prior to the 3rd February, 2004, to a person other than a regulated entity, contract for such transaction shall expire on maturity of the instrument or within a period of five years from the 3rd February, 2004, whichever is earlier.

(2) A Foreign Institutional Investor or sub-account shall ensure that no further downstream issue or transfer of any instrument referred to in sub-regulation (1) is made to any person other than a regulated entity.

Hon'ble SAT found that even Regulation 15 A (which was introduced subsequently in 2004) too did not impose any prohibition on the FIIs from dealing in PNs with the aforesaid class of persons. Regulation 15A, according to SAT, was introduced only to restrict their dealings with such entities which are regulated by any relevant regulatory authority in the countries of their incorporation or establishment, subject to compliance of "know your client" requirements.

Therefore, Hon'ble SAT was agreeable to the proposition of Goldman Sachs that "even today" there is no bar on the FIIs. All this made "the requirement of furnishing the undertaking even more incomprehensible" to SAT. Accordingly, in its view, SEBI was not justified in asking for the undertaking prescribed by the revised reporting format.

Intriguingly, Hon'ble SAT made a very interesting observation on the powers of the Board (SEBI). It said, "Before we conclude on this issue, we hasten to add a caveat here. Not even for a moment are we suggesting that the Board could not have called upon the FIIs to report about their activities or furnish to it the information required of them under the Regulations."

Nevertheless, Hon'ble SAT finally concluded, "We are only disapproving the action of the Board in so far as it requires them to furnish the undertaking as prescribed for the first time in the revised reporting format in the absence of a bar prohibiting them from dealing in ODIs with Indian residents/NRIs/PIOs/OCBs."

In finality, Hon'ble SAT not only reversed the penalty of Rs one crores levied on Goldman Sachs by SEBI but rubbed salt on the wounds of SEBI by stating that Goldman Sachs could recover the costs from SEBI which were assessed at Rs one lakh. No wonder, it is often remarked, if SEBI proposes, SAT disposes.

But the larger question remains: Is SEBI yet to fully comprehend its role, powers and its position as a regulator?

Crucially, the Goldman Sachs case exposes two important lacunae in the regulation of PNs by SEBI. For starters, it demonstrates that there is no legal bar to the FIIs to issue PNs to OCBs, resident Indians, NRIs and PIOs. Secondly, in the absence of this bar, SEBI cannot get any meaningful information about the issue of PNs by FIIs. To this extent, the Goldman Sachs order by the Hon'ble SAT has clearly demonstrated the gaps in the FII Regulations vis-à-vis PNs. It also reveals that the recommendation of the JPC report has been given short shrift, both by the Government of India and SEBI. It may also be pertinent to note that SEBI has not rectified the regulations in the aftermath of this SAT order.

Yet, all this does not explain the belated action of SEBI against Goldman Sachs. For an alleged infraction of its own regulation, it is difficult to believe that SEBI waited almost three years before proceeding to act against Goldman Sachs. The moot point is: who will regulate the regulators, hold them responsible for such shoddy regulations and make them accountable for such serious lapses? It is time someone bells the cat.

References

1. Adjudication order issued by SEBI in respect of Goldman Sachs (Mauritius) Limited [Adjudication Order No AP/AO-16/2006-07]
2. Order of the Hon'ble SAT in respect of Goldman Sachs (Mauritius) Limited Versus SEBI [Appeal No. 153 of 2006 and date of decision : 15.5.2008]
3. The SEBI Act, 1992
4. The Report of the Joint Parliamentary Committee on the stock market scam and matters relating thereto.
5. In contrast to these assertions of Goldman Sachs, it may be noted that the RBI vide its Master Circular on Investment has stated, "OCBs have been de-recognised as a class of investors with effect from September 16, 2003".

CHAPTER 7

KYC: Know Your Controversy

What's in a name? That which we call a rose, by any other name would smell as sweet.

—William Shakespeare in Romeo and Juliet

The first tryst of Indian stock markets with the PNs resulted in the stock market scam of 2001. As explained in the earlier chapters of this book, this resulted in the setting up of the JPC that went into a host of issues which triggered the scam in the first place. Since then, PNs have been significantly occupying the media and policy space.

The JPC's finding was that through PNs, various layers are created which make it easier for the holders to keep their identities undisclosed and, at the same time, purchase shares in Indian markets. The JPC suspected that some of the Indian promoters have purchased shares of their own companies, in the process using the PN route for a variety of reasons, including manipulating the markets, recycling their ill-gotten wealth back into India and bypassing various regulations of SEBI. In such cases, the JPC prescribed tighter regulatory norms to be exercised by SEBI. [Para 8.81 of the JPC Report.]

It is in this connection that SEBI introduced vide circular IMD/CUST/8/2003 dated August 8, 2003, a fortnightly reporting of PNs issued by FIIs against underlying securities from August 2003. Accordingly, all FIIs were required to submit an undertaking stating *inter alia* that the FIIs have not issued PNs directly or indirectly to any Indian resident, NRI, PIO or OCB. The efficacy or the lack of it was examined in greater detail in the previous chapter.

However, post the JPC report, PNs have once again come to dominate the Indian stock markets. Increasingly, it is suspected that PNs are used or rather misused by many several resident Indians. These include politicians, industrialists, bureaucrats, celebrities, media houses and, in some extreme cases, foreign banks too. What was adding further consternation to a well-meaning minority of this country was that the PNs offer enormous scope for narco-terrorists to park their money in the Indian markets without any let or fear of any authority investigating their investments.

In effect, as it was for the JPC then and to many even now, the PN is a mystery wrapped in a puzzle, packed in an enigma, parked inside a conundrum and delivered through a riddle. The JPC rightly believed that the markets could well understand the power of the hidden hand of Adam Smith but not the prejudices of the "Invisible Man."

Therefore, it is in this context that SEBI brought about large scale regulatory changes in the FIIs Regulations vis-à-vis the issue, monitoring and reporting of PNs issued by FIIs. The first one was in October 2001 followed by certain improvements to the same in August 2003 and February 2004.

While all these were unfolding in front of us, albeit at a glacial pace, in May 2004, the National Democratic Alliance (NDA) was voted out of office. All hell broke loose immediately. With the United Progressive Alliance (UPA) yet to be formed, the second week of May 2004 was indeed tumultuous for Indian politics. Naturally, that reflected in the Indian stock markets. What was worrying for the market players, especially the FIIs, was that the results indicated a larger political role for the leftists. To add fuel to the fire, the Communist Party leader Mr. A. B. Baradhan precisely in those very turbulent times made a statement hostile to the market sentiments.

But the issue was not of the markets going to hell. Rather, it was all about finding who sold shares in such a significant quantity, leading to the crash of the stock markets on that particular day. In the process, it was a test for all regulatory changes brought about till then by SEBI on the basis of the recommendations of the JPC.

It was time to test whether the changes made were appropriate, functional and effective. In the process, the obscure yet dangerous, faceless yet fancied, PNs were dragged once again onto the national centre-stage. These were both testing as well as interesting times for the Indian markets, regulators and, of course, policy analysts.

The Markets Really Went to Hell

Markets abhor uncertainty, especially political uncertainty. When political uncertainty hits the markets, they recoil as they did on May 17, 2004, when they literally had a free fall. The bell-weather Indian stock index – the Sensex – fell by 568 points (intra-day, the Sensex fell by 842 points) and the NIFTY fell by 197 points from their previous close. Such a steep fall in the stock market resulted in temporary stoppage of trading twice on the major stock exchanges on that day in India viz. the BSE and the NSE. The chaos was unprecedented, with fears of several market players going bankrupt, or in the least, defaulting on their commitments to the respective stock exchanges. The Indian market had come under unparalleled strain on that particular day.

In view of this crash in the Indian stock markets, SEBI sought to investigate what and who triggered the events leading to the crash. As a regulator, it was duty bound to do so for the orderly conduct of the market. It was simultaneously expected to investigate and explain the reasons behind the crash to the pubic as well as to the investors, both in India and abroad. Given the severity of the fall, it had to assure investors globally that Indian markets were functioning efficiently, transparently and were not susceptible to any manipulation. Remember, markets worldwide detest manipulation as it upsets the level playing field amongst market participants. Manipulation unduly enriches the manipulator at the cost of the honest market participant.

SEBI, on the first blush of stock exchange records, found that UBS Securities Asia Limited, a registered FII dealing through its sub-account Swiss Finance Corporation (Mauritius) Limited, sold in the cash market segment to the extent of Rs. 188 crores on that fateful day.

On further investigation, SEBI determined that as on May 14, 2004, the short position of UBS in NIFTY futures was to the tune of Rs. 434 crores and stock short positions in the futures market was to the tune of Rs. 292 crores. The data obtained from the stock exchanges revealed that while UBS incurred a loss of Rs. 18 crores on May 17, 2004, on account of its sale in the cash segment, its short positions in the futures segment earned it a mark to market credit of Rs. 60 crores on that day alone, resulting in a net overall gain of approximately Rs. 42 crores. The strategy of UBS was that large scale sale in the cash market would depress the prices of stocks and shares both in the cash as well futures markets. It is, therefore, likely that it would even suffer losses in the cash segment. However, the short positions created by it in the futures markets prior to March 17, 2004, would turn profitable.

SEBI, on a *prima facie* reading of the situation, suspected UBS of manipulating the Indian market to serve its own purposes. The large scale sales effectuated on May 17 were a ruse to create panic amongst the market players. Sales data on that day suggested that due to the huge volume of sale in the cash market, the concomitant effect was also felt in the futures market, which too was depressed. Obviously, the crash of the market favourably impacted those holding short positions prior to the crash. And UBS was one of the players with the highest short positions in the futures market prior to the fateful day. For all these reasons, the needle of suspicion for the said crash pointed towards UBS.

SEBI now began attempting to solve the jigsaw puzzle about the crash of the stock markets in May 2004. It put the entire picture in perspective as it began its investigation. As a preliminary step, it sought information from UBS, which, as explained above, was amongst the largest sellers in the cash segment on that particular day.

Strangely, while at the outset, UBS informed SEBI on May 27, 2004, that all the transactions were on their proprietary account, subsequently UBS "revealed" that it had also sold a large value of securities on May 17, 2004, on behalf of various entities to which its affiliate, namely, UBS AG, London, had issued Offshore Derivative Instruments (ODIs) or popularly known as PNs, with underlying Indian securities.

SEBI was not at all amused by such shifting of stand by UBS. Given the gravity of the situation, it had to necessarily investigate and find out whether the sale of shares in such large volumes by the holders of PNs had triggered the crash.

The reasons for calling for such investigations are not far to seek. SEBI could not even by any illogical reasoning link the fall in the stock market on that particular day to the fundamentals of the economy or the performance of any specific corporate or group of corporates. Crucially, it sought to know as a market regulator who sold the shares. And the needle of suspicion on who triggered the crash now turned from UBS to the unknown beneficiaries who held the PNs and exited from their short positions on that eventful day. But the key to finding these ultimate beneficiaries lay with UBS as all these transactions were routed through UBS.

The obvious legal question for SEBI was whether any market participant violated the rules of the game and violated the Prohibition of Fraudulent and Unfair Trade Practices (PFUTP) Regulations relating to the securities market or for that matter any of its regulations.

What's in a Name?

During the course of this investigation, SEBI initially called for information from UBS relating to its major PN holders, in terms of their addresses, the names of their directors, fund managers, major shareholders, top five investors in case they were a corporate entity and such other fundamental details. It may be noted that such information is usually called for by the relevant authorities as a matter of routine in every investigation. UBS were also advised by SEBI to confirm, in line with the extant regulations (explained below in greater detail), issued by SEBI relating to the issue of PNs that none of the investors of its clients are Indian nationals, PIOs or OCBs being majority owned or controlled by NRIs.

In short, what SEBI had asked for were the following two details:

- Names of the beneficial ownership of those who held PNs and sold on May 17, 2004.
- Secondly, in line with what the JPC had originally suggested and the SEBI guidelines had mandated, a confirmation that none of the major investors of its clients were Indian nationals, PIOs or OCBs being majority owned or controlled by NRIs.

It may be surprising to know that UBS did not provide this information forthwith. In fact, it procrastinated and dawdled, hummed and hawed. It was only after several months that UBS wrote to its clients and requested them to provide SEBI with the abovementioned particulars in relation to their trading during the relevant days in May 2004.

UBS simultaneously sought an extension of time for their response, stating that the majority of investment managers were located in North America and Europe, who must "review this matter" and seek their own "internal approvals" wherever necessary. Review of the matter? One fails to appreciate what is the "matter" that needs to be reviewed when it comes to providing fundamental details to a market regulator. "Internal approvals" for providing basic information to the market regulator! Surely, things cannot get more bizarre than this. But this is how UBS reacted to this investigation. The stonewalling had begun in right earnest.

UBS further replied to SEBI that some of the investment managers may not be able to respond due to "confidentiality constraints." It may be noted that the confidentiality issue arose not on any private matters but relating to the basic issue of providing names and related details to a market regulator. Further, UBS assured SEBI that they were using their "best endeavours" to ensure that responses are received from the investment managers wherever it was possible. Best endeavour, it may be noted is a persuasive clause and a diplomatic way of saying that it is not possible to comply with the request at all. Though completely out of context, it is here that one is reminded of the "best endeavours" of the then ruling Taliban dispensation in Afghanistan in releasing the passengers from the hijackers of the ill-fated IC-814 at Kandahar.

As a matter of detail, SEBI had sought information relating to twelve major clients on behalf of whom UBS had dealt with in May 2004. While UBS furnished the requisite information regarding six of its clients, in respect of the remaining six clients, it did not furnish the particulars as sought by SEBI. What is crucial here for the reader to note is that SEBI for all purposes even at this point did not go in for a full-fledged investigation. After all, the information sought by it even at this point in time was rudimentary. There was nothing vindictive about it. Neither did it seek to precipitate the issue. In hindsight, given the gravity of the situation, it appears that SEBI initially approached the investigation, at least at the preliminary stages, with kid gloves.

As noted above, UBS initially did not furnish the information, citing client confidentiality. For every dogged attempt of SEBI, UBS began to stonewall with greater force. Nevertheless, UBS began to yield and started furnishing bits and pieces of information relating to some of its PN clients. Even these details, to SEBI's discomfort, were furnished by UBS over a period of several months and in driblets. This was obtained after several reminders and stern warnings by SEBI. With UBS remaining economical with the truth, SEBI was unable to make much headway in these investigations, even after several months, SEBI could not obtain basic information about the sellers who triggered the crash of the markets in May 2004, especially in the case of the following six clients.

1. Caxton International Limited.
2. Indus Asia Pacific Fund Ltd.
3. ROHATYN.
4. Indea Capital Pte Ltd.
5. PMA Prospect Fund.
6. Sattva Asia Opportunities Master Fund.

On all these cases, either UBS or its clients did not furnish the names and addresses of the top five largest investors in the respective funds, names of directors, etc as requested by SEBI and the value of portfolio held in May 2004, citing "reasons of confidentiality."

Interestingly, some of the answers provided in this context were not only humorous but also indicate the extent to which global players like UBS go to protect their business models, clients and their interests. In this connection, some of the names of the beneficiaries provided to SEBI by UBS are highlighted hereunder:

- A USA-based global fund of funds organisation.
- A major Northeastern USA university.
- A major Southwestern USA university.
- A European-based bank and investment organisation.
- A European-based fund of funds organisation.

Look at the irony: as the regulator demands the names – the specific name as well as precise attendant details and nothing more – the answers made out by UBS merely provide vague clues to the beneficial owners of the PNs. Surely, no one was seeking clues to a crossword puzzle, definitely not SEBI. Yet, it would seem that this is precisely what was attempted by UBS. But what is often forgotten in the melee is that if UBS could provide the clue as to the beneficial ownership of the PN, then why not disclose their names as well?

Subsequently, with respect to some of these funds, SEBI was able to extract the names but not the addresses and other particulars. However, in respect of its most prominent client, namely Caxton International Ltd., UBS did not provide the names of its top five investors or their addresses. And even when they came about, according to SEBI, it was too late. A year is too long a period for even a lame horse to bolt. This approach of SEBI needs to be contrasted with the fact that as a market regulator, it has the legal authority to lock the stable doors of the swiftest of horses at very short notice, sometimes even presumptively too. This delay, once again symbolises the manner in which SEBI functions.

PNs: Participatory Notes or Phantom Notes

Never in the history of regulations and regulators has a market player treated a regulator in such lackadaisical manner as UBS did SEBI in the instant case. And as one may note, this is not merely an issue that concerns the regulator and the regulated but involves larger issues, involving but not limited to the very powers of the market regulator to regulate capital markets.

What is interesting for the reader to note is that instead of providing the necessary information details to SEBI, UBS questioned SEBI's legal approach. For instance, in response to a query by SEBI as to whether PN holders are Indian nationals, PIOs or OCBs (which are majority owned or controlled by NRIs), UBS replied that such a query "seems to be inconsistent in the context of the scope of the FII Regulations." Stating that such legal position assumed by SEBI presumes the existence of a regulation that restricts an FII from issuing PNs to an entity that may have a shareholder who is an Indian national, NRI, PIO or OCB, UBS was loath to provide any further details on this issue.

SEBI was now feeling increasingly challenged.

SEBI, in the context of this interference in the Indian stock markets by UBS, felt that the repeated failure of UBS to give the complete information as sought by the market regulator, itself raised serious issues concerning regulatory powers in India. SEBI thought it was time that it bared its fangs a bit more to demonstrate its powers – not only with respect to the FII Regulations but under the overall scheme of the SEBI Act. One suspects that though this act was rather belated, it was spot on.

On the flip side, one can argue on similar lines that what UBS sought to do was perhaps acceptable behaviour. Given the fact that regulators in India have historically played ball with foreigners, especially foreign investors who brought in "precious" foreign exchange into the country, UBS like many others, did not take the initial threatening postures of SEBI seriously. In fact, one can distinctly understand and visualise how surprised, perhaps even amused, UBS must have been to know that Indian regulators can bark, at the least, if not bite. Naturally, the outcome of these developments in India was watched across continents in great excitement. Here was a regulator of a developing country that was taking on the might of an international financial giant head on. Strangely, a case of this magnitude and importance did not get the attention it deserved of the Indian professional class, media and policy analysts.

SEBI could, by now, as would the reader, smell that something was terribly amiss in the events that led to the massive sale of stocks by UBS. Equally, it was peeved at the manner in which UBS sought to play "duck and drakes" with it. Perturbed at the continued thumbing of its nose by UBS, SEBI ultimately decided enough was enough. The stench was becoming increasingly unbearable for it by the day. It finally mustered enough regulatory courage to get to the "bottom" of the issue. On the one hand, it was duty bound to investigate the crash of the markets in May 2004 while, on the other, it was also important to establish itself as a powerful market regulator. Importantly, for SEBI, both these objectives seem to be co-terminus with each other.

If curiosity killed the cat, UBS has only itself to blame for arousing the curiosity in the first place. It may be recalled that originally SEBI never sought to get to the bottom of the issue but wanted perhaps to carry out a simple enquiry. After all, what SEBI had asked for was not the moon but simple information that was denied to it through plain defiance, convoluted logic and, of course, ingenious interpretation of the regulations.

Naturally, given this position of UBS; the following issues arose for the consideration for SEBI:

- Was UBS was dealing with phantoms in the issue of PNs? Had it failed to identify its clients through what is commonly referred to as "Know Your Client" (KYC) requirements as laid down in Regulation 15A of the FII Regulations? One may well recall that when ordinary citizens proceed to open bank accounts in the neighbourhood, they are mandated to provide certain details so as to facilitate the banks in identifying the customer. This is a universal practice, especially in the aftermath of the tragic events in the USA on 9/11, when the authorities realised that terrorists could well be using normal banking channels to fund their operations. The global developments regarding money laundering and combating terror financing was discussed in some detail in the earlier chapters. India too was no exception to this global development. Hence, it was crucial that banks have complete details of every customer so as to trace their identity should the need arise. What applies to the banker, applies in equal measure to every other player in the financial market, in the instant case to UBS, as it should have had all the details and particulars of all its clients even before commencing operations on their accounts. This is the quintessence of KYC requirements under Regulation 15A of the FII Regulations.

- The other possibility is equally consternating. UBS could possibly have obtained the necessary information i.e. it could have met the obligations cast on it under Regulation 15A of the FII Regulations and, yet, for some reasons best known to it, it failed to furnish the same as sought by SEBI and thereby violated Regulation 20A of the FII Regulations. In the process, the crucial question was whether UBS had failed to comply with the clauses pertaining to the Code of Conduct as prescribed under the FII Regulations by refusing to part with the information pertaining to its clients.

One is quite certain that phantoms do not have names. And even if they do, one is more often than not forced to deny their existence. When existence is denied, where is the question of providing names? Either way, whenever phantoms are involved, the story does get absolutely scary.

From now on, PNs denote Phantom Notes.

Doomed if it did, Damned if did not

There were only two possibilities from this point in time: either UBS did not collect the KYC information from its clients in the first place and thereby violated Rule 15A of the FII Regulations. In the alternative, it did comply with the KYC norms and did collect the same, but refused to part with them to SEBI and thereby violated Rules 20 and 20A of the FII Regulations which cast an onerous responsibility on the FII to maintain the highest level of ethics in all its transactions, notably with SEBI.

Either way, UBS was doomed if it had failed to collect the information as required by the KYC norms. In the alternative, it was damned if it had collected the same and refused to part with them. Doomed if it did, damned if it did not! That made SEBI's contention against UBS to that extent watertight. Or was SEBI all along lulled into a false sense of legal security? We will examine the issue as we proceed.

SEBI's contention on this matter was that it is the duty of UBS to ensure that prior to the issue of PNs, it should have fulfilled the 'KYC' requirements. Instead, as is evident from the approach of UBS, it approached its clients only after the information was sought by SEBI. SEBI claimed, and, in my opinion, rightly so, that UBS violated some of the cardinal principles applicable to market players. SEBI also felt that UBS was evasive and providing "convoluted" explanations in order to wriggle out of the responsibility cast on it by the regulations.

It is in this connection that one may appreciate the import of Regulation 15A (already dealt with elaborately in the previous chapter) of the FII Regulations. The rationale of Regulation 15A, included the following:

- To facilitate the disclosure of names of the beneficial owners of PNs to SEBI by the FIIs who issued them.
- PNs were allowed to be issued by FIIs only to regulated entities, i.e. entities which were under some formal supervision of a regulator. This is a fundamental safeguard against "dirty money" getting into the Indian capital markets. Further, since India and SEBI are duty bound under the FATF regime to provide details of the market participants to other regulators across the world, it is important for SEBI to be aware of the ultimate beneficiaries of these PNs.
- Since the hedge funds are unregulated, it follows that the identity of the PN holders need to be, disclosed at least to SEBI, so as to effectuate the policy decision of the Government to keep the unregulated hedge funds out of the Indian capital markets.
- A plain reading of the above regulation suggests that it is not possible to issue PNs to further downstream entities and ensure multi-layering. Needless to emphasise, this is to ensure that SEBI would always be in a position to track down the beneficial holders of such PNs.
- Since the source of external funds would necessarily be a matter of relevance, especially in the context of terrorist and drug money being increasingly laundered across continents, the issue of transparency become crucial. All these sources are the fountainheads of "dirty money." Hence, it becomes crucial to identify the ultimate beneficiary of every PN so as to prevent such flow of dirty money into the Indian capital markets.

Over and above this, one of the primary objectives of the investigation was to ascertain whether any Indian nationals, PIOs or OCBs have dealt in the Indian securities market in a manner of hiding their identity behind the entities to whom the PNs were issued by UBS. Obviously, this was to find out whether Indians were laundering money out of India and investing into the Indian stock market through the PN route. Again, this was possible only if SEBI had some concrete particulars about the ultimate beneficiaries of the PNs issued.

It may be noted that this responsibility of identifying and knowing their clients was cast on the FIIs operating in India by amending the FII Regulations with effect from February 3, 2004, by the insertion of Regulation 15A in the FII Regulations. Obviously, it is pertinent at this point to appreciate the sequence of events that led to the amendment, as well as understand the rationale behind these requirements of the law.

SEBI's argument, given the provisions of this regulation was that it could very well be within its rights to ask for information up to the ultimate beneficiary. It believed that it had the regulatory power to do so. Surely, in SEBI's opinion, as I am sure it would be of any reader, any non-disclosure on this count would have seriously undermined its position as a market regulator.

Additionally, SEBI held that "it should not have been a matter of insuperable difficulty for UBS to give the full and complete information with proper documentation at the first level of its business relationship.....UBS is required to have the necessary due diligence and client verification at the first level. In such a context, the delay of one year has something more to it than what is made out in terms of touted difficulties, which peter out to be imaginary in the ultimate analysis."

Another interesting explanation forwarded by UBS was with respect to Regulation 20, which states, "Every Foreign Institutional Investor shall, as and when required by the Board or the Reserve Bank of India, submit to the Board or the Reserve Bank of India, as the case may be, any information, record or documents in relation to his activities as a Foreign Institutional Investor as the Board or as the Reserve Bank of India may require."

In a communication to SEBI, UBS argued, "The scope of Regulation 20 of the FII Regulations is limited to the information, records or documents that are in the possession of the FII in relation to its activities as an FII. However, in the present circumstances, UBS does not have the information sought by SEBI. Therefore, in such circumstances, it cannot be said that UBS has failed to comply with the requirements of Regulation 20 of the FII Regulations."

In short, the argument, reduced to simple terms, was that as UBS did not have the requisite information, there was no regulatory obligation cast on UBS to provide SEBI the information at all! This was as duplicitous an argument as a person claiming amnesty of the murder of his parents on account of being an orphan now! How could it (even if legally mandated) provide information when it did not have it in the first place?

All these arguments may be acceptable in our daily conversation; unfortunately, regulatory requirements are far more simple, plain and logical. Lawyers are engaged precisely for reducing complex subjects into simpler ones. More often than not, legal cases require simple understanding or facile interpretation of the law, of course, peppered with some small measure of common sense. In direct contrast, lawyers end up complicating simple issues into complex ones! In the process, most arguments in courts are on ultra-technicalities of the law, forgetting the larger picture. Unfortunately, simplicity has been made into a complex subject by the legal profession, especially in India. It is in this test of simplicity that UBS repeatedly fails. No wonder, it is accused of resorting to convoluted interpretations, quixotic logic and, of course, perverse reasoning. Or did it? Let us find out.

Five is a Four Letter Word

Regulation 20A of the FII Regulations reads as follows: "Foreign Institutional Investors shall fully disclose information concerning the terms of, and parties to, offshore derivative instruments such as participatory notes, equity linked notes or any other such instruments, by whatever names they are called, entered into by it or its sub- accounts or affiliates relating to any securities listed or proposed to be listed in any stock exchange in India, as and when and in such forms as the Board may require."

UBS argued, "As per Regulation 20A of the FII Regulations, the obligation of UBS is to disclose only the 'terms of and parties to' offshore derivative instruments such as participatory notes, equity linked notes entered into by it or its sub-accounts or affiliates relating to any securities listed or proposed to be listed in any stock exchange in India."

UBS argued that "information in relation to the 'parties' to offshore derivative instruments that must be disclosed is:"

- Name and location of the person to whom the PNs are issued.
- Name and location of other persons in the case of back to back issues of PNs.
- Type of investor (e.g. Hedge funds, corporate, individual, pension fund, trust, etc.).

In the light of the above, UBS contended that there was no requirement in either Regulation 20A of the FII Regulations or the circular for an FII or a sub-account of an FII to obtain from the parties to the PNs details of their investors and major shareholders. In effect, according to UBS, merely knowing the names of the PN holders would meet the regulatory requirement and there is no need to look into its ownership and management details beyond the first level.

In direct contrast to this legal positioning by UBS, SEBI sought the names of top five investors of every client who sold their positions in May 2004 from UBS.

In this connection, UBS contended that "pursuant to Regulation 20A of the FII Regulations, there is no obligation on the part of UBS to maintain records / details of top five investors and major shareholding of the clients. It is submitted that in the absence of any such obligation, it cannot under any circumstances be said that UBS has breached any obligations pursuant to Regulations 20 and 20A of the FII Regulations."

It is interesting to note that nowhere do the regulations call for the details pertaining to the top five investors or shareholders. In fact, the regulations call for compete details. What SEBI had called for was minimal information and basic details. Put differently, how could someone who was not even prepared to provide details about the top five shareholders proceed to provide details about the entire lot? Surely, SEBI cannot be faulted for this approach. And it is this liberal approach of SEBI that continues to haunt it, as we would see, even today. We will revert to this subject in greater detail shortly when we discuss how the Hon'ble SAT came down heavily on this line of thinking by SEBI. But suffice to say at this point in time that five had indeed become a four letter word during the course of this investigation.

Consequently, UBS confidently, asserted, "In such circumstances, it cannot be said that details of major shareholders and top five investors are required to be maintained under Regulation 20A of the FII Regulations." Little did UBS realise that SEBI was providing it a huge leeway by seeking to symbolically comply with the request. Obviously, UBS was not prepared to meet even this diluted requirement. Strangely, it is this attitude of compromise and the age old Indian phenomenon of compromising from a position of absolute strength that turned into the Achilles' heel of SEBI.

Needless to emphasise, Regulation 20 of the FII Regulations casts an obligation on the FIIs to submit to the Board "*any information* (emphasis mine) record or documents in relation to his activities as a Foreign Institutional Investor as the Board may require." "Any information," as may be noted above, includes the top five investors. According to UBS, since the FII Regulations in their entirety did not mandate the FII to keep or provide the information pertaining to the "top five" investors, it was not duty bound under the regulations to part with such information.

Clearly, as per the FII Regulations, it was the obligation of UBS to furnish the information. That is my understanding of the regulatory powers. Yet UBS dithered, argued, wavered, protested and did everything under the sun but provide the details to SEBI. And that, in a nutshell, brings about the role of SEBI as a market regulator into sharp focus vis-à-vis the issue of PNs by FIIs.

Violating the Code of Conduct

SEBI's investigation also focussed on violation of Clauses 1, 2, 5 and 6 of the Code of Conduct as specified in Regulation 7A of the FII Regulations by UBS. To understand the issue, a brief reference to this code is crucial to our understanding of the issue.

Clause 1 of the Code of Conduct states, "A Foreign Institutional Investor and its key personnel shall observe high standards of integrity, fairness and professionalism in all dealings in the Indian securities market with intermediaries, regulatory and other Government authorities." Integrity, as any standard dictionary would tell us, means truthfulness, honour or reliability. Read in conjunction with fairness and professionalism, one can safely surmise the responsibility cast on an FII registered with SEBI. This one does not require any further explanation.

Clause 2 of the Code of Conduct states, "A Foreign Institutional Investor shall, at all times, render high standards of service, exercise high due diligence and independent professional judgement." Again, due diligence means meticulousness and conscientiousness. By legislating these codes in such explicit terms, the high standard of expectation set by the legislation is only too obvious. Forget UBS for the moment, even SEBI cannot dilute the same.

Clause 5 states, "A Foreign Institutional Investor shall maintain an appropriate level of knowledge and competency and abide by the provisions of the Act, regulations made hereunder and the circulars and guidelines, which may be applicable and relevant to the activities carried on by it." Again, SEBI does not expect any FII to be ignorant of the law, regulation or circular issued by it. In contrast, the level of knowledge and competency expected by SEBI of an FII shall be "appropriate."

Amplified further, that could mean that an FII is expected by SEBI to display conduct that would be commensurate of a responsible, knowledgeable and law-abiding market player. SEBI does not expect any market player, definitely not an FII, to nitpick, quibble and equivocate on the very rules it has drafted.

Clause 6 states, "A Foreign Institutional Investor shall not make any untrue statement or suppress any material fact in any documents, reports or information furnished to the Board." Again, this clause makes interesting reading. One way of interpreting the entire clause would be to suggest that when an FII is in the know of a "material" fact, it cannot suppress the same from SEBI. Now the question could be as to whether the names of the top five investors of the clients of UBS comprise a material fact or whether they are immaterial and whether UBS was in the know of it or was not, and if it was in the know of the same, whether it was incumbent on it to pass it on to SEBI or not.

If one contends that the names and addresses of the top five investors are not material or till there are exact guidelines from SEBI as to what constitutes "material" information, any FII can withhold any information from SEBI, on the grounds that such information is not "material" and, hence, does not fall within the scope of the said clause. Whatever it may be, such interpretations are often accepted by the courts and at times rejected. In the process, the courts too have become highly subjective.

Further, Regulation 7A of the FII Regulations states, "A foreign institutional investor holding a certificate shall, at all times, abide by the Code of Conduct as specified in the Third Schedule."

On this charge, UBS contended:

- There was no obligation under the FII Regulations for UBS to obtain from the holders of PNs the details of their major shareholders or top five investors.
- It had made all necessary efforts to procure the relevant information from its clients for SEBI. However, it was prevented from disclosing the required information to SEBI on account of the confidentiality clauses in its agreements with its clients.
- UBS further stated that under the FII Regulations, it is not obliged to obtain the above information from the holders of PNs.
- Finally, it contended that it has not made any untrue statement or suppressed any material fact in any document, report or information furnished to SEBI and, accordingly, it has not breached Clauses 1, 2, 5 and 6 of the Code of Conduct. How could it have said something untrue when it did not say anything in the first place? How could it have suppressed any information when it claims it never had any information in the first place? How could it have provided information when it was not required to provide information in the first place? Brilliant, but in my considered opinion, convoluted legal arguments.

In short, the contention of UBS was that the information requested by SEBI was not within the control or power of UBS to provide such information as it was exclusively in the domain of third parties. In such circumstances, it cannot be held liable for failures which arise for no fault of its and which are as a result of factors beyond its control.

A Reference to the JPC Report yet Again

A bit of digression at this point is necessary. It may be recalled that the issue of PNs has been haunting the Indian capital markets for over a decade or so. May 2004 is merely a stopover. The JPC that went exclusively into the operations frowned on the manner in which the PNs were regulated by SEBI and suggested certain regulatory mechanisms to monitor PNs. It was only after the constitution of the JPC that SEBI took the first steps in regulating FIIs on the vexed issue of PNs. Naturally, this evolution needs to be traced, albeit briefly, to understand what is stated above.

In this connection, the relevant excerpts specifically on PNs by the Hon'ble JPC on the stock market scam (2001) are quoted hereunder: "Investigations have shown that entities connected with some of the Sub-Accounts issue Participatory Notes (PNs) as Derivative Instruments outside India. It is suspected that these instruments enabled entities, which may not be eligible to get registered as FIIs to transact in the Indian capital market. This instrument enables the holders to hide their identities. Through PNs, various layers are created which make it easier for the holders to keep their identities undisclosed and, at the same time, purchase shares in the Indian market. It is suspected that some of the Indian promoters have purchased shares of their own companies in this way. It appears that shares purchased through this route were shifted to Ketan Parekh entities through OCBs. SEBI has now asked FIIs to report about the details of the PNs as and when issued by them." [Para 8.66.]

The report further adds, "Participatory Notes are Derivative Instruments issued against underlying securities of investments in shares. A PN is issued outside India and represents a transaction between two non-residents, who are not subject to the Indian laws. PNs are extra-territorial instruments and SEBI has no regulatory jurisdiction over them. SEBI has expressed suspicion that some of the Indian promoters have purchased shares of their own companies through Participatory Notes issued by sub-accounts of FIIs. This mechanism enables the holders to hide their identities and enables them to transact in the Indian capital market". [Para 8.67.]

Apparently, the 2001 JPC report centres on identifying the ultimate beneficiary of the PNs with a view to prevent unauthorised entry of participants into the Indian stock markets. SEBI examined the issue of FIIs issuing PNs to a multi-layered structure (that is, a PN passes on from one entity to several layers) and, more particularly, the need for identifying the ultimate beneficiary of these instruments. It was felt that only known and regulated entities should be allowed to invest in the Indian securities market through the FIIs, and non-verifiable sources should not be allowed.

It was in this context that SEBI had first issued a circular dated 31/10/2001 (even as the JPC was investigating the 2001 stock market scam) directing FIIs (that have been issuing PNs with Indian securities as its underlying) to report issuance / renewal / cancellation / redemption of the aforesaid instruments to SEBI, as per the format prescribed in the circular.

This was the first step in "regulating" the PNs issued by the FIIs. Further, the above-mentioned circular required the FIIs to give an undertaking that the FIIs / associates / clients have not issued / subscribed / purchased any PNs directly or indirectly to/from Indian residents / NRIs / PIOs / OCBs. Evidently, it can be deduced from the above that the FIIs would have to first know the ultimate beneficiaries of the respective clients on whose behalf they were transacting in the capital market. And surely, residents, NRI and PIOs do not figure in the eligible category to whom FII could issue PNs. Else, the entire undertaking would become an exercise in futility. (But as we saw in the previous chapter, this reporting was ultimately reduced to an exercise in futility)

Thereafter, in order to strengthen the policy decision flowing in the aftermath of the JPC report and to ensure better regulatory supervision of the October 2001 circular, SEBI introduced Regulation 15A. The idea contained in this regulation and its implications have been explained in greater detail in the previous pages.

It may once again be noted that issuing PNs to the regulated entities and meeting the KYC norms are not alternatives. Rather, they are cumulative conditions and need to be met concurrently. Therefore, it could not be taken as compliance of Regulation 15A merely if ODIs were issued to the regulated entities. The compliance of KYC was equally an important part of the regulations and has to be complied with simultaneously and not as an alternative.

Nevertheless, despite all the arguments put forth by SEBI, UBS contented that SEBI has not prescribed any format for KYC norms to be followed by FIIs. Put bluntly, in the absence of a regulation "detailing the requirements" to be met for the purposes of KYC norms, according to UBS, meeting a hypothetical requirement of SEBI is irrelevant, why even impossible. But is the matter so ridiculously simple? Let us examine the issue, especially given the fact that the KYC norms are understood globally by all those with even an accidental tryst with the world of finance.

Worldwide there are different regulators who insist on a wide range of information to be collected under the KYC norms. Yet names, addresses and other basic details are the uniform standard prevalent worldwide. Of course, there are several variations of the KYC norms, yet fundamentals of KYC are constant.

Yet, this is what UBS raised in its defence with SEBI – that it could not provide the names as it could not fully comprehend the meaning of the KYC norms. Remember, the Code of Conduct for FIIs. Recall that it had prescribed professionalism as part of the conduct expected of FIIs. Little did SEBI realise that such prescription was displayed in abundant measure while extending legal arguments but not while providing information. Professionalism, yes, for defence and non-compliance but not for compliance!

Big Men do not Make Small Mistakes

Before we proceed further, it is essential that we get to know what UBS is, its capacities, its financial clout worldwide and, of course, its global reach and presence. Today's UBS, its brochure tells us, took shape in the course of the 1990s through a series of mergers and acquisitions. These initiatives transformed a predominantly Swiss business into a top-ranking global institution.

In June 1998, the Union Bank of Switzerland and Swiss Bank Corporation (SBC) completed their merger. Just two years later, UBS acquired the US brokerage firm Paine Webber, greatly increasing the size and scope of its business. Then the new firm set the seal on these achievements by proclaiming a single brand. In this light, UBS is both a new institution and a new brand. At the same time, its history extends to many generations into the past, particularly in Switzerland, the US, and the UK, even up to the eighteenth century.

Its catch phrase explains its reach and presence succinctly as well as eloquently: "UBS is one of the world's leading financial firms. And we operate in two locations – everywhere and right next to you." That, in essence, is UBS.

Some of the facts and figures about it are startling and stunning. WWW.UBS.ORG lists out the following as some of its key facts:

- UBS is one of the world's leading financial firms and is headquartered in Zurich and Basel, Switzerland.
- UBS serves a discerning, international client base with its wealth management, investment banking and asset management businesses.
- In Switzerland, UBS is the market leader in retail and commercial banking.
- UBS is present in all major financial centres worldwide. It has offices in over 50 countries.
- UBS employs more than 75,000 people around the world.

Interestingly, UBS, being one of the world's largest and financial firms of great repute, does have an internal mechanism to meet the KYC norms. Some of these are provided in the abovementioned website and reproduced here to ensure a comprehensive understanding of the arguments made out by UBS. The website states, "UBS takes its responsibility to preserve the integrity of the financial system, and its own operations, very seriously. The firm has developed extensive policies intended to prevent, detect and report money laundering, corruption and terrorist financing. These policies seek to protect the firm, and its reputation, from those who may intend to legitimize their ill-gotten gains through UBS." One may note that all these are possible if and only if UBS has a robust KYC norm.

That is not all. UBS has a separate wing to counter money laundering. The UBS website adds, "The Group Money Laundering Prevention Unit (GMLPU) leads UBS' efforts to fight money laundering, corruption and the financing of terrorism. It does so by continuously assessing the threats and risks that UBS faces with respect to AML in all its businesses. It takes a risk-based approach, ensuring the firm's policies and procedures are commensurate with those risks, and that relationships that are classified as higher risk are dealt with appropriately."

Further, "UBS also seeks to ensure its employees adhere to the firm's strict know-your-customer regulations, while, at the same time, not treating clients *a priori* as criminals or undermining their right to privacy. Employees regularly undergo training in AML-related issues and new trends, be it through online training, awareness campaigns or seminars. UBS also utilizes advanced technology to assist in the identification of transaction patterns or unusual dealings."

That is not all. It has a policy of desisting from dealing with certain countries which have heightened risks. In this connection, UBS states, "Over the last few years, and as a core part of its risk-based approach, UBS has been particularly vigilant about enhancing controls with regard to regimes and countries with heightened risks. The need for increased vigilance has been underscored by the acknowledgement by the Financial Action Task Force (FATF) of the importance of country risk considerations in the risk-based approach, increasing international focus on corruption, and the need for the firm to manage its global security risk activity. As a result of these considerations, UBS has implemented a global sanctions policy, ceasing all business activities with a limited number of countries."

Yet, surprisingly, when it came to the instant case, UBS, the global financial giant did not know what KYC norms are. Surprising!

Further, UBS is also a member of the reputed Wolfsberg Group[1] of financial institutions which is committed to contributing to the fight against terrorism.

1. The Wolfsberg Group consists of the following leading international banks ABN Amro N.V., Banco Santander Central Hispano, S.A., Bank of Tokyo-Mitsubishi, Ltd., Barclays Bank, Citigroup, Credit Suisse Group, Deutsche Bank AG, Goldman Sachs, HSBC, J.P. Morgan Chase, Socié"té Générale, UBS AG and became known when they, together with Transparency International and Mark Pieth, agreed to a set of global anti-money-laundering guidelines for international private banks in October 2000. Wolfsberg is the location in Switzerland where an important working session to formulate the guidelines was held.

This group seeks to ensure that financial institutions prevent the flow of terrorist funds through the world's financial system.

Incidentally, the Wolfsberg Statement on "The Suppression of the Financing of Terrorism" states in right earnestness, "The Wolfsberg Group recognises that adherence to existing Know Your Customer policies and procedures are important to the fight against terrorism. Specifically, the proper identification of customers by financial institutions can improve the efficacy of searches against lists of known or suspected terrorists issued by competent authorities having jurisdiction over the relevant financial institution."

And, pray, when was this statement issued by the Wolfsberg Group of which UBS remains an integral part even to this date? January 2002. Yet, surprisingly, when it came to the instant case in 2004, UBS, the global financial giant did not know what KYC norms are.

Cheese for the Goose is not Cheese for the Gander

How and why did UBS fail to recognise the KYC norms when it is accepted as a fundamental business and regulatory requirement worldwide? Why did UBS take this stand of stating that since KYC norms are not precisely defined in any SEBI Regulations, it was not required to follow any KYC norms? How is it that UBS had set up an internal KYC norm (which in more ways than one corresponded to the international norms of identifying clients) and yet did not part with the information to SEBI? One is not sure.

Importantly, an organisation of repute such as UBS and one which is having an international presence, surely could have done with far more credible explanations. But what about those who advised UBS, both within and outside the courts, especially lawyers? Recall the problem with students of law – they take legal interpretations into hair-splitting detail. Modern court craft is all about taking legal arguments to the extreme, little realising that lawyers, especially senior advocates, have as much a responsibility as judges have to society at large. But the moot point is whether our lawyers recognise this responsibility?

Crucially, the question remains. Would UBS have attempted to answer in a similar vein when confronted with a similar request under similar circumstances in a developed country like, say, the USA? One is not sure. Nevertheless, the contrasting approach of UBS (where it literally was made to go on all fours) in similar circumstances to the Inland Revenue Service (IRS) Department of the USA has been detailed in the earlier chapters.

One may note that KYC norms are met at the threshold, that is, when one walks into a bank for the first time and seeks to open an account, not later. Therefore, it is expected that the bank should have detailed information on any account once the account is opened, not six or eight months down the line. The bank cannot and should not collect information at its own convenience. Nor should it be collected in driblets. KYC norms obviously have a temporal relevance too – they cannot be collected at the free will of the market participants who have to adhere to this discipline of timing on this matter. Naturally, by prescribing the KYC norms, SEBI expected UBS to comply with the same prior to the issue of PNs, by ensuring that it gets at least basic information from clients that the regulator probably could ask for, and not go in search of the same when SEBI wants such information.

Instead, UBS claims to have approached its respective clients after SEBI sought the information regarding these clients. This shows that UBS diluted the essence of KYC requirements. Or was there something more than what was repeatedly remonstrated in all innocence? Was UBS protecting someone high and mighty in India even if it was to risk a debilitating dent on its credibility? Again, one is not sure.

Equally, one is intrigued by the constant shifting stand of UBS on this issue. First, UBS undertook to furnish the requisite information in respect of its clients through its London and New York offices as the PNs were issued from there. Then, it changed its stance and claimed that the clients were unwilling to disclose the information, citing confidentiality reasons.

Surely, in such circumstances, especially in the aftermath of the tragic events in America on September 11, 2001, it is often seen that organisations rush to (and, in some cases, act in tandem with the regulators in coming with the necessary regulations) adhere to what is prescribed by regulators to maintain security. Strangely, when it comes to the developing countries, these very organisations that pontificate endlessly on the virtues of transparency, openness and ethics, suddenly seem to be oblivious to what constitutes KYC – the grandmother of all these norms in the first place.

Isn't it a classical case of cheese for the goose not being cheese for the gander?

Naturally, the issue is not merely SEBI's power to regulate the FIIs or the PNs issued by them. Rather, this concerns the physical and financial security of the country. As it may be noted, we are dealing with this issue right through the length and breadth of this book.

Conclusion by SEBI

Based on what was explained above, SEBI arrived at the following conclusion:

- UBS totally failed to discharge its obligations to regulatory requirements, with a design to withhold critical information for stultifying the investigation.

- UBS has not complied with Regulations 15A, 20 and 20A of the FII Regulations and Clauses 1, 2, 5 and 6 of the Code of Conduct applicable to FIIs, as found in the course of collecting information for the investigation.
- There has been no proper exercise of due diligence in compliance with KYC norms by UBS. UBS was required to give such information in relation to its clients, as mandated by Regulation 15A read with 20 and 20A. Consequently, UBS failed to discharge even the onus cast upon it in terms of these regulatory requirements.
- In view of the above and in the light of its acts of omission and commission, UBS is guilty of non-compliance of Regulations 15A, 20 and 20A and Clauses 1,2, 5 and 6 of the Code of Conduct applicable to FIIs as laid down in the FII Regulations.

The order of SEBI in the final analysis stated, "The findings in this case have highlighted serious regulatory concerns in that the PN / ODI route and its cover of anonymity is being used by certain entities without there being any real time check, control and due diligence on their credentials. Such a lapse has very grim portents as far as the market integrity and interest of investors are concerned. The mechanism of opening up the Indian securities market through the PN / ODI route to entities outside India imposes a commensurate onus on the registered intermediaries (FIIs) of maintaining high standards of regulatory compliance, exercise of high due diligence and independent professional judgment and, therefore, any gaps in measuring up to the onus may be fraught with critical repercussions in the market."

SEBI's order added, "Therefore, in light of the above, SEBI prohibited UBS / its affiliates / agents from issuing PNs for a period of one year." SEBI also prohibited UBS / its affiliates / agents from renewing or rolling over any of the ODIs already issued against the positions held by it in the Indian securities market for a period of one year. Finally, SEBI also directed UBS to establish the highest standards of the customer due diligence process in line with the requirements of the FII Regulations.

In a remarkable turn of events, the order of SEBI was passed on May 17, 2005, exactly a year after the stock markets crashed. Was it planned that way or was it a sheer coincidence – one is not sure.

SAT Views the Issue Differently

Immediately, UBS appealed against this order of SEBI to the SAT, the appellate forum. Most of the issues raised by UBS have been dealt with extensively in the earlier portion of this chapter when UBS responded to the Show Cause Notice issued by SEBI. However, some of the principal arguments of UBS in SAT are highlighted once again to draw attention of the readers to this vexatious subject.

UBS submitted that the main charge against it was that it did not furnish information of top five clients / investors to SEBI for conducting the investigation, and that it violated the KYC requirements as prescribed in Regulation 15A of the FII Regulations. It further submitted that a plain reading of Regulation 15A makes it quite clear that it does not call for knowing the ultimate beneficiary or the persons behind the client who has entered into an agreement. Nowhere, it contended, is it mentioned that the names and addresses of the top five investors / clients should be maintained by the FII and provided to the regulator. It interpreted Regulation 15A to state that derivatives such as PNs could be issued by FIIs in favour of those entities which are regulated in the countries of their incorporation, subject to compliance of KYC.

In effect, what SEBI wanted was details of a sample. In the process, UBS twisted the entire issue to seek "absence of legal sanctity" on the sampling methodology called for by SEBI. It is well accepted in law that whenever a regulator calls for some detail in totality, it could also call for a part of it.

What is interesting to note here is that UBS held on to its argument that nowhere have the KYC requirements been defined in the FII Regulations or for that matter in any other laws/rules/regulations/circulars relating to FIIs. It pointed out that it is not possible to give a definite and certain meaning to the KYC, as mentioned in Regulation 15A. It argued that neither the FII Regulations nor any other available indicators of the standards of KYC requirements could support the findings in the impugned order that identity of the top five investors / shareholders of a corporate client was an essential requirement of KYC in terms of Regulation 15A of the FII Regulations.

UBS pointed out to the SEBI order which said, "Know Your Client is a very basic commercial requirement which does not require a formal prescription." It submitted that in the light of such KYC requirement which has not been defined by SEBI, there could not be any legal obligation on the part of the appellant to maintain and obtain information pertaining to the names and addresses of the major shareholders / top five investors.

While it is, indeed, accepted that the extant KYC norms are surely vague, it is a trite argument that one does not understand them – especially UBS, given its stature as a global financial giant. Recall that we discussed about this issue earlier in this chapter and how UBS was a signatory to the Wolfsberg Group on the very same issue. It is also true that KYC norms differ from one jurisdiction to the other, but that does not offer scope to a regulated entity to get away by not providing any details to the regulator.

According to UBS, SEBI had sought to impose an indeterminate standard as it expected the appellant to anticipate correctly all the questions that the respondent was "likely to ask or may ask in future." It further submitted that it was legally impossible to satisfy such a requirement. SEBI should have made known the questions which are likely to be complied with by the FIIs instead of leaving them to be imagined by the FIIs to respond when SEBI asked such questions. In short, the argument of UBS was that the KYC requirement in terms of Regulation 15A of the FII Regulations should have been more exact and precise.

UBS also submitted that in the absence of any clear guidance from the respondent and the regulations, the scope and extent of the KYC requirements under Regulation 15A of the FII Regulations would be highly inexact and flexible because the interpretation would be left to the respondent at subsequent points of time. It went on to argue that the phrase "know your client" has not been defined by SEBI anywhere.

UBS further argued that the requirement of verifying that the first level of clients are regulated entities is stipulated in Regulation 15A (1) of the FII Regulations. According to UBS, such a definition included an entity incorporated in a jurisdiction that requires filing of constitutional and/or other documents with a registrar of companies or comparable regulatory agency or body under the applicable companies legislation in that jurisdiction or an entity that is regulated, authorised or supervised by a central bank, or any other similar body.

UBS contended that if the law required that the ultimate beneficiaries of PNs should also be ascertained by the FIIs, the FII Regulations should have specifically said so and should have prescribed the requirement of a compliance report in this respect also. The FII Regulations, according to it, had not stated any such requirement. Regulation 15A(2) of the FII Regulations clearly stated that the only requirement for any further downstream issue or transfer of ODI is to ascertain that further downstream issue or transferring of such PNs was only to be done to a regulated entity. Therefore, it contended that the order of SEBI was beyond the scope of Regulation 15A of the FII Regulations.

UBS also submitted that PNs were issued by UBS AG, London, which was regulated by the FSA. It argued that the undertaking only required UBS, London, to ensure the compliance of the abovementioned undertaking as to the first level of subscribers / purchasers, namely, as to the identity of the clients to whom PNs were issued and not as to the top five investors or ultimate beneficial owners. It also submitted that the world over, financial markets relied upon certificates, representation and warranties of clients. It also pointed out that since the investors and the clients "keep on changing" it was practically difficult to maintain this information. This argument is acceptable with a caveat. It is possible that investors or beneficial owners would keep changing constantly. Therefore, it would be impossible to provide details of the same on a real-time basis. Nevertheless, it is possible to provide such details with some time lag. Difficulty is not an alternative to impossibility – UBS seemed to have consciously diffused the two.

Nevertheless, as conceded by UBS, if the PNs were indeed issued by its London counterpart, and regulated by the FSA, why then could it not provide details? Was it arguing merely on technicality and incurring the wrath of SEBI or was it a fact that it did not have the necessary details? Or was it acting at someone's behest and in the process, protecting the high and mighty? Well, we may never get any answer to any of these questions.

UBS further submitted that the KYC requirement of the FSA, UK, SEC, USA, and the Hong Kong Securities Futures Commission who are signatories to the FATF Forty Recommendations, did not require information on the ultimate beneficial owners' major shareholders or top five investors in all cases. It is a classical case of a glass partially filled with water being termed half full or half empty. Surely, it is in the eye of the beholder. While admittedly, the FATF Recommendations (we have discussed the same in earlier chapters) do provide some operational leeway, they do, in most circumstances, call for outmost transparency. This is an issue that remains un-debated even to this day.

UBS also submitted that the FII industry, "even to that date," was not clear about the KYC requirements. It pointed out to the letters dated June 8, 2005, of ISDA which is a Global Trade Association representing over 600 institutions from 47 countries, including India, the letter dated May 18, 2005, of Merrill Lynch and the Citi Group letter dated May 16, 2005, and pleaded that there were areas of uncertainty and ambiguity about the KYC requirements under Regulation 15A of the FII Regulations which are causing great concerns for market participants in the FII industry. They were not quite sure of the KYC requirements under the FII Regulations. A request was made in the said letter for "guidelines setting out the minimum KYC requirements that FIIs should meet under the Regulations." The timing of these letters – coinciding with the order of SEBI – is as intriguing as the contents of the letters.

UBS interestingly pointed out that the SEBI (Stock Brokers) Regulations have been modified in October, 2004 which stipulated the KYC requirement but under Regulation 15A of the FII Regulations there was no requirement to obtain the same type of details of the shareholders or ultimate beneficiaries.

UBS stated that it was required to provide a monthly undertaking as to the ODIs being issued / subscribed / purchased directly or indirectly by Indian residents, NRIs, OCBs, PIOs. It submitted that it had ensured in all circumstances that the PNs were not issued / subscribed / purchased by such persons as mentioned above and it was fully aware of the identity of the purchasers / subscribers of such PNs. Furthermore, UBS AG, London, had obtained warranties from the clients on the basis of which it was in a position to give a monthly undertaking in compliance with SEBI. The undertaking only required UBS AG, London, to be satisfied as to the first level of information about the identity of the clients to whom PNs were issued. There was no mention of the top five investors or ultimate beneficial owners because UBS AG, London, only required confirming that the clients to whom PNs were issued were not NRIs or PIOs or OCBs, with major shareholding of PIOs. As per Regulation 15A(2) of the FII Regulations, the only requirement for any further downstream issue or transfer of PNs is to ascertain that further downstream issue or transferring of such PNs was only to a "regulated entity."

Agreeing with this proposition of UBS, the SAT concluded, "The objectives of the regulator in inserting new Regulation 15A are unexceptionable and quite right. It is always the legitimate right of the regulator who is entrusted with the responsibilities of maintaining orderly development of the securities market to enforce regulations and seek any information which it considers essential for the discharge of its responsibilities. The contentious issue was whether Regulation 15A entailing upon the FIIs the KYC obligation meant maintaining and submitting the information of top five investors / and whether this information fell within the ambit of Regulation 15A. From perusal of the regulation and other circulars and guidelines issued by SEBI, we find that the KYC requirements are vague. It has not been defined anywhere by the respondent. Even when the Tribunal, during the course of the hearing, asked the respondent to define what they meant by the 'Know Your Client' requirement, it had not been clarified by the respondent but reiterated what was mentioned in the impugned order."

SAT further added, "From the above, we find that the regulator did not have a clear and explicit understanding of the KYC requirements. Had it been so, it would have been spelt out unequivocally instead of expecting the appellant to visualise and imagine the questions SEBI is likely to ask. It is an accepted principle of law that if anyone is to be punished for violation or infringement of any Act or Regulation, he should clearly know the obligations which are required to be met under the law. If the legislature or the respondent had wanted to make the KYC unambiguous, it could have easily inserted or added the necessary words such as 'ultimate beneficiaries.' Alternatively, it could have been prescribed as a part of the Compliance Report to be submitted by the FIIs."

In finality, SAT declared, "In any case, it is the violation of FII Regulations of the country which would be relevant because there may be different regulations and KYC requirements for different FIIs in their own countries which could not be subject to enforcement and monitoring or compliance in this country. SEBI circular dated 08/08/2003 prescribed the details of items to be disclosed about the offshore derivative instruments. Nowhere is it mentioned that the names of the top five investors / major shareholders are also required to be disclosed while submitting the ODI statement. It is felt that any law which has to be enforced, has to be clearly made known to the persons who are supposed to abide by the regulations or law. Regulation 15A(2) prescribes that the FII or sub-account shall ensure that no further downstream issue or transfer of any instrument referred to in sub-regulation (1) is made to any person other than a 'regulated entity'. It is nobody's case that UBS has not given or has not obtained the undertaking from their clients that purchase or sell or offer to purchase and sale by it or to its clients will not cause or result in violation of any provision of applicable law/ regulation. It would not be offered to or sold directly or indirectly in India for the account of any resident Indian, NRI, OCB. It will not be in violation of any Indian exchange control regulations. It is also stated that the purchase or sale or offer of purchase or sale by it or its clients of the notes will be made to entities which are 'regulated by any relevant regulatory' authorities as permitted from time to time by SEBI. Such monthly undertakings have been given by the appellant which is not disputed by the appellant. It has to be agreed that worldwide financial markets and dealings rely on certificates and warranties of clients. In the absence of anything proved otherwise, it has to be taken as an acceptable standard document in the financial world."

SAT also observed, "There is a disclosure requirement of ODIs as per SEBI circular IMD/Cust/8/2003 dated 08/08/2003 which is being regularly submitted by the appellant, but there is no requirement as per the circular to provide the details of the top five investors / major shareholders. We find that it was only the information pertaining to KYC particularly, Caxton International Limited, that was not provided by the appellant and the respondent has charged the appellant for violation of Regulation 20 of the FII Regulations for the aforesaid lapse. It needs to be stressed that it has already been dealt with by us while discussing the requirement under Regulation 15A and we came to the conclusion that there was no requirement under Regulation 15A in terms of KYC requirements to give the names of top five investors / shareholders of the clients of UBS. Hence, there is no violation of Regulation 20."

Finally, SAT adjudicated that in view of the above-mentioned facts, it did not find any reason to uphold the orders of SEBI. Consequently, the Hon'ble SAT set aside the order of SEBI.

Finally, the Matter is Diffused in the Supreme Court

Not agreeing with the order of the Hon'ble SAT, SEBI preferred an appeal in the Hon'ble Supreme Court.

Strangely, a consent petition was filed between both UBS and SEBI to "amicably settle the matter." Accordingly, UBS agreed to pay of a sum of Rs. 50,00,000 in full and final settlement of all proceedings initiated against it in the instant case by SEBI without admission or denial of guilt. Further, the court ordered that the SAT judgement shall not be relied upon as precedent in any future proceedings in any matter by any person.

Nevertheless, the following questions remain unanswered to this day:

- Does SEBI have a right to call for "complete details" from market players, including FIIs?
- What are the precise KYC norms that needs to be respected by FIIs especially in the context of PNs?
- Is it sufficient if an overseas entity is a "regulated" enterprise and, thus, could continue to be the beneficial owner of PNs issued without providing any details to SEBI?
- And if so, to whom can the PNs be issued and how does SEBI monitor them in the light of the observations in the Goldman Sachs case and JPC recommendations discussed in the earlier chapters?
- How should an overseas enterprise be held to be liable under the extant law and SEBI regulations to provide details about downstream holders of PNs?

The wheel has turned full circle. The developments in the UBS as well as Goldman Sachs cases sadly demonstrate that the regulatory changes attempted post the JPC report, have failed miserably. It is time for a complete overhaul of the SEBI regulations regarding FIIs. Else, PNs will continue to play "ducks and drakes" with the Indian stock markets. In the Indian context, KYC has come to be known as Know Your Controversy.

References

1. Order of the SEBI in the matter of UBS dated May 17, 2005 (WTM/GA/1/ISD/5/05).
2. Order of the Hon'ble SAT in the Appeal (No 97 of 2005) filed by UBS against the Order of SEBI.
3. Consent terms filed in the Hon'ble Supreme Court by SEBI and UBS in connection with the Appeals filed by SEBI against the Order of the Hon'ble SAT, February 2009.
4. The Making of UBS from www.ubs.com.
5. Wolfsberg Statement on The Suppression of the Financing of Terrorism, September 2003.
6. Non-Cooperation with the Regulator led to Ban on UBS", *The Hindu,* May 23, 2005.

CHAPTER **8**

Monetary Policy Management: A Tight-Rope Walk for RBI

Hegel remarks somewhere that history tends to repeat itself. He forgot to add: the first time as tragedy, the second time as farce.

— Karl Marx

Nothing is unmixed good or bad in economics, especially, macroeconomics. For every policy decision aimed at some beneficiaries, there would be an equal number of people who would claim to be victims. Therefore, the challenge before policy framers is to constantly evaluate whether the beneficiaries of their policy exceed those who are not.

The moot point addressed right through the book is whether the beneficiaries exceed the victims. This has been sought to be addressed through three different dimensions: manipulation of capital markets, maintaining the independence of our monetary policy, and the threat to national security. Chapters 5, 6 and 7 have dealt with the issue of manipulation to our capital markets through PNs. Chapter 9 would deal with the threat to national security caused by PNs. This chapter now focusses on the macroeconomic impact of allowing PNs.

Managing macroeconomic functions, notably managing Foreign Exchange (Forex) reserves, ensuring appropriate exchange rates, and tempering the impact of Forex flows on the domestic economy is one of the most challenging tasks at the best of times. It blurs the difference between the causes and effects, and the correlation between the two. It is an intricate balancing job, nay, an impossible one. It is often remarked in jest that like the mythical Yeti, a successful central banker too is a fictional character. Fantasising about the ultimate central banker is the pastime of many policy analysts across continents. You may hear about him, appreciate him, but cannot see him.

Most central bankers fall by the wayside, attempting to achieve this intricate balance between several contradictory pulls and pressures. They fail not merely because they have misread the internal or the external situation. Rather, they fail because the modern world of finance and capital is far too complex for even the best of minds to comprehend. Naturally, the established laws of economics do not work in situations where the economic crisis in one country may originate in one, manifest in another and probably have a solution in yet another. In the process, global financial crises mirrors, more often than not, some of the well-known pandemics in their origination, proliferation and, of course, even in their solution. Let us not forget that we are in a globalised world where the world of finance is "virtually" global, where billions of dollars of capital move in and out of a country at the click of a mouse. Yet, the regulation of the movement of this global capital is national and not global. Consequently, this gives rise to an unequal battle between the regulated and the regulator. *This, to many, is the Achilles' heel of the globalised world.*

Given this paradigm, the challenges that often confront a central banker are:

- Whether a currency should be a "strong" or a "weak" one.
- If so, how should it be valued or bench-marked against other global currencies, notably against the US dollar?
- How to maintain parity with the commodities market, especially crude, which is seemingly linked to currency movements?
- How to react to the sudden surges in capital flows – both inflows and outflows?
- Should the central banker interfere in the Forex markets to maintain the value of a currency?
- What is the level of Forex reserves that is appropriate for a country?
- Finally, how much do all of these impact inflation and ensure independence of monetary policy?

The answers to these vexed questions are attempted in this chapter by providing a broad overview of the issue by analysing the impact of sudden surges in Forex flows, especially through the anonymous PN route, on the domestic economy. This requires some detailed explanation.

It may be noted that providing theoretical answers to all these is impossible at the best of times. Yet, central bankers need to answer them in real life situations, sometimes in real-time, which, more often than not, are extremely hostile, volatile and unpredictable. To that extent, the quality of information flows becomes crucial. And when their information line is cut or when the quality of information is dubious, they are often clueless as to how to tackle the emergent situation. Information or no information, central bankers have to manage several factors viz., ensure adequate liquidity within the economy, manage the exchange rate of their currency vis-à-vis other currencies, interest rates and, of course, control inflation. All these, it is to be noted, are interlinked, integrated and intertwined. Naturally, a solution for one issue could dynamite other factors. Consequently, central bankers need to provide "comprehensive" solutions to the challenges faced by them,

Therefore, central bankers are, more often than not, loath to allow secrecy in any dealing with the macroeconomic arrangement of the country. They abhor confidentiality. It puts paid to their best laid plans and compounds the issues on hand. Yet, we have allowed PNs to proliferate, little realising how PNs (and, by extension, surges in the flow of foreign capital into and from India) impact our domestic economic management. *Naturally, if money enters and exits the country with the central banker not having a clue, one can well comprehend the quality of economic management of the country.*

Understanding Global Imbalance

To appreciate the challenge of macroeconomic management in a country like India, let us at the outset understand the context – the functioning of the global economy, which itself is in a state of extreme imbalance. This is because the developed economies, particularly the US, are consuming on a massive scale, leading to gargantuan trade deficits. Their extreme levels of consumption and imports are matched by the proclivity of the developing countries in having an export driven economic model sustained by their low cost labour, labour productivity, product innovation, leveraging economies of scale and, of course, through a weak currency.

Thus, while a set of developing countries produce and export, the developed countries are importing and consuming. But that is not all. This export surplus in the hands of the exporting countries is invested back into countries that are importing in the first place. In the process, these countries export their savings – read capital – to these developed countries. After all, at the global level, the Forex reserves of one country get mirrored as the borrowings of another. In the process, the poor developing countries are, in effect, funding the rich developed countries for their imports, sustenance and development!

But there is a counter-argument to this story. Through their gargantuan consumption and concomitant import, the rich countries, in more ways than one, operate the wheels of commerce of the exporting countries. To that extent, both of them are made for each other.

Either way, that makes economies dependent on others' consumption, to rely on an export driven model for their growth. That would explain the fetish of the Asian countries to maintain a weak currency and why their central banks often intervene in the international currency markets to ensure a stronger dollar and correspondingly a weaker domestic currency. Implicitly, it means that the developing world is subsidising the rich developed world through its weak currency policy that sustains its own export competitiveness.

These are the imperatives of globalisation, especially for an Asian country which needs to ensure that its currency does not appreciate when compared to its peers. Should it break ranks from its other Asian peers, it could well lose its export competitiveness. *India, an Asian country, is no exception to this global prescription of contriving to have a weak currency.* It is this peer pressure of competing countries that has largely provided the philosophical support to our policy framers when it comes to keeping down the value of the rupee. Needless to emphasise, this has it own share of complications. Let me amplify.

The annual US current account deficit is estimated to be approximately 7 per cent of the GDP (2009 was an exception when the deficit came down marginally due to the economic crisis in the US) and stands at approximately USD 900 billion. Obviously, the current account deficit of the US becomes the current account surplus of other exporting countries viz., China, Japan, as well as other oil producing and exporting countries.

The reason for this imbalance in the global economy is the fact that post the Asian currency crisis, many countries discovered the virtues of a weak currency and engaged in "competitive devaluation." Under this scenario, many countries simply leveraged their weak currency vis-à-vis the US dollar to gain access to the global (read US) markets. This mercantilist policy of accumulating export surplus is through accumulation of Forex reserves, notably the US dollar.

Commenting on this paradigm, the RBI Governor Dr. D. Subbarao, stated in a lecture in New Delhi on July 31, 2009, "Global macro imbalances got built up because of the large savings and current account surpluses in China and much of Asia in the wake of the East Asian crisis a decade ago. These were mirrored by large increases in leveraged consumption and current account deficits in the US. In short, Asia produced and America consumed. There is a raging debate on what was the cause, and what the effect – the US consumption boom and the Asian savings glut? Regardless, the bottom line is that one was simply the mirror of the other and the two share a symbiotic relationship."

The key operative word here is "symbiotic relationship" that resulted in such global imbalances. It is to be noted that this "symbiotic relationship" also goes by the sexed up appellation of globalisation – a mechanism that translates national imbalances into global imbalances and local problems into global ones.

This idea of sustaining an export driven model suited the Asian countries for over a decade. This arrangement of countries lining up to produce and export to select countries had its own impact on their domestic economies. *And within a decade or so, this idea seemed to have run its full course. It is often remarked that linearity rarely works in life, much less in economics.*

While countries battled to keep the value of their currency down, the US dollar too, in the face of the mounting external debt of the US, confronted a different set of problems, leading analysts to predict an impending fall in the value of the dollar. That meant that other currencies had to rise in value vis-à-vis the US dollar. But that idea, as already explained, is unacceptable to many. Moreover, such a paradigm shift could alter the fundamental assumptions of globalisation. A stronger currency could possibly erode the export competitiveness of several Asian countries. That meant that even if the value of the dollar fell, the value of other currencies was adjusted automatically by their respective central banks to negate such fall in the US dollar.

The reason for the same is obvious. As countries (through their Forex reserves) hold enormous quantities of dollars, allowing a fall in the value of the dollar would mean committing hara-kiri. And unless they are prepared to take a big hit in the value of dollar reserves held by them, they cannot allow the US dollar to depreciate. In effect, that means that the US has outsourced even defending the US dollar to these countries, for a collapse of the US dollar would hurt these countries holding billions of dollars as reserves, more than perhaps the US itself!

It is, indeed, pertinent to note that while countries succeeded in ensuring a weak currency, they could not escape the inevitable consequences of their own actions. Remember, in both physics and economics, every action has an equal and opposite reaction. It is interesting to note that by following a weak currency policy, they facilitated exports to the US, on the one hand, while accumulating Forex reserves, on the other. This, in turn, meant that for every dollar accumulated, the central bank had to release a corresponding amount of domestic currency into its national economy. This resulted in excessive liquidity in the national economy, leading to inflation, asset bubbles and, of course, derailment of the monetary policy management.

Simultaneously, for some reason, should the tide turn, as it did during the second half of 2008-09, the situation becomes far more challenging because of exactly the opposite set of factors. We will examine both these contrasting issues in greater detail in the context of surges in inflows and outflows of Forex into India on the capital account and FII flows (more specifically on flows originating through PNs).

In this connection, commenting on the above phenomenon in *Power and Interest News Report*, Jephraim P. Gundzik wrote that the world growth "was hardly sufficient to be behind the further rise of commodity prices in the first five months of this year (i.e. in 2006). Rather than demand pushing the value of commodities higher in the past 18 months, it has been the (impending) dollar's devaluation against commodities that has pushed commodity prices to record highs." Naturally, as the players fear the (impending) fall in the value of the dollar, and reach out to various assets and commodities, the prices of these commodities and assets rise.

What Gundzik wrote in 2006 will hold true till all nations collectively address the issue of global imbalance, American debt and the value of the US dollar.

The Psychological Dimension

But as the imbalance shows no sign of correcting, market players seek to shift to commodities and assets (instead of financial assets, especially dollar denominated ones) across continents to hedge against the impending fall in the value of the US dollar. Why should one invest in a dollar whose supply seems to increase by the day? After all, when supply increases – as is the case with the US dollar – the value is expected to fall. This is fundamental economics. Yet, in real life, basic economics is attempted to be suspended by the consistent action of central banks in sustaining the value of the US dollar through persistent market interventions.

In direct contrast to such actions that dominate the Forex markets, commodity markets are not constrained by such interventions of central banks. On account of a surge in the supply of the dollar, commodities markets "seemingly" apply the laws of economics by ensuring the appreciation in the prices of commodities in dollar terms. That implicitly symbolises depreciation of the dollar. Put simply, while central bankers do not seek an appreciation of their currency vis-à-vis the dollar, with no intervention of central bankers, the rise in the prices of commodities more or less reflects the fall in the value of the US dollar.

Naturally, all these have profound implications for the management of currencies across the world. As the prices of commodities are more or less market determined, the value of the dollar or for that matter other currencies, could be well linked to the value of some commodity (or a basket of commodities). This is simply because most central banks of Asian countries intervene in the Forex market and artificially determine the value of their respective currency. Therefore, commodity prices determined by free markets "theoretically" emerge as an efficient benchmark for the determination of the value of the dollar. The moot point is: are prices of commodities determined freely?

To amplify further, if the value of the commodities falls in dollar terms, it implies a rise in the value of the US dollar which, in turn, could signify depreciation in the value of the rupee. Likewise, a rise in the value of commodities indicates depreciation in the value of the dollar. Naturally, that would be a signal for the rupee to appreciate in tandem with the commodities. But real life is not so simple. Nor are commodity markets free of manipulations. We shall revert to this subject shortly.

First, let us examine the net consequence of this imbalance on the domestic economies of various countries. As a corrective measure to address the global imbalance explained above, experts are coming to the conclusion that most of the currencies across the globe are highly undervalued vis-à-vis the US dollar. For instance, a consensus exists amongst currency traders that the Yen is one of the most highly undervalued currencies (estimated at around 60 per cent) along with the Chinese Yuan (estimated at 50 per cent) followed by other countries in Asia. This artificial undervaluation of currencies is the fundamental cause for increasing global liquidity, inflation and asset booms between 2001-02 and 2008-09.

To get an idea of the enormity of the aggregation of these two factors on the world's supply of dollars, Jephraim P. Gundzik calculates the increased dollar circulation and rising prices of just one commodity – crude oil. In 2004, global demand for crude oil grew by a mere 4 percent. Nevertheless, oil prices advanced by as much as 34 percent. Simultaneously, the world's dollar supply increased by about USD 330 billion in that period in time. Similarly, in 2005, international crude oil prices gained another 35 percent and global demand for oil grew by only 1.6 percent. Nonetheless, the world's supply of dollars increased by a further USD 460 billion.

The link in the rise in oil prices and dollar supply is ominous. Yet, most analysts seem to miss this point.

With most countries refusing to revalue their currencies along with a continued increase in supply of US dollars, it is, in effect, leading to a surge in global liquidity. To correct this extraordinary global liquidity situation, two policy interventions seems inevitable – one, the dollar supply by the US must stop and two, countries must revalue their currencies. Both these prescriptions are untenable.

Obviously, this excessive liquidity has undoubtedly found its way into the asset markets of other countries. Most of it has been parked in alternative investments such as commodities, stocks, real estate and other markets across continents, leveraged many times over by the financial sector.

The twin causes – excessive liquidity due to undervaluation of various currencies (technical) and fear of a possible fall in the value of the US dollar, leading to increased purchase of various commodities to hedge against a fall in the US dollar (psychological) – need to be tackled upfront if this asset, commodity and real estate bubble has to be confronted at a global level.

Unfortunately, in the foreseeable future, one cannot see both these solutions effectuated. And that in effect means that the Forex markets would remain volatile and would constantly be a sourse of asset bubbles.

Forex Flow and its Link to National Economics

The excessive global liquidity, as explained above, has facilitated the buoyant growth of money and credit since 2001. It may be recalled that the US adopted a soft money policy in the aftermath of the terrorist attacks on its soil. The net effect of all these resulted in a net accretion to the Forex reserves of India (and, for that matter, several Asian countries) between 2001 and 2008, aggregating to in excess of USD 250 billion (approximately Rs 12,00,000 crores of which approximately Rs 5,00,000 crores accrued in the year 2007-08 alone). Crucially, this incremental flow of foreign exchange into the country has resulted in increased credit flow by our banks, fuelling the stock market, real estate and commodity prices. And when the going was good, every manager of the national economy claimed credit for the sustained bull run in our stock markets between 2003 and 2008, little realising that such run was triggered more by liquidity caused by a weak rupee, as explained above, rather than sound macroeconomic management.

It may not be out of place to mention that most economists make us believe in a universal law where price and demand are inversely related. But in the real world, it need not be so. That is because economists do not take into account the impact of the collective psychology of market players, which is difficult to predict. For instance, when prices rise, more people are tempted to buy more shares of a particular company in anticipation of greater price increases. Similarly, when prices fall, there is a stampede to exit. The seeming infallibility of an argument that sustains a bull run is simply turned on its head once there is a bear run. In the process, the fundamentals of economics – of prices being a function of demand and supply – no longer exist.

This is what is rationalised by economists as sentiments.

Moreover, economists rationalise speculation as "healthy" and one that is "vital" for the orderly functioning of the markets. Speculation supposedly provides liquidity to illiquid markets. Naturally, in the absence of a clear understanding of the impact of collective psychology, classical solutions may not work.

When investors turn into speculators, they are insensitive to prices and continue to buy at elevated or sell at depressed prices, be it stocks, commodities or currencies. After all, the net effect of all this theory has been to elevate commodities normally destined for consumption into an investment category. This, in turn, has led to hoarding of these commodities. This explains the price spiral as the demand for these commodities for investment purposes far exceeds the normal supply. Whatever it may be, the consequences of all these are inescapable in any economy. That would explain how we had a stock market boom between 2005 and 2008, with a concomitant real estate boom and commodities boom coupled with runway inflation in prices of food grains, pulses and edible oil.

This phenomenon is not limited to India alone. Nor is our polity alone guilty of this mess. Rather, this sustained undervaluation of Asian currencies, coupled with the impending fall in the value of the US dollar, is at the centre of the present macroeconomic conundrum across the globe. Undervalued currency in a way attracts sustained capital flows as well as aids and abets export growth. This simultaneously increases the Forex accumulation across continents.

However, there is an untold downside to this magnificent story – all this results in internal economic turbulence in every country. Sustained Forex inflows – capital or revenue – lead to increased liquidity within several countries as for every dollar's arrival at the central bank, the central bank of that country has to release the corresponding value of local currency. That is why it is often remarked that by definition, exports are inflationary. In contrast, imports, to some extent, are anti-inflationary.

When local currency is issued for every dollar received, that too on a sustained basis, it becomes a case of too much money chasing too few goods. This is the classical definition of inflation. In such a scenario, central banks are forced to necessarily step in and suck out the excess liquidity through macroeconomic instruments (discussed in detail in the later half of this chapter), including but not limited to, raising interest rates. But raising interest rates could by itself be a double edged weapon as such increase in rates could fuel further flow of capital on account of interest rate differentials. To that extent, it could be a double jeopardy!

Economic policy rests in the triumvirate of fiscal, monetary and trade policies. Theoretical understanding of economics means that these policies are interdependent. Also, one needs to appreciate that growth naturally comes with its attendant costs and consequences. While these policies are usually interlinked, intertwined and typically compensatory, one has to understand that the issues, with respect to macroeconomic management, cannot be subjected to conventional wisdom or template ideas in the era of globalisation.

One way of handling this issue in a globalised world is to prevent capital inflows and outflows. That would mean the end of a globalised world. But there is a larger dimension to this debate, especially in the context of movement of capital. Recall what we discussed about the IMF in earlier chapters wherein the undiluted preference of the IMF to encourage such capital flows[1] (both inflows as well as outflows) was discussed in greater detail. What needs to factored in here is that free flow of capital especially in these troubled times, often contains the seeds of several macroeconomic disturbances.

The next best alternative would seem to ensure appreciation and depreciation in the value of the rupee to match the external flows. But that again, has its own share of complications. First, what is the arrangement to plot such adjustments to the value of the rupee? Secondly, even if an arrangement were to be worked out through an external benchmark, the issue central to the discussion on hand is that if the rupee appreciates too fast due to a surge in the flow of capital into India from the outside world, exports from India would suffer. In contrast, a flow of capital away from India could result in rapid weakening of the rupee. In such a scenario, imports take a hit. Either way – a strong rupee or a weak rupee – could have a debilitating impact on the domestic economy. The RBI could do precious little as we have witnessed in 2008-09 when the country faced sustained inflows in the first half and dramatic outflows in the second.

It may be noted that we are a highly import dependent country for our energy requirements. A weak rupee, in turn, means a high landed price for crude in rupee terms. That, in effect, makes the Indian economy, structurally prone to bouts of inflation. The only way to counter the high crude prices in the international markets is to allow concomitant appreciation of the rupee to counter the rise in the prices of crude and allow the rupee to depreciate whenever crude falls. In a way, this is logical. A rise in the prices of crude denotes the fall in the value of the

1. Interestingly, the IMF has come out with a Staff Position Note on February 19, 2010 (SPN/10/04) suggesting that capital account controls can be accepted in certain circumstances. This U turn of the IMF, albeit belated, is welcome as it provides more policy elbow room to the Central Bank at a "philosophical level." In fact, the RBI and more specifically the Tarapore Committee on Fuller Capital Account Convertibility stand completely vindicated.

dollar. Naturally, the rupee too, along with crude, has to appreciate. Similarly, if the dollar registers an appreciation against crude, it must do so against the rupee too. But as I briefly noted earlier, economics is not so simple.

It may be recalled that in earlier chapters of this book, we had referred to the collapse of the Bretton Woods arrangement in 1971. That meant the end of the gold standard. The chary Americans since then knew that while the world had, by 1971, used the dollar and would continue to use the dollar as a global currency, the fact of the matter remained that the dollar required some backing – explicitly or implicitly. The manner in which the crude oil was substituted for gold has been dealt with in earlier chapters of this book. This may not be a *de-jure* standard but can still be used as a *de-facto* one to comprehend the complexity faced by national economies in a globalised scenario.

It may further be stated that as the limitations within the crude standard had begun to manifest, the crude standard of the 1970s gave way to the multi-commodity standard of the mid-1990s.

In this context, let us analyse the rise in the prices of crude (again used as a benchmark) between 2004 and 2008 from approximately 30 dollars per barrel to 147 dollars per barrel, its near spectacular fall from such highs recorded to 30 dollar per barrel in the beginning of 2009 and its subsequent rise to in excess of 70 dollars per barrel in the middle of 2009. This analysis is crucial to understand why benchmarking the rupee against commodities is virtually impossible.

The Rise, Fall and Rise of Crude Oil

Given this paradigm of a weak dollar and a possible appreciation of the commodities market (in dollar terms), it was natural that the US financial sector had begun to turn its attention from currency and stock markets to commodity markets. According to *The Economist*, about USD 260 billion had been invested into the commodity market in 2008 – up nearly 20 times from what it was in 2003. Coinciding with a weak dollar and this speculative interest of the US financial sector, the prices of commodities had soared globally.

And most of these investments are bets placed by hedge and pension funds, always on the lookout for risky but high-yielding investments. What is indeed interesting to note here is that unlike margin requirement for stocks which is as high as 50 per cent in several countries, the margin requirement for commodities is a mere 5-7 per cent. This implies that with an outlay of a mere USD 250 billion, these speculators would be able to take positions of approximately USD 5 trillion – yes, USD 5 trillion! - in the futures markets. *It was estimated by mid-2008 that half of these were bets placed on oil.*

Readers may note that oil is internationally traded in New York and London and denominated in the US dollar only. Naturally, it has been opined by experts that since the advent of oil futures, oil prices are no longer controlled by OPEC (Organisation of Petroleum Exporting Countries). Rather, it is now done by Wall Street. This tectonic shift in the determination of international oil prices from the hands of producers to the hands of speculators is crucial in understanding the spectacular rise in oil prices between 2006 and 2008.

Today, oil prices are believed to be determined by the four Anglo-American financial companies-turned-oil traders, viz., Goldman Sachs, Citigroup, J. P. Morgan Chase, and Morgan Stanley. It is only they who have any idea about who is entering into oil futures or derivative contracts. It is also they who are placing bets on oil prices and in the process, ensuring that the prices of oil futures go up (or come down) by the day. But how does the increase in the price of this oil in the futures market determine the price of oil in the spot markets? Crucially, does speculation in oil influence and determine the price of oil in the spot markets?

Answering these questions as to whether speculation has "supercharged" the demand for oil, *The Economist*, in its issue in mid-2008 states: "But that is plain wrong. Such speculators do not own real oil. Every barrel they buy in the futures markets, they sell back again before the contract ends. That may raise the price of 'paper barrels,' but not of the black stuff refiners turn into petrol. It is true that high futures prices could lead someone to hoard oil today in the hope of a higher price tomorrow. But inventories are not especially full just now and there are few signs of hoarding."

On both counts – that speculation in oil is not pushing up oil prices, as well as on the issue of the build-up of inventories – the venerable *Economist* could possibly be wrong.

In June 2006, when the oil price in the futures markets was about USD 60 a barrel (indicating a cost of USD 35 per barrel), a Senate Committee in the US probed the role of market speculation in oil and gas prices. The report points out that large purchases of crude oil futures contracts by speculators have, in effect, created an additional demand for oil and, in the process, driven up the future prices of oil. The report further stated that it was "difficult to quantify the effect of speculation on prices," but concluded that "there is substantial evidence that the large amount of speculation in the current market has significantly increased prices."

The report further estimated that speculative purchases of oil futures had added as much as USD 20-25 per barrel to the then prevailing price of USD 60 per barrel (indicating a cost of USD 35 per barrel). When the oil prices peaked to

USD 147 per barrel in mid-2008, approximately USD 110 per barrel alone could be attributed to speculation! But the report found a serious loophole in the US regulation of oil derivatives trading, which, according to experts, could allow even a "herd of elephants to walk to through it." The report pointed out that US energy futures were traded on regulated exchanges within the US and subjected to extensive oversight by the Commodities Future Trading Commission (CFTC) – the US regulator for commodity futures market.

The report also pointed out to the tremendous growth in the trading of contracts which were traded on unregulated OTC (Over-The-Counter) electronic markets. Interestingly, the report pointed out that the trading of energy commodities by large firms on OTC electronic exchanges was exempted from CFTC oversight by a provision inserted at the behest of Enron into the Commodity Futures Modernisation Act in 2000. The report concludes that the consequential impact on account of lack of market oversight has been "substantial."

NYMEX (New York Mercantile Exchange) traders are required to keep records of all trades and report large trades to the CFTC, enabling it to gauge the extent of speculation in the markets and to detect, prevent, and prosecute price manipulation. In contrast, traders on unregulated OTC electronic exchanges are not required to keep records or file any information with the CFTC as these trades are exempt from its oversight.

Consequently, as there is no monitoring of such trading by any oversight body, the committee believes that it allows speculators to indulge in price manipulation. Finally, the report concludes that to a certain extent, whether or not any level of speculation is "excessive" lies entirely in the eye of the beholder. In the absence of data, however, it is impossible to begin the analysis or engage in an informed debate over whether energy markets are functioning properly or are constantly in the midst of a speculative bubble.

That was a few years back. And much water has flowed in the Mississippi since then. Now to answer the second part of the question: how are speculators able to translate the future prices into spot prices? The answer to this question is fairly simple. After all, oil price is highly inelastic i.e. even a substantial increase in price does not alter the consumption pattern. No wonder, a mere 3-4 per cent annual global growth has translated into more than a compounded 40 per cent annual increase in prices for the three or four years between 2004 and 2008.

But there is more to it. One may note that the world supply and demand is evenly matched at about 85-87 million barrels every day. Only if supplies exceed demand by a substantial margin can any downward pressure on oil prices be created. In contrast, if someone with deep pockets picks up even a small quantity of oil, it dramatically alters the delicate global demand-supply gap, creating enormous upward pressure on prices. The obvious question is: who is this someone with deep pockets?

It is interesting to note that the US strategic oil reserves were at approximately 350 million barrels for a decade till 2006. However, by mid-2008, these reserves had doubled to more than 700 million barrels. Naturally, this build-up of strategic oil reserves by the US (of 350 million barrels between 2007 and 2008 i.e. close to one million barrels a day) was adding enormous pressure on the oil demand and, consequently, its prices.

Did the oil speculators know of this reserves build-up by the US and were they, therefore, indulging in rampant speculation? Were they acting in tandem with the US Government? But who foots the bill at such high prices? At an average price of even USD 100 per barrel, the entire cost for the purchase of this additional 350 million barrels by the US worked out to a mere USD 35 billion. Needless to emphasise, this can be funded by the US. After all, it has a currency that is acceptable globally and people worldwide are willing to exchange it for precious oil.

No wonder, Goldman Sachs predicted in early 2008 that oil would touch USD 200 a barrel shortly, perhaps anticipating that the US Government would fully back its prediction. And, in the past three years alone, the world has paid an estimated additional USD 3 trillion (the premium due to this manoeuvring and resultant speculation on conservative basis) for its oil purchases. Oil speculators (and not oil producers) are the biggest beneficiaries of this price increase. That would explain why OPEC countries, notably Saudi Arabia, were crying hoarse over the rise of the crude prices when in effect they should have celebrated.

The global crude oil price rise is complex, sinister and beyond innocent economic theories of demand and supply. It is speculation, geo-politics and much more. Obviously, there is a symbiotic link among the US, the US dollar and oil prices. And unless this truth is understood and the link somehow broken, oil prices cannot be controlled.

Oil Economics Beyond Comprehension of Analysts

It is, thus, obvious that this spectacular gyration in the oil prices since 2004 has flummoxed the world. Nothing, it would seem, explains the phenomenal rise in crude oil prices – from a mere USD 30 per barrel a few years back to well above USD 147 per barrel in July 2008 – a rise in excess of 350 per cent. Some economists had rationalised this consistent and spectacular rise in the price of oil for the past few years as one being caused by a steep demand and supply mismatch.

The standard explanation for the increase in the oil prices between 2006 and 2008 was that either oil supply was falling or that global demand at that time was rising. Better still, it was predicted to be a combination of both. The most prominent factor for the oil price rise, according to these economists, that fuelled global demand was the rapid growth of major economies, notably, the booming economies of China and India. Beyond China and India, it was also pointed out that emerging economies across the globe were also recording robust growth, and along with it, creating their own pressure on global oil demand.

Simultaneously, economists have also been fair to the supply side with equally smooth arguments. The fundamental assumption was that oil supplies could never match the burgeoning growth of the global economy as the planet had run out of oil. The brighter ones came with up with theories of "peak oil" being behind us. That implied that we had used more oil than available with Mother Nature.

Often supply disruptions (Nigeria, for instance) or potential ones (like in Iran) were repeatedly pointed out to buttress these arguments. It is in this connection that one notes that, for instance, a supply disruption, caused by terrorism in Nigeria, of 2,00,000 barrels a day (the global supply is approximately 85-87 million barrels) – less than a mere 0.2 per cent of the daily global supply – was sufficient to cause a significant spike in the global oil prices. If oil prices were so sensitive to such minor supply disruptions, terrorism backed by oil speculation (or is it the other way around) must, indeed, be a profitable business.

In hindsight, it seems to be with a purpose.

It would seem that the lines differentiating terrorists and oil speculators are indeed getting blurred. And did such economists play a vital role in blurring those lines – a question that seemed to have escaped most of us in the rise and fall in oil prices.

This requires some references to certain geo-political developments that happened in those heady times of 2008. One may recall that in mid-2008, the entire world feared a serious conflagration in the Gulf. Analysts, geo-strategists and political analysts (surprisingly all at once, simultaneously and in an orchestrated manner) believed that Israel would launch a presumptive strike on the Iranian nuclear facility. This war psychosis was built-up step by step till it reached a crescendo in June-July 2008.

Analysts, along with oil speculation naturally began playing (should I say leveraging?) on the fears of the entire world to this possible scenario. And as a possible retaliation to the Israeli attack, it was even openly advised by many that Iran should not retaliate by bombing Israel, but by drowning its own ships in the Hormuz Strait. Why the Hormuz Strait? The reason for the same is not far to seek. The Hormuz Strait is a very narrow sea passage, yet it facilitates significant movement of oil – 40 per cent of global oil, as per some estimates, passes through the Hormuz Strait in huge oil tankers. Obviously, when this narrow passage would be blocked by Iran by sinking its own ships, the assumption was that there would be a huge supply constraint. Logically, it was explained that such a strategic strike on its own ships by Iran would block oil to the rest of the world. Given this possible paradigm, these economists predicted, oil prices would shoot up well over USD 200 per barrel.

Further, at that price, it was implicitly held by these analysts that Iran, more than anyone else, could profit – implying that even a war was good for Iran!

It is in this connection that everything the Iranians did was analysed ruthlessly by analysts. Every rise of the Israeli eyebrow was clinically dissected by these economists. And virtually everyone across the globe came to the near unanimous conclusion – Israel would (and should) attack Iran shortly. Crucially, it would lead to a significant rise in the prices of oil.

It may be recalled that in the first half of 2008 when the oil prices were rising substantially, a report from Goldman Sachs stunned the world with a prediction of oil at USD 200 per barrel. And, naturally, coming from such financial houses, such predictions were carried "faithfully" by the mainstream media in every country. And that would explain how all the data – or seemingly unconnected information – was interpreted to mean global supply constraints or exaggerated global demand with a sole intention of psychologically tutoring the minds of people across the world. Given the prevalent mood in those weeks, it was sacrilege for anyone to voice any contrary thoughts. And even independent media houses of repute became victims of such constant tutoring on oil prices.

For instance, mirroring the mainstream opinion, on June 23, 2008, BBC, in a report, stated, "Despite an emerging global consensus that oil prices are dangerously high, there seems little chance of the cost of oil falling significantly in the near future." It was an opinion, no doubt, but coming from BBC, it had an aura of invincibility about it. Let us not miss the wood for the trees here. It is well known that many of these financial institutions (surely the honourable BBC is an exception) had taken huge exposures in the futures markets in oil in the first place. Naturally, it was in their interest to see the rise of oil prices. In the process, nowhere did I ever come across any declaration by any of these institutions, analysts or economists providing details of their interests or exposure to oil before providing such forecasts! Obviously, it is an ethical issue that needs to be tackled by the world sooner than later.

The interests of these financial houses in, first, speculating on oil prices, and second, how they could continue to finance their operations through their relationship with the US Federal Reserve and the continued build-up of the strategic reserve stock by the United States Government has been briefly explained above. It is a remarkable coincidence that this build-up of reserves increased allocation by the financial sector to the oil futures market, and the oil price hike in the spot markets occurred simultaneously.

But what made oil prices come down in the later half of 2008? Perhaps the US had run out of storage capacity by then. In the process, that could have eased demand pressures, leading to the easing of the oil prices. In the absence of authentic data pertaining to the unfilled reserve oil storage capacities in the US, one is not sure. Yet, this is one possibility that cannot be ruled out. Whatever the case may be, slowly but steadily, analysts began, without batting an eye-lid, convincing counter-arguments for the unwinding of oil prices in the second half of 2008!

Nevertheless, it may be noted that some countries, by then ostensibly under enormous pressure created by these predictions, had already turned into oil speculators and taken positions in the futures market at high prices. In the process, it does seem that some of these oil speculators exited at such high prices, pocketing huge profits. No wonder, as oil prices unwound, the entire reasoning of some economists, built up assiduously over the past few years, was turned on its head. Suddenly, demand-supply mismatch was no longer offered as the plausible explanation. Similarly, the fears about an Israel-Iran conflict have miraculously receded. In the spring of 2010, the world, it seems, has forgotten about oil.

As already pointed out, oil had fallen 75 per cent since July 2008 and risen once again since then. Global demand, by any stretch of the imagination, has not recorded a concomitant fall or rise. Clearly, if it was speculation all the way up, it is speculation all the way down and speculation once again. Yet most economists continue to offer standard theoretical explanations, little realising that whatever may be the reason for the rise and fall of oil and commodity prices, in the process their credibility has registered a huge fall.

No wonder, it is often remarked that those who maintain these sentiments, sustain the prices of their investments. The key to profits from investment is to ensure sustained positive sentiments.

Let us see examine the impact of all these on national economies. Writing his weekly column in *The Times of India* on June 22, 2008, titled "Oil will Fall Below USD 100 per Barrel", India's foremost economist Swaminathan S. Anklesaria Aiyar noted with authority that the prices would definitely take a downward spiral. Aiyar noted in his column, "For these reasons, I predict a modest rise in the production of, and modest cooling of the demand for, oil in the second half of 2008. That should suffice to bring the price down to USD 100/barrel. That is not exactly low. And it may go up again if the world economy grows strongly in 2009. But let us be thankful for any decline, even a temporary one."

Aiyar went on to add, "My prediction could be wrong for several reasons – a US/Israeli attack on Iran, terrorist attacks on US oil installations, hurricanes in the Gulf of Mexico that destroy oil platforms. But let me not take refuge in ifs and buts. Let me stick my neck out and shout, oil at USD 100/barrel."

That was in June 2008. Barely a fortnight later, in the first week of July 2008, Aiyar was, given the rapid rise in the prices of crude, compelled to revisit the subject once again. In his article titled "India Should Turn Oil Speculator", Aiyar suggested that "politicians in India and abroad have lambasted traders who buy oil contracts for future delivery as speculators that have driven oil to USD 145/barrel. In fact, India itself should start buying oil futures and options. This will be a sensible risk management, not villainous speculation."

It may be noted that only a fortnight earlier, Aiyar had "stuck his neck out" on the fall in the prices of crude to less than USD 100 per barrel. But as the prices rose to USD 145, perhaps the ever composed Aiyar was unnerved. Concluding in his inimitable style, Aiyer noted that "all speculation may not be insurance. But all insurance is a speculative bet on possible disasters." But the crux of the arguments made by Aiyer was that India should purchase oil at that high price in the futures market to partially offset the uncontrolled hike in crude oil prices in mid-2008. Aiyar, the economist, was in effect prescribing the speculative route as an antidote to cure the unprecedented price rise of crude oil (which was at USD 145 a barrel) when it was only a fortnight earlier that he had pointed out that the prices (when it was 100 dollars to a barrel) would not hold out.

One is not clear as to whether speculation causes a price rise or whether speculation can cure a price rise! Crucially, speculation is linked to sentiments. It would seem that by manipulating sentiments, one can exaggerate boom and exacerbate gloom.

Challenges in the Management of the Value of the Rupee

This elaborate reference to the global oil economy (and to the world of speculation) is merely to highlight the fact that in a globalised era, macroeconomic management of national economies, maintaining the value of the respective national currency with reference to commodities (more specifically crude) is virtually impossible. What compounds the problem of the central bank is that abrupt surges in inflows and outflows have a debilitating impact on the national economic management. As a consequence, managing the value of the rupee in tandem with its Asian peers too, as demonstrated earlier in this chapter in the context of global imbalance, is fraught with its share of complications. But in such a scenario, India becomes a part of the global imbalance and is left holding Forex reserves whose value gyrates by the minute. Also, it has been our experience that there is an implicit cost for maintaining such huge reserves.

Whatever be the basis of exchange rate valuation of the rupee, sudden surges in flows can make or mar the value of a domestic currency, create inflationary pressures and, of course, create tremendous macroeconomic instability. All these pose immense challenges to the domestic economy if the rupee does not appreciate or depreciate concomitantly. But if the rupee appreciates on account of tremendous surges in capital flows, as seems to have happened in 2007-08 and 2008-09[2], the impact on the national economy, especially its manufacturing sector, is indeed debilitating.

Exchange rate management, in the context of a liberalised economy, calls for dextrous and transparent management of the rupee. We lack both in our exchange rate management. It may be noted that large capital inflows and equally large outflows could well dynamite the exchange rate movement of a currency. The experiences of the past few years clearly indicate the fact that sudden surges of capital inflows led to a sharp appreciation of the rupee in 2007-08 while the abrupt outflows led to a steep depreciation of the rupee in 2008-09. While the sudden appreciation resulted in the loss of India's international competitiveness, the sharp depreciation of the currency has proved to be extremely "dislocative" to the economy. A developing economy can hardly afford such volatility of its currency.

Readers may well recall that China pegged its Yuan at 8.28 to the US dollar for well over a decade since 1994 till 2005. As this exchange rate of the Yuan was cast in stone, China experienced spectacular growth of its economy. Given this paradigm of a stable Yuan, its concept of Special Economic Zone (SEZ) and an export driven macroeconomic model made real sense. The

2. The manufacturing growth recorded during 2008-09 was a mere 2.8 percent.

Indian experience is a study in contrast. Illustratively, Indian exporters had not hedged their receivables at the prevailing rates in March 2007, on the assumption that the rupee could not appreciate further. When the rupee actually appreciated (under the pressure of sustained capital flows – mostly PNs into the Indian economy) to Rs 39 to a dollar in 2007, exporters were caught totally unawares.

Similarly, when the rupee depreciated once again from Rs 39 in late 2007 to well in excess of Rs 50 in early 2009, exporters as well importers were once again caught unawares. Both exporters and importers were anticipating further strengthening of the Indian rupee to Rs 35 to a US dollar when the rupee actually depreciated to Rs 50 to a dollar.

This sudden gyration of the rupee was on account of an inexplicable yet sudden strengthening of the US dollar at the global level since March 2008 as well as the sudden flow of capital away from India. Even global analysts could not anticipate this sudden change in the value of the rupee (and the US dollar). Therefore, to expect ordinary exporters of the country to take appropriate corrective steps in anticipation of the exchange rate movements is a joke, if not a cruel one. The collateral damage of a gyrating rupee is so huge that some exporters across the country are bankrupt.

All this is having a significant bearing on the national economy in these grim times. It was in this context that the Confederation of Indian Industry (CII) had suggested in 2008-09 that the rupee should be pegged at Rs 45 to the dollar in the "greater interests of the economy." While such an approach can definitely be explored, the truth of the matter is that the exchange rate cannot be determined (and pegged) in such a simplistic manner in these complex times. Yet, one cannot dismiss the suggestion of CII. Therefore, we need to fall back to a more predictable and reliable exchange rate mechanism rather than one that encourages volatility or a fixed exchange rate system that allows build-up of pressure points (inflation, for instance) in the economy.

It may be noted that the Indian exchange rate regime is classified by the International Monetary Fund as a "managed float with no predetermined path for the exchange rate." Certain exchange rate managers have argued that our exchange rate policy must centre on managing volatility and not on pegging it. It can be noted that the RBI announces the movement in its exchange rate through a process of computing the Real Effective Exchange Rate (REER). This is the weighted average of nominal exchange rates adjusted for relative price differential between the domestic and foreign countries, drawing upon the purchasing power parity hypothesis.

While this may be complex economics for the common man, simply put, the exchange rate of the rupee is based on a 6-country index comprising (i) the share in India's exports and trade; (ii) regional representation; and (iii) the availability of data on the exchange rate and prices on a monthly basis. The 6-currency index includes the US, EU, UK, Japan, China and Hong Kong. The index uses the wholesale price index as a proxy for Indian prices and the consumer price index as a proxy for foreign partner countries and uses these factors to indicate excessive exchange rate movement of the rupee. Unfortunately, REER does not have a policy status right now apart from being a theoretical reference point for researchers. Nevertheless, many policy framers have suggested that the exchange rate management of the rupee must centre through the REER.

In fact, the 1997 Tarapore Committee that suggested the constitution of a roadmap for full capital account convertibility, had recommended using REER for exchange rate management. The committee then recommended: "The RBI should have a Monitoring Exchange Rate Band of +/- 5.0 per cent around the neutral REER. The RBI should ordinarily intervene as and when the REER is outside the band. The RBI should ordinarily not intervene when the REER is within the band. The RBI could, however, use its judgment to intervene even within the band to obviate speculative forces and unwarranted volatility."

The subsequent Tarapore Committee formed in 2007 and revisiting the same subject, stressed in finality that the REER should also be a valuable input into the formulation of the RBI's exchange rate policy and fully endorsed the recommendations of the 1997 Committee. It may be noted that the rupee was well outside this suggested band since early 2007. The REER for 2007-08 was 114, implying the overvaluation of the rupee vis-à-vis its global peers. While it is easy to blame global recession for the slump in our manufacturing in 2008, the debilitating impact of the poor exchange rate management in 2007 in the context of our manufacturing sector is too obvious to be missed. But why did the RBI allow the rupee to appreciate in 2007-08? Why did the RBI go against the well thought out advice of the Tarapore Committee of maintaining within the REER band? Why was the rupee allowed to appreciate abruptly? What were the policy alternatives to the Government? Why they were not pursued?

Unanswered Questions that Lead to an Inference

The answers to these questions bring us to the subject matter of our discussion: Forex flows, especially through PNs. It may be recalled that India had to appreciate her rupee to manage the surge in Forex inflows, a substantial portion of which as we know now is through the PNs, which, in turn, powered the spectacular rally in our stock markets. India, it is to be noted, is still unprepared for its financial sector liberalisation to power the real economy. The financial sector tail cannot wag the manufacturing sector dog, at least in the Indian context.

Inexplicably, when India's manufacturing sector was facing difficulty and losing its export competitiveness (because of the rupee appreciation between March and December 2007), the Indian stock markets actually boomed and reached unprecedented highs. Isn't it strange that this should have happened when the manufacturing sector hit road blocks? Is this phenomenon to be dismissed as one of the several paradoxes that define India? Or is it that the manufacturing sector was made the sacrificial goat at the altar of expeditious financial sector management – read stock market boom? Was the unhindered flow of Forex allowed by the Government to sustain the stock markets even at the cost of rupee appreciation and resultant negative impact on the exports of the country? Questions that beg answers to this day!

In retrospective analysis, it would seem that the Government of the day had a clear choice – to curb capital flows, especially through the PN route, prevent abrupt rupee appreciation, and tackle the resultant monetary expansion leading to building of inflationary pressures. What was done was exactly the opposite of what the text-book ordered. In the process, we allowed our export sector to be dynamited through a rapidly appreciating rupee. The Government could have very well curbed the flow of capital flows through PNs and saved our manufacturing sector. Nevertheless, the collateral damage in such a scenario would have been localised within the stock market. In hindsight, it would seem that this policy alternative was never actively considered by the Government.

The only inference that one can draw from all this is that powerful people within the Government, media, intellectuals, industry and our polity have a direct interest in our stock markets and stand invested through the PN route. In the process, if the real economy be damned, so be it.

Gyrations: The Challenge to the Central Banker

The gyrations of crude in the past few years provide the text and context to the discussions on hand. It is clear that the rise of the crude oil price, its fall and rise subsequently provide references to the discussion on hand. As already pointed out earlier in this chapter, if the rupee appreciates, exports lose their competitiveness in the international markets. That also makes imports cheaper. Cheap imports hurt the domestic industry. On the other hand, a weak rupee could make imports, especially those of crude, costlier. That could trigger inflation in India, which could, in effect, erode the competitiveness of our industry, while a strong rupee could impact our imports, inflation and, in the aggregate, the national economy.

The above discussions are merely intended to highlight the fact that several factors impact the value of the rupee. Some of these are far beyond the control of even the RBI. From a macroeconomic perspective, the most important issue for the RBI is to maintain the value of the rupee at a stable level. Allow it to appreciate too fast, exporters are damned. Allow it to depreciate, importers and domestic industry are doomed. Apparently, at any given level of the rupee, the RBI – the central bank in the Indian context – either ends up displeasing the exporters or the importers, mostly both.

If the RBI accumulates too much of Forex reserves, the North Block (where the Finance Ministry in Delhi is seated) may rejoice over the success of its economic policies. The accumulation of Forex reserves over the years has become the conclusive proof of the "inherent strength of the Indian economy." Ever since we underwent the Forex crisis in the early Nineties, successive finance ministers have been fixated to the accumulation of Forex reserves[3]. The reason for the same is not far to seek. This Forex crisis of the Nineties (as did the East Asian Economic Crisis) had a profound impact on the collective psyche of the country. A paranoid nation has since then developed an extreme sense of trepidation on the issue of accumulating Forex reserves or better still, the lack of it.

After the balance of payments crisis in the early 1990s, the extent of dependence on external finance for financing domestic growth has been limited to the sustainable level of the current account deficit. Simultaneously, capital flows were encouraged to ensure that such flows exceeded current account deficit. In the process, the RBI ensured that this resulted in a "comfortable build-up of foreign exchange reserves." But somewhere down the line, policy framers could not determine how much of Forex reserves was comfortable in the Indian context. Was it 100 billion, 200 billion or 300 billion?

3. Our reserves largely comprise capital flows and are not built out of trade surpluses. Since 1991, we have been running current account deficits for most years. Consequently, our reserve build-up has been primarily through the capital account which has not only funded the current account deficit but also allowed us the luxury of a Forex reserve. This composition of our Forex reserves, built through capital accounts comprising "hot money" (one that can flow out any time) in substantial quantities, lends itself to greater instability.

Surely, having opened the capital account tap for inflows, the country could not turn the clock back either. Or is it a case of having caught the tiger by the tail and being reluctant of letting it go?

The reserve management policy also assumes importance in the context of the exchange rate regime of India where the RBI avowedly aims at containing undue volatility. Obviously, the RBI recognises the adverse effects of a volatile exchange rate on trade, investment and growth. Consequently, the RBI intervenes in the Forex markets to sell or buy foreign exchange merely to curb volatility.

However, it is the reaction to a temporary crisis of the early 90s that has come to stay as an official policy close to two decades since then. What seems to have been forgotten is the fact that a policy to counter a crisis has in effect become a policy for normal times too. In the process, we have failed to appreciate a fundamental law of economics – excess in an economy brings about its own challenges as much as deficits do. *The economics of managing excesses is an emerging frontier in modern economics.* And this has been brilliantly dealt with by the former US Federal Reserve Chairman, Alan Greenspan, in the *Age of Turbulence* in the context of budgetary surpluses in the American economy. The moral of the story is that managing shortage is as difficult as managing excess, be it in the US or in India. (This is not to state that we have excess Forex reserves).

Crucially, used as we are to deficits, we as a nation have not been able to develop appropriate reflexes to the issue of surpluses on several matters. For instance, an excess of Forex is actually a problem of plenty for the RBI. One, it has to ensure that it deploys the said reserves profitably. Two, it has to balance a wide range of monetary policies which are the subject matter of greater examination in this chapter. Every dollar that flows into the economy actually results in increased rupee circulation.

Given this scenario, the RBI is under tremendous pressure to protect the value of the rupee from gyrations while ensuring sustained and uniform Forex inflows into the country. This may not be exactly the definition of perfection, but falls just short of it.

As explained earlier, managing Forex flows is not a simple issue. Rather it is a complex subject that has constantly engaged the attention of central bankers. That does not mean that central bankers have hit upon a magic formula to address this issue. Quite the contrary, central bankers are often found to dawdle, dither and grope in the dark in a constant search for some answers to the vexed questions that they face in the context of sustained Forex inflows into a country. The final solution often arrived at is akin to feeling for stones while crossing a river – a subject that is learnt while one is on the job, not otherwise. In most cases, it is observed that events overtake central bankers, often presenting them with a *fait accompli.*

Put pithily, there are several dilemmas in the process of managing the Forex reserves. It is a resolution of several conflicts. Abrupt inflows result in a surge in domestic liquidity. That could well lead to inflationary pressures and concomitant increase in interest rates. The central bank has to use a host of measures to neutralise such increase in liquidity. Likewise, a sudden withdrawal could dry up liquidity, paradoxically leading to a spurt in interest rates. That could force the central bankers to adopt contrarian measures to increase liquidity. What compounds matters is that this entry and exit of capital alternates far too rapidly for the comfort of the central bankers. It is this volatility that intensifies the pressures for the central bankers. They need to manage the currency rates while simultaneously balancing monetary issues. It is this delicate balance that often goes awry in macroeconomic management for the central bankers. Sudden surges, either way, could propel the economy out of control. Global uncertainties make the task significantly complex and critical.

Forex flows, therefore, have significant implications for the domestic economy. On the one hand, they leave the central bankers with very little choice but to maintain competitive exchange rates. Post the East Asian crisis, every central bank across the globe is under compulsion to maintain adequate Forex reserves commensurate with its needs. That is primarily to protect the economy from extreme gyrations in the value of its currency with respect to the other currencies, mostly the US dollar. A surge in inflow of Forex or an abrupt outflow impacts domestic liquidity. This, in turn, influences the independence of the domestic monetary policy. Balancing these three factors remains at the core of the functioning of any central bank. It is often found that every central banker, India's included, is successful at best in meeting the imperial demands of two of the three factors listed above, but not all of them simultaneously. The balancing of these three factors all at once remains at the core of every central banking mandate. Colourfully, it is explained as an "impossible trinity" or a "trilemma" of a central banker.

The Dilemma of Trilemma

Explaining the policy issues that need to be tackled on account of foreign capital flows, the Ministry of Finance, Government of India, stated in 2007, "The management of capital flows is a complex process encompassing a spectrum of policy choices, which *inter alia,* include: the appropriate level of reserves; monetary policy objectives related to liquidity management and interest rates; and maintenance of healthy financial market conditions with financial stability."

Commenting on the issue of trilemma, the 11th Five-Year Plan of the Government of India states, "The problem posed by having to manage large inflows has been discussed in Chapter 10. It arises because of the well known 'trilemma' that it is not possible to achieve three objectives simultaneously, i.e. free capital mobility, an independent monetary policy and a stable exchange rate. Attention should be given to measures to restrain these capital flows and enhance the absorptive capacity in the economy to avoid running into the classical 'Dutch Disease' situation where non-tradable become overpriced and erodes the competitiveness of the economy in the tradable sector."

What makes the job of the central banker unenviable is that capital flowing into India as well as away from India cannot be easily predicted. It can enter and exit even in the presence of sound fundamentals. This entry and exit of capital is highly prejudiced by investor sentiments, global developments and, of course, inexplicable reasons. *Interestingly, the logic for entry of foreign capital can be the logic for exit too.* Nothing is certain in this entire exercise. That makes the job of predicting flows of capital into a country extremely difficult. Analysts and the pundits in the media are often caught analysing the reasons only after the horse has bolted from the stable. In this game, there are no rules and definitely no referees. Central bankers across the globe believe that they are the referees and empowered to provide the rules. In the war with those engaged in moving their capital globally, central bankers are found to invariably come second best.

The reason for the same is very obvious. Capital flow, especially international capital, is extremely volatile. It is an extremely tough task-master. Unlike central bankers, it is ruthless, cold and calculative. It is controlled by the best of minds, coupled with the best of technology. On the slightest provocation, it would move from one jurisdiction to another, without any remorse or emotions. *Better still, global capital can manage the environment that justifies its movement.* A hint of a negative report from the Government, a possible delay in the monsoon, a probable political uncertainty, strained international relations, the impact of multilateral decisions, domestic economic policies and several other factors can make or break the capital flow into an economy. Sometimes, even a loaded statement from the Government is sufficient to make or mar the markets in a country.

Naturally, central bankers are often on the lookout for causes that can lead to increased inflows as well as sudden outflows of Forex from a country. When they occur, they do so both abruptly and in plenty, leaving very little head room for manoeuvre as well as reaction time. Central bankers are constantly chary of this phenomenon.

It has to be noted that all Forex flows are not volatile. For instance, FDIs are less volatile than say the portfolio flows into the stock markets. It has been repeated by several economists that there is a positive hierarchy of preferences to the capital flows into an economy. What adds to the pressure of managing capital flows is that the capital emanating from tax havens (often managed by some popular hedge funds) enters an economy and this capital is extremely volatile. Equally, it is very difficult to judge as to what could make this capital move. As we have seen in the previous chapters, one cannot fathom the mind of the phantom that operates this capital from obscure tax havens. Naturally, the science of monetary policy management includes the art of reading the mind of the phantoms in the tax havens. This is virtually impossible.

The entire paradigm was succinctly captured by Shankar Acharya in his Working Paper titled *India's Macroeconomic Performance and Policies since 2000* wherein he states, "From 2002-03 to 2007-08, India experienced a sustained and unprecedented surge in net foreign capital inflows, which soared ten-fold from USD 10.8 billion in 2002-03 to USD 108 billion in 2007-08. As a proportion of GDP, the increase was from 2.1 percent of GDP to 9.2 percent. The surge was particularly strong in the two years between 2005-06 and 2007-08, when net inflows jumped four-fold from USD 25 billion to USD 108 billion. Since over the period 2002-03 to 2007-08, the current account was close to balance, the bulk of the net inflows went to swell the country's foreign exchange reserves. These reserves rose from USD 76 billion in March 2003 to USD 310 billion in March 2008, with nearly USD 160 billion being added in the last two years. The main forms of capital inflow were foreign direct and portfolio investment and external commercial borrowing by Indian companies. The capital surge and the resultant reserves build-up posed major challenges and choices for the country's macroeconomic policies, especially in regard to the exchange rate, convertibility and monetary policies."

But as we would see shortly, it is this sustained flow of capital into the Indian stock markets, especially from tax havens, that dynamites the monetary policy management. In the alternative, money flowing into the Indian economy through any route that allows anonymity to the owners of such funds raises similar concerns. However, there is a serious difference between the two. While getting details of the ultimate beneficiaries is fraught with uncertainties for the Government of India, in the case of tax havens, surely, it cannot blame anyone else for the anonymous route offered by it through PNs! And till it rectifies the same, it has very little moral authority in compelling other countries to disclose the names of Indian having such accounts abroad. *To me, this is the soft underbelly in our debate concerning tax havens.* In this connection, one is reminded of the Holy Bible which tells us rather philosophically that we should not remove the mole from other man's eye till we remove the beam from our own.

Volatility and its Impact on Monetary Policy

To amplify what has been stated above in brief, an overview of a typical monetary policy would be in order. When the central banker intervenes in the foreign exchange market through purchase of foreign exchange (this purchase aggregates to form the foreign exchange reserve of India), it injects liquidity into the system through the corresponding sales of domestic currency. For instance, whenever the RBI receives one dollar on account of export or capital flow, it is bound to release the corresponding rupees at the prevailing exchange rate into the national economy. Conversely, when it sells foreign exchange (either for imports or capital outflows), domestic liquidity is absorbed from the system. However, what is of constant worry for the RBI is the "unanticipated expansion or contraction" of money supply. Such abrupt disruptions have the calculated effect of disturbing the monetary policy of an economy.

One classical way to manage such flows is to allow the rupee to appreciate rapidly in the surge in inflows or depreciate in the case of surge in outflows. While in theory, such adjustments may be possible, they are impossible to carry out in practice. Abrupt adjustments in the exchange rates have been found to have a debilitating impact on the domestic economy. A sudden appreciation of the rupee, as happened in 2007, instantly dynamited the Indian export sector. Similarly, any depreciation in the value of the rupee too seems to affect the domestic players, especially importers, very heavily. Policy analysts are veering to the conclusion that an emerging economy – especially its manufacturing sector – profits more from a stable exchange rate mechanism than one that allows significant gyration of its currency.

Therefore, the overall monetary policy management includes neutralising the sudden impact on domestic liquidity arising out of capital flows. Most techniques to offset the impact of such Forex flows are classified as either market-based or non-market-based approaches. The market-based approach involves either withdrawal or injection of liquidity, as the case may be. The non-market-based approach involves the use of quantitative barriers, rules or restrictions in market activity, which attempt to keep the potential injection or withdrawal of liquidity outside the domestic financial system. The market-based approach, aimed at neutralising the monetary impact of foreign inflows, is termed as sterilisation.

The scope of sterilisation operations is circumscribed by the Reserve Bank of India Act, 1934. First, the Reserve Bank is not allowed to borrow beyond its paid-up capital of Rs. 5 crores without collateral. This requires Government securities to be furnished as underlying collateral in virtually all cases. Second, the Reserve Bank cannot issue its own paper under the extant provisions of the Act. The stock of marketable Government paper with the Reserve Bank being finite can, thus, affect the extent of its monetary policy operations.

This challenge to India arises in the context of increasing liberalisation of the Indian economy and integrating the same with the global economy. Naturally, inward Forex flow results in increased liquidity, leading to challenges in the management of domestic liquidity. Needless to emphasise there is a trade-off between the excessive volatility in the financial markets, exchange rates and interest rates. Tinkering with any of these could result in erosion in the competitiveness of the Indian economy. On the other hand, there is sterilisation – in effect, withdrawing liquidity from the economy by issuing the appropriate instruments. *This is borrowings by the RBI when it is not in need of such borrowings.* The RBI has to properly balance between the two. If it relies too much on sterilisation, it may have to pay a heavy cost. If it relies too much on tinkering with one of the three parameters constituting the "trilemma," it actually shoots itself. Either way, it is not a happy prospect for the RBI.

In short, in the face of sustained capital flows, India's Forex reserves had been burgeoning till at least early 2008 (we will deal with the issue of reversal of capital outflows from India in 2008 and 2009 shortly). It is in this connection and due to the imperative need to manage the concomitant increase in domestic liquidity that the RBI, with enormous foresight, constituted an internal group on the Instruments of Sterilisation in 2002-03.

Sterilisation

Addressing the issue of volatility on the monetary policy management, the working group, at the outset, stated, "In emerging markets, capital flows are often relatively more volatile and sentiment driven, not necessarily being related to the fundamentals in these markets. Such volatility imposes substantial risks on the market agents, which they may not be able to sustain or manage. Where the exchange rate is essentially market determined, the authorities intervene in order to contain volatility and reduce risks to the market participants and for the economy as a whole, some difficult choices need to be made."

The difficult choices available to the RBI to deal with volatility are whether to intervene so as to curb the same. Secondly, the next logical question to the RBI is how to intervene, that is, what are the instruments available to the RBI to carry out such intervention. Finally, the next policy choice that needs to be discussed is the determination of the quantum of intervention.

In this connection, the group suggested that a view has to be taken by the authorities for operational purposes on:

- The extent of Forex market intervention and consequent build-up of reserves; and
- Whether to sterilise or not, and if so, to what extent.

The report of the group correctly summarised, "It is evident that operations involving sterilisation are undertaken in the context of a policy response which has to be viewed as a package encompassing exchange rate policy, level of reserves, interest rate policy, along with considerations related to domestic liquidity, financial market conditions as a whole, and degree of openness of the economy."

Therefore, the policy response of the RBI, the working group correctly concluded, depends on several policy level trade-offs. These trade-offs are also expected to be between the short-term and the long-term. It may well be appreciated that judgement on whether capital flows are temporary ones or investments for the long-term are extremely difficult. The working group correctly states that this distinction between short-term and long-term flows could be conceptually clear. But in practice, it admits that it is not always easy to distinguish between the two for operational purposes. On this, the group concludes, stating, "Moreover, at any given time, some flows could be of an enduring nature whereas others could be short-term and, hence, reversible. More important, what appears to be short-term could tend to last longer and vice versa, imparting a dynamic dimension to judgment about their relative composition."

The group also noted that unsterilised intervention in Forex markets could lead to an alignment of domestic interest rates with international interest rates. Further, it was argued that this could have beneficial effects on investment and growth. Nevertheless, on the downside, such unrestrained capital flows, could lead to asset price volatility caused through imprudent lending. In such a scenario, there is a constant fear in our economists that it could have adverse effects, with possibilities of abrupt capital reversals. Consequently, there is greater convergence on sterilisation as a policy response simply because being a temporary measure, it addresses short-term, fleeting and passing inflows effectively. Furthermore, it can be implemented quickly.

What is crucial to the management of inflation caused through excessive liquidity is that sterilisation ensures that base money and money supply remain unchanged, thereby avoiding the undesirable expansionary effects of capital inflows. Furthermore, Forex market intervention accompanied by sterilisation allows the monetary authority to build international reserves that will help withstand future shocks. However, prolonged sterilisation runs the risk of upward pressure on interest rates, which could itself attract further Forex inflows, neutralising the impact of sterilisation.

Sterilisation also has its costs. The net cost of sterilisation to the central bank is the difference between the interest rate on domestic securities and the rate of return on foreign exchange reserves adjusted for any exchange rate change. The larger the extent of sterilisation and the greater the yield differentials, the higher is the cost. Commenting on the above as a cost of sterilisation, the then finance minister in his budget speech of 2008 stated, "Merchandise exports have come under some pressure due to the appreciation of the rupee and may fall just short of the target of USD 160 billion, although the growth rate was strong at 21.8 per cent during April-December 2007-08. I may note that the interest cost of sterilisation through Market Stabilisation Bonds (MSS), estimated at Rs. 8,351 crores for the whole year is, in a sense, subsidy to the export sector. Government is sensitive to the needs of the export sector and will continue to respond sympathetically as the situation demands."

The increasing openness of the Indian economy and the management of liquidity, following strong capital inflows, is indeed a challenge to the RBI to manage the macroeconomic balances within the national economy. As explained above, there is a definite trade-off between curbing excessive volatility in the financial markets and managing the exchange and interest rates. Further, some of these could result in erosion in the competitiveness of the economy, on the one hand, and the financial cost of sterilisation, on the other. All these require some dextrous handling and a very delicate approach, as for every action proposed by the RBI, there are some inevitable consequences.

Following the adoption of structural reforms and external sector liberalisation in the early 1990s, the Indian economy experienced surges of capital flows. While the capital inflows eased the external financing constraint, naturally they, as noted above, also posed dilemmas for the conduct of the monetary policy. Under the circumstances, the objectives of containing exchange rate volatility, inflation and sustained increase in Forex reserves become increasingly difficult to achieve. More particularly, if capital inflows outstrip the demand for foreign exchange, the situation often necessitates interventions by the central bank

Fig 1: Coping with Surges in Capital Inflows: Macroeconomic and Prudential Considerations

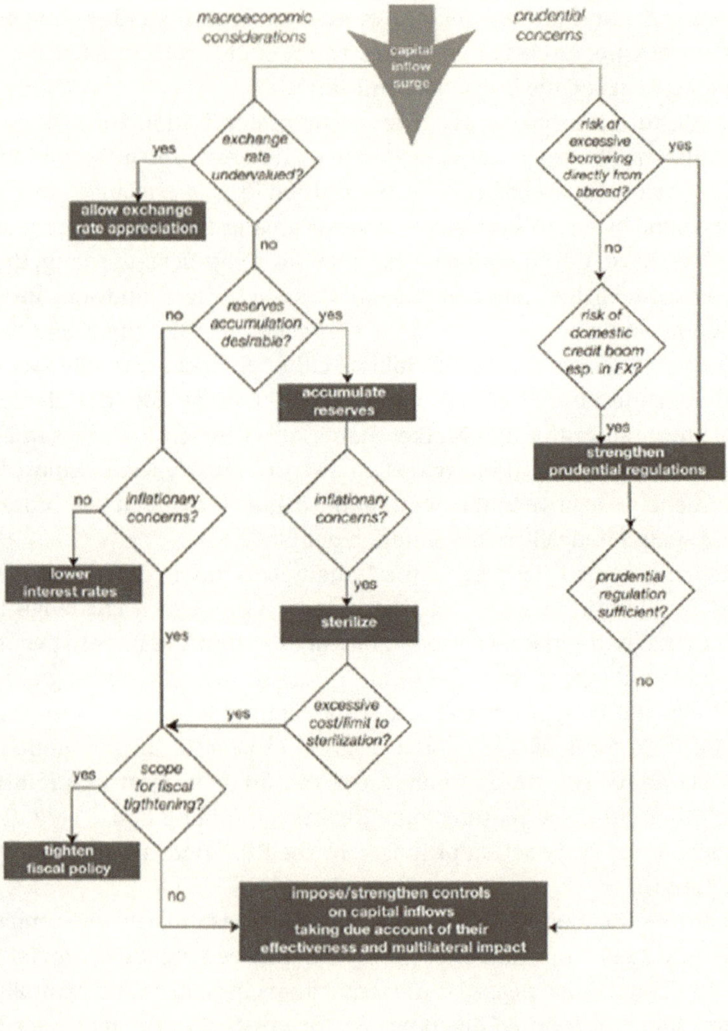

1/ From the perspective of an individual country, without taking account of multilateral considerations; on the effectiveness of controls, see Section III.

to drain off the excess supply of foreign currency. In doing so, the accretion to official reserves implies an immediate expansion in primary money supply, with attendant consequences for domestic inflation.

In the event of tight liquidity conditions, the RBI's liquidity support to primary dealers enables it to directly intervene in the market, thereby moderating pressures on the overnight call money rates. Thus, the Liquidity Adjustment Facility (LAF) has emerged as the principal operating instrument of monetary policy, enabling the RBI to modulate short-term liquidity under varied financial market conditions. The LAF operates through daily repo and reverse repo auctions that set a corridor for the short-term interest rates, consistent with the policy objectives

Apart from the LAF, which is essentially an instrument of day-to-day liquidity management, sterilisation operations are conducted through several other means. In the past, the RBI had augmented its ability to carry out Open Market Operations (OMOs) by converting non-marketable special securities into marketable paper. With the full conversion of the entire stock of such paper in September 2003, the RBI was unable to further resort to such operations. The RBI cannot issue its own paper under the extant provisions of the Reserve Bank of India Act, 1934, and such an option has generally not been favoured in India.

The Market Stabilisation Scheme (MSS) was subsequently introduced in April 2004 to provide the RBI (under recommendations of the group constituted by the RBI to recommend instruments of sterilisation) with an additional instrument of liquidity management and to relieve the LAF from the burden of sterilisation operations. The MSS is an arrangement between the Government of India and the Reserve Bank of India to mop up the excess liquidity generated on account of the accretion of the foreign exchange assets of the bank to neutralise the monetary impact of capital flows. Under the scheme, the RBI issues treasury bills/dated Government securities by way of auctions and the cost of sterilisation is borne by the Government.

The IMF puts the entire debate of liberalising capital flows in the proper perspective. The appropriate policy response obviously cannot be put through a straitjacket formula and is likely to be "multifaceted," according to the circumstances facing the country. In this connection, the IMF in a staff position paper examines the series of options available to a central banker as hereunder:

"Exchange rate appreciation: The first question is whether the exchange rate should be allowed to appreciate. Although countries are frequently concerned that an appreciation will damage competitiveness of the tradable sector, the

multilateral context is paramount here: if the exchange rate is undervalued from a multilateral perspective, the appropriate response would be to allow the nominal exchange rate to appreciate passively in response to the capital inflows.

Reserve accumulation... The next question is whether the country has a relatively low level of foreign exchange reserves and whether some further reserve accumulation would be desirable. If so, the capital inflows may present a useful opportunity to augment the central bank's reserve holdings.

...and sterilization: If there are inflation concerns, the resulting increase in the money supply can be sterilized through open-market operations or, more generally, a corresponding decrease in domestic credit. There are, however, limits to sterilization.

Monetary and fiscal policies: The policy response would be to lower interest rates, thus, reducing incentives for inflows, and to tighten fiscal policy – particularly when capital inflows are driven by fiscal expansion – thus, reducing currency appreciation pressures.

Controls on capital inflows: In the face of substantial inflows, a purely macroeconomic policy response may not suffice in some country circumstances (as described above), and controls on capital inflows may form a useful part of the policy toolkit. "

The matrix of the policy responses available in the IMF document is available in the previous page.

The Lessons of 2008-09

To understand the efficacy of all these policy formulations in the context of Forex flow to and from India, let us make a brief study of the challenges to the Indian economy in 2008-09. It is often remarked that 2008-09 was a peculiar year. Since September 2008, the world witnessed an economic crisis followed by a recession unknown since the great depression of the 1930s. This economic crisis was a sequel to the period of sustained bull runs in virtually all markets in most economies.

In effect, there were "two distinct phases" – each one as challenging as the other for the RBI. In the first half of the year, the world experienced a simultaneous increase in food and commodity prices as a consequence to the unrestrained bull run in the real estate markets, commodity markets and stock markets. In the second half of the year, the emerging global financial crisis and the consequent global recession emerged as a key challenge to national economies. In effect, globalisation – the key idea to de-risking an economy – emerged as a major risk to these economies. Obviously, the abrupt plunge to "dysfunctional markets" from a phase of "sustained high growth trajectory" challenged the very idea of globalisation.

Commenting on the above issue, the RBI in its annual report for 2008-09 states rather candidly, "Post-September 2008, developments in the financial systems of advanced countries revealed that irrespective of the degree of globalisation of a country and the soundness of its domestic policies, a global crisis could spread to every economy." In effect, the antidote to the risks of globalisation is contained in the time honoured economic principles of sound risk management policies and, of course, the extent of resilience embedded within the national economy.

The financial crisis[4] of the US translated into an economic crisis of the West at the first stage. The transmutation of this economic crisis into a global recession happened in the second stage. This was virtually instantaneous and was transmitted through reversal of capital flows that defined globalisation. Recall that we have been repeatedly discussing how the global flow of capital dominates the idea of globalisation.

In this connection, Governor of the RBI, D. Subbarao, tracing the origins of this crisis in the events of the past decade, begins with the issue of global imbalances that we discussed earlier in this chapter. The governor puts it succinctly, "And how did these imbalances build up? The answer lies in globalisation – globalisation of trade, of labour and of finance. The world witnessed a phenomenal expansion in global trade over the last 50 years; global trade as a proportion of global GDP more than doubled from 24 per cent in 1960 to 57 per cent in 2006, just before the crisis hit us. Globalisation of finance was even more prolific, especially over the last decade. For the world taken together, the ratio of foreign assets and foreign liabilities to GDP rose from 45 per cent in 1970 to over 300 per cent in 2004." It is obvious that it is this globalisation of finance that has emerged as the singular risk to the very idea of globalisation. Unfortunately, more often than not, analysts and policy-makers fail to see the link between the two.

Equally vital is the link between global imbalance and the economic crisis of 2008-09. The RBI governor states, "The chain of causation from these imbalances to the financial crisis is interesting although not obvious. As Asia accumulated savings and simultaneously maintained competitive exchange rates, the savings turned into central bank reserves. Central banks, in turn, invested these savings not in any large, diversified portfolio but in Government bonds of the advanced economies. This, in turn, drove down risk free real interest rates to historically low levels, triggering a phenomenal credit expansion and

4. The cause of the US financial crisis is beyond the scope of the current discussions.

dropping of the guard on credit standards, erosion of credit quality and search for yield, all of which combined to brew the crisis to its explosive dimensions." Perfect analysis, indeed!

All these resulted in increased national liquidity, along with global liquidity. With falling asset prices, the long pending de-leveraging process (caused primarily through bubbles built during the seeming "prosperous period" prior to September 2008) began in right earnest. In the process, it tightened the liquidity which, in turn, escalated into solvency problems for market players, banks and financial institutions.

India was no exception to this phenomenon witnessed in 2008-09, albeit at a relatively minor scale.

With the gradual surge in the capital flows since 2004, India witnessed a strange phenomenon of increased domestic liquidity. This was unprecedented and perhaps an understated problem of our successful attempts at globalisation. Consequently, the RBI had taken measures to counter this build-up of liquidity overhang that was (gradually) happening within the Indian economy. To this effect, the RBI ensured gradual increase in both repo and reverse repo rates since 2004. Further, since April 2005, the RBI had also been expressing its concerns over the fast growth in credit, and the overdrawn state of the banking system to sustain the credit disbursement, given the mismatches between sources and uses of funds, and the associated increase in the credit-deposit ratios for certain banks. Recognising the unprecedented credit growth to the real estate sector during 2004-07, the provisioning requirements and risk weights were increased to prevent a build-up of asset bubble.

But how much of this global crisis impacted India? Did we panic too much in the face of a Forex reserve in excess of USD 300 billion? Or did we have a different crisis of sorts within India? To answer these questions, let us look at some cold figures. India's foreign exchange reserves recorded a decline of USD 57 billion during 2008-09 to USD 252 billion as at end-March 2009. This includes a valuation loss of USD 37 billion representing the fall in the value of Forex assets held by the RBI in dollar terms. What should interest us here is not this valuation loss (which in accountants' language is a mere book entry i.e. one that does not entail any flow of funds whatsoever), but the balance USD 20 billion – a sum of say, Rs one lakh crores.

It may be noted that since independence, India had current account deficits, barring a few years in the interregnum. The year 2008-09 was no exception as it ran a deficit of approximately USD 30 billion. To fund this deficit, India, like in previous years, attracted foreign capital which includes USD 17 billion through the FDI route and external commercial borrowings to the extent of USD 8 billion. This flow of foreign money brings down the net Forex deficit for the year to a mere USD 5 billion. Then, how come we talked of USD 20 billion above?

The answer to this is contained in the fact that approximately USD 15 billion moved out of India on account of FII money. And it is this USD 15 billion movement away from India that was at the root of our financial consternation in the later half of 2008-09. Of this, how much was PN money that went out of India is anybody's guess.

Consider the following policy interventions by the Government of India and RBI in the second half of 2008:

- Cut in the repo rate under the LAF by a cumulative 425 basis points from 9.0 per cent to 4.75 per cent. Cut in the reverse repo rate by a cumulative 275 basis points from 6.0 per cent to 3.25 per cent.
- The RBI reduced CRR by 400 basis points since October 2008. This resulted in a release of Rs. 1,60,000 crores of liquidity to the Indian banking system. This was aimed at addressing the liquidity crunch faced by the economy.
- Further, the reduction in the repo rates and in reverse repo rates (along with other monetary measures), resulted in a further availability of more than Rs. 2,40,000 crores of additional actual/ potential liquidity to the system by the end of the year. In the aggregate, a sum of Rs 4,00,000 crores was released into the system between October 2008 and March 2009.
- The BSE Sensex fell to a low of 8160 on March 9, 2009, witnessing a decline of 61 per cent from the peak of January 8, 2008. The corresponding decline in market capitalisation was 63 per cent.
- The exchange rate of the rupee vis-à-vis the US dollar depreciated sharply from Rs. 40 per US dollar at the beginning of April 2008 to Rs. 51 per US dollar in March 2009, signifying depreciation in excess of 25 per cent.
- Reduction in Statutory Liquidity Ratio (SLR) from 25 per cent to 24 per cent of Net Demand and Time Liabilities (NDTL) with effect from the fortnight beginning November 8, 2008
- Unwinding of MSS from a peak of approximately Rs 1,75,000 crores in September 2008 to approximately Rs 22,000 crores by July 2009.

Simply put, is the monetary policy of India decided by the FIIs – read PN – flows?

USD 15 Billion to Dynamite the Indian Capital Markets?

An exit of a mere USD 15 billion through the FII route was sufficient to collapse the Indian stock market and dry up the domestic liquidity. Unlike the Forex crisis of the early 1990s, this time around we had a Forex reserve of USD 300 billion to tackle the emergent situation. Yet, it significantly impacted the real economy. It may be noted that the total Forex outflow during 2008-09 aggregated to USD 20 billion which includes the USD 15 billion through the FII route. In rupee terms, this works out to Rs 1,00,000 crores. For this outflow, we need to pump in liquidity in excess of Rs 4,00,000 crores through the cuts in CRR, repo and reverse repo rates, and unwinding of the MSS and LAF schemes. Despite all these, even in the second half of 2009-10, the impact of the outflow of USD 15 billion was acutely felt.

All these are important pointers to the fact that even a small fraction of FII outflows is sufficient to hold the entire economy to ransom. That makes the study of the flows arising into and from India through the PN route extremely important. It is believed that of the USD 15 billion outflow on account of FIIs, a significant portion could have been of the PN money. In the absence of appropriate information about the beneficiary holders of such PNs, the following questions will come to haunt us with unfailing regularity:

- Who are the FIIs that moved money aggregating to USD 15 billion from India in 2008-09? Of this, how much is through the PN route?
- Of this, how much belonged to genuine investors or institutional investors who exited India because of genuine reasons?
- Of the balance, how much exited India on account of "non-economic strategic" reasons?

The answers to these questions lie in getting at the names of the PN holders. It is quite possible that they are genuine holders and exited our stock markets. Equally, it is possible that they are forces inimical to India, conducting a dry run. Unless we answer these questions, the Indian economy would constantly be under the threat of serious disruption by such abrupt outflows. Domestic monetary policy and our stock markets cannot and should not be allowed to be at the mercy of such FII flows, more particularly anonymous flows through the PNs.

The lessons of 2008-09 are compelling – all that it takes is USD 15 billion to dynamite the Indian economy!

The dreaded Pakistani Inter-Services Intelligence (ISI) (or for that matter any other enemy of the country) must be chuckling on reading this analysis in its headquarters and plotting something sinister against India. But why blame the ISI when we have such injudicious economic policies in the first place?

Enter the Dragon and the Idea of Strategic Interventions

But Pakistan (and its ISI) is at best a minor irritant. It would, till it exists, continue to attempt to effectuate a thousand cuts on India. Of course, a bleeding India rationalises the partition and existence of Pakistan. But the real danger is from China which has territorial as well geo-political ambitions. To understand the size of the risk of China to the Indian economy, a reference to the Chinese threat to the American economy is imperative.

The net consequence of the global imbalance, explained earlier in this chapter, has led to a gargantuan build-up of Forex reserves by China. This has strangely received very little attention from economists, policy analysts, currency traders and, of course, geo-strategists around the world. Why is China engaged in this exercise? What could be its implications on the ongoing global financial crisis? Could China trip the US economy? Crucially, what are the implications for the existing global order?

What is intriguing in the Chinese Forex reserve build-up is that both trade surplus and foreign direct investment account only for a part of this gargantuan pile. But this is not a two-way trade as would be commonly believed. Most of this is unilateral – i.e. exports from China to the US. This is the fundamental reason for the burgeoning current account surplus that, in turn, translates into China's Forex reserves. In the process, over the years, the US has become extremely dependent on China not only for supplying cheap goods but also for the Chinese to fund such imports by parking their Forex surplus within the US.

This twin-dependency on China for goods and money to finance its deficits has always engaged the attention of the US policy framers who are not at all comfortable with this arrangement. And now, added to this, the latest aggressive build-up of Forex reserves by China surely has the Americans in a bind. A good portion of this build-up is inexplicable. However, any discussion on the global imbalance, notably the US-China trade imbalance, invariably gets focussed on the valuation of the Yuan. Some economists in the US till recently believed that a weak Yuan implicitly subsidises the Chinese exports, leading to huge trade imbalances between the two countries. Consequently, they have been pointing out to the imperative need for a substantial appreciation of the Yuan by a minimum of 20-25 per cent vis-à-vis the US dollar to remedy the situation. In the alternative, they have suggested a countervailing duty of a similar scale on imports from China.

Further, economists are of the opinion that by constant intervention in the Forex market, not only does the Chinese Central Bank ensure a weak

Yuan, it also causes competitive devaluation of various currencies in Asia. The net consequence is a domino effect, with the result that the US dollar is artificially valued at higher level vis-à-vis most Asian currencies. Experts believe that a significant Yuan revaluation will ensure a more realistic exchange rate mechanism in Asia as it could force other countries to follow suit.

It is in this connection that C. Fred Bergsten of the Peterson Institute, in a testimony before the hearing on the Treasury Department's Report to Congress on International Economic and Exchange Rate Policy, in early 2007, stated: "By keeping its own currency undervalued, China has also deterred a number of other Asian countries from letting their currencies rise very much against dollar for fear of losing the competitive position against China."

Naturally, China's trade strategy of Forex build-up is engaging the attention of security strategists. Is China maintaining trade competitiveness through a weak Yuan? Or is there something more to it than meets the eye? Are the Chinese acquiring the dollars with some sinister motive? In effect, is the Chinese strategy of a weak currency over the years, an unstated policy of dynamiting the American economy?

What is worrying the Americans is that China accounts for about one-fourth of the global Forex surpluses and is the counterpart of the US current account deficit. Put simply, while China accumulates Forex reserves, the US accumulates a corresponding debt. And the Americans are aware that the Chinese are the biggest accumulators of the US treasury bonds. What is indeed intriguing is that a country – the US – that prides on being "independent" of other countries, especially in security affairs, is now caught in a quagmire as it has to be constantly in the good books of the Chinese Government if it wants to avoid a sudden shock.

Countries that hold large US dollar denominated Forex reserves have a powerful tool in their arsenal – they could wreck the American financial markets at a mere click of a mouse by selling their dollar holdings. Imagine China with a holding nearly USD 2.5 trillion worth of treasury bonds, deciding to sell the same overnight. And that could instantaneously dynamite the global financial system as it could suck out liquidity and cause interest rates to shoot through the roof.

China, of course, would well know that this operation could be tricky and costly. But the Chinese know that no country can ever become a global superpower without a cost. As and when the Chinese decide to take a hit on their dollar holdings, global finance could indeed take a roller coaster ride. Obviously, the Americans borrowing from China and the Chinese supply of money to the US is indeed an intriguing geo-political game. This cannot be simple economics by any stretch of the imagination. Given this paradigm, experts opine that both are locked in a tight bear hug. According to Lawrence Summers, "It is a new form of mutually assured destruction that has quietly emerged over the last few years." This implies that China needs the US (for its exports and to park its Forex reserves) as much as the US needs China (for imports and borrowings). Political analysts call this a Mutually Assured Destruction (MAD) syndrome.

So have the Americans played into the hands of the Chinese? Recent events in the US have turned this MAD paradigm upside down. It is in this context that the recent bailout package in the US needs to be viewed, which seeks to increase liquidity over a period of time by the US Government taking over sub-prime assets from financial institutions. That, according to the American thinking, is expected to provide liquidity to the US economy. But it is all these happenings within the US that make this accumulation of Forex reserves by China extremely interesting. It may be noted that the Chinese, unlike the others, have always questioned the global order, with the US at the helm of affairs. And the Chinese accumulation of Forex reserves is surely a strategy that perhaps has an ominous side to it. Incidentally, the Chinese attempts to remove the peg for its currency in the summer of 2010 have not impressed many. It is, in my opinion, the age old Chinese strategy of lulling the opponents into a sense of complacency.

All this is not pure economics as it is made out to be. Rather, it was and remains a well-planned economic, political and military strategy of the Chinese. And, in a way, it is the mirror image of the Star Wars programme that the then US President Reagan unleashed on the erstwhile USSR in the early Eighties that eventually bankrupted the latter within a few years as it engaged in a competitive arms build-up with the former. Statecraft is all about engaging other countries at one's own terms, pace, time and cost. This is what the US did to the USSR in the Eighties and succeeded in dynamiting that country. And that is what China could do to a vulnerable US in the coming years. Crucially, if it doesn't, from China's perspective, it might well rue this moment forever.

The US, till date, was depending on the Chinese for imports and to finance them as well as for such imports. Now they will have to be considerably dependent on the Chinese to protect their currency as well as to ensure liquidity in their money markets. And that completely alters the existing global order. As each side waits for the other to blink, there are some significant lessons for other countries, notably India.

But what has all this got to do with India? How will it affect India? Does China pose a security risk through its Forex reserves to India? How will China deploy its Forex reserves? Can it do so in the Indian stock markets, especially through the PN route? We will seek to answer these questions.

Sovereign Wealth Funds as an Instrument of Terror

The reference to Forex reserves emerging as a foreign policy tool (strategic, military as well as diplomatic) offers significant lessons for India. With such gargantuan Forex assets at their command, countries had repeatedly faced the problem of putting the same to profitable use. With lower interest rates prevailing worldwide, countries obviously began exploring alternative avenues to park their Forex reserves profitably. This has resulted in the creation of a new instrument – the Sovereign Wealth Fund (SWF).

SWFs are clearly a subset of the massive increase in official assets – read Forex reserves – of emerging economies in recent years. That implies that the Communist states have become the biggest investor in equity markets!

The ostensible purpose behind such a fund is to ensure increased return on such sovereign wealth primarily invested in United States treasury bonds thus far. With global interest rates heading southwards, sovereign funds are now being constituted by countries having significant Forex reserves, to invest in capital markets across the globe profitably. Is it merely an instrument of maximising the wealth of a nation? Some analysts are unambiguous in their view – countries that hold large US dollar-denominated Forex reserves have a powerful tool in their arsenal – they could wreck financial markets worldwide at the mere click of a mouse. Surely, they may have no obvious intent to do so as it would be suicidal. That could well mean that the Forex assets that they are holding could diminish in value. But if the Chinese so desire, they could well "engage" others and discuss "issues" with them on their own terms.

What has indeed set the cat among the pigeons is the fact that the Chinese Government has proposed in June 2007 to inject USD 200 billion into a new Government company that will buy assets abroad. Beijing calls this as an effort to make more profitable use of its USD 2 trillion plus Forex reserves. What will distinguish this Chinese fund is not just its size, but that it will be a Government entity, owned and run by the Government of China. Apparently, all this positioning is part of a well-orchestrated plan of the Chinese Government to use its reserves profitably as well as strategically.

Ever since China announced the launch of its SWFs, these have come to dominate the headlines and are rapidly becoming a key preoccupation of policy-makers globally. The size of these funds and the quantum of Forex reserves held by countries now point out to the emergence of a new geo-political instrument in the hands of the policy framers. This requires some examination, policy response and strategic positioning.

Incidentally, India has a huge border issue with China. The fear is the China could use a small fraction of its Forex reserves for investment into the Indian stock markets through the anonymous PN route and could probably "talk" to the Indian counterparts from a position of strength. After all, as we saw earlier, a mere USD 15 billion is sufficient to hold India, the Indian economy and Indian capital markets to ransom.

While China continues to hog the limelight for a variety of reasons, including the reasons stated above, what is adding fuel to the fire is that two-thirds of the world's oil comes from troubled global hot spots. What is causing alarm in the US is the growing financial clout of Russia, Venezuela and Middle Eastern countries as a result of sustained high oil prices and their build-up of foreign assets. It is estimated that the Forex reserves of such countries are expected to increase substantially in future. And they could also begin to increasingly use SWFs. Some of these countries may not be particularly enamoured with India.

Naturally, these surpluses are having a huge impact on international capital flows. Commenting on the net impact of the high oil prices and their impact on the global financial markets, economists have observed that the net result of this increased liquidity is once again stirring up frothy financial markets. Further, such capital emerging from these countries is much harder to track as a large chunk of foreign assets are held not as official reserves but in secretive Government investment funds in several offshore accounts.

Notice the silence of some of these regimes to the global movement against such tax havens. And that too should agitate India in significant measure. (In a classical case of pot calling the kettle black, Switzerland has objected to the lack of transparency in the operation of the SWF!)

SWFs are not about economics, as it seems on a superficial level. As SWFs deploy their assets, it is bound to generate political heat. No wonder, many countries have now put in place well-defined foreign investment review processes. It is indeed time that the Indian regulators too discuss this issue and ensure an appropriate policy response to this vexatious issue. Obviously, the challenge to the policy-makers is to find a balance for Government-backed funds that contain geo-political issues without discouraging orderly global movement of capital – a Herculean task, considering the inherent paradox contained in the idea. Naturally, issues get blurred when questions are raised concerning direct or strategic investment by SWFs i.e. when management stakes, sensitivity and security risks, size and, of course, strategic interests are involved. The response would naturally be equally blurred, diffused and, to that extent, arbitrary.

Who said capital did not have colour or for that matter, intent? The earlier we realise the same, the better. No wonder, many countries have now put in place well defined foreign investment review processes. For instance, the US has one of the most well-defined foreign investment review processes. Similarly, many EU states are not far behind in ensuring such review processes are in place. What, is indeed, paradoxical to note here is that globalisation had contained the seeds of this protectionist state of play.

Global response has been predictable and on proven lines. The G-7 leaders have suggested that the OECD, IMF, World Bank and such multilateral institutions take the lead on risk management, transparency and accountability. Needless to emphasise, with several new countries announcing plans for sovereign funds, it is very clear that SWF flows will play an increasingly important part of bilateral and multilateral relations.

It may be interesting to note that very few SWFs disclose their holdings, strategy, corporate governance and risk control – or, in some cases, even their size. These trigger several concerns.

Perhaps learning from the likes of Dubai Ports World and CNOOC's bid for UNOCAL, some state-backed investors (China, for instance) have taken non-voting shares and restricted stakes to avoid blocked deals. Further, state-backed institutions take on more risks as they benefit from Government support. This is simply because SWFs could possibly be prepared to take more than conventional risks as they could be heavily subsidised by the state. In the process, the very idea of market functioning gets dynamited.

The concerns of the policy framers can be gauged by the fact that for the first time in 2007, the US Treasury Department's semi-annual report on exchange rates included an appendix on Sovereign Wealth Funds. The possible response to this could reflect a two-fold policy initiative:

- One, to encourage more transparency and regulation of existing SWFs and;
- Two, to encourage exchange rate flexibility to foster adjustment and discourage the build-up of official foreign assets.

The European Commission has floated the idea of suggested golden shares by which countries could prevent an outright takeover of strategic holdings and politically sensitive companies. In case the SWFs do not increase transparency, tighter controls are proposed on strategic sectors.

Another policy conundrum confronting law-makers and policy-makers is that though most SWFs are long-term investors who tend to be less leveraged than private funds and potentially less likely to engage in dramatic asset allocation shifts, it is uncertain how sovereign investors might react to losses. Nevertheless, the concerns remain as their size might move markets. Yet, we in India, seem to be strangely oblivious to this monster.

By allowing PNs, we are in effect encouraging this monster. And the monster will invariably feed on PNs.

Needless to emphasise, prescriptions can follow only if we are clear about the diagnosis. Unfortunately, we are not clear about either the diagnosis or prescriptions. With Indian capital markets too subject to gargantuan capital flows (both inwards and outwards) in recent years (in relation to its size), it is imperative that India comes out with a detailed policy response sooner than later on the issue of SWFs. But before that, it has to address the convoluted issue of PNs. Else, the Indian economy and capital markets could well be in the control of forces inimical to us.

The lessons of 2008-09 are too compelling for us to ignore. The next war, probably with some of our neighbours, may not be fought in the Himalayan peaks but could well be in fought in Dalal Street (where the Bombay Stock Exchange is located) and Shahid Bhagat Singh Road (where the Central Office of the RBI is located).

Capital markets can ignore the economic thoughts of Karl Marx but not his views on history.

References

1. Annual Report of the RBI for the year 2004-05, 2005-06, 200-07, 2007-08 and 2008-09.
2. Akiko Terada-Hagiwara, Economist in the Macroeconomics and Finance Research Division, Economics and Research Department, Asian Development Bank, *Reserve Accumulation, Sterilization, and Policy Dilemma.*
3. Ila Patnaik, "The Consequences of Currency Intervention in India" ICRIER, New Delhi, 2003.
4. RBI Report of the Working Group on Instruments of Sterilisation.
5. Speech on Financial Sector Reforms and RBI's Balance Sheet Management by Dr. Y.V. Reddy, at Bengaluru on November 14, 1997.
6. Shankar Acharya, *India's Macroeconomic Performance and Policies Since 2000,* ICRIER Working Paper No 225, 2008.
7. "Global Financial Crisis - Questioning the Questions", JRD Tata Memorial Lecture delivered by Dr. D. Subbarao, Governor, RBI, New Delhi, on July 31, 2009.
8. Reserve Bank of India, Annual Policy Statement 2009-10, April 21, 2009.

9. "India : Managing the Impact of the Global Financial Crisis", Speech by Dr. D. Subbarao, delivered at the Confederation of Indian Industry's National Conference and Annual Session, 2009, in New Delhi, on March 26, 2009.
10. "Management of the Capital Account in India: Some Perspectives", Inaugural address delivered by Dr. Y. V. Reddy, Governor, Reserve Bank of India, at the Annual Conference of the Indian Econometric Society, Hyderabad, on January 3, 2008.
11. Discussion paper prepared by RGE Monitor on SWFs.
12. CII, "Dealing with the Impact of the Global Financial Crisis", 2008.
13. United States Senate Permanent Subcommittee on Investigations – the Role of Market Speculation in rising Oil and Gas Prices – a Need to put the Cop back on the Beat – 2006.
14. IMF Staff Position Note, February 19, 2010 (SPN/10/04).
15. "What is Keeping Oil Prices so High" BBC, dated June 23, 2008.

CHAPTER 9

Indian Policy Responses

Make the lie big, make it simple, keep saying it, and eventually they will believe it.

— Adolf Hitler

Not many Indians may know about Munich, the third largest city in Germany after Berlin and Hamburg. Further still, a smaller number of Indians may know of an annual event in that city – the Munich Conference on Security Policy. This was founded in 1962 by German publisher Ewald-Heinrich von Kleist-Schmenzin under a tongue twisting title, *Wehrkundetagung.* Over the years, this conference has become a prestigious meeting point of men (and women) at the helm of national security to discuss and exchange views on foreign and security policy challenges faced by their respective countries as well as globally. Ministers, Members of Parliament, high-ranking representatives of the armed forces, scientist, and the media are invited to the discussion forum, which focusses on foreign and security policy challenges, primarily in European and American relations.

Each year, in the first week of February, some 250 participants from 40 countries discuss in depth their views on the development of "transatlantic relations as well as European and global security." (One needs to be reminded that both sides of the Atlantic Ocean do not constitute the globe. Yet, that is how people usually on both sides of the Atlantic define it.) This international conference prides itself in being a unique forum for discussions on security and peace policy. At the beginning of the 21st century, with its global challenges, this conference makes important contributions in shaping the future of international security architecture.

All these make the Munich Conference an exciting annual event to discuss issues relating to security. It invites the very best from various countries to discuss "global security." For all the reasons stated above, it is the most unlikely place to discuss something specifically relating to India. Consequently, for over four decades, this conference has never attracted the attention of our media, with the sole exception of 2007. Speaking at the 43rd Munich Conference on security policy in 2007, the then National Security Adviser (NSA) M. K. Narayanan chose to address "the issue of financing of terrorism in the context of a sustained and multi-pronged combat against international terrorism." Of course, this was a very pertinent issue and was perfectly in sync with the conference theme of Global Crisis – Global Responsibility. There were three underlying assumptions to this invitation – one that terrorism was global; two, it required a globally orchestrated response; and three, the West finally agreed that India was part of the globe.

It is often remarked that this issue of eliminating financing that is linked to terrorism is the single largest challenge to all Governments in a civilised world. What was particularly spectacular about the entire address is that the NSA drew on the experiences of Asia, more particularly India, to explain how South Asian terror groups fund their operations. It may be noted that the entire focus of the NSA was rooted to the issue of disseminating the experiences gained by India on the operational strategies adopted by these terror groups.

Explaining the potential opportunity to reduce terrorism by eliminating the known means of terrorist financing, the NSA, in his well drafted speech, elaborated, "Reducing the flow of funds and money supply to terrorist outfits and organisations is perhaps the most vital aspect after penetration of these outfits. Reducing the flow of funds would limit terrorist capability to acquire weapons, recruit cadres, establish training facilities and state-of-the-art secure communications." In effect, the NSA hit the nail right on the head – to curb terrorism, it is vital that nation states cut or at least reduce, the flow of funds to the terror groups. Unless terror groups are starved of their funds, it is impossible to contain terror.

Explaining in greater detail in his address about the common methods employed by terrorist outfits to generate funds, as experienced in the context of South Asia, the NSA highlighted eleven such methods. Briefly stated these include:

- Voluntary contributions: From individuals, members of expatriate communities, and organisations that sympathise with the broad objectives of the terrorist organisation.
- Forced/compulsory donations: Ethnic, ideological and religious terrorists are known to use the technique of forced or compulsory donations.
- State support/sponsorship: The Lashkar-e-Tayyeba, Hizbul Mujahideen and Al Badr (which operate in India), are well patronised, including through provision of funds, by certain official agencies across the border.

- Extortion and use of coercive methods: Many terrorist outfits today imitate criminal enterprises.
- Association with criminal syndicates: *Jehadi* and non-*jehadi* terrorist outfits seek, and enter into, partnerships with organised criminal syndicates and outsource fund-raising to the latter.
- Utilisation of legitimate business enterprises: Terrorist outfits set up legitimate business enterprises viz. restaurants, real estate, shipping, etc. and utilise part of the proceeds to siphon off funds for terrorist activities.
- Stock market operations: Isolated instances of terrorist outfits manipulating the stock markets to raise funds for their operations have been reported. Stock exchanges in Mumbai and Chennai (India) have, on occasions, reported that fictitious or notional companies were engaging in stock market operations. Some of these companies were later traced to terrorist outfits.
- Misuse of banking channels: Legitimate banking channels are regularly being used to fund terrorist operations. Use of both real and fraudulent ATM cards has also been resorted to at times.
- Narcotics: Funds from drug cultivation and trafficking in narcotics are extensively used to fund terrorist outfits.
- Counterfeit currency: Counterfeiting of currency is currently a favourite method being adopted (by agencies across the border) to fund terrorist activities directed at India.
- Charities: An important source of funds to *jehadi* terrorist outfits are religious charities. Sincere believers contributing to charities are perhaps unaware that a sizeable portion of the funds go to finance terrorist activities and terrorist outfits. Many of the charities are already designated as "Terrorist Front Organisations"; yet most continue to operate under new labels.

One fails to understand why our leaders should use a foreign land or an international forum to state something that relates to the domestic audience back home. One wonders whether the thrill of added media attention makes one go berserk abroad. It is incomprehensible why Mr. Narayanan chose the Munich Conference to reveal something so important about the manner in which our stock markets functioned or how terror outfits penetrated the stock markets. The same could have been done in India with or without much ado. Yet, what he talked about are profound issues. Let us dwell on them.

Two Intelligent Malayalees and Three Opinions

It may be noted that the NSA highlighted eleven common methods employed by terrorist outfits to generate funds. Of this, the seventh method – the manner of manipulating the stock markets, was the highlight of his address and is of direct relevance to the discussion on hand. The NSA, it may be, recalled pointed out the Indian experience of:

- How terrorist outfits were manipulating the stock markets to raise funds for their operations.
- How fictitious or notional companies were engaging in stock market operations and how some of these companies were owned by terrorist outfits.

Questions were instantly raised back home in India. Was the NSA hinting at the use of PNs by terror groups in our stock markets? If such isolated instances of terrorist outfits "manipulating the stock markets to raise funds for their operations" were "reported," what action did the Government or for that matter, market regulators, SEBI and RBI, take to remedy the situation? It may be noted that this conference was hosted in February 2007. Yet, one is yet to see some concrete action on this score despite the gravity of the charge and a reasonable passage of time. Welcome to India where the most serious of charges attract minimal attention and, in direct contrast, trivial issues attract maximum attention. Nevertheless, it must be conceded that as an exception to this general rule, the statements of the NSA did set the Yamuna on fire, albeit briefly.

The crucial issue to note here is that the NSA's apprehensions were not merely hypothetical. Nor was he speaking on the issue casually. He was representing India in one of the most prestigious global summits on security. It is obvious that the NSA was indeed referring to the manipulation of the Indian stock markets by the terrorists. Whether such manipulation was orchestrated through the PN route or not is secondary to the issue on hand. Importantly, the language used by the NSA clearly indicates a temporal link in the manipulation of stock markets between the past, present and possibly the future. Simply stated, all these representations by the NSA at the Munich Conference seem to be based on hard facts, unequivocal experiences and hard-nosed evidences gathered by our intelligence services.

In direct contrast, responding to the queries of an anxious press, the then SEBI Chairman Mr. M. Damodaran, is reported to have summarily dismissed the views of the NSA. But that added further fuel to the already blazing fire on the issue of PNs. Stating that the NSA's remarks were used by the media out of context, he opined on several occasions to repeated questioning by journalists: "We do not have any evidence that money raised from the Indian capital market has been used for terrorist activities," and went on to compound the confusion by adding, "His comments were not country-specific." (In a meeting organised by the Institute of Chartered Accountants of India in Chennai in December 2007, I did bring this issue to the attention of Mr. M. Damodaran. Though it was an informal meeting with the Chennai press, Mr. Damodaran held on to his stated position that the views expressed by the NSA were hypothetical.)

What worries security analysts and market players is that the source of the huge amount of foreign money that is flowing into the country is virtually unknown to any of the regulators. Is it genuine foreign institutional investment? Or is it domestic black money being re-routed by way of PNs? Is it aggressive "hedge funds" targeting the Indian market for their "pump and dump moves?" Or is it funds by terrorist outfits who have abused the PN route to finance their operations in India? Questions that repeatedly haunt us after every sudden surge in capital flows into the economy or abrupt crash in our stock markets, and after every terrorist attack carried out on our soil. Yet, we as a nation are clueless.

It may be noted that globalisation of terror, proliferation of modern technologies in our banks and the innate ability of terrorists to exploit these technologies ensure movement of terror funds across international borders. Terror funding is an elaborate exercise involving several sub–plots, with the final user of such funds not even aware of its origins. These involve several layers of allowing a transaction to pass so as to frustrate any investigation, provide several false leads and destroy evidence about the actual source of its origin. All these were stated in the context of our discussions in the previous chapters. It is in this connection that the NSA conceded in the Munich Conference, "The most popular means employed in South Asia for laundering funds is the underground and parallel banking system which ensures placing of funds without actual or visible movement of money."

That was in February 2007. Assuming that the observations of the NSA were indeed hypothetical, the fact remains that the Government of India has not taken any visible concrete steps to address this issue of parallel banking to this day. If the observations of the NSA were based on some experiences, the situation is all the more alarming.

Obviously, money laundering exercises utilising the "underground and parallel banking system" have made it extremely difficult for enforcement agencies to detect, track or trace funds destined for the use of terrorists, since there is no audit or paper trail available for the authorities to investigate the matter. And even when these are available, the evidence is so diffused that it is as difficult as finding a non-existent black cat in a dark alley on a moonless night.

It is indeed bizarre for a nation that often claims to be one of the worst victims of global terror to dismiss the statements of its own NSA or to endlessly debate whether the same were hypothetical or not. The shrillness of our claims of being a victim of terror is not matched by our actions in tackling terror, especially funding of terror. This is not to say that we are doing nothing. But such stray incidences of foiling terrorists are the outcome of our intelligence and brave security personnel, rather than concerted action by the Government of India. Any nation seeking to assert itself as an emerging global power would be keen to ensure that the others consider it seriously. And for that perception to gain currency, India needs to act against terror, especially terror funding. For that, we need to think honestly, act decisively.

We as a nation seem to fail on both fronts.

Pointed Questioning by the Nation

All that has been stated till now pertains to the debate between the NSA and the SEBI chairman. If one was befuddled by their arguments and counter-arguments, the debate attracted the attention of Ms. J. Jayalalithaa in mid-2008. She was the former Chief Minister of Tamil Nadu and a tall political leader of the country. She zeroed in on the issue of flow of funds through the PN route. Given the fact that the Parliament has not undertaken to debate the concerns expressed by the NSA, PN and terror funding, this debate initiated by Ms Jayalalithaa becomes crucial to comprehend the collective concerns of the nation on these subjects and the corresponding response by the Government of India.

For starters Ms. Jayalalithaa could not have chosen a better time – it was barely days after the serial blasts that rocked the city of Jaipur in May 2008. It was precisely when the monster of inflation in India too was rearing its ugly head. It may be recalled that inflation continued to surge on a weekly basis, much to the consternation of the Government. Similarly, the stock markets, after registering dizzy heights in January 2008, had begun to show signs of moderation then. Obviously, the Government was seemingly defensive on the subjects of terrorism, volatility in stock markets and inflation.

In her statement on May 27, 2008, Ms Jayalalithaa noted the steps taken by Governments worldwide to tackle the scourge of terrorism and curb funding of terror activities. In comparison, she noted that in India, "acts of terrorism are taking place with monotonous regularity, everywhere. Practically, every state in the country has experienced the phenomenon of senseless, wanton violence. Crowded railway trains and railway stations, bus stands, bazaars, places of worship, tourist destinations, even India's Parliament House have been used by sundry terrorist outfits as their playground, often with devastating effect. So many innocent people have died. So many valiant personnel from our security forces have also perished."

Ms Jayalalithaa attacked the Government where it hurts most. Pointing out to the fact that an Indian citizen in India has to provide his/her address proof, photo ID proof, PAN details, etc to open even an ordinary savings bank account in a local bank, she contrasted this to the lax prevailing norms for investment through the PN route. It was repeatedly pointed out in previous chapters how investors can hide their identity under a sub-account by making use of the PN route. Further, she rounded her statement on that day by saying, "Investments through the PNs route are believed to be largely responsible for sudden, unexplained fluctuations in the stock market indices, including the huge falls which have even resulted in suicides in Dalal Street."

Obviously, Ms Jayalalithaa was seeking to connect several seemingly disconnected issues – terror funding, inflation and, of course, volatility in the Indian stock markets – all in one Toynbee-like sweep. For her, as it seems to many policy analysts, the villain of the piece was unambiguous. It was the PN.

Ms Jayalalithaa is not alone on this matter. In fact, there are several well-meaning Indians who have constantly questioned the Government on this crucial issue. Some of the questions are listed out hereunder:

- What prevents the Government from invoking the provisions of the Benami Transactions (Prohibition) Act, 1988, to obtain the names of all beneficial owners of PNs issued?
- What are the surveillance mechanisms to ensure that no Indian is re-routing investments through PNs?
- What steps has the Government taken to ensure that slush funds from India and terrorist funds from abroad are not entering the Indian market through PNs or the Mauritius route?
- What is the evidence that the terrorists are not manipulating the stock markets and misusing the PN route?
- To what extent is the inflation in the Indian economy caused by FII flows, especially through PNs?

There were several related questions raised by experts on the subject about the efficacy of the extant regulations about PNs in India. Surely, Ms Jayalalithaa was voicing the views of a concerned citizenry. She concluded her statement of May 2008 by demanding that the Government had to necessarily do something tangible about these issues.

One may or may not agree with these observations of Ms Jayalalithaa. Nevertheless, it would be seen that in effect, she was more or less mirroring the concerns of the NSA, spelt out in the Munich Conference. In the process, she had pitch-forked into the Indian political theatre the subject of terror funding through the PN route, the possibility of market manipulation caused by the anonymity offered by the PNs and its symbiotic link to inflation. It is pertinent to note that several neutral observers too had begun to question the impact of the PNs on the Indian stock markets which was exhibiting significant volatility at monstrous regularity.

In a carefully worded rejoinder by the Finance Ministry, the Government refuted the allegations made by Ms. Jayalalithaa on the vexatious issue of funds flowing into the country through the PN route as "totally baseless besides betraying a complete lack of understanding of the FII regime that is in force." The Finance Ministry, as is its wont, attempted to shoot the messenger instead of the message. The explicit idea put forth in this rejoinder was that global financial flows, rules and regulations that govern the FII regime in India as well as the PNs are complex subjects. Consequently, they cannot and should not be subject to scrutiny in any ordinary or casual manner. Implicit in the argument was that one has to have a degree of practical understanding of the Indian economy to comment on the same – PN, in effect seemed to be a grand idea that was propelling the Indian economy with some mild, irrelevant side effects.

National security, terror funding, inflation, market manipulation and their link to PNs had indeed become a popular subject by now!

Claiming that FIIs are regulated by SEBI, the Finance Ministry clarified that in terms of the SEBI (FII) Regulations, 1995, an FII may issue Participatory Notes (PNs) with Indian instruments as the underlying securities, subject to the subscriber being a "regulated entity." Further downstream issue of PNs, if any, may also be done only to "regulated entities." Brushing aside the fears of Ms Jayalalithaa on the issue of anonymity, the Finance Ministry clarified that FIIs are required to report at the end of every month, in a prescribed format, all information relating to PNs issued by them, including the names of subscribers to the said PNs. FIIs are also required to give an undertaking that the FII or its associates have not issued, subscribed or purchased any PNs to/from an Indian resident or NRI or PIO or OCB during the reporting period.

Obviously, the Finance Ministry was referring to the report to be submitted by FIIs to SEBI on a fortnightly basis since 2003. But as we know and as decided by the Hon'ble SAT in the Goldman Sachs case, the report was legally unenforceable by SEBI. In the instant case, the Hon'ble SAT, pointing out to the lack of regulation that empowers the Board to seek appropriate information, stated, "Not even for a moment are we suggesting that the Board could not have called upon the FIIs to report about their activities or furnish to it the information required of them under the Regulations. We are only disapproving the action of the Board in so far as it requires them to furnish the undertaking as prescribed for the first time in the revised reporting format in the absence of a bar prohibiting them from dealing in ODIs with Indian residents /NRIs/PIOs/OCBs."

What is interesting is the timing of this rejoinder and the judgement of the Hon'ble SAT in the Goldman Sachs case. The rejoinder by the Finance Ministry was issued on June 2, 2008, while the order of the SAT was issued a few days earlier i.e. on May 15, 2008. Clearly, the Finance Ministry had not factored the decision of the Hon'ble SAT in their reply. Else, they would not have held the reporting format issued by SEBI as a defence. The issue here is that by May 15, 2008, any student of law would have known that the formal reporting format for FIIs on a fortnightly basis was completely dynamited by the SAT order.

Therefore, as Goldman Sachs did, several FIIs could have bypassed the well intended but legally untenable reporting directions of SEBI. That was the only instrumentality of obtaining information from FIIs on the issue of knowing the ultimate beneficiaries of PNs and whether PNs were issued to regulated entities. Yet, it is inexplicable that the Finance Ministry relied on this defunct reporting format in their defence of the extant FII regime in India.

On the issue of terrorist funds finding their way into the stock markets, the Finance Ministry dismissed the charge by stating that the "matter has been clarified in Parliament." This clarification was issued in August 2007 in the aftermath of the discussion of the statement of the NSA. Does that mean the end of the matter? Nevertheless, on the issue of terror groups manipulating the stock markets, the Finance Ministry categorically clarified in this rejoinder once again, "Information available with the Government and the regulators does not indicate any surreptitious entry of terrorist outfits into the stock market. Besides, there are adequate provisions in the laws such as FEMA and PMLA to deal with unauthorised or suspicious transactions involving currency or foreign exchange." That was in June 2008.

But what was missed by the Finance Ministry in its rejoinder was the then finance minister's admission in the Parliament in November 2007 expressing "apprehensions" that our stock markets were being used by terror groups to raise funds for their operations. Further, he pointed out that the Government was probing *one possible* terror funding in share markets and was "keeping a close watch on a person" who was suspected to have used the "booming Indian share market for terror funding."

Using the booming share market for terror funding? Well that was the charge of the NSA in the Munich Conference in February 2007. And in November 2007, the then finance minister stated, "Recently, one case has come to our notice. It is suspected that it may be linked to a person under watch. I cannot divulge further details," This was the first time the Government had made an admission, that too in the Parliament, of suspected links between terror outfits and our stock markets. Not much was heard after that on the identity of the person or any action precipitated on the said person. After making it to the headlines of a few dailies and breaking news in news channels, the subject was forgotten within a few days. Like the Nagarwala case of the Sixties, and Bofors of the Eighties, will the identity of this person too remain a secret forever?

Or did the terror funding cause the boom in our stock markets in the first place?

Finally, answering the charge of PNs causing volatility in our stock markets, the rejoinder of the Finance Ministry went on to add that the belief that investments through PNs were largely responsible for the sudden and unexplained fluctuations in the stock market indices demonstrated a total lack of understanding of both PNs and the movement in the stock market.

While one does not seek to take sides in this debate between Ms Jayalalithaa and the Finance Ministry, the fact remains that the former was merely echoing some of the concerns of even well-meaning analysts. Were they all reflecting a total lack of understanding of PNs and the movement in the stock markets? But pray what was the correct understanding, especially in the context of the two decisions of the Hon'ble SAT in the UBS and Goldman Sachs cases? Was the Finance Ministry implying that PNs were an elixir for the stock markets that could not be done away with even if the terrorists used them and unscrupulous promoters manipulated the markets? Or is the protest of those against the PNs motivated?

Your guess is as good as mine.

The Haunting Questions

Indian democracy may not yet be a fully matured one like its Western counterparts. Yet, at times, the quality of debate is often found to be sharper, more interesting and illuminating than debates elsewhere in democracies across the globe. In the process, several administrative lacunae are addressed and policy developments take place. For all these, each one of us has to, individually as well as collectively, thank the sublime features of our Constitution and the manner in which Indians have taken to democracy.

It is precisely for this reason that this debate is crucial on the subject of PNs. It was a rare debate, it was intense and it virtually captured the arguments of both sides like never before. Rarely has a political debate on an economic issue in recent times been so sharp, factual and reasoned from both sides. This would explain the elaborate reference to the same at this point in time, especially in the absence of a debate in the Parliament or elsewhere encapsulating the entire range of issues.

Naturally, in these circumstances, there is a distinct Indian flavour to the approach, of course, fashioned by several of our noted parliamentarians. One such happens to shoot a torrent of questions that would drown a political adversary. This practice, readers may note, became part of the Indian political folklore after the noted criminal lawyer and eminent parliamentarian, Mr. Ram Jethmalani, posed ten inconvenient questions every day to the former Prime Minister Rajiv Gandhi at the height of the Bofors scandal. Subsequently, it has become a benchmark of sorts for every Indian politician whenever a gauntlet is thrown by his or her political adversary to retort through a torrent of questions – preferably ten.

If you have not asked your political adversary in India, ten rapid, successive questions, you have not made the grade as a serious politician.

Why this fixation with the number ten? Well there is another Indian twist to this too. Indian politicians are often guided by astrologers. Ten, astrologers point out, is the numerological link to the seat of power. "10 Downing Street" they would say as a matter of fact. "But the address of White House is 1600 Pennsylvania Avenue", I have argued with several astrologers. "10 Janpath" would be the instant retort. I have found that argument compelling as well logical.

Let me once again return to the debate in June 2008 on the issue of PNs. In the instant case, the gauntlet was thrown. The attack was perceived to be personal by Ms Jayalalithaa. Therefore, the rebuttal was swift, calculated and pointed. Terming the rejoinder as "a personal diatribe against me," Ms. Jayalalithaa, stated that the Finance Ministry's failure to answer to the questions posed by her were an elaborate "exercise in obfuscation." She further requested the Finance Ministry to rise above pedantry and not resort to "skulduggery," at least on matters concerning "national security and the credibility of our financial sector."

In her rebuttal, Ms. Jayalalithaa pointed out to the reply of the rejoinder issued by the Finance Ministry which stated *inter alia* that FIIs are regulated entities, with SEBI being the regulator. FIIs are required to report at the end of every month, in the prescribed format, all the information relating to PNs issued by them, including the names of subscribers to the said PNs.

From this, she claimed, "One has to assume that SEBI has the names and details of all the foreign investors who have invested in India through these PNs." Given this stated position, she went on to seek answers to the following questions:

- Will the Union Finance Ministry publish the complete list of PN holders, along with their details and the amount of investment on its website or on the website of SEBI? What has prevented the Union Finance Ministry from doing so?

  When PNs are subscribed to by a company, does the Union Finance Ministry track the names of the owners/promoters or beneficiaries of that company? Can it authentically say that the company in question is not promoted or funded in any way by an Osama bin Laden, a Dawood Ibrahim or a Velupillai Pirabhakaran? If so, how and what are the mechanisms and internal checks it has put in place to ensure that narco-terrorist money does not find its way into the Indian stock market?
- If everything about PNs is so transparent and above board as the Union Finance Ministry claims, why did Mr M. Damodaran, who then headed SEBI (who ought to have had all the details about the PN holders if the Union Finance Ministry is to be believed), tell the *Business Standard* in September 2007 that he was not "entirely comfortable[1]" that one-fourth of the market was being held by anonymous PNs investors?
- The Union Finance Ministry claims that "Ms Jayalalithaa's allegation that investments through PNs are believed to be largely responsible for the

1. Actually, Mr. M. Damodaran had stated that he was not "entirely uncomfortable." The use of double negatives was perhaps interpreted by Ms. Jayalalithaa to mean that he was not entirely comfortable either.

sudden and unexplained fluctuations in the stock market indices betrays a total lack of understanding of both PNs and the movement in the stock market". Does India's NSA, Mr M. K. Narayanan also suffer from the same lack of understanding?

Since the Union Finance Ministry has all the answers, can it state with authority that no terrorist outfit has ever manipulated the stock markets in India? Does it imply that the NSA was lying or was not abreast of these facts?

- The Union Finance Ministry may remember that on the assumption of office by the UPA Government on May 17, 2004, it was greeted with a steep fall in the Indian stock market (the Sensex fell by 567.74 points). It was later on found that UBS Securities Asia Ltd, which is a SEBI registered FII dealing through its SEBI registered proprietary sub-account Swiss Finance Corporation (Mauritius) Ltd, had sold stocks in the cash market segment to the extent of Rs.188.35 crores. SEBI decided to investigate. During the investigation, SEBI called for further information from UBS relating to its major PN clients in terms of their addresses, the names of their directors, fund managers, major shareholders, top five investors, etc. UBS did not furnish the information, citing reasons such as client confidentiality. This is not a wild, unsubstantiated allegation I am making. On the contrary, I am referring to what is contained in Order no WTM/GA/1/ISD/5/05 of SEBI.
- If, as the Union Finance Ministry claims, all the information relating to FIIs and PNs is available with SEBI, then why the impotent helplessness on the part of SEBI when it found that the stock market had been manipulated? Crucially, what steps, legislative or otherwise, has the Union Finance Ministry taken since May 2004 when this Government assumed office to ensure that SEBI was armed with appropriate legal teeth to face such situations in future?
- I now quote from the dissenting note to the Report of the Expert Group[2] on Encouraging FII Flows and Checking the Vulnerability of Capital Markets to Speculative flows by the Reserve Bank of India sent to Dr Ashok Lahiri, Chief Economic Adviser, Department of Economic Affairs, Ministry of Finance, Government of India: "The Reserve Bank's stance has been that the issue of Participatory Notes should not be permitted. In this context, we would like to point out that the main concerns regarding issue of PNs are that the nature of the beneficial ownership or the identity of the investor will not be known, unlike in the case of FIIs registered with a financial regulator. Trading of these PNs will lead to multi-layering which will make it difficult

2. We will discuss this report in greater detail shortly.

to identify the ultimate holder of PNs. Both conceptually and in practice, restriction on suspicious flows enhance the reputation of markets and lead to healthy flows."

- Is the Union Finance Ministry going to dismiss the RBI's dissent note as quoted above too as "lack of complete understanding on the FII regime" as it seeks to do to me? Is the Union Finance Ministry suggesting that the RBI is incompetent? Or is it dismissive of the RBI simply because it had dared to send a dissent note on an issue that the Finance Minister himself has a lot to explain?
- Will the Union Finance Ministry tell whether it has the names of all foreign investors who had sold stocks on the January 23 and 24, 2008, aggregating to Rs 18,600 crores? Who are these people who sold in such massive quantities, which led to an unprecedented fall of the Indian stock market on these two days leading to massive loss to the ordinary Indian investors, even leading to suicides by several investors who lost all?

Two more questions ensured that the aggregate totalled to ten. Being politically loaded ones, we shall side-step the same.

A few days later, Ms Jayalalithaa once again sought answers to a further set of questions. This time around, she used the judgement of the Hon'ble SAT in the Goldman Sachs case to further her case. According to her, the judgement in the Goldman Sachs was the "documented proof of the impotence of the Union Finance Ministry and its market regulating agencies like SEBI when it comes to regulating investments from abroad."

Crucially, she claimed, "The case (Goldman Sachs) is not only a loss of face for SEBI, it is also a clear indication that the Union Finance Minister's claim that investments from abroad are being adequately monitored is a lie." Once again, a series of questions followed. This time, they were direct and political. Consequently, we will side-step them too. But let us not lose track of the issues raised by Ms Jayalalithaa.

In short, she was relying on the judgment of the Hon'ble SAT in both the UBS case[3] and the Goldman Sachs case to buttress her point. While the judgment in the UBS case demonstrated the inability of SEBI in ferreting out information about the ultimate beneficiaries who own the PNs, the Goldman Sachs case demonstrated that the voluntary compliance by FIIs through the fortnightly reporting format was legally untenable. Naturally, the regulation of PNs by SEBI

3. The UBS matter in May 2008 was in the Supreme Court and the consent order was made out only in February 2009.

was illusory, something that could well be taken to be non-existent, especially in the context of the extant FII regime relating to PNs.

Patented Negligence?

Once again, the Union Finance Ministry replied to the issues raised by Ms. Jayalalithaa about the FII regime in India and more particularly about the possibility of the misuse of the PN system. Let us examine the issue dispassionately in the light of the pointed questions of Ms Jayalalithaa and the replies made out by the Finance Ministry.

On the question of the misuse of the Indo-Mauritius Double Taxation Avoidance Treaty, the Finance Ministry replied that "efforts were underway to prevent misuse" – tacitly admitting to some misuse taking place. The issue was one of putting official machinery in place to prevent money laundering from India into Mauritius and then bringing back the money into India as investments into our stock markets through the PN route.

On the suggestion to the Finance Ministry to publish the complete list of PN holders on its website or on the SEBI website, the reply states *inter alia,* "The information about PNs is with SEBI and not with the Ministry of Finance..." So, will SEBI publish the list on its website? Only when such names are published in some authentic website, can one is sure of the efficacy of the regulations being put in place by SEBI to tackle the extant issue.

Crucially, given the judgements of Goldman Sachs and the setback faced by SEBI in the UBS case, one suspects it cannot.

Obviously, this leads us to the next issue – could the Union Finance Ministry track the names of beneficial holders of all the PNs issued by FIIs? Did the Union Finance Ministry know the names of owners/promoters or beneficiaries of a company holding PNs? Could it authentically say that no PN holder had any narco-terrorist connections? The Finance Ministry states that "information available with the Government and the regulators does not indicate any surreptitious entry by terrorist outfits into the stock market." The key issue is: does the Union Government have all the relevant information to come to such definitive conclusions on this matter to expose the link between terror modules operating in India and their counterparts abroad? Questions of how terrorists in India have received funds from abroad to perpetrate violence on Indian soil remain unanswered in several cases.

But the answer to this too is obvious. But let us hear it from the horse's mouth. In an interview provided to the media (*The Hindu,* dated April 9, 2007) on the sidelines of the annual conference of the International Organisation of Securities Commissions in April 2007 in Mumbai, Mr Damodaran, the then chairman of SEBI, when questioned about the quality of investments from abroad through the PN route, candidly admitted: "We know money is coming through banking channels. Is it money that has escaped tax, gone overseas and come back? This is something that SEBI cannot say... It is beyond us to check the quality of money coming to the markets. All that we know is that it is coming through people who are supposed to know their clients, including FIIs..."

Pray who checks the "quality" of money that comes into India? Mr Damodaran further elaborated, "All the money comes into the markets only through bank accounts. All investors are brought to the market through market intermediaries, brokers and depository participants. All of them are subject to KYC (Know Your Customer) norms. We know money is coming through banking channels. Is it money that has escaped tax, gone overseas and come back? This is something that SEBI cannot say. There are other regulators who deal with issues of flow of money into India and its quality and we are in close touch with them. This is not our direct responsibility."

Who then is responsible for the quality of the money flowing into the Indian capital markets? The RBI, as it involves cross-border movement of funds, is ideally placed to monitor the same. But the RBI has consistently been ill at ease with PNs. We would examine the position of the RBI shortly on this vexatious issue.

Mr. Damodaran also referred to terror funding in his interview. "There is a financial intelligence unit, an Income Tax Department, apart from other investigating agencies. We will assist them with whatever information we have. But it is beyond us to check the quality of money coming to the markets. All that we know is that it is coming through people who are supposed to know their clients, including FIIs which give us regular certificates saying they know to whom the Notes are issued and that they do not include PIOs, NRIs and OCBs. So PNs being equated with money of dubious quality is not based on a one-to-one relationship. There are different reasons for different people to invest through PNs."

Obviously, these are tacit admissions that SEBI was not in control of the money that goes abroad and comes back through the PN route. Surely, these are *not* confident assertions of a market regulator. Quite the contrary, they reflect the helplessness experienced by our regulators.

On the issue of the statements made by the NSA during the course of his address in the Munich Conference, the Union Finance Ministry claimed that no specific companies had been named by the NSA. Naturally, the questions arise: did the Finance Ministry request for more details from the NSA? Did it seek confirmation from the stock exchanges of Chennai and Mumbai, on whether they had reported such instances directly to the NSA? In the alternative, what was the source of the information of the NSA? And if all these were unsubstantiated, how could the NSA discuss the same at an international forum? Surely, there is more than meets the eye in the entire episode.

Further, the Finance Ministry asserted that there was no evidence with it to suggest the view that terrorist groups were manipulating the stock markets in India. But this assertion flew in the face of the statement made by the NSA in Munich as well as by the finance minister himself in the Parliament in November 2007. Obviously, someone in the Finance Ministry has not got the facts right.

The decisions of the Hon'ble SAT in the Goldman Sachs case and the UBS case as well as the manner in which SEBI accepted for a consent in the Hon'ble Supreme Court are clear pointers to the regulatory gaps in addressing the issue of FII regulations in the context of PNs. Till date, successive Governments have failed to recognise these issues and address the same in a planned manner.

The billion dollar question that remains unanswered here is whether all these comprise patented callousness on the part of the Government of India on such vital matters?

The RBI is opposed to PNs, as seen in the dissent note provided to the Ashok Lahiri Panel (we will be discussing about the same shortly). SEBI has reservations about it, especially in the aftermath of the decisions in both the cases referred to above. So has the NSA. The major political parties and some economists have also expressed disapproval of the PN concept. Yet the Union Finance Ministry repeatedly seems to assure the nation that there is nothing amiss in the issue of PNs. Why? Is the Government trying to tell us that the nation has misunderstood the issue of PNs? In fact, it has been repeatedly observed that at every stage, the Finance Ministry tends to take a hostile view of anyone who has a contrary view about PNs or questions their fallibility.

In the third week of January 2008, the Sensex experienced huge fall along with other markets around the world. On January 21, 2008, the Sensex saw its highest ever loss of 1,408 points at the end of the session. The next day, the BSE Sensex index went into a free fall. It hit the lower circuit breaker barely a minute after the markets opened at 10 am. Trading was suspended for an hour.

On reopening at 10.55 am, the market saw its biggest intra-day fall when it hit a low of 15,332, down 2,273 points. However, after reassurance from the finance minister (FM), the market bounced back to close at 16,730 with a net loss of 875 points.

If SEBI could investigate the fall in the shares on May 17, 2004, why has it not investigated into such huge sales effected on these two days? Crucially, who sold the shares on these two days? These questions remain unanswered to this day. Were they genuine investors who had taken purely investment decisions? If so, what was the economic development within the country that led to such a free fall in the markets? One is not aware of any. Or was this fall in the market orchestrated by someone with some specific purpose?

Whatever it may be, someone (or a group) was toying on those two days with the overall sentiments of the markets. In the process, the Sensex was getting manipulated. The earlier we realise this, the better.

Lahiri Panel – Contriving to Lose

Readers may recall that the UPA Government was formed in 2004. This Government was supported from outside by the Leftists who were ideologically chary of speculative capital flows into the national economy. In contrast, the Congress Party favoured a liberal approach of allowing foreign capital into the economy. Consequently, to resolve the policy divergence between the two political groups, the Common Minimum Programme (CMP) – the arrangement between the Congress Party led ruling alliance and the Left parties was drafted – so as to guide the UPA Government on all contentious issues. The CMP sought to balance between the two contradictory approaches to free flow of foreign capital by adopting policies, which, while continuing to encourage investment through the FII route, ostensibly sought to reduce the vulnerability of the financial system to the flow of speculative capital.

Accordingly, an Expert Group under the chairmanship of Ashok Lahiri was constituted to advise on an action plan for implementation of the above mentioned commitment made in the CMP. The report of this Expert Group was submitted in November 2005. The broad terms of reference of this Expert Group are laid out hereunder:

- To consider how FII inflows into the country can be encouraged;
- To examine whether the existing regulatory framework adequately addresses the concern for reducing the vulnerability of capital markets to the flow of speculative capital; and

- To suggest further regulatory measures as may be considered necessary.

On the issue of PNs the report of the Expert Group notes that these are instruments used by foreign funds, not registered in the country, for trading in the domestic market. They are derivative instruments issued against an underlying security which permits the holder to share in the capital appreciation/income from the underlying security. PNs are like contract notes and are issued by FIIs, registered in the country, to their overseas clients who may not be eligible to invest in the Indian stock markets. PNs are used as an alternative to sub-accounts by ultimate investors, generally based on considerations related to transactions costs and record-keeping overheads.

Explaining how the names of the beneficiary holders of the PNs are kept anonymous because of its very structuring, the report of the Expert Group notes that the associates of these FIIs generally issue these notes overseas. The investors, who buy these notes, deposit their funds abroad in the international account of the FII, which also operates in India. The FII then buys stocks in the domestic market on behalf of these investors on their account. In this case, the FII or the broker acts like an exchange: it executes the trade and uses its internal accounts to settle the trade. This helps in keeping the investor's name anonymous, unless the FII discloses the names of the holders of the PNs. What makes it difficult for the FII to disclose the names of PN holders is that PNs are subject to multi-layering and could be sold downstream. The FII would have very little control over such transactions and have practical difficulty in identifying the names of the ultimate holders at any given point in time.

The report of the Expert Group noted that some genuine foreign investors (institutional as well as individual) often find it expensive to operate in India and comply with all legal formalities, especially in cases where their total exposure is not going to be very large. Such investors look for PNs to gain exposure in the Indian stock markets. , the PN mechanism is favoured by such investors on the grounds of lower transactions costs and overheads.

The Expert Group noted that of the 733 entities registered as FIIs with SEBI at the end of June 2005, "only" 17 entities had issued PNs. The total value of underlying investments in equity represented by the PNs was approximately Rs. 67,000 crores, representing about 26 per cent (we shall shortly look into how the share of PNs exploded in the next few years and began to dominate the aggregate FII flows into India) of the cumulative net investments in equities by FIIs of Rs. 2,61,000 crores at the end of June, 2005.

But the issue of anonymity associated with PNs remained unaddressed. Interestingly, the Expert Group noted that FIIs invest funds on behalf of such investors, who "prefer to avoid making disclosures required by various regulators." Small individual investors, as also certain institutional investors, as explained in the previous paragraphs, on account of cutting costs and overheads, would use the PN route for their investment into India. Such cases would definitely be few and far between. Nevertheless, if they are genuine investors, even they would not mind making appropriate disclosures to any regulator.

Needless to state only shady investors with dubious links viz, those with narco-terror links would, as the report of the Expert Group claims, "prefer to avoid making disclosures required by various regulators." The report of the Expert Group seems to have missed this obvious point. In fact, a plain reading of the report seems to suggest that the Expert Group justifies persons and entities in maintaining their identity as a secret from our regulator! The Expert Group eventually concedes that while the Indian regulatory structure would like to have information about the end-investors, there is a need to recognise that there are innate limits to the extent to which these regulations can achieve their goals.

But one needs to realise that the Indian bureaucracy is known for such diffused drafting, one that could be interpreted by anyone to his advantage. However, the Expert Group failed to realise that if free and fair markets were to flourish, the regulator cannot be looking into the preferences, likes or dislikes of every investor group and tailoring their policies accordingly. It is only the healthy and robust capital market that ensures a sustained flow of capital.

After championing the cause of those investors who "prefer to avoid making disclosures required by various regulators," the Expert Group does deal with the issue of anonymity offered by the investment through the PN route. This report also notes that the anonymity afforded by the PN route has led to three concerns about the desirability of PNs. These include:

- First, with PNs issued to various types of entities abroad, the identity of the actual investor may not necessarily be known to the regulatory bodies. These investors are not subject to Indian laws. This has given rise to concerns that some of the money coming into the market via PNs could be the unaccounted wealth of some rich Indians camouflaged under the guise of FII investment. The money might even be tainted and linked with such illegal activities as smuggling and drug-running.
- Second, concerns have also been raised about the potential for enhanced volatility in the Indian markets with substantial issuance/redemption of these derivative instruments abroad.

- Third, hedge funds may be using the devices of PNs and sub-accounts of the FIIs to play in the Indian market.

The report allayed the general apprehension that routing of unaccounted money and its use by unscrupulous individuals to ramp up share prices could be achieved by rigorously enforcing the KYC requirement. Further, this could be addressed by "tightening the regulatory regime" and "doing some vigorous investigations" in cases where there is *prima facie* evidence of wrong-doing. How many vigorous investigations were carried out by SEBI or the Finance Ministry after November 2005 when the report of the Expert Group was issued is anybody's guess. Whatever it may be, this report of the Expert Group after a few years in retrospect appears to be a futile exercise.

It is pertinent to know that the report was issued in November 2005, a few months after the UBS case was decided by the Hon'ble SAT. The central issue on hand was whether SEBI had defined KYC norms in an unambiguous manner so as to ensure compliance of the same by FIIs in the context of PNs issued by them. The terms of reference clearly indicate that the Expert Group was empowered to suggest regulatory measures as it may consider necessary. Yet the Expert Group chose to ignore the ratio that led to the judgement of the Hon'ble SAT in the UBS case. The crux of the issue is that the confusion in the FII Regulations vis-à-vis KYC norms exists to this day. No wonder, SEBI has, since the infamous UBS case, never commenced investigation on any market crash, especially involving FII and PNs. Have all FIIs turned into saints since May 2004 and desisted from manipulating the Indian stock markets? *One is not sure.*

The Expert Group further noted with great satisfaction that with effect from February 3, 2004, PNs could be issued only to regulated entities and further transfers, if any, of these instruments could also be done to other regulated entities only. It also noted that the FIIs issuing such derivative instruments are, therefore, required to exercise due diligence and maintain complete details of the investors, based strictly on the KYC principles.

The Expert Group also noted that SEBI had indicated in February 2004 that the existing non-eligible PNs will be permitted to expire or be wound down on maturity, or within a period of five years, whichever is earlier. The said period of five years came to an end in early 2009. How much of this was actually wound down within this period and how much was done in 2009 remains a mystery. Equally, one is not clear whether every single non-eligible PN was wound down by February 2009. Also, one is equally uncertain whether in the absence of any clear cut guidelines, FIIs could once again issue PNs to unregulated entities.

Someone could, as was done successfully in the Goldman Sachs case, ask as to where is the legal prohibition after 2009 to prohibit such issue of PNs to unregulated entities?

In net effect, the Expert Group contrived to conclude that PNs were necessary for the Indian economy, more particularly the Indian stock markets. It suggested that the current dispensation for PNs, which was approved after careful examination of the High Level Coordination Committee for Capital and Financial Markets and SEBI's Board, may continue. However, as a precaution, it noted that SEBI should have full powers to obtain information regarding the final holders/beneficiaries at any point of time in case of any investigation or surveillance action. And as a final bargain for continuing the practice of allowing FIIs to issue PNs, it ordered, "FIIs should be obliged to provide the information to SEBI." The element of tokenism in this report of the Expert Group is too palpable, especially in the aftermath of the decisions of the Hon'ble SAT in the UBS and Goldman Sachs cases.

The Lahiri panel seems to have contrived to lose the war even before the battle had begun.

RBI: The Odd Man Out

The report of the Expert Group included representatives from the Finance Ministry, SEBI and RBI. While representatives of SEBI chose to maintain a strategic silence, the RBI disagreed with the conclusion of the Expert Group that PNs may continue. Is it because SEBI is directly under control of the Finance Ministry while the RBI, despite such a handicap, has learnt to be an autonomous organisation? It is perhaps precisely these reasons that emboldened the RBI which obviously felt enough was enough and decided to issue an unambiguous dissent note to the report of the Expert Group. As a rule, our Government functions through an elaborate charade of discussions, meetings and noting. Dissent, if at all, is never demonstrated, especially in writing. Such a positioning is extremely rare, perhaps unprecedented in the Indian context. *One fails to recollect any other instance where one arm of the Government disagreed with a policy formulation of the other arm. Yet, that is what the RBI chose to do in the context of PNs.*

On this issue, the RBI categorically stated, "The Reserve Bank's stance has been that the issue of Participatory Notes should not be permitted." The reasons that followed were equally sharp: "In this context, we would like to point out that the main concerns regarding issue of PNs are that the nature of the beneficial ownership or the identity of the investor will not be known, unlike in the case of FIIs registered with a financial regulator. Trading of these PNs will lead to multi-layering which will make it difficult to identify the ultimate holder of PNs."

More was to follow. For the RBI, allowing PNs was akin to administering steroids to a child. The child would register spectacular growth in the first instance. But that is neither healthy nor sustainable in the long run. In order to sustain the healthy functioning of our markets, it was important, according to the RBI, that the Government restricts suspicious fund flows. The logic that drove the RBI to this conclusion was Gresham's economic maxim which roughly states, "When the good circulates with the bad, the bad drives out the good." The RBI feared bad money brought in through the PN route could destabilise the Indian stock markets in the medium to long term. That explains its insistence on clean investments.

Needless to emphasise, in this globalised world, flow of good clean money takes time and is dependent on the sustained performance of the national economy over several years, measured through several parameters. Given the proclivity of the Indian Governments to show instant success, the PNs despite its obvious handicaps, emerged as a preferred choice. At the altar of political expediency, sustainability and national interests were given short shrift. Given this economic logic and constraints, the RBI concluded, "Both conceptually and in practice, restrictions on suspicious flows enhance the reputation of markets and lead to healthy flows. We, therefore, reiterate that issuance of Participatory Notes should not be permitted."

That was not all. The RBI was apprehensive about the very purpose for which the Expert Group was constituted viz., encouraging FII flows and checking the vulnerability of capital markets to speculative flows. To the RBI, as to any unbiased observer, it seemed, as to the Expert Group was keen on the issue of encouraging FII flows into India and was reluctant to check the vulnerability of capital markets to speculative flows. According to the RBI, the very purpose of the Expert Group was not met and the terms of reference of the Government were not respected. Obviously, peeved at the attitude of the Expert Group, the RBI suggested the formation of another "special group" as a priority to look into the "unfinished agenda" of the Expert Group.

Volatility in any market is a byproduct of several factors in an economy. These include the exchange rate of the rupee, fiscal stance, monetary management including but not limited to the domestic interest rates and their difference with interest rates prevailing abroad. In this connection, the RBI noted, "In view of macroeconomic implications, impact on financial stability, especially on the exchange rate, and fiscal vulnerability, apart from monetary management, a special group may be constituted to study measures to contain large volatility in FII flows as a priority." The failure of the Expert Group can be well appreciated when we analyse the events in 2007-08 (when there was a surge in capital flows into the economy) and in 2008-09 (when India recorded a reversal of capital flows).

In 2007-08, the surge in capital flows resulted in the appreciation of the rupee in excess of 10 per cent leading to several disruptive consequences. Similarly, when capital flows reversed, the consequences were equally painful as the rupee depreciated in excess of 25 per cent. The ill-effects of volatility were discussed in greater detail in the previous chapter. It is precisely these issues of volatility that, according to the RBI, were not addressed by the Expert Group. Was it extraordinary clairvoyance or sheer professionalism on the part of the RBI that guided it to come to these conclusions? Whatever it may be, the fact remains that the conclusions of the Expert Group in controlling volatility were inconclusive.

The RBI, therefore, realised that the recommendations of the Expert Group, especially the policy decision to allow the further issue of PNs, did not address the very purpose for which it was formed – i.e. to address the issue of volatility comprehensively. The RBI's dissent note was scathing as well as candid enough to state, "The recommendations of such a special group may be finalised and further actions considered together. Such a package is necessary since the present report does not address the issue of volatility comprehensively." *In effect, the Expert Group, according to the RBI, lacked the expertise to address the issue of volatility in the first place!* No wonder, it failed to address the issue of volatility comprehensively. Yet, it is the view of this "Expert Group" with such severe faultlines amongst its own members, that has come to be the stated official policy on PNs of the Government of India.

The RBI had an opportunity to visit the vexed subject of PNs once again in 2006. It may be recalled that the Government had requested the RBI to suggest a roadmap to fuller capital account convertibility. The RBI had set up a committee under the chairmanship of Mr. Tarapore. The Report of the Committee on Fuller Capital Account Convertibility was submitted on July 31, 2006. In this report, the RBI examined the role of PNs in the context of ushering fuller capital account convertibility and observed the following:

- In the case of Participatory Notes (PNs), the nature of the beneficial ownership or the identity is not known unlike in the case of FIIs.
- These PNs are freely transferable and trading of these instruments makes it all the more difficult to know the identity of the owner.

- The committee is, therefore, of the view that FIIs should be prohibited from investing fresh money raised through PNs.
- Further, existing PN holders may be provided an exit route and phased out completely within one year

This reiteration by the RBI in 2006 in the report of the committee to examine fuller capital account convertibility followed its dissenting note to the report of the Expert Group. One may or may not agree with the stance of the RBI in so far as it pertains to the issue of allowing PNs, but it is absolutely apparent that the RBI is not in doubt over this issue.

At least on clarity and especially on this issue, the RBI scores a perfect ten.

SEBI Suddenly Wakes up in October 2007

Given this policy formulation of the Government of India, PNs continued to proliferate between November 2005 when the report of the Expert Group was submitted and October 2007 when SEBI chose to revisit the subject. It may be recalled that the report of the Expert Group pointed out that the total value of underlying investments in equity represented by the PNs was approximately Rs. 67,000 crores representing about 26 per cent of the cumulative net investments in equities by FIIs of Rs. 2,61,000 crores at the end of June 2005. This had increased to approximately Rs 3,53,000 crores in August 2007, representing about 52 per cent of the cumulative net investments of the FIIs.

Concerned with the proliferation of PNs and with a view to monitoring the investment by FIIs through PNs, SEBI, in consultation with the Government, proposed the following measures, to be implemented "urgently:"

1. FIIs and their sub-accounts shall not issue/renew PNs with immediate effect. They are required to wind up the current position over 18 months, during which period SEBI will review the position from time to time.
2. Further issuance of PNs by FIIs will be discontinued with immediate effect. They will be required to wind up the current position over 18 months, during which period SEBI will review the position from time to time.
3. The FIIs that are currently issuing PNs with notional value of PNs outstanding (excluding derivatives) as a percentage of their assets in India of less than 40 per cent, shall be allowed to issue further PNs only at the incremental rate of 5 per cent of their assets in India.
4. Those FIIs with notional value of PNs outstanding (excluding derivatives) as a percentage of their assets in India of more than 40 per cent, shall issue

PNs only against cancellation / redemption / closing out of the existing PNs of at least an equivalent amount.

SEBI's proposed measures were calculated to discontinue new issuance of PNs by FIIs with immediate effect. It further mandated that existing positions will be required to wind up within 18 months. For once, SEBI began to assert itself on the issue of PNs.

All hell broke loose instantly. Nothing else illustrates the stranglehold of the PNs on the Indian stock markets than the reaction of the stock markets to these measures. When the market opened the following day, within a minute of opening trade, the Sensex crashed by 1,744 points or about 9 per cent of its value – the biggest intra-day fall in Indian securities markets in absolute terms till then. This led to automatic suspension of trading for one hour. The then finance minister had to immediately step in and issue clarifications in the meantime that the Government was not against FIIs and was not immediately banning PNs.

Interestingly, there were "several reactions" by "market participants." Note how a policy change was greeted by a crash of the stock markets. Editorials lamented about how the Government had acted in great haste. Columnists rushed to advise caution to the Government. Experts opined in channel after channel that it would spell disaster for the Indian economy as a whole.

It would seem that PNs were sentiments and sentiments constituted Sensex in the Indian context.

Some of the reactions are highlighted hereunder:

- On behalf of the hedge fund industry, the Managed Funds Association (MFA) expressed concern to SEBI that its proposals may cause the Indian markets to "effectively be closed to a substantial pool of investors, thereby leading to greater, rather than diminished, market instability and inefficiency."
- The MFA further stated in its response to SEBI, "Specifically, there should be clear measures adopted to clarify applicable standards and expedite the FII registration process for hedge funds, in order to ensure that hedge funds are not prohibited from investing for an extended time period due to administrative or technical reasons."
- The International Swaps and Derivatives Association (ISDA) also cautioned SEBI that the proposed measures could be highly disruptive. "Market participants who have conducted their business and dealings on the basis of the current FII regulations would face great difficulty in changing their

arrangements overnight to comply with the proposed measures." Whose cause the ISDA was championing is anybody's guess.

- ISDA further added, "This is exacerbated by the retroactive nature of the proposed measures in regard to the requirement to wind up current Offshore Derivative Instruments with derivatives underlying within 18 months ... The proposed measures, if adopted immediately and without substantial modifications, have the potential to disrupt the market and impose significant losses and economic costs on market participants."

Of course, the markets returned to normalcy within a few days and peaked during January 2008. Nevertheless, the issues raised by these measures of SEBI remained unaddressed. Would banning the PNs rob the Indian capital markets of liquidity? Was the eighteen-month window sufficient for unwinding of the existing positions? Will it affect the Sensex? Will it impair capital flows into the economy? A scholarly review of these measures was carried out in December 2007 by Mr. Manmohan Singh for an IMF Working Paper titled Use of "Participatory Notes in Indian Equity Markets and Recent Regulatory Changes."

Apart from discussing other contentious issues associated with PNs, this Working Paper threw up an open secret of the Indian corporate world – the use of overseas affiliates to fund stock market operations through the PNs. The Working Paper pointed out to certain corporate structuring that allowed large Indian corporates with overseas affiliates to get around the then prevailing ECB caps. This involved the promoters of the Indian corporates pledging their shares with an Indian bank's offshore subsidiary. In turn, the subsidiary of the Indian bank offshore provides a loan to the affiliate of the Indian corporate offshore. The offshore Indian corporate routes the money into the Indian stock markets through the PN route. The Working Paper notes in conclusion, "Market sources suggest that the large size of the present PNs on derivatives may in part be stemming from such structures."

Naturally, such structures fuel capital inflows which can never be anticipated. Nor can the RBI or for that matter, any regulator, anticipate their exit. These inflows, along with the regular capital inflows, had placed an additional upward pressure on the rupee, over and above the pressures from onshore FII flows in 2007. The impact of these flows on the overall economy was covered in the earlier chapter.

That would explain why several leading corporates floated several foreign affiliates or subsidiaries between 2005 and 2007. They were not only going global, some of them were obviously going to take the PN route. It is thus no surprise that since 2006-07, India recorded significant FDI flows into several other countries – approximately USD 14 billion in 2006-07, USD 19 billion in 2007-08 and USD 17 billion in 2008-09. How much of this was routed back into the Indian stock market through the PNs is anybody's guess. Also, by incorporating affiliates and foreign subsidiaries, one could also have the luxury of over and underinvoicing between group companies. With the proliferation of the services industry, any meaningful detection of any such manipulation becomes difficult. All these funds generated in such foreign companies are then transferred to some tax havens under the watchful guidance of some FII and multinational audit firms.

Commenting on the possible impact from the regulatory changes, the IMF Working Paper referred to above concluded that SEBI's ban on the issuance of PNs on derivatives will "reshuffle the investor base on portfolio inflows." According to the Working Paper, SEBI's proposal could increase the "inflows onshore by the apparent interest from real money accounts to register onshore; however, inflows from margin accounts i.e. from investors who use PNs on derivatives are likely to disappear along with some investors from the PN cash market." In effect, the IMF Paper concluded that the near-term impact depended on how staggered the unwinding was likely to be. Once the reshuffling of the investor base in favour of the real money account takes place over the next 18 months, capital flows are likely to be more stable. This is what the RBI too wanted implicitly in its dissent report to the Expert Group.

Response of Political Parties to Tax Havens and PNs

It is indeed strange that the politically explosive subject of tax havens does not find even a cursory mention by our political parties except during elections. And whenever the question was addressed, it was not backed with adequate understanding of the subject. Further, since every political party across the political spectrum has been in power at one time or the other in the past decade or so, or, at least, been providing outside support to the Government of the day, it is virtually impossible for any one of these political parties to accuse the other of any misdoing on this subject. As the Buddha said, only the unsinned can thrown a stone on the other! In the case of PNs, every political party has sinned, only the degree varies.

Nevertheless, the issue of tax havens and with it, of PNs, did occupy the political space in the run-up to the 2009 general elections. It is in this period that the BJP constituted a Task Force comprising eminent persons outside of the BJP who included:

- S. Gurumurthy – Chartered accountant and noted columnist.
- Ajit Doval – Noted security expert.

- Dr. R. Vaidyanathan – Professor of finance, IIM, Bangalore.
- Mahesh Jethmalani – Senior lawyer, Mumbai.

The Task Force came out with its interim recommendations in April 2009, which included certain specific suggestions on the steps to be taken by the Indian Government to bring the funds illegally stashed away in secret tax havens, particularly Switzerland. In the context of allowing overseas investment into India through the anonymous PN route, this Task Force questioned the moral authority of India in pursuing the matter with countries like Switzerland. In this connection, the Task Force states, "For this purpose, it has to change the rules like allowing investments in Indian stocks through the Participatory Notes method which is secretive and allows secret funds into India like the Swiss banks do! Actually, the Indian rules permit a Switzerland in India. How can India call for action against Switzerland when it permits a mini-Switzerland in India?"

In short, the Task Force constituted by experts outside the BJP had hit the nail right on the head. How can India have the moral authority to compel tax havens to part with the details of account holders when India itself has a policy of encouraging anonymity through the PN route? Unless we address this issue, it is unlikely that the tax havens would take our requests seriously. Conversely, if we sort out the PN conundrum, there is a moral authority in pursuing the tax havens to fall in line. Therefore, the solution to the vexed issue of obtaining details from these jurisdictions lies in tackling the PNs at home.

The moot question is: are we ready to tackle PNs internally so as to tackle tax havens externally?

If the BJP was taking such strong positions in the run-up to the elections, could the Leftists be far behind? Claiming that the Task Force report was a hoax, the CPI (M) in a press release in April 2009 questioned the commitment of the BJP leadership to bring back the money stashed in tax havens abroad. Quoting from the Task Force report, the press release noted, "The GFI study shows that during the period from 2002 to 2006, annually USD 27.3 billion were stashed away from India. If this is true, then nearly USD 55 billion worth of illicit transfers occurred in the two-year period, 2002 to 2004, under the BJP-led NDA Government itself, in which Mr. Advani was the deputy prime minister and the home minister. What did he do to prevent such illegal transfers when he was in power?"

This is the standard operating procedure of the Leftists. First question the timing, then the integrity of the messenger, discredit both and, finally, claim the only solution lies in the prescriptions of Karl Marx. The press release seemed to be more focussed on the actions (or the lack of them) during the NDA rule rather than the fast emerging global situation in early 2009. But the CPI (M) failed to realise that it was de-facto in power till mid-2008 when it virtually had the veto powers and naturally these questions can be put to it too. Let us not forget that the silence of the Communists on the issue of PNs between 2004 and 2008 is deafening. It may be recalled that the report of the Expert Group on Encouraging FII Flows and Checking the Vulnerability of Capital Markets to Speculative Flows virtually allowed PNs. This was in 2005 and the Leftists were silent. It is pertinent to note that till the Leftists parted ways with the ruling alliance in 2008, they remained quiet.

Only in the run-up to the general elections (thanks to the global developments as well as competitive political compulsions) did the Leftists wake up and make their usual noises, peppered with their template slogans. Nevertheless, they claim full credit for all these political initiatives. Did the Leftists rake this up issue merely as an election issue in 2009 and was their silence between 2005 and 2008 simply because of some possible Chinese investments (through the Sovereign Wealth Funds, as discussed in the previous chapter) through the PN route! Strangely, after the 2009 election, the Leftists have once again remained silent on this issue.

The behaviour of the Leftists, with their diffused loyalties, is often intriguing, to say the least, on matters of vital national interest.

SEBI Continues to Score Self-Goal

By October 2008, that is, exactly a year after it took the "bull" by its horns, SEBI chose to revisit the vexed subject of PNs all over once again. Just as one thought that the scourge of PNs was well behind us, on October 6, 2008, SEBI did a volte face on its October 2007 stand on the issue of PNs. Of course, too much water had flowed under the bridge, since October 2007. The collapse of several financial institutions in America, including Lehman Brothers and Bear Sterns, had a debilitating impact on global capital markets. Simultaneously, the commodity markets had collapsed, leading to de-leveraging of large positions by major financial players. This, in turn, caused a severe liquidity crisis across continents.

India was no exception to this global meltdown and the Sensex had virtually crashed by 50-55 per cent from its all time highs recorded only in January 2008. Capital flows began to reverse and the rupee which recorded handsome gains in 2007-08 began to depreciate dramatically. Further, on account of this reversal in cash flow, India too began to experience domestic liquidity crunch.

The manner in which the RBI tackled the liquidity crunch in this period has been dealt with in greater detail in the previous chapter.

SEBI too, for its part, needed to do "something." SEBI felt that it was time to review the decision that was taken on the issue of PNs in October 2007. The SEBI website cryptically notes that "it decided to do away with restrictions on issue of PNs by FIIs against securities, including derivatives, as underlying." Surely, when the dust was settling on the issue and India it seemed had finally got rid of the monkey from its back, SEBI scored this infamous self-goal.

And unlike the media furore that greeted it in October 2007, this time around, the decision was greeted with a thundering silence by one and all.

This reversal in the policy decision was, however, vehemently opposed by the Leftists only. The press note issued by the CPI (M) noted, "The decision of the SEBI to relax the restrictions on the issuance of Participatory Notes (PNs) by the FIIs announced yesterday is a retrograde and illogical move. The Reserve Bank of India has been advocating a ban on these non-transparent derivative instruments used by the FIIs to invest money in the Indian capital market on behalf of undisclosed entities and individuals. SEBI, while refusing to prohibit PNs, had applied a 40 per cent cap on total assets held by FIIs under PNs in October 2007."

Pointing out that "SEBI has summarily removed all its earlier restrictions in one stroke in order to woo the FIIs back," the press release, pointing out to the flip-flop of SEBI, stated in clear terms, "Such an intervention by the SEBI to favour of a set of players, who are holding the market to ransom, is grossly violative of the role of a market regulator." The apparent reason for SEBI to do a policy about-turn was simply to shore up the sagging market that was crashing by the hour. For once, the Leftists were spot on.

SEBI seems to have neither understood the contours of the prevailing global financial crisis nor learnt from past Indian experiences. While Governments the world over were plotting to tighten the regulation of financial markets following the crisis, SEBI seemed to take an entirely different route. In the process, *status quo ante* that prevailed prior to October 2007 was restored.

But SEBI did not mind all these and stop there. It continued to have its dose of flip-flops. All of a sudden, in December 2008 (further refined on September 1, 2009), it recalled the Prevention of Money Laundering Act which was passed in July 2005 (and further amended in early 2009). SEBI through its master circular in December 2008, mandated all registered intermediaries to maintain a record of such transactions, the nature and value of which has been prescribed in the rules notified under the PMLA. Such transactions include:

- All cash transactions of the value of more than Rs 10 lakhs or its equivalent in foreign currency.
- All series of cash transactions integrally connected to each other which have been valued below Rs 10 lakhs or its equivalent in foreign currency where such series of transactions take place within one calendar month.
- All suspicious transactions, whether or not made in cash.

SEBI further laid down the minimum requirements and emphasised that the intermediaries may, according to their requirements, specify additional disclosures to be made by clients to address concerns of money laundering and suspicious transactions undertaken by clients. In order to fulfil these requirements, SEBI mandates registered intermediaries to have a system in place for identifying, monitoring and reporting suspected money laundering or terrorist financing transactions to the law enforcement authorities. Each of the registered intermediaries is expected by SEBI to adopt written procedures so as to implement the anti-money laundering provisions which should include the following three specific parameters, which are related to the overall concept of "Client Due Diligence Process" and includes the following:

- Policy for acceptance of clients.
- Procedure for identifying the clients.
- Reporting suspicious transactions.

Further, in order to further strengthen the KYC norms and identify every participant in the securities market with their respective PAN, thereby ensuring a sound audit trail of all the transactions, PAN has been made sole identification number for all participants transacting in the securities market, irrespective of the amount of transactions.

All these efforts of SEBI to tackle money laundering look particularly spectacular if and only if seen in isolation. By allowing PNs to once again enter the Indian stock markets and to undo its own policy initiative of October 2007, SEBI seems to have done incalculable harm to the financial integrity of the Indian stock markets. Where is the question of tackling money laundering, on the one hand, when we are allowing PNs, especially from tax havens, on the other?

Allowing PNs and simultaneously issuing guidelines on prevention of money laundering is akin to running with the hares and hunting with the hounds. Successive Governments in India seem to believe that by repeating lies, they could convert lies into truth. To that extent, the Government of India seems to accept Hitler's view point on making the lie big, making it simple, keep repeating it, and hoping eventually everyone will believe.

That in sum and substance defines the Indian approach to the issue of PNs – the lie is big, it is kept simple and repeated several times over. The net effect it is that an innocent nation has come to believe that PNs are good for the country. The media, thanks to the nexus with the stock markets and compulsions to play ball with the Government, is silent. Equally strange is the silence of our intellectuals, chambers of trade and commerce, industry bodies and, of course, the entire professional class. Barring occasional protests, all of them have been, by and large silent on this issue. Either they do not understand or because of their beneficial interests, feign ignorance on this matter.

The net effect of all these is that India's stand on the crucial issue of recovering our stolen wealth from the tax havens could be seriously compromised in the coming years, especially when the global initiative gathers steam. And in such a scenario, we as a nation could possibly face some acute embarrassment.

References

1. Speech of the NSA in the Munich Conference, 2007.
2. *The Hindu*, several issues.
3. *The Economic Times*, several issues.
4. *Business Standard*, several issues.
5. Indo-Asian News Service, November 2007.
6. Guidelines on Prevention of Money Laundering, issued by SEBI on December 19, 2008, September 1, 2009, and January 16, 2006.
7. Paper for discussion on Offshore Derivative Instruments (Participatory Notes) issued by SEBI on October 16, 2007.
8. Report of the Expert Group on Encouraging FII Flows and Checking the Vulnerability of Capital Markets to Speculative Flows, Government of India, Ministry of Finance Department of Economic Affairs, November, 2005.
9. Report of the Committee on Fuller Capital Account Convertibility
10. IMF Working Paper "Use of Participatory Notes in Indian Equity Markets and Recent Regulatory Changes", Prepared by Manmohan Singh.
11. Interim recommendations of the Task Force constituted by the BJP on the steps to be taken by the Indian Government to bring Indian funds illegally stashed away illegally in secret Swiss bank accounts and other tax havens around the world.
12. Press release of the CPI (M) dated April 18, 2009.
13. Press release of the CPI (M) dated October 7, 2008.
14. Lauren Teigland-Hunt, *India: The Problem with P-Notes* .

CHAPTER **10**

Manipulate Sentiments, Manage Markets

The greatest sin of our time is not the few who have destroyed but the vast majority who sat idly by.

— Martin Luther King

The core idea of this book contained in the previous chapters centres around three distinct yet interrelated issues - crime, corruption and capital market manipulation. It was demonstrably seen that the channels and conduits used by one of these were often also used by the other. The natural argument that follows is that unless all the three are comprehensively tackled, we cannot deal with each one of these individually. While at a superficial level, the operational dynamics of one may apparently differ from the other, the fact of the matter is that at a functional level, each one of these issues relies significantly on concealment, systemic suppression and camouflage. All these are ostensibly aimed to coverup any audit trail or investigation by the authorities. Therefore, it is often remarked that a Hawala channel could probably be used by a corrupt minister to launder money or a terrorist to fund terror activities. Unless the Hawala conduit is completely uprooted, we cannot deal with corruption or terror funding. Put differently, unless we eradicate corruption and terrorism, we cannot tackle the scourge of Hawala.

India, as we saw in the previous chapters, is one of the worst victims of terror. Yet India's fight against terror, corruption and market manipulation continues to be an elaborate exercise in self-deception. Repeated attacks of terror occur with monstrous regularity across the country with deadly precision. In contrast, the global fight against terror is simultaneously getting bigger. Despite our demonstrable lack of will to fight terror, it is certain that India will be pitchforked into the forefront on this war on terror sooner rather than later. This will happen thanks to our geo-positioning. Similarly, as India procrastinates in her fight against tax havens as the global fight against tax havens gains momentum across continents, it is certain that India may well be compelled to lead the global movement against tax havens. But this will be more by default – read compulsions of geo-political developments – than design by our Government.

Strangely, despite these possible as well as positive developments, we seem to be in a self-denial mode. Information of accounts in tax havens of Indians in high places could have profound implications on the security of India. It is only a matter of time that a numbered account of a prominent Indian in a tax haven finds its way to the Chinese, American or Pakistani intelligence. That opens up a huge potential for blackmail and compromise, and could well determine the manner in which we conduct future negotiations with the Chinese on the convoluted border dispute or with the Pakistanis on the complex Kashmir issue or with the Americans on the complicated nuclear issue. In all these future negotiations, we could well end up second best.

Let me amplify my fears. In November 1991, six months after the assassination of former Prime Minister Rajiv Gandhi, a Swiss magazine, carried a story alleging that there was a numbered Swiss bank account in the name of Rajiv Gandhi roughly equivalent to USD 2 billion. As Rajiv Gandhi was dead by then, there could be no possible denial or verification. Similarly, Dr. Yevgeniya Albats, the author of *The State Within a State: KGB and Its Hold on Russia*, too has pointed out to the payments by the KGB to several prominent Indians in the Seventies and the Eighties through such accounts. The pro-Soviet tilt in India's foreign policy during those heady times is too well known to warrant a repetition here.

Nevertheless, these allegations leave us with an uncomfortable question: are India's top politicians, bureaucrats, judges, industrialists, media personalities, celebrities vulnerable to blackmail? *If so, how independent are our policy formulations?*

The Swiss magazine has not carried any further story on the said numbered account since then. What happened to the money? Is it still lying with the Swiss bank? What have successive Governments done to follow up on this story? Has anyone claimed the money after Rajiv's death? Interestingly, after Rajiv's death, several political combinations have come to power in the past nineteen years at Delhi. Yet, none have seriously pursued the matter to a logical end with the Swiss authorities. Is it a strategic truce prevailing amongst the Indian political class?

Or was the reputed *Schweitzer Illustrate* completely wrong on this matter? If so, why is it that the Government of India has not sought an official apology from the Swiss magazine, especially given the fact that the person – a former prime minister of the country, no less – is not around to defend his honour? Fascinatingly, his party has been in power for eleven of the nineteen years since then. Yet, there is complete silence from his party. More interesting is the fact that in the rest of the period, his political opponents have been in power. They too remained silent when they could have easily pursued the matter. On such matters, it is silence that unites the otherwise warring Indian political class.

Similarly, what if a probe or a report reveals the fact that a prominent business house was rigging the prices of its own shares using the PN route? Would it not devastate the integrity of India's capital markets? Equally crucial is the devastating impact of all these possible revelations on the collective psyche of the nation. Naturally, we need to handle the issue with outmost care. On the one hand, we cannot allow the continued loot of the country. Nor can we allow our establishment to be tarnished in one stroke. In such scenario, the next generation could lose faith in the "system." We need to precisely prevent both. And for that, the Parliament is best suited to debate. But strangely, the major political parties (as well as prominent political personalities) refuse to entertain any debate on this vital issue.

When it comes to tax havens, ostrich and not peacock, would seem to be the national bird.

L' affair Hassan Ali

Nothing illustrates the approach of our political class better than the story of Hassan Ali. And to explain this story a reference to the budget documents of 2010 becomes crucial. The budget documents contain a statement on the tax revenues raised but not realised by the Government of India. This is a legal obligation under the Fiscal Responsibility and Budget Management (FRBM) Act. This statement provides the details of the unrealised dues on major taxes and duties levied by the Central Government viz., income tax, excise, customs and service tax. These are further categorised under amounts under disputes, that is, where the assessee has gone on an appeal, and those not under any dispute. With the revenue departments of the Government of India having a demonstrated penchant for undue litigation and the stakes on tax litigation getting higher by the day, it is common knowledge that those under disputes may well get settled after several years in the Supreme Court. What is important is the undisputed tax amount – one wherein the assessee has accepted the department's view point and has agreed to pay his tax.

As per the Budget 2010-11, the tax revenues raised but not realised aggregate to Rs 1,17,065 crores. Given this paradigm, let me return once again to the unfinished story of Hassan Ali. It may be recalled that in January 2007, the Income Tax Department had first raided one Hassan Ali Khan's residences across the country and seized certain incriminating documents. The department also found that Khan had not filed income tax returns since 1999. Later, the Enforcement Directorate (ED) started investigating as it was also a case of suspected money laundering, and revealed that he had a sum of USD 8 billion deposited in the UBS AG, Zurich. ED has also been probing Khan and his associate Tapuriah for violating the Foreign Exchange Management Act and laws against money laundering.

Subsequently, the Income Tax Department had issued notices to Hassan Ali Khan and a few others, alleging money laundering to the tune of several billion dollars and for suspected tax evasion. According to press reports, a show-cause notice was issued by the IT Department demanding Rs 40,000 crores (on taxes alone) against Hassan Ali for not disclosing funds in several foreign bank accounts, including the abovementioned USD 8 billion in an account in UBS AG, Zurich. Further, his associates were also alleged by the ED to have an account at Credit Suisse, and that between 2001 and 2005, two transactions worth USD 1.6 billion were made through it.

It is interesting to note that Hassan Ali Khan is out on a bail on a fake passport case. According to various press reports of February 10, 2010, the Bombay High Court had dismissed the appeal of the state government to cancel this bail. The court observed that the state government itself was not interested in cancelling the bail granted to Hassan Ali Khan. In this connection, Justice D. G. Karnik said, "The state government is not interested in serving notice [to the accused and other parties] even after six months of filing an appeal." Justice Karnik also added that if the Government was not keen on pursuing its own appeal, then the court had no reason to waste time on it. This is the power of the man and his ability to move the levers of power at the state level. Naturally, it is interesting to note his influence at the Central level.

The tax liability of Hassan Ali was not merely speculation in the press. It was confirmed by the Government – no less – as late as August 4, 2009, and that too in the Parliament. The Government, while disclosing the list of tax defaulters in the Rajya Sabha, stated that Hassan Ali Khan topped the list of tax defaulters with an outstanding arrear of "*more*" (emphasis mine) than Rs 50,000 crores. Simultaneously, the affidavit of the Government to the Hon'ble Supreme Court in the PIL filed on the tax havens case stated, "The Income Tax Department, on the basis of seized documents and other materials gathered during investigations, have raised total demand of Rs. 71,848.59 crores against the said Ali Khan, his wife Raheema Khan and other associates." That was in the middle of 2009. That could well be close to Rs. 1,00,000 crores by February 2010 when the budget was presented on account of tax dues and accumulated interest.

Yet, the entire tax dues of the Government of India as per the budget documents (both disputed and non-disputed) for all taxes as per the statement of tax revenues raised but not realised aggregates to a mere Rs 117,065 crores. It is pertinent to note that the income tax due from non-corporates (both disputed and undisputed) as per the statement of the Government is a much lower sum of approximately Rs 50,000 crores (the balance of Rs 67,065 is due from corporates – both disputed and undisputed). This is the amount relevant for comparison with the tax due from Hassan Ali and his associates as they are non-corporate assessees. Despite such huge demands against Hassan Ali Khan, his wife and his associates, someone in the Finance Ministry has missed them out. Whether this was an error of omission or one of commission is the moot point.

But there is yet another possibility – what if Hassan Ali and his associates had paid their taxes by February 26, 2010, when the budget for 2010-11 was delivered in the Parliament? Interestingly, *The Week*, in its issue dated March 14, 2010, has carried an interview with the Hon'ble FM precisely on this subject. The Hon'ble FM seems to categorically assert that the Government seems to have recovered the tax dues from Hassan Ali. Excerpts of the relevant portion of this interview are as hereunder:

Q. *Last year, the minister of state for finance told the Lok Sabha about the huge tax money that horse breeder Hassan Ali Khan owed the government.Any progress on that?*

A: *We have done something; we have shared the information with Parliament. But certain information we cannot share because the German authorities gave it to us. On the basis of that, you can realise the tax but you cannot share the information with anybody. Therefore, we have got back the tax.*

Q. *You've got back the tax?*

A. *Yes, we've got back the tax. But the details we cannot share because that is the international commitment we have given. If we violate it, nobody else will give us any information.*

Unfortunately, this cannot be true, as the revised estimates for 2009-10 do not reflect the same. Rs 1,00,000 crores is too large a sum to be lost even in the

Government of India's budget. Either, the Hon'ble FM is mistaken or has been misquoted by *The Week*. In a subsequent rejoinder, issued by the Central Board of Direct Taxes (CBDT), it was clarified that the Hon'ble FM was indeed wrong. But that it is a tacit admission that tax due from Hassan Ali was missed out by the Government in the budget papers.

There is yet another dimension to this issue: the amendment to the Income Tax Act relating to the provisions of the Settlement Commission. Under the provisions of Section 245A(b) of the Income Tax Act, the term "case", in relation to which an application to the Settlement Commission can be made, excludes assessment proceedings arising from a search initiated under the Act. The budget of 2010 had sought to include proceedings for assessments resulting from a search within the definition of a "case" which can be admitted by the Settlement Commission.

Some tax experts opine that the direct beneficiary of this amendment seems to be Hassan Ali Khan who was hitherto excluded by the law from approaching the Settlement Commission, but now, thanks to this amendment[1] contained in the Budget of 2010, can do so without any let or fear. But why should the Government be in such tearing hurry in granting this escape route to Hassan Ali Khan?

The answer to the same lies in Para 124 of the budget speech of 2010 wherein the Hon'ble FM states, "Last year, amendments to the statute enabled Government to enter into tax treaties with specified territories besides sovereign states. We have commenced bilateral discussions to enhance the exchange of bank related and other information to effectively track tax evasion and identify undisclosed assets of resident Indians lying abroad."

The impetus to go after the illicit wealth parked in tax havens is gathering global momentum. India cannot remain a mute spectator to these developments as the international pressure mounts on tax havens to disclose the names of those who have their accounts in such places. Consequently, India has to perform its role in the proverbial rain dance of the African tribal chief on this subject. One way of doing it is to "seemingly" go after tax defaulters who have parked their wealth abroad. It is in this connection that the Government seeks to pursue cases of wealth secreted abroad in proven cases of tax evasion. This is what is effectively confirmed in Para 124 of the budget.

---

1. There are contrarian opinions by experts that this amendment may not actually benefit Hassan Ali. Needless to emphasise, both opinions are based on facts available in the public domain. It has to be remembered that income tax is a highly technical matter where any opinion on the subject could change based on the facts involved. Nevertheless, this amendment to the Income Tax Act seems that there is more than meets the eye.

Now that the Hon'ble FM has confirmed to *The Week* that the Government has collected taxes from Hassan Ali, there is no case for the Government to pursue this case any further in other countries. In case he has not yet paid the taxes (as is most likely the case), the escape chutes (by amending the Income Tax Act pertaining to the Settlement Commission) are already opened. Where is the question of Hassan Ali being a defaulter when he has settled his tax dues with the Government? Either way, the Government has done enough spade work to ensure that the curious case of Hassan Ali and his associate is diluted.

What makes the Hassan Ali case interesting is that money was allegedly laundered from India using the Hawala route. Those in the world of finance know that a stud farm owner could not have been an originator of such gargantuan income. Obviously, it was not his money that was laundered. At best, he could well have been a conduit for several (prominent?) Indians who could have used the Hassan Ali (read Hawala) route to transfer their ill-gotten wealth abroad.

Naturally, the source of money in India to Hassan Ali is as interesting as the ultimate beneficiaries of the laundered money.

But all these inconvenient questions can be side-stepped if Hassan Ali comes to the Settlement Commission and settles his case. In fact, the Settlement Commission is precisely aimed at cases that are complex and where the Income Tax Department finds it tough to determine even the sources of income of an assessee. Hassan Ali's case squarely fits the bill. In such a scenario, where Hassan Ali's case could be effectively settled through the Settlement Commission, it must be noted that in the books of the Government of India, he would no longer be a tax defaulter in India. To that extent, there is no *locus standi* for the Government to pursue his case any further with any other country, much less in the case of tax havens.

Surely, Hassan Ali must be having huge clout. Or is it a case of a paranoid Government acting with great alacrity. What are his sources of such a staggering amount of wealth? How was he able to dodge the Government by not even filing his income tax return for so long? How and why did the intelligence of the Government fail for such long period of time that allowed him to launder the money? How is that he has not been arrested till date on this matter? What are the steps taken by the Government to retrieve this money from abroad? Remember, if the tax due is in excess of Rs 70,000 crores, the income could well be approximately Rs 2,00,000 crores! Where is the balance? Has a portion been brought into India through the anonymous PN route? Who has ensured protection to Hassan Ali for so long from within the establishment? Is it the corrupt money of some politicians that was laundered by Hassan Ali? Does he have terror links? More importantly, is there only one Hassan Ali in this country?

These questions incessantly keep haunting us and may well haunt us during the coming decade too.

The Moral of the Immoral Story of Hassan Ali

Nevertheless, L'affair Hassan Ali once again signifies the extent of the rot that has set into our public life. India is not the only country to be plagued by corruption. While corruption affects several countries, India seems to be taking an ambivalent position against the same. In 2003, the United Nations adopted a Convention Against Corruption. In this connection, the then secretary general of the UN, in his statement to the General Assembly stated, "Corruption is an insidious plague that has a wide range of corrosive effects on societies. It undermines democracy and the rule of law, leads to violations of human rights, distorts markets, erodes the quality of life, and allows organized crime, terrorism and other threats to human security to flourish. This evil phenomenon is found in all countries, big and small, rich and poor but it is in the developing world that its effects are most destructive."

What is forgotten in the entire debate is that corruption hurts the poor significantly, especially in a developing country like India. It ends up diverting development funds and thereby undermines the developmental work of the Government. Naturally, that retards growth and pushes poor people into a vicious cycle of poverty and corruption. In conclusion, the then secretary general put it succinctly, "Corruption is a key element in economic underperformance, and a major obstacle to poverty alleviation and development."

The adoption of the United Nations Convention Against Corruption also sends an unambiguous message to the entire world that the international community is determined to prevent and control corruption. The convention introduced a comprehensive set of standards which were applicable to all signatory countries in order to strengthen their regulatory regimes to fight corruption. It called for preventive measures and the criminalisation of the most prevalent forms of corruption. What is important is that the convention makes a major breakthrough by requiring member countries to return assets obtained through corruption. Consequently, it was estimated that the corrupt would find it difficult to hide their illicit gains.

These provisions were expected to ensure stronger cooperation between states to prevent, detect, and return the proceeds of corruption. This is a particularly important issue for many developing countries where corrupt high officials have plundered the national wealth, and where Governments badly need resources to reconstruct and rehabilitate their societies. India, with her high level of corruption in public places, was expected to be a prime beneficiary of this convention, provided it ratified this convention.

Interestingly, India has not yet ratified this convention.[2]

Naturally, the likes of Hassan Ali will continue to proliferate. It is very clear to anyone with some understanding of the world of finance that the sums of money in his foreign accounts do not merely represent his personal wealth. In all probability, it is the corrupt money of the rich and famous that has been laundered abroad and deposited into the accounts of Hassan Ali. It would be equally interesting to know the "ultimate beneficiaries" of this money. This can be done by tracing the accounts to which the money was ultimately transferred from his accounts abroad. But to do all this, some experts opine, India must first ratify the UN Convention Against Corruption. That would give India the legal teeth and the moral authority to pursue the matter effectively in these countries.

Commenting on the issue of corruption, Mr. Rajinder Puri, a senior political columnist, writing his column titled, "Pranab Mukherjee's Dilemma: Black Money, Blue Funk", stated, "The worst aspect of the Bofors case was not its corruption. Corruption in varying degrees is worldwide. The worst aspect was the cover-up of the corruption. Cover-ups too happen worldwide. But nowhere are they as brazen and shameless as they are in India. Bofors set a new standard of shamelessness. After the Bofors case, there followed a whole stream of scandalous crimes that were consistently covered up, with equal shamelessness. HDW Submarine case, Jain Hawala case, Oil for Food scam – there is a long list of scandals covered up with contempt for public opinion. The politicians, the investigators, the judiciary and the media all got badly tainted in this process."

Mr Puri perhaps is still living in the past. The collective conscience of the nation got agitated for a mere Rs 64 crores. That was in the mid-Eighties. In the ensuing general elections, corruption was the main issue, with Bofors dominating the political discourse along with few other scandals. And that

2. Some the prominent countries that have not yet ratified this convention include Switzerland, Singapore, Liechtenstein, Myanmar, Sudan, and Saudi Arabia.

was sufficient to bring down the Rajiv Gandhi Government in 1989. Allowing for the time value of money, and devaluation of the Indian rupee against the US dollar that would at best be Rs 1,000 crores in today's prices. But strangely, today's scams run into several thousands of crores. Interestingly, while the entire opposition thought corruption to be a serious issue in the Eighties, it is strangely silent on the issue of corruption now. The media that aroused the collective conscience of the nation on the issue of corruption, is inexplicably quiet on these issues today. The response of our intellectuals who voiced concerns about corruption in high places then, is muted this time around. It is, indeed, a remarkable coincidence that since the 1989 general elections, corruption has ceased to be a prime election issue.

If Bofors as Mr Rajinder Puri opines, tainted the reputation of politicians, investigators, judiciary and the media, the Hassan Ali case and other scams of the past decade or so increasingly demonstrate the direct nexus between the looters on the one hand, and the politicians, investigators, judiciary and sections of the media, on the other.

India, as already pointed out, is yet to ratify the United Nations Convention Against Transnational Organised Crime. It may be noted that this convention is the main international instrument to fight against transnational organised crime. The convention represents a major step in the fight against transnational organised crime and signifies the recognition of the seriousness of the issue by the UN. It points out to the need for closer international cooperation in order to tackle these problems. Importantly, states that ratify this instrument, commit themselves to taking a series of measures against transnational organised crime, including the creation of domestic criminal offences (participation in an organised criminal group, money laundering, corruption and obstruction of justice); the adoption of new and sweeping frameworks for extradition, mutual legal assistance and law enforcement cooperation; and the promotion of training and technical assistance for building or upgrading the necessary capacity of national authorities

Yet, the Government of India for some inexplicable reason, refuses to ratify this convention. This ratification can be done through the executive without even consulting the Parliament. This is the stated position of the Indian Constitution. It is time that the Parliament, the opposition parties, media, intellectuals, professionals and citizens exert pressure on the Government to ratify the said convention. Let us not forget that the channels for terror funding and those who launder money arising out of corruption are one and the same.

Remember the serial blasts in Bombay in 1993? The ammunition for the blasts was smuggled into the country by using the conduits used by ordinary smugglers. For a petty smuggler, smuggling the dreaded RDX is virtually no different from smuggling gold or antiques.

Cynics may argue that ratifying such conventions could at best be symbolic, with hardly any possibility of real gains accruing to the country. But, more importantly, by ratifying it, India could be sending a positive message to the international community as well as to those who continue to launder her wealth from within and terrorise her. It could be symbolic, no doubt. But that symbolism can provide the moral authority to the country in her grand pursuit of her stolen wealth. Unfortunately, India today lacks conviction in her quest for getting back her stolen wealth from abroad. Adopting the UN Convention could be a small but sure step in regaining the moral authority.

And till that time, the stories of Hassan Ali can make interesting headlines for the media but not provide any concrete action at the ground level.

Not About Corruption but Security

But there is more to it. In February 2010, the Hon'ble President Mrs. Pratibha Patil made a reference to the tax havens in her address to the Parliament. In this connection, she stated, "My Government has undertaken a number of steps to unearth unaccounted money parked outside India. These include amendment of the Income Tax Act, 1961, to enable the Central Government to enter into tax agreements with non-sovereign jurisdictions. Steps have already been initiated for negotiations for entering into Agreements for the Exchange of Information with major jurisdictions. Renegotiation of the Tax Treaty with Switzerland is in process. India is an active part of the global efforts to facilitate exchange of tax information, and to take action against tax evasion." Obviously, the Government assumes that the entire loot in tax havens is money that has evaded tax.

But that is one facet of the entire debate relating to tax havens. What about corruption? What about cross-border terrorism? What about the possibility of this money entering our capital markets through the PN route and destabilising our capital markets? The issue, as the Hon'ble President makes out in her speech, is not one of tax evasion alone. If that be the case, the Government shall be entitled to recover only those amounts of tax dues raised (for which the assessee has not preferred any appeal) but not realised by it. The budget documents of 2010 demonstrates that this aggregates to a mere Rs 46,000 crore[3] (USD 10 billion) only! This is simply because unless tax evasion is demonstrated by our

3. The balance Rs 71,065 crores is under dispute, where technically the money is legally due to the Government but under appeal in various courts or tribunals.

Government in the first instance, we cannot have a tenable claim on such money. Assuming that the entire Rs 46,000 crores is parked outside India in Switzerland, the Government can in all probability recover at best ten billion dollars.

Naturally, there is yet another angle to this story. Replying to the discussion on the motion of thanks to the president for her address in March 2010 to both Houses of Parliament, the Prime Minister stated that while no official data is available on the quantum of slush funds, it is estimated that such black money stashed away by Indian nationals in tax havens overseas could be worth nearly USD 140 billion. Now how come the Government arrived at this conclusion? What was the source that propelled the Government to point out to a neat sum of money? Crucially, what steps has the Government taken to recover the said money from these tax havens? The answers, as usual, remain inconclusive.

The Hon'ble PM in his reply to the motion of thanks adopted by the Parliament in the first week of March 2010, stated, "Steps have been taken for signing of agreements. We have also approached Switzerland for renegotiation of our tax treaty so that we can have access to the information." According to him, the Government was also pursuing the matter with respect to a new protocol for sharing of information on tax evaders, and that such a mechanism would be put in place soon. But one is unclear as to why the Government fails to ratify the UN Convention Against Corruption and simultaneously ratify the UN Convention on Transnational Organised Crime.

What makes all these efforts of the Government suspect is the allegation by the Swiss authorities – no less – on the manner in which the Government has sought to handle the entire case. The Swiss authorities have reportedly announced that documents submitted by the Indian authorities in January 2007 in the case Hassan Ali Khan were "forged." Quoting a communication from Folco Galli, information chief of the Swiss Department of Justice and Police, Berne, the magazine *Hardnews* claims that the Indian authorities had submitted "forged" documents to seek assistance on the Hassan Ali Khan case.

In its May 2009 issue, the magazine reported, "Swiss authorities want to provide further assistance in that case if the Indian authorities could satisfy the Swiss government's demand to establish dual criminality – what is a crime in India is a crime in Switzerland. The Swiss also wanted to know whether Hassan Ali Khan's offence was an object of Indian money laundering. Since April 2007, the Indian Government has not responded to Swiss authorities on this issue," the magazine report claimed.

The response of the Government was swift but as usual diffused. In a tersely worded rejoinder, the Ministry of Finance stated, "It needs to be pointed out that the documents forwarded to the Swiss authorities were those seized from Mr. Khan's/his associates' premises and it would, therefore, be improper to suggest that the Indian Government has forged any document or Government of India submitted forged documents." Does that mean that the documents were forged even before they were seized? In that case, it makes the curious case of Hassan Ali a wild goose chase.

But what makes this issue all the more interesting is that the Government went on to affirm, "The insinuation that the Government of India doctored any document is false and contrary to facts. It is further relevant to point out that a letter by Mr. Hassan Ali Khan duly notarised by a notary in London had also been obtained by the Enforcement Directorate which is being used against Mr. Khan since the notary concerned has confirmed that the document does have his certification." If that is the case, is the Swiss Government attempting to pull wool over our eyes? Remember, Governments are Governments. The credibility of the Swiss Government is as good or as bad as that of the Indian Government. Whether one believes the Swiss or the Indian Government, the take is entirely theirs.

Nevertheless, the Hon'ble PM himself has admitted in Parliament - part one of the debate comes to an end. For some inexplicable reason, successive Indian Governments are endlessly in a denial mode on the very existence of this Indian wealth in tax havens. At least, this admission of the Hon'ble PM puts the matter to rest. It may be noted that against the estimates of this loot being in the order of USD 1.4 trillion by various economists, the figures of the Government are a mere fraction. Be that as it may, let us welcome this wholeheartedly and pray that the Government will decisively follow up on its own figures and recover at least this money in the next few years.

However, this debate, unfortunately, is not related merely to the extent of the loot stashed in tax havens abroad. If the money does exist - and it does, as affirmed by the Hon'ble PM - and data on the same is available, there are good chances that such data could find its way into the hands of forces inimical to the sovereignty of India. It could be a secret now but for how long? Obviously, we need to act quickly. And in these matters, there is no scope for being secretive unless, of course, the Government has some vested interest in doing so.

Naturally, all these issues raise profound questions relating to national security and, of course, the possibility of some foreign powers blackmailing the high and mighty of the land with respect to their accounts in tax havens. Recall that the Government affirmed to the Hon'ble Supreme Court that it had received the information about the LGT Bank from the German authorities on March 18, 2009. One year later, not much action is visible on this account except that income tax notices have been issued.

This has many right thinking citizens worried. Putting the matter in the right perspective Mr Rajinder Puri states, "The Finance Ministry had claimed that it was trying to recover black money stashed abroad. But its actions belied its words. The German Government had given a list of names of Indians whose money is lying in the LGT Bank of Liechtenstein. The Indian Government refused to disclose the names provided by Germany. It claimed that it was prevented by certain legal hurdles put up by Germany. Did the Finance Ministry deliberately create those legal hurdles? Germany itself has released its own list. How can it prevent India from releasing the list which it provided to India?"

Brilliant questions. It is indeed inexplicable as to why the Government is keen on not publishing the names of those in the said disc provided by the Germans. But the Government has neatly sidestepped these questions and has come up with its own fuzzy logic, save, of course, for its admission of USD 140 billion in tax havens.

But noted jurist and the petitioner to the Supreme Court, Mr Ram Jethmalani is not amused. Speaking in a panel discussion organised by the Delhi Administration Officers' Academic Forum on the occasion of the release of the India chapter of an International Guide to Money Laundering: Law and Practice, brought out by Bloomsbury Professional, London, he said, "The Government has filed an affidavit in the Court that it has received a list of account holders in Swiss banks. But, it is not divulging the names. This is fraud." To many, it is.

Need to Relook at the Root Assumptions Governing the Global Economy

Now let us examine the issues relating to the global macroeconomic management in the past decade or so. The character of global economics has changed completely in the past decade or two. If the thrust two decades back in the Western economies was on manufacturing, the priority today is the financial sector. This tectonic shift in the strategic interests of the Western economies, notably the US, from the manufacturing sector to the financial sector is perhaps the most defining movement in modern history and economics. Clearly, the supremacy of the sole surviving superpower of the post Cold War is getting increasingly challenged, more now than ever before. In hindsight and with the experience of the past two years or so, one can safely affirm that this strategic shift from the manufacturing sector to the financial sector has made the US strategically more vulnerable than ever before.

Importantly, the root assumptions of post Cold War economics are also getting greater scrutiny. People who hailed the end of the Cold War as conclusive evidence of the triumph of democracy and markets are now flummoxed. The reasons are not far to seek. The economic crisis of 2008-09 is perhaps a preview of a full-length horror movie. Neither was it totally unanticipated. In the process, it exposed the soft underbelly of the Western economies. But what has been attempted as a solution to deal with the extant situation is merely symptomatic. Naturally, economists are worried.

As explained in greater detail about global imbalance in the earlier chapters, this economic crisis was the manifestation of a huge imbalance among the major national economies. The large current account deficits in the United States and the United Kingdom, on the one hand, were counter-balanced by current account surpluses in China, Japan and the oil-exporting countries, on the other. Growth, it may be repeated, in several Western countries, was driven to a large extent by debt-driven consumption, made possible by reckless lending. This, in turn, fuelled inflation of assets and increased private consumption. After 2001, household debt increased rapidly in those countries, where current-account deficits had widened, leading to an accumulation of external liabilities. No wonder, it is often remarked that if the US is the engine of global growth, its housing industry is the compressor of that engine.

Simultaneously, macroeconomic policies (by an artificial suppression of interest rates, especially in the US) ensured bubbles in the housing and stock markets. The ingenuity of the financial sector took over from now on with the proliferation of derivatives and other instruments of mass financial destruction. That made the crisis widespread and resulted in a contagion across continents. The financial sector deregulation was an outcome of a misplaced belief (or was the belief itself manipulated?) in the efficacy of the markets mechanism that ensured the proliferation of casino capitalism. It was obvious to several economists that this situation could not continue forever.

As a readjustment policy, multilateral institutions suggested a globally coordinated adjustment programme whereby surplus countries would increase domestic consumption while deficit countries would bring down their consumption. As early as in 2004, for example, the UNCTAD's Trade and Development Report stated: "Large disparities in the strength of domestic demand persist among the major industrial countries, and increasing trade imbalances between the major economic block could ... increase instability in currency and financial markets." But who cared to see the writing on the wall, especially in those heady times?

The net result is an unprecedented economic crisis that has hit several countries. The only solution that seems to have been worked out by these countries is to lower interest rates to near zero while allowing enormous latitude to their financial sector by running gargantuan deficits. And all these are aimed at providing succour to all those stakeholders – borrowers as well as lenders – who were party to this credit extravaganza for the past several years. If it was an American loan *mela* till 2008-09, it is a global subsidies *mela* since then.

Importantly, there is growing realisation across the world that in a globalised world, there are no Chinese walls to control "shocks" emanating in one part of the world. Naturally, this has raised fundamental questions about the very idea of global financial integration. In this connection, the 2009 Trade and Development Report of the UNCTAD states, "The experience with the current financial crisis calls into question the conventional wisdom that dismantling all obstacles to cross-border private capital flows is the best recipe for countries to advance their economic development. While it is agreed that global finance has caused the current crisis, surprisingly little attention is being given to the management of global finance, and in particular speculative capital flows." Further, the report adds, "The experience of this financial crisis also supports the case for a more fundamental rethinking of global financial governance with a view to stabilising trade and financial relations by reducing the potential for gains from speculative capital flows."

Obviously, if allowing free capital flows was considered the last mile connectivity to a globalised economy in the Nineties, today, the pendulum seems to have swung the other way. Post economic crisis of 2008, some (albeit in minority even to this day) are of the view that it is better to restrict unhindered flow of capital than be a victim of such finance. In this connection, the IMF Staff Position Paper published on February 19, 2010, in its concluding para states, "The perspective of this note is thus that capital controls are a legitimate part of the toolkit to manage capital inflows in certain circumstances." That in itself constitutes a huge policy turn for it was the IMF that was championing the cause of unbridled capital flows in the not so distant past.

Further, the global economic crisis has spawned a new debate on the ability of the developed countries to invest in other countries. After all, the developed countries are saddled with gargantuan debts and are in poor financial health. Moreover, these debts are actually the lending of the developing countries, made at extraordinarily low rates of interest to such developed countries. The inability of these developing countries due to a variety of reasons to absorb their huge domestic savings results in this movement of capital from their hands into the developed countries.

Naturally, what is lending for the developing countries becomes borrowing for the developed countries. What is missed in the melee is that in effect foreign investment is nothing but recycled savings of the developing countries – first lent at low rates to the developed world that reenters the developing countries with certain tough terms and conditions. While one is not against foreign capital entering India, let us not forget that in the current global context, it is our own domestic savings that are substantially rerouted back into India as foreign investment.

Strangely, in India, we seem to have missed out these fundamental issues in our debate of allowing foreign money into India. Capital inflows have their own associated cost. *It is no longer a case of allowing PNs and attempting endlessly to know about their ultimate beneficiaries. Rather, we need to revisit the entire policy relating to FII flows. The earlier we realise the same, the better it will be.*

The Mother of all Subsidies?

Modern economics has another unexplored dimension of artificially lowering interest rates as a one-stop-shop cure to all the ills facing the economy. By repeatedly lowering interest rates for the past several years or so, the US Federal System (Fed) expects to stimulate consumption, crucially lower mortgage payments and, in the process, trigger a recovery in the US. That by extension possibly includes the global economy. After the economic crisis exploded in September 2008, the US Fed has lowered interest rates to historic lows. However, experts, including Noble Laureate Joseph Stiglitz, point out to the futility of this exercise, opining that this cut in interest rates will have little impact on the overall scenario. According to them, it is a case of too little and too late – akin to applying pain balm when chemotherapy is the need of the hour. Even as the interest rate cuts are carried out, experts opine that the US Fed could be charged with creating a "moral hazard." After all, in sum and substance, the act of the Fed is rewarding all those who were party to reckless borrowings and lending.

That takes us to the most important question – was the Federal Reserve motivated in lowering the interest rates within the US? In the process, was it not protecting someone? Is bailing out the reckless lenders and borrowers more important than controlling inflation in the US? Crucial questions that stare at us in the extant global scenario.

The answers to these questions are revealing. The approach of the Fed to savings, investments, stock markets and the symbiotic link provided to all these is central to understanding its motives, its responses to situations, and what drives its decisions. It may be noted that despite being dependent on other countries for funding its trade deficits, the US establishment has never been bothered about increasing its domestic savings. It is in this connection that Ben Bernanke, who was the head of George Bush's Council of Economic Advisers and subsequently became the Fed chief, had suggested in 2005 that the world suffers from excessive savings – what he termed as "savings glut," implying lack of investment opportunities within the developing countries. Further, he argued that people save less in the developed countries, especially in the Anglo-Saxon ones because of the sophistication in their financial markets – read investments in stock markets – and that higher savings in other countries are because of the "poor returns" and "underdeveloped markets."

And Bernanke is not alone on this matter. In fact, this is the thinking within the Fed – why it could well be termed as the official thinking of the Fed. Bernanke's predecessor, Alan Greenspan, a celebrated economist and a Fed chief for over eighteen years between 1987 and 2005, in his book *The Age of Turbulence* goes a step further and theorises that the propensity of people to save is a sign of underdevelopment. In contrast, he points out how the developed countries, through their vast financial networks, enable a "significant fraction of the consumers to spend beyond their current incomes." In short, according to Mr. Greenspan, Mr. Bernanke and the Fed, savings is a sin, spending a virtue.

This paradigm was captured brilliantly by *The Economist* which in a paper published on April 7, 2005, points out, "It may be a virtue, but in much of the rich world, thrift has become unfashionable. Household saving rates in many OECD countries have fallen sharply in recent years. Anglo-Saxon countries – America, Canada, Britain, Australia and New Zealand – have the lowest rates of household savings. Americans on average, save less than 1% of their after-tax income today compared with 7% at the beginning of the 1990s. In Australia and New Zealand, personal saving rates are negative as people borrow to consume more than they earn." By 2008, (i.e. just before the onset of the global economic crisis) the less than one per cent savings had turned negative.

All this is not as simple as it seems on a superficial examination – an issue related to savings in an economy and the concomitant interest rates. What is crucial to remember at this point is the fact that it if the developing countries do not fund the developed ones for the requirement of their capital, these "developed" countries could come to a grinding halt. And contrary to the popular belief, it is this export of capital from the developing countries that is sustaining the developed ones, not the other way around. This is one issue that Alan Greenspan or for that matter Ben Bernanke have failed to answer. But that has other implications too. As savings are scarce in the Western countries and remain only in the hands of the developing countries, it is in the interest of the developed countries to pay lower rates of interest for such "import of capital." And being a virtual monopoly borrower at the global level, the US has been successful in determining the terms of such borrowings. Interesting, isn't it?

But that is not the end of the matter. Crucially, by lowering interest rates, Ben Bernanke and his predecessor at the Fed have been batting openly for the routing of capital from the developing to the developed countries and from investments bearing fixed rates of interest to the stock markets, not only within the US but even outside the US. With substantial US investments in global corporates and in stock markets across the globe, a cut in interest rates is in the interest of the US corporates, notably its financial sector.

No wonder, this transfer of wealth from the developing world to the developed world at very low interest rates is the mother of all subsidies – aimed at sustaining the global stock market. And if this is the central idea that sustains global economics, can India be far behind?

To understand this paradigm, a return to the textbooks is necessary. Fundamental economics tells us that interest rate cut leads to two consequences. First, it acts as a disincentive to savings and simultaneously encourages spending. The second consequence directly impacts the capital markets. It moves money from the hands of individuals to the corporates as lower interest rate acts as a dampener for interest-related savings, but, encourages investments into stock markets. By a single policy measure of lowering interest rates, the corporate economy is sustained.

The calculated effort of the US Federal system (and its financial sector) to shift savings from the households to the corporates, not only within the US but also outside the US, as briefly explained above, is central to modern economics. It would seem that the Fed is wedded to the cause of the American corporates, especially its financial sector. American corporates, along with the US Fed, therefore, are on a joint mission – while the US Fed battles for lower interest rates, the US corporates are the beneficiaries of lower interest rates. Naturally, it is in their interest to lower the interest rates across the globe. Near zero rates of interest in effect means zero risks.

As mentioned above, this paradigm of low interest rates favours investment in stocks as compared to those who seek to invest in deposits bearing fixed but low rates of return on their investments. In India, we do not have a near zero rate regime as in the US. Also, the Indian rupee may not enjoy the global currency status of the US dollar. That effectively means that India cannot borrow like the US from the outside world. But like the US, we too have an implicit need to subsidise our stock markets. After all, both in the US and India, the hold of the financial sector on the polity is extraordinary.

This subsidy regime is simply achieved through domestic policy interventions. It may be interesting to note that inflation rates in India are calculated at a wholesale price level. That means that inflation at the consumer price level is ignored. Moreover, the inflation rates are heavily doctored by the Government. That is how inflation is "controlled" by the Government in India. In comparison, even to the official inflation rates, it is often found that the return on bank deposits could well be negative. Yet, our policy framers consistently persist with a low interest rate regime. In the process, they brush aside the obvious disconnect between domestic inflation and interest rates.

The reason for this policy machination is obvious. India has huge domestic savings – estimated to be approximately 38 percent of her GDP. Further, it is estimated that nearly three-fourths of this savings is generated by the households in India – a sector that has very little voice or lobbying power. What is causing consternation to the pro-corporate and pro-stock market lobbyists is that only a small fraction of this savings is routed to the capital markets or to the corporates. Therefore, while money is indeed available in domestic markets, lobbyists work overtime to plot appropriate policy formulations that need to be carried out to ensure that this savings of the Indian households is channelled into the capital markets. What better way of doing it than to suppress macro-economic parameters (inflation, for instance) so as to ensure a soft interest rate regime in India to benefit the stock markets? The disconnect between the near-administered interest rates of India and the elevated inflation rates prevailing in the country since 2006-07 is evidence of policy orientations favouring the markets.

Further, of late, even some banks fund individuals for their purchase of shares. This was unthinkable even a decade ago. All this was done right under the direct knowledge of the RBI. Again, this was pro-market policy intervention. All this was marketed by banks as "personal loans" which were usually secured on the basis of the stocks purchased out of such lending. And when the stock markets gyrated, the banks played Shylock and invariably squeezed their clients for margins to fall in the value of their shares. In the alternative, banks sold these shares at suppressed values. Having given personal guarantees, many such borrowers were forced to make good their loss. Alternatively, banks are also known to use strong arm tactics to recover money from their customers.

One is not sure as to why the Government remains silent to all these issues. The only reason that can be put forth is that such policies encourage people to invest in capital markets. Interest rates are no longer seen by analysts as a monetary policy tool to control inflation and trigger growth, but as a powerful policy tool to ensure a shift in domestic savings from the hands of the households to corporates.

Analysts view this soft money and pro-market policy as a clear subsidy to the stock markets and market participants. While the US does this at the cost of the poor and developing countries, India seems to do it at the cost of its savers.

Markets and its Interest in Interest Rates

This policy orientation of shifting household savings into the hands of the corporates has the open blessings of the mainstream media, economists and, of course, academicians. Their common refrain is that lower interest rates are a prerequisite to growth. Contrarian or alternative views are simply rejected, ridiculed and snubbed. All this is done with a calculated objective of preparing the minds of the people to accept a shift in savings from the households into the hands of the corporates. Remember, this is a twenty-four by seven job, with no holidays in between. And any policy that ensures the routing of the household savings into the hands of the corporates or the stock markets is welcome.

Nothing illustrates the link of the popular media to such alternative economics than an article in mid-2009 by the CNBC titled "Higher Savings is Great, But What About the Economy." While the title of the article itself was intriguing, the logic that ran through the entire article was even stranger. "Households pushed their savings rate to the highest level in more than 15 years in May as a big boost in incomes from the government's stimulus program was devoted more to bolstering nest eggs than increased spending." It went on to put modern economics in a succinct yet brazen manner, "The higher savings rate is healthy in the long-term, economists said. But without vigorous consumer spending, the Government may have to do more to revive the economy, possibly through further tax breaks and spending."

In short, thrift is bad for the economy. But what do we mean by "economy?" Obviously, economy refers to corporate economy – not the economy as a whole. In a sharp rejoinder to this article, Robert P. Murphy an economist wrote, "I realize it must be difficult to maintain a constant barrage of 'just breaking' financial news stories, but CNBC really puts out some doozies. Take, for example, a recent article titled, 'Higher Savings Rate is Great, But What About the Economy?' When the title itself is nonsense – why would high savings be great if they destroyed the economy? – you know the article will be chock full of entertaining assertions and faulty logic."

Asserting that for the first time in 15 years, he was "proud to be an American," Murphy hits the nail right on the head when he states, "Most people in this country were living beyond their means from 2002 to 2006, in part because of an unsustainable housing boom set in motion through easy credit from the Fed." And the obvious solution to Murphy was for people in the US to live *below* their means for several years from now on. Pointing out to the fact that the Government had failed to increase interest rates after the housing bubble popped, Murphy suggests that such fall in "aggregate demand" would have been in the larger interest of the US economy.

But the most profound question put forward by Murphy was, "If households across the country are opting for less consumption today in order to have more wealth in the future, why are the politicians (and CNBC) trying to thwart their plans?" That indeed is the moot point. Murphy is not done yet. In conclusion, he puts it all in the proper perspective when he states, "It's understandable that the politicians would get up there and propose that we lend them a few trillion dollars to hand out to their friends. But why do sober economists lend their voice to the madness, and why do financial reporters continue to quote them? Let's just hope it's all an honest mistake."

Honest mistake? Well, that is putting things rather mildly. Perhaps Murphy sought to be politically correct. Nevertheless, this idea of transferring the savings of the households into the hands of the corporates has been the single most economic thought that has occupied the central policy stage for over two decades now not only within the US but in several countries across the globe. In the process, economic success or failure is reduced to a single mathematical expression – the rise or fall of the index in the stock markets of which the lower interest rates plays a determinant role. Interest rates are no more the outcome of the macro-economic state of play of the economy and increasingly bear little or no causal relationship with inflation rates prevailing in the economy. Rather, they remain as policy interventions to make mar markets. And this has the tacit blessings, as Murphy points out, of sober economists and the media too.

Given the dominance of this thought at a global level, can India lag behind? Or can it be credited with any fresh thinking? Remember, CNBC operates in India through an affiliate. Naturally, the Sensex is more important than farm production, the NIFTY more sacred than industry. All these make the study of "fixing" interest rates in India fascinating, especially given the prevailing high rates of inflation and low interest rates. Benign interest rates undeniably appear to be the biggest subsidy to boost sentiments so as to boost stock markets in India.

Markets or Rigged Casinos?

One may recall the discussion in the context of the oil price increase between 2006 and 2008, its fall in the later half of 2008, and the subsequent rise in 2008-09 in the earlier chapters. It would have been noticed that the rise, fall and rise of the crude oil prices had nothing to do with the demand and supply of crude oil. It is often seen that markets not linked by economic fundamentals are invariably under the disruptive influence of strong speculative forces. This is modern economics at work where the fundamental laws of economics are suspended. And in this economics, it is the confluence of greed, speculation and deceit, all played out in the full glare of the regulators, with little or no relation to fundamentals.

In the process, little do we realise that the grammar of speculators is significantly different from the grammar of investors, producers or consumers. Speculators aim for short-term (sometimes on an hourly basis) gains only through the first mover advantage. For them, news is important, interpreting it instantly becomes crucial. Every bit of news has to be "discounted" even before others assimilate the news. Fascinatingly, it is often noticed that a large majority of speculators react uniformly to "news." This is simply because when one of the players, especially a large influential one, exits a particular market, others necessarily have to follow even if it were to create a stampede at the exit. Similarly, when large players enter a market, others necessarily have to follow suit.

In the Indian context, the ultimate beneficiaries of all these policies to play up (and play down) market sentiments are those who manipulate markets. At the cost of repetition, it is once again stated: manage sentiments and manipulate the Sensex – or, for that matter, any index.

In such a situation where prices are strongly influenced by speculative flows, little do Governments and regulators realise that markets function inefficiently. The disproportionate influence of the large players can been seen when they determine the "favourable conditions" for their entry or exit from a market. Smaller players with contrarian views do not matter as they cannot make or mar the markets. But what adds fat to the fire is the media acting in tandem with such large players. Recall what we discussed just now – every bit of news is important and interpreting it is crucial. That makes it a heady concoction, with little or no antidote to the Government or the regulators. Once the media takes up a story, competition within the media ensures a momentum of its own; especially, given the fact that the media, more often than not, is also an active market participant. That, in turn, makes or mars the markets, making them extremely volatile.

The claim that the financial markets can ever be stable was debunked by George Soros himself in a testimony before the Banking Committee of the US House of Representatives. Soros told the committee that when a speculator bets, a price will rise and it falls instead when he is forced into selling, which accelerates the downward spiral and thereby increases market volatility. His testimony also revealed the perspective of the financial speculator, for whom volatility is a source of profits. He also spoke about his experience of how speculators could shape the directions of the market price and create instability. He is one of the legends who have made and unmade so many markets – commodities, currencies, stock, interest and others – that a New York Times article, "When Soros speaks, World Markets Listen" credited him with being able to increase the price of his investments. After taking a position against the German mark, he was quoted as saying that he expected the mark to fall against all major world currencies. And the mark did indeed fall as the world over, traders agreed that this was a Soros market. Similarly, on November 5, 1993, the *New York Times* Business pages carried a story titled "Rumours of Buying by Soros Send Gold Prices Surging." Remember, that was nearly two decades back. Things have definitely not improved since than.

The reach of these "financial players" is not restricted to any specific commodity, currency or stock markets. In September 1992, Soros sold USD 10 billion worth of British pounds. In doing so he was credited with forcing a devaluation of the pound that contributed to the breaking of the system of the fixed exchange rates in the UK. The resulting gyrations in the markets led the British pound to fall 41 percent against the Japanese Yen over the next year or so. To sum up, in the words of Felix Rahatyn, a senior partner with Lazard Feres & Co, "In many cases, the hedge funds and speculative activity in general, may now be more responsible for foreign exchange and interest rate movements than intervention by Central Banks."

Obviously, speculators thrive on volatility and abhor stability.

In contrast, where there is stability in any market, it is in their interest to dynamite it and usher in volatility at the earliest. This leads to price movement not justified by fundamentals, causing significant damage to the real economy.

Some economists innocently argue that a bit of speculation is good for the markets as it would provide liquidity. That is acceptable when the markets are perfect. But when have the markets been perfect? Economists, more often than not, do not realise the innate power of these speculators in moulding the minds – read sentiments – of the market players. In the process, it is these sentiments that determine the demand and supply of the markets and, therefore, the prices. With a pliable media playing ball, speculators and market manipulators never had it so easy, especially in the Indian context. And that requires some reference to real life situations in India.

Of late, there is a new class of investors – investment by the financial sector into the commodities futures market. In doing so, the fundamental laws of economics, the price of a commodity and its relationship between supply and demand seems to have been suspended. What is worrying analysts is the growing influence of these players, "who tend to take only long positions that exert upward pressure on prices." Consequently, it is observed that the size of their positions has become so large that they can significantly influence prices and create speculative bubbles. Moreover, their activities are obviously coordinated across currency, stock and commodity markets. In this connection, the Trade and Development Report of 2009 of the UNCTAD observed, "Commodity prices, stock prices and the exchange rates of currencies affected by carry trade speculation moved in parallel during much of the period of the commodity price hike in 2005–2008, during the subsequent sharp correction in the second half of 2008 and again during the rebound phase in the second quarter of 2009."

Consequently, the rise and fall in commodity prices over the past few years has nothing to do with demand and supply or for that matter, well-established laws of economics. This issue is of particular importance for food commodities in a country like India, with constant supply side constraints. Naturally, speculating on the weather and its impact on food production has assumed big business world over. A "Report" published in some remote corner on the El-Nino flows or its impact on the Indian monsoon pattern could well trigger a spurt in the food grain prices in India merely in anticipation of a failure of the monsoon. That, when repeated by vested interests in the media at prime time or on the front pages of national dailies, instantly becomes an "impending food disaster waiting to explode." In addition, experts of various hues are called by different sections of the media in competition with each other to comment on the "food crisis caused by the failure of the monsoon." Being "experts" they have no option but to prophesise on crisis, calamity and devastation. And "bad" news is also "good" news for the media as it is increases readership or viewership, as the case may be.

Naturally, all these add to the overall panic in the economy. This, in turn, leads to hoarding by the "common man." People hoard in *anticipation* of shortages and not when there is an *actual* shortage. It is this hoarding by the common man that generates demand at the aggregate level, leading to increase in the prices of a commodity. Once the necessary threshold level of panic is created, the rest is easy. Rumours, black marketers and hoarders at the retail level then take over and ensure a price rise. In India, it is far easier with underdeveloped spot markets and poor infrastructure to create demand supply gaps easily through this process of creating panic. Financial investors and their partners in investment the media, act in tandem to create this panic. After all, they have taken long positions in the futures market quite early, knowing pretty well it is they who have the ability to hype the failure of the monsoon, leverage it and profit from it.

Commenting on this issue of overhyping the failure of the monsoon in 2009, the Economic Survey for 2009-10 was particularly critical of the Government's failure in not being able to check the "hype" over the *Kharif* crop failure, caused by an erratic monsoon, which did not take into account the comfortable food stocks and prospects of *Rabi* production. The survey further notes that this "may have exacerbated inflationary expectations, encouraging hoarding and resulting in a higher inflation in food items." What is lost in this debate of the absurd is that the Government allowed such speculation in the first place and then kept quiet when the players hyped up the monsoon failure.

Some analysts argue that whatever may be the impact of such "intervention" by the speculators, it would be purely temporary and prices would return to normal so as to reflect the fundamentals. That is, provided the fundamentals themselves are not subject to such intervention. But the more important question is: what prevents the Government from preventing such hyping in the first place?

That makes the study of speculators and their linkages to the corridors of power all the more fascinating in India. The answer to this question requires a reference once again to the Economic Survey of 2009-10. The Economic Survey further points out to the fact that the minimum buffer stock of rice and wheat required to be maintained in the month of January 2010 was 20 million tonnes. Against the same, the Survey points out that the actual buffer stock of rice and wheat was approximately 47 million tonnes. In contrast, the buffer stock in January 2009 was 35 million tonnes. In short, in a "drought year", the Government actually procured 12 million tonnes from the markets. Conventional economics suggests otherwise – that the

Government should release buffer stocks to ensure more supply to meet the possible surge in prices.[4]

Nevertheless, this action of the Government ensured a shortfall in supply to that extent. With such a huge supply shortage, there was an apparent demand-supply gap at the ground level. Anyone oblivious to these facts would blame the price rise on the monsoon (or retail hoarders), little realising that it was the Government that had created an artificial shortage by hoarding such a huge quantity of food grains in the first place. No wonder, the food inflation, even as per official admission, was 20 percent in January 2010 and is expected to be elevated for the foreseeable future even in June 2010. Welcome to the theatre of the absurd! But questions remain. Who in the Government authored this pernicious policy? Who benefited from it? Who in the Government ensured the vital link among hype, hoarding and hyper-inflation?

No wonder, given this scenario, rumours of even senior Cabinet ministers being a part of the speculation cabal gains credence. That makes markets in India increasingly resemble a rigged casino.

Now SEBI Sidesteps the Ownership Issue

Now let us return to the stock markets and their possible manipulation through PNs. SEBI was once again forced to revisit the issue of PNs in two similar cases, one in late 2009 and the other in early 2010. Interestingly, the facts of both cases are similar and the approach of SEBI typical. The order of SEBI (December 2009) directed "Barclays Bank PLC not to issue/subscribe or otherwise transact in any fresh/new Offshore Derivative Instrument till such time as Barclays satisfies SEBI that it has put adequate systems, processes and controls in place to ensure true and correct reporting of its ODI transactions to SEBI." Participatory Notes, it may be noted are technically called ODIs.

That once again brought the vexatious issue of FII Regulations, especially with respect to PNs, into sharp focus. The crux of the charge made out by SEBI is that Barclays had not only failed to provide "true, fair and complete" details of the PN activity undertaken by it but had also violated the provisions of the FII Regulations by furnishing false and incorrect information to SEBI. In a strongly worded order, SEBI went on to explain the rationale for this order. It stated, "As the source of funds available with an FII comes from offshore, by its very nature SEBI has no direct access to verifying the nature of the funds or

4. It is pertinent to note that the Government had banned futures trading in rice and wheat in early 2007. Subsequently, the ban on futures trading in wheat was lifted in mid-2009, coinciding with the hype.

whether the funds will be misused for the purpose of market manipulation or for perpetrating any type of fraud in the market."

According to SEBI, the introduction of Regulations 15A and 20A reflects "this pressing regulatory concern on the part of SEBI." In short, SEBI conceded that it places almost absolute faith and unqualified reliance on the ability of an FII to carry out the basic regulatory and prudential oversight. Once this faith is violated and the integrity of the process vitiated, SEBI concluded that FII inflows can potentially become "conduits for large scale manipulation and fraud in the market."

It may be noted that Barclays had issued four PNs in 2006 to UBS AG with Reliance Communications Limited as the underlying. Inexplicably, SEBI had sought certain specific information with respect to these PNs in September 2009. During this entire period, in their periodic reports to SEBI, Barclays had claimed that these PNs were issued to UBS AG. Subsequently, Barclays, in November 2009, submitted that the counterparty of the transactions was not UBS AG as earlier reported by it but Hythe Securities Limited – an entirely new entity which did not form part of any of the earlier periodical submissions made by Barclays to SEBI.

In this connection, SEBI advised Barclays to reconcile the records of beneficial owners of all PNs and confirm that there are no further re-statements required in the matter. In response to this query, Barclays submitted in early December 2009 that the PNs under reference were originally issued to Hythe and that they were "onward issued" to another entity viz., Pluri Emerging Companies PCC Cell E Emerging Markets Growth Fund (Pluri).

It may be noted that the reporting format of SEBI specifically requires FIIs to provide the name and location of the entity to whom the PNs are issued, the name and the location of the entity in case the PNs are onward issued back to back to another entity. Further, this reporting format requires the FIIs to provide the information about the regulated status of the entity to whom the PNs have been issued, including the jurisdiction and the regulator with whom the entity is regulated. It may be noted that SEBI has ostensibly cast a responsibility on FIIs to ensure that any downstream issuance of PN is in strict compliance with FII Regulations.

According to regulation 15A(1) of the FII regulations, an FII may issue PNs against underlying securities, only in favour of those entities which are regulated by any relevant regulatory authority in the countries of their incorporation or establishment, subject to compliance of "know your client" requirements. Further, according to 15A(2) of the FII Regulations, an FII shall ensure that no further downstream issue or transfer of any instrument referred to in sub-regulation (1) is made to any person other than a regulated entity. This provision was further amended in May 2008. Accordingly, *"A foreign institutional investor shall ensure that no further issue or transfer is made of any offshore derivative instruments issued by or on behalf of it to any person other than a person regulated by an appropriate foreign regulatory authority."*

From the information provided by Barclays, SEBI concluded that the PNs that were issued by it to Hythe Securities Limited (originally stated to be issued to UBS AG) were in effect issued to Pluri. This, according to SEBI, was in contravention of Regulation 15A(2) of the FII Regulations as Barclays misrepresented that the PNs were not issued "back to back" to any other entity when in fact they were.

It may be interesting to note that all the information between the issue of the PNs by Barclays in 2006 and September 2009 (when SEBI began to peruse the matter) were made by Barclays through a fortnightly reporting mechanism to SEBI. In these reports, Barclays had repeatedly stated that it had not issued PNs on a back-to-back basis when, in fact, it had precisely done so. Barclays attempted to blame all this on manual compilation of the PN reports in December 2006 and error at the data entry level which continued till this error was discovered during the extant investigation.

While SEBI was not impressed by the attempt of Barclays to downplay the issue, it precisely chose to needle Barclays on trivia. Consequently, in the face of such "blatant disregard" for the FII Regulations, SEBI concluded that Barclays failed in complying with the provisions of the FII Regulations. Apparently, it seems that SEBI was miffed on the "back-to-back" issue rather than on the beneficial ownership of Pluri and whether an appropriate regulatory authority regulates it. In fact, it is pertinent to note that SEBI's order is silent about the ownership of Pluri. But this, in my opinion, is the crux of the issue.

It is important to note that if Barclays were to prove that Pluri is regulated by an "appropriate foreign regulatory authority" as required by Regulation 15A(2), it could turn out to be a classical case of much ado about nothing. Everything else being the smaller order of smalls could be explained as a clerical error. Equally, one hastens to add that if Pluri were not regulated by an appropriate authority, surely, it raises several inconvenient questions on the manner in which FIIs are regulated by SEBI. Perhaps that explains why SEBI has sought to sidestep this crucial issue – especially on the ownership of Pluri – in the first place.

Nevertheless, one is unclear as to what SEBI means by "appropriate foreign regulatory authority." In this connection, one is constrained to recall that the Hon'ble Securities Appellate Tribunal (SAT) in the UBS case had agreed to the contention of UBS that the KYC norms were not defined in the FII Regulations. To this day, SEBI has inexplicably not defined the KYC norms as applicable for FIIs in India. Similarly, in the absence of a precise definition or guidelines on what constitutes "appropriate foreign regulatory authority", it may be rationalised that even simple police verification could pass muster.

Naturally, this raises the next interesting question – what if Pluri (given the fact that its ownership details are unknown) fits into one of the four categories. Given the ratio of the Goldman Sachs case as explained above, SEBI does not have a case in the first place in such circumstances, as the fortnightly undertaking submitted by Barclays itself is legally untenable. Strangely, SEBI has failed to seek answers these questions. Given these enormous constraints, one wonders what could be the fate of this order.

PNs Continue to Hoodwink SEBI

Simultaneously, SEBI began investigating another FII operating in India – Societe Generale (SG). The facts were more or less similar to the Barclays case. During the period January 2006 to January 2008, it was observed that SG had issued certain PNs to Hythe Securities Limited with Reliance Communications Limited as the underlying. On an investigation by SEBI, SG admitted that out of forty-eight transactions with Hythe, it misreported fourteen such transactions. SEBI also sought to know whether PNs were issued to downstream entities, the beneficial owner and the regulatory status of such entity. In reply, SG stated that it had established a relationship with Hythe for dealing on a 'principal' basis. On further investigations, it transpired that PNs were issued to "designations" by the name of Pluri Emerging Co PPC Cell E, Pluri Cell E, or just Cell E. Regarding these PNs, the reporting by SG of Hythe as the end beneficiary was obviously not true.

When SEBI sought to get at the beneficial holders of such PNs, SG acknowledged that it was unable to obtain the details of the beneficial owners, stating, *"Hythe is not willing to provide such information to us. They would rather provide you (SEBI) the details directly." The charade was played out all over once again.*

SEBI contended that it has permitted issuance of PNs by FIIs with an explicit obligation that the issuance of PNs comes with an inalienable responsibility to maintain a complete audit trail of onward issuances of PNs right up to the end beneficiary. SEBI was not amused about not coming to know of the beneficial owners of such PNs. In its order in January 2010, SEBI noted that "SG has failed to satisfy the basic tenet of know your client compliance" in respect of the PNs issued by it.

SEBI further opined that "such information should have been well in the possession of SG itself in the first instance." According to SEBI, SG, being a registered entity which has been permitted to issue PNs, cannot throw up its hands in "sheer helplessness and put forward a plea that it is unable to furnish the required information, because its client is unwilling to part with the same." To SEBI, such a stand was clearly unacceptable as it indeed makes a mockery of the regulatory requirements.

SEBI finally concluded:

- SG has failed to provide true, fair and complete details of the PN activity undertaken by it and also *prima facie* violated the provisions of FII Regulations by furnishing false and incorrect information to SEBI.
- It, *prima facie*, has not even been able to ascertain whether the entity to which PNs were issued onward are themselves regulated.
- It has failed in its due diligence expected in the observance of 'know your client' norms.

Consequently, SEBI directed SG not to issue or otherwise transact in any new PNs till such time it provides true and correct reporting of PNs to SEBI. Given the track record of SEBI with regard to PNs, the final outcome of these cases is anybody's guess.

In June 2010, SEBI accepted the consent filed by RBS Asia limited (formerly ABN Amro Asia Limited) in the matter of the market crash of May 2004. The allegations *inter alia* were almost similar – RBS failed to carry out due diligence in respect of clients and issued PNs without complying with the KYC norms. A show cause notice was issued in May 2005 and the hearings as well as enquiry were held in the following months. Strangely, SEBI kept silent (as is its wont) for the next three years. In 2010, RBS proposed a consent to SEBI and agreed to pay Rs 60 lakhs as settlement charges for the settling the enforcement actions. SEBI agreed for the same in June 2010. Well, it is more or less a remake of UBS with a same climax – tragedy coupled with farce.

In the Indian context, KYC (especially vis-à-vis PNs) has come to be understood as something is completely negotiable for a small official fine (with possibly large unofficial payments). The actions of SEBI in the UBS and RBS Asia Limited cases demonstrate this paradigm.

More Allegations but Very Little Action

But more was to follow. Surprises never cease in India, do they? According to *Moneylife* (issue dated March 26, 2010) a Member of Parliament (MP) from the Congress Party had alleged that the Anil Dhirubhai Ambani Group (ADAG) was carrying out unauthorised trading in the accounts of a couple of diamond traders out of the London branch of Union Bank of Switzerland (UBS). The crux of the allegation contained in that particular issue of *Moneylife* was that ADAG diverted funds raised through External Commercial Borrowings (ECB) and Foreign Currency Convertible Bonds (FCCB) into stock market operations through UBS. The funds were moved by UBS into the dormant accounts of some diamond merchants and then used to conduct large-scale unauthorised trade running into several billions of dollars. This was done by routing the money into the Indian capital market in the form of PNs through a Mauritius-based entity called Pluri Emerging Company PCC. The MP claims to have written to all the regulatory agencies, including the RBI and SEBI and the chairman of the Central Board of Direct Taxes (CBDT) asking them why they were uninterested in pursuing the investigation.

Given the record of SEBI in tracking the ultimate beneficiaries of PNs, one is not sure about the effectiveness of these investigations. Whatever be the outcome of the Barclays and SG cases, it is pertinent to note that the issue of PNs is a politically sensitive one in the country. Given the regulatory gaps (where herds of elephants can pass through), and as exposed by the judgements of the Hon'ble SAT in the Goldman Sachs case as well as the UBS case, as explained above, it is time that SEBI comprehensively overhauls the FII regulations vis-à-vis PNs and recalibrates its mindset. Should SEBI fail to do so, it would be left questioning FIIs merely on trivial issues.

The Rot Within

All these are crucial to understand the rise, fall and rise of the Sensex, in the Indian context. Fundamental market functioning tells us that any gyration in the prices of stocks depends on the following factors:

- Information: Markets love information – good or bad is immaterial. Every bit of news has value. It is this flow of information that creates demand, or in the alternative, selling pressure. Naturally, that is crucial to tackle every corporate at a micro level.
- Liquidity: When there is sufficient liquidity in the hands of the players, stock markets react positively. This, as we observed in the earlier portion of this chapter, needs to be available at substantially lower rates of interest. This is equally important to translate buying interest into demand.

- Policy decisions: The third factor that determines the rise or fall in the stock markets is the policy decisions taken by the Government. For instance, should the RBI decide to increase the interest rates, it may impact the functioning of the stock markets.

The sudden rise and fall of the stock markets in 2001 led to the formation of the JPC in 2001. Since then, especially in 2007 and 2008, there have been several instances of sudden falls followed by steep increase in the stock markets. Or it could well be the other way around. Stock markets rationalise it as increased volatility on account of its linkages with the global capital markets. In comparison, the events that led to the formation of the JPC in 2001 look like a walk in the park.

This requires some elaboration. In 2009, we were witness to a strange spectacle. Due to certain security constraints caused by electoral compulsions, the Indian Premier League (IPL-2) T-20 cricket was shifted out of India. It was cricket, played predominantly with Indian players and an Indian flavour but in South Africa. Barring a few cheerleaders, there was nothing South African about it. What is interesting is that the Indian stock markets reflect that peculiar chapter of the IPL. It is Indian stocks, Indian companies but it is increasingly the foreign money that determines the rise and fall of the Indian stock markets. It seems that like the South African Cricket Board provided all the logistics (and, of course, a few players) during the IPL-2, the Indian stock markets provide all the logistics to these foreign investors, with investment through domestic mutual funds thrown in for good measure.

But the moot question remains in the context of Indian stock markets: are they foreign institutional investors or foreign indirect investments of the rich and mighty of the land? Is this wealth first taken out of India through the Hawala route, and subsequently re-routed into India through the tax haven-PN route? As we repeatedly saw, SEBI or for that matter any other regulator or the Government is not fully aware of the ultimate beneficiaries of these PNs. What is more galling is that international banks and financial institutions of repute (UBS, Societe Generale or Barclays, for instance) have risked their reputation to ensure that the ultimate beneficiaries are protected. SEBI is unwilling to get to the bottom of the matter, so much so, that no one is willing to take it up seriously.

The case of Hassan Ali is evidence of the rot that has set in high places in India. It is a confluence of crime, corruption and capital market manipulation in India. The reluctant response of the Government in pursuing our money is indeed bewildering to say the least. The manner in which the UBS case was given an indecent burial demonstrates all that is wrong with SEBI. The Goldman

Sachs case exposes the regulatory limitation vis-à-vis FIIs in India. The Societe Generale and the Barclays Bank cases discussed earlier in this chapter comprise conclusive evidence, despite all the tall claims of the Government – between 2001 (when the JPC was constituted) and now, nothing seems to have changed with respect to PN Regulations.

In 2009, India brought out a Report on its Financial Sector Assessment Programme (FSAP). The FSAP is a joint initiative of the IMF and the World Bank. The primary idea of the FSAP is to assess the stability and resilience of financial systems in member countries. India first participated in an FSAP in 2001. In September 2005, the IMF and the World Bank jointly brought out methodologies for FSAP that could enable countries themselves to undertake self-assessments. Subsequently, India decided to constitute a Committee on Financial Sector Assessment (CFSA) to undertake a comprehensive self-assessment of India's financial sector. Overall, the assessment has found that the financial system is essentially sound and resilient, and that systemic stability is robust.

With gaping holes in our regulatory regime on the issue of PNs and other related issued discussed above, one is not sure as to how we can evaluate our financial system to be sound. Experiences during 2008-09 demonstrate that India could well be having a resilient financial system whose stability could well be robust. But can it be classified as a sound one? Given the track record of our regulators, and the high decibel levels usually associated with any public discourse in India, one can safely surmise that the Indian financial system is all sound but not *sound.*

So What Needs to be Done?

Indian money in tax havens poses a new security and macroeconomic risk to India. It is time we recognise this. Similarly, PNs and their anonymity pose a significant challenge to the Indian economy. If we do not act now, our opponents will. That may have a debilitating impact on the integrity of the country, its economy and security. Strangely, the Government seems to be acting at a glacial pace. Inexplicably, the opposition seems to be playing ball with the Government. The media, intellectuals and intelligentsia all seem to be in a suspended sense of disbelief on these matters of vital importance.

Obviously, it is a terrible mess out there. The Government must act, and act forthwith. It cannot diffuse the matter any longer. The reply of the Government to the PIL filed in the Hon'ble Supreme Court is an empty exercise in semantics and a complete one in obfuscation.

However, on this sensitive matter, we cannot wash all our dirty linen in public. We need to be practical as well morally correct. We need to strike a balance. One way out is that the Hon'ble Supreme Court intervenes in the matter and ensures a comprehensive probe into these issues by constituting a committee of experts with a proven track record of integrity to look into the matter. The Government has to necessarily confide to this select committee – about what has been done till date and what it seeks to do. It has to share the information available with it on the LGT Bank, the source of information about the deposits aggregating to USD 140 billion in tax havens (including the Liechtenstein data) as disclosed by the Hon'ble PM and other relevant information to this committee if not with the nation at large.

Similarly, SEBI as well as the RBI must be asked to get at the root of the PN conundrum. We need to ensure that the PN holders are appropriately identified. Else, the Government must nationalise these investments and credit them to the Consolidated Fund of the Union. Only genuine PN investors must be allowed to take their money back from India. In the alternative, we need to get another Joint Parliamentary Committee to probe into all these issues. And this time around we have to fix all the "fixers."

All these actions are merely illustrative of what needs to be done. We as a nation need to do "something" to deal with this issue that is getting out of hand by the day. Desperate times call for desperate measures. The time to act on all these issue is *now*. Else the words of Martin Luther King shall continue to haunt the silent majority of this country, perhaps eternally. This book is merely an effort to ignite the imagination of the silent majority so that they no longer remain silent.

Reference

1. *The Week*, issue dated March 14, 2010.
2. Reply of the Government of India to the Hon'ble Supreme Court to the PIL filed on the issue of tax havens.
3. Budget Speech of the Hon'ble FM delivered in the Parliament on February 26, 2010, and budget paper of the Government of India, 2010.
4. United Nations Convention Against Transnational Organised Crime.
5. United Nations Convention Against Corruption.
6. IMF Staff Position Note, February 19, 2010 (SPN/10/04).
7. UNCTAD Trade and Development Report 2009.
8. Rajinder Puri, "Pranab Mukherjee's Dilemma: Black Money, Blue Funk?", Boloji.com dated October 20, 2009
9. Economic Survey of the Government of India for 2008-09 and 2009-10.
10. United Nations Convention against Corruption, 2004.
11. Order of SEBI on Societe Generale dated January 15, 2010. (WTM/KMA/IMD/207/01/2010).

12. Order of SEBI on Barclays Bank dated December 9, 2009 (WTM/KMA/IMD/ 184 /12/2009).
13. Address by the Hon'ble President of India, Mrs. Pratiba Devsingh Patil, to Parliament, New Delhi, February 22, 2010.
14. "Will Ensure Return of Black Money", IANS, dated March 5, 2010.
15. "Report: Centre Submitted Forged Documents in Hassan Ali Case", *The Hindu,* May 08, 2009.
16. Clarification on Reports of Allegations about Indian Black Money in Swiss Bank Accounts, PIB release of the Ministry of Finance, May 13, 2009.
17. "Jethmalani Attacks Inaction on Money Laundering", *The Hindu,* March 28, 2010.
18. Consent Order of SEBI in the matter of RBS Asia Limited issued on June 24, 2010.
19. *When Corporations Rule the World* by David C. Korten.

INDEX

www.ingramcontent.com/pod-product-compliance
Lightning Source LLC
Chambersburg PA
CBHW031335230926
51848CB00002B/248
9789380502496